W9-ALW-479

Gleim Publications, Inc., offers five university-level study manuals:

Auditing & Systems Exam Questions and Explanations	$19.95
Business Law/Legal Studies Exam Questions and Explanations	19.95
Federal Tax Exam Questions and Explanations	19.95
Financial Accounting Exam Questions and Explanations	19.95
Cost/Managerial Accounting Exam Questions and Explanations	19.95

Exam Prep Software also available @ $20 each

The following is a list of Gleim examination review books:

CIA Review: Part I, Internal Audit's Role in Governance, Risk, and Control	$29.95
CIA Review: Part II, Conducting the Internal Audit Engagement	29.95
CIA Review: Part III, Business Analysis and Information Technology.	29.95
CIA Review: Part IV, Business Management Skills	29.95

CIA Test Prep software ($49.95 per section) is also available to complement your study.

CMA/CFM Review: Part 1, Economics, Finance, and Management.	$26.95
CFM Review: Part 2CFM, Corporate Financial Management.	26.95
CMA Review: Part 2CMA, Financial Accounting and Reporting	26.95
CMA/CFM Review: Part 3, Mgmt. Reporting, Analysis, and Behavioral Issues	26.95
CMA/CFM Review: Part 4, Decision Analysis, Information Systems, and Management Controls. . . .	26.95

CMA/CFM Test Prep software ($44.95 per section) and CMA/CFM Review audios ($69.95 per section) are also available to complement your study.

CPA Review: Financial.	$39.95
CPA Review: Auditing	39.95
CPA Review: Business	39.95
CPA Review: Regulation	39.95

CPA Test Prep software ($49.95 per section) and CPA Review audios ($89.95 per section) are also available to complement your study.

EA Review: Part 1, Individuals	$29.95
EA Review: Part 2, Sole Proprietorships and Partnerships.	29.95
EA Review: Part 3, Corporations, Fiduciaries, Estate and Gift Tax, and Trusts	29.95
EA Review: Part 4, IRS Administration and Other Topics.	29.95

EA Test Prep software ($49.95 per section) is also available to complement your study.

Order forms are provided at the back of this book or contact us at www.gleim.com or (800) 87-GLEIM.

REVIEWERS AND CONTRIBUTORS

Caitlin M. Bourdon, B.A., University of Florida, is our book production coordinator. Ms. Bourdon coordinated the production staff, reviewed the manuscript, and provided production assistance throughout the project.

Kimberly Solvang Hamm, J.D., University of Washington, is our quality control editor. Ms. Hamm reviewed the manuscript, revised it for readability, and provided extensive editorial assistance.

Grady M. Irwin, J.D., is a graduate of the University of Florida College of Law, and he has taught in the University of Florida College of Business. Mr. Irwin provided substantial editorial assistance throughout the project.

Bruce S. Masingil, B.S., Florida International University, is our book production assistant. Mr. Masingil provided assistance throughout the project.

John F. Rebstock, CIA, is a graduate of the Fisher School of Accounting at the University of Florida. Mr. Rebstock reviewed portions of the manuscript.

A PERSONAL THANKS

This manual would not have been possible without the extraordinary effort and dedication of Rachael Goodwin, Terry Hall, Jean Marzullo, and Teresa Soard, who typed the entire manuscript and all revisions; prepared the camera-ready pages; and drafted, scanned, and laid out the diagrams and illustrations in this book.

The authors also appreciate the production and editorial assistance of Matthew Carty, Katharine Cicatelli, Laura Heston, Nicolas Medina, Eloise Pinto, Chiquita Pratt, Shane Rapp, Mittal Shah, Christina Smart and Jan Strickland.

The authors also appreciate the critical reading assistance of Ben Arundel, Kendra Brewer, Jose Carrasco, Lance Mathew, Christopher North, Dhruven Parikh, Chirag Patel, Christopher Pavilonis, John Taldi, and Keith Williams.

Finally, we appreciate the encouragement, support, and tolerance of our families throughout this project.

ELEVENTH EDITION

CIA REVIEW

PART I

INTERNAL AUDIT'S ROLE IN GOVERNANCE, RISK, AND CONTROL

by

Irvin N. Gleim, Ph.D., CPA, CIA, CMA, CFM

with the assistance of
Grady M. Irwin, J.D.

ABOUT THE AUTHOR

Irvin N. Gleim is Professor Emeritus in the Fisher School of Accounting at the University of Florida and is a member of the American Accounting Association, Academy of Legal Studies in Business, American Institute of Certified Public Accountants, Association of Government Accountants, Florida Institute of Certified Public Accountants, The Institute of Internal Auditors, and the Institute of Management Accountants. He has had articles published in the *Journal of Accountancy, The Accounting Review,* and *The American Business Law Journal* and is author/coauthor of numerous accounting and aviation books and CPE courses.

iv

Gleim Publications, Inc.
P.O. Box 12848
University Station
Gainesville, Florida 32604
(800) 87-GLEIM or (800) 874-5346
(352) 375-0772
FAX: (352) 375-6940
Internet: www.gleim.com
E-mail: admin@gleim.com

This is the first printing of the eleventh edition of *CIA Review: Part I, Internal Audit's Role in Governance, Risk, and Control*. Please e-mail update@gleim.com with CIA I 11-1 included in the subject or text. You will receive our current update as a reply.

EXAMPLE:

To: update@gleim.com
From: your e-mail address
Subject: CIA I 11-1

ISSN: 1547-8041

ISBN: 1-58194-331-8

ACKNOWLEDGMENTS FOR PART I

The author is grateful for permission to reproduce the following materials copyrighted by The Institute of Internal Auditors: Certified Internal Auditor Examination Questions and Suggested Solutions, excerpts from *The Practice of Modern Internal Auditing, Statements of Responsibilities of Internal Auditors, Code of Ethics, Standards for the Professional Practice of Internal Auditing, Professional Standards Practice Releases*, and *Statements on Internal Auditing Standards*, copyright © 1980 - 1998 by The Institute of Internal Auditors, Inc.

The authors also appreciate and than the Institute of Certified Management Accountants for permission to use questions from past CMA examination, copyright © 1982 - 1990 by the Institute of Management Accountants.

Visit our website (www.gleim.com) for the latest updates and information on all of our products.

TABLE OF CONTENTS

PREFACE

The purpose of this book is to help **you** prepare **yourself** to pass Part I of the CIA examination. The overriding consideration is to provide an inexpensive, effective, and easy-to-use study program. This manual

1. Defines topics tested on Part I of the CIA examination.

2. Includes all recent changes in Part I of the CIA program.

3. Explains how to optimize your grade by analyzing how the CIA exam is constructed and graded.

4. Suggests exam taking techniques to help you maximize your exam score.

5. Outlines all of the subject matter tested on Part I of the CIA exam in 10 easy-to-use study units, including all relevant authoritative pronouncements.

6. Reorganizes past exam questions according to the subunits within each of the 10 study units and presents an intuitively appealing explanation of each objective question answer.

7. Provides an opportunity for professional accountants to obtain CPE credit while preparing to pass the CIA exam. See the opposite page for more information.

Even though Gleim's four-volume *CIA Review* constitutes a complete self-study program for the CIA exam, candidates should consider enrolling in a formal review program. Local IIA chapters throughout the world have, in the past, coordinated CIA review programs and will probably continue to do so. In addition, all candidates should invest in our *CIA Test Prep* software, which is a powerful supplemental study aid to any review books or courses. Call (800) 87-GLEIM for more information.

Thank you for your interest in our materials. We deeply appreciate the thousands of letters and suggestions we have received from CIA, CMA, CFM, and CPA candidates and accounting students during the last four decades.

Please send us your suggestions, comments, and corrections concerning *CIA Review: Part I*. The last page in this book has been designed to help you note corrections and suggestions throughout your study process. It is imperative that we receive your feedback after you take the CIA exam. We pledge to continue to improve the product (with your suggestions, we hope) in the twelfth and subsequent editions.

The outline format and spacing and the question and answer formats are designed to facilitate learning, understanding, and readability. Please read the introduction of this book carefully.

To continue providing our customers with first-rate service, we request that questions about our books and software be sent to us via mail, e-mail, or fax. The appropriate staff member will give each question thorough consideration and a prompt response. Questions concerning orders, prices, shipments, or payments will be handled via telephone by our competent and courteous customer service staff.

Good Luck on the Exam,

Irvin N. Gleim

January 2004

USING THIS MANUAL TO EARN CPE CREDITS

The Gleim approach to CPE is both interactive and intense. You should be continually challenged to answer each question correctly. When you answer a question incorrectly or have difficulty, you should pursue a complete understanding by reading the answer explanation and consulting reference sources as necessary.

We offer CPE credit online that correlates with this Eleventh Edition text. Visit www.gleim.com/accounting/cpe/onlinecpe for more information. You can register for either the Interactive or WebCPE Grading online.

Most of the questions in the study guide were taken from various professional examinations. Each question is revised, adapted, etc., to provide broader, up-to-date coverage of the internal auditing body of technical knowledge. In addition, publisher questions cover material added since examinations became "closed."

Finally, we ask for any supplemental comments, reactions, suggestions, etc., that you may have as you complete our CPE program. Please attach them to the online Course Evaluation or send an e-mail to cpeinfo@gleim.com.

To continue providing our customers with first-rate service, we request that questions about our books and software be sent to us via mail, e-mail, or fax. The appropriate staff member will give each question thorough consideration and a prompt response. Questions concerning orders, prices, shipments, or payments will be handled via telephone by our competent and courteous customer service staff.

Thank you for your interest, and we look forward to hearing from you.

Best Wishes in Your CPE Endeavors,

Irvin N. Gleim

January 2004

PREPARING FOR AND TAKING THE CIA EXAM

ABOUT THE CIA EXAM

Introduction

CIA is the acronym for Certified Internal Auditor. The CIA designation is international, with the examination administered in numerous countries. The CIA exam has been administered by The Institute of Internal Auditors since 1974. The exam consists of four 3 1/2-hour parts that are given on the third Thursday and its preceding Wednesday in May and November. Each part consists of 125 four-answer multiple-choice questions.

Part I	The Internal Audit Activity's Role in Governance, Risk, and Control	Wednesday	8:30 - 12:00	3 1/2 hours
Part II	Conducting the Internal Audit Engagement	Wednesday	1:30 - 5:00	3 1/2 hours
Part III	Business Analysis and Information Technology	Thursday	8:30 - 12:00	3 1/2 hours
Part IV	Business Management Skills	Thursday	1:30 - 5:00	3 1/2 hours
				14 hours

Please note as you read through this introduction that CIA program rules and prices are subject to change. Please visit The IIA web site at www.theiia.org for the most up-to-date information.

Internal Auditing

Internal auditing is an independent, objective assurance and consulting activity designed to add value and improve an organization's operations. It helps an organization accomplish its objectives by bringing a systematic, disciplined approach to evaluate and improve the effectiveness of risk management, control, and governance processes.

Internal auditing reviews the reliability and integrity of information, compliance with policies and regulations, the safeguarding of assets, the economical and efficient use of resources, and established operational goals and objectives. Internal audits encompass financial activities and operations including systems, production, engineering, marketing, and human resources.

The Institute of Internal Auditors (IIA)

The IIA was organized in 1941 to develop the professional status of internal auditing. The organization's headquarters was in New York City until 1972, when it moved to Altamonte Springs, about 5 miles north of Orlando, Florida.

The IIA has an annual budget of approximately $17 million and employs a full-time staff of 100+. Presently, over 40,000 individuals have attained The Institute of Internal Auditors' CIA designation.

The IIA has chapters in more than 200 metropolitan areas and has affiliated national institutes in many countries around the world. The chapters and institutes hold regular meetings, seminars, and conferences that encourage members to network with peers, develop professional contacts, and stay informed about current issues and practices in internal auditing.

The Institute of Internal Auditors' mission is to be the primary international professional association, organized on a worldwide basis, dedicated to the promotion and development of the practice of internal auditing.

The IIA is committed to:

- Providing, on an international scale, comprehensive professional development activities, standards for the practice of internal auditing, and certification.
- Researching, disseminating, and promoting to its members and to the public throughout the world, knowledge and information concerning internal auditing, including internal control and related subjects.
- Establishing meetings worldwide in order to educate members and others as to the practice of internal auditing as it exists in various countries throughout the world.
- Bringing together internal auditors from all countries to share information and experiences in internal auditing and promoting education in the field of internal auditing.

IIA annual dues in the United States and Canada:

1.	Regular members	$115
2.	Sustaining	$50
3.	Educational Member	$65
4.	Life Member	$2,100
5.	Retired Member	$30
6.	Student Member	$30

For non-Chapter members outside the United States, Canada, and the Caribbean nations, dues are $115. These members are also required to pay a $30 bank collection charge for drafts drawn on banks outside the U.S., Canada, and the Caribbean. Applicants, except students and sustaining members, must also pay an application fee of $25.

CIA Board of Regents

The Board of Regents is a special committee of The Institute of Internal Auditors established to direct the certification program for internal auditors as established and/or modified by The IIA's Board of Directors.

The Board of Regents consists of at least nine regents. The regents are appointed by the Chairman of the Board of Directors to serve 3-year terms. Membership on the Board of Regents rotates, with two or three regents being appointed each year. The responsibilities of the Board of Regents include

a. Define the common body of knowledge for the Certified Internal Auditor examination and other Institute certification examinations.
b. Define the education, experience, character, examination, and other program requirements relating to The Institute certifications.
c. Define continuing professional education (CPE) requirements for Institute certifications.
d. Maintain the quality and security of examinations.
e. Promote The Institute's certifications globally.

IIA Certification Department

The Vice President of the Learning Center and the Certification Department staff, who are located in The IIA's Florida offices, administer the program. They undertake all of the day-to-day work with respect to the Board of Regents' responsibilities.

The chair of the Board of Regents divides the members into subcommittees. Each subcommittee is responsible for one part of the exam; i.e., each subcommittee makes the initial recommendations concerning the content and grading of its part of the examination to the Board of Regents as a whole.

Well-Planned Evolution Rather than Abrupt Change

One of the responsibilities of The IIA Board of Regents is to continually update and enhance the sources of exam questions, which in their entirety constitute the **common body of knowledge**.

At the same time, the scope and content of the CIA exam appear to evolve so as to be predictable to CIA candidates. Addition of new topics and deletion of currently tested topics are announced at least one year in advance so candidates may plan and prepare accordingly.

Pass rates on the exam are low enough to give the examination credibility relative to the CMA and CPA exams but are high enough to encourage accounting and auditing professionals to participate in the CIA certification program. Everyone, including The IIA Board of Directors, the Board of Regents, the certification staff, CIAs, noncertified internal auditors, and the accounting/auditing profession in general, is interested in the continual upgrading and improvement of the CIA exam.

Objectives and Content of the CIA Examination

The CIA exam tests a candidate's knowledge and ability regarding the current practice of internal auditing. It enables candidates and prospective managers to adapt to professional changes and challenges by:

- Addressing nearly all management skills.
- Focusing on the principles of management control.
- Measuring a candidate's understanding of risk management and internal controls.

The exam tests candidates' knowledge and ability with respect to the current state of the art of internal auditing practice. The **common body of knowledge**, referred to in The IIA's materials, is reflected in this edition of *CIA Review*.

THE IIA'S CIA CONTENT SPECIFICATION OUTLINES

Part I: The Internal Audit Activity's Role in Governance, Risk, and Control

A.	Comply with the IIA's Attribute Standards	20%
B.	Establish a risk-based plan to determine the priorities of the internal audit activity	20%
C.	Understand the internal audit activity's role in organizational governance	15%
D.	Perform other internal audit roles and responsibilities	5%
E.	Governance, risk, and control knowledge elements	20%
F.	Plan Engagements	20%

Part II: Conducting the Internal Audit Engagement

A.	Conduct Engagements	30%
B.	Conduct Specific Engagements	30%
C.	Monitor Engagement Outcomes	10%
D.	Fraud Knowledge Elements	10%
E.	Engagement Tools	20%

Part III: Business Analysis and Information Technology

A.	Business Processes	20%
B.	Financial Accounting and Finance	20%
C.	Managerial Accounting	15%
D.	Regulatory, Legal, and Economics	10%
E.	Information Technology (IT)	35%

Part IV: Business Management Skills

A.	Strategic Management	25%
B.	Global Business Environments	20%
C.	Organizational Behavior	25%
D.	Management Skills	25%
E.	Negotiating	5%

The IIA publishes Content Specification Outlines (CSOs) that outline topics covered on the CIA exam. The percentage coverage of each exam part is indicated to the right of each topic. (Note that The IIA "percentage coverage" is given in ranges, e.g., 15-25%, as presented in Appendix A. On page 4, we present the midpoint of each range to simplify and provide more relevant information to CIA candidates, e.g., 20% instead of 15-25%.) We continually adjust the content of our books and software to changes in The IIA's CSOs.

Appendix A contains the CSOs in their entirety. Remember that we have studied and restudied the CSOs in developing our *CIA Review* books and software. Accordingly, you do not need to spend time with Appendix A. Rather, it should give you confidence that Gleim's *CIA Review* is the best review source available to help you PASS the CIA exam. The CSOs refer to proficiency and awareness levels. The IIA definitions of these levels are presented below.

> **Proficiency** -- Candidate is able to exhibit the competency in understanding and applying the subject matter in the workplace on a regular basis with skill and expertise.

> **Awareness** -- Candidate exhibits awareness and knowledge. Candidate is able to define terms, recognize issues, and recall facts about the issues.

Gleim Study Unit Listing

We believe our 10 study unit titles better describe the content of each part of the CIA exam. Our study unit titles and content also reflect feedback from CIA candidates. Please use the last page in this book to give us feedback after each exam. Thank you.

LISTING OF GLEIM STUDY UNITS

Part I: Internal Audit's Role in Governance, Risk, and Control

1. Introduction to Internal Auditing
2. Charter, Independence, & Objectivity
3. Standards & Proficiency
4. Internal Audit Roles & Responsibility
5. Control I
6. Control II
7. Planning & Supervising the Engagement
8. Managing the Internal Audit Activity I
9. Managing the Internal Audit Activity II
10. Engagement Procedures

Part II: Planning and Conducting the Internal Audit Engagement

1. Engagement Information
2. Working Papers
3. Communicating Results and Monitoring Progress
4. Specific Engagements
5. Information Technology Audit Engagements I
6. Information Technology Audit Engagements II
7. Statistics and Sampling
8. Other Engagement Tools
9. Ethics
10. Fraud

Part III: Analytical Concepts and Information Technology in Internal Auditing

1. Business Performance
2. Managing Resources & Pricing
3. Financial Accounting Basic Concepts
4. Financial Accounting Assets, Liabilities, and Equity
5. Financial Accounting -- Special Topics
6. Finance
7. Managerial Accounting
8. Regulatory, Legal, & Economic Issues
9. Information Technology I
10. Information Technology II

Part IV: Business Management Skills

1. Industry Environments
2. Analytical Techniques
3. Strategic Analysis
4. Global Business Environments
5. Motivation & Communication
6. Organizational Structure & Effectiveness
7. Group Dynamics & Team Building
8. Influence & Leadership
9. Time Management
10. Negotiation

Admission to the CIA Program

Anyone who satisfies these character, educational, and professional requirements may sit for the examination.

1. **Bachelor's degree or equivalent**. Candidates must have an undergraduate (4-year) degree or its equivalent from an accredited college-level institution.

   a. Educational programs outside the United States and the qualifications of candidates who have completed most but not all of a degree program are evaluated by The IIA's Board of Regents to determine equivalency.

   b. IIA affiliates have been given the authority to recommend educational and experience criteria for their countries to ensure adequate consideration of cultural and societal differences around the world. In addition, certain international professional designations (such as Chartered Accountant) may be accepted as equivalent to a bachelor's degree.

   c. A major in accounting is not required.

2. **Character reference**. CIA candidates must exhibit high moral and professional character and must submit a character reference from a responsible person such as a CIA, supervisor, manager, or educator. The character reference must accompany the candidate's application.

3. **Work experience**. Candidates are required to have 24 months of internal auditing experience (or the equivalent) prior to receiving the CIA certificate. However, a candidate may sit for the exam before completing the work experience requirements, but (s)he will not be certified until the experience requirement is met.

   a. An advanced academic degree beyond the bachelor's or work experience in related business professions (such as accounting, law, finance) can be substituted for one year of work experience (1-year maximum).

   b. Equivalent work experience means experience in audit/assessment disciplines, including external auditing, quality assurance, compliance, and internal control.

   c. Full-time college or university-level teaching in the subject matter of the examination is considered equivalent to work experience. Two years of teaching equals one year of internal auditing work experience.

   d. Work experience must be verified by a CIA or the candidate's supervisor. An Experience Verification Form is available on The IIA web site or in the CIA brochure for use in verifying professional experience. This may accompany the candidate's application or be submitted later when criteria have been met.

If you have questions about the acceptability of your work experience, contact The IIA Certification Department at certification@theiia.org or by fax at (407) 937-1313. If you do not possess a bachelor's degree and are unsure whether your educational achievements or professional designation qualify as equivalents to a bachelor's degree, you should submit related educational/professional information with your application and include a cover letter requesting review by the Board of Regents. Include a complete description of your situation. Please submit these materials to

Certification Department
The Institute of Internal Auditors
247 Maitland Avenue
Altamonte Springs, FL 32701-4201

You will receive a response from The IIA as soon as the certification staff or the Board of Regents evaluates your request. Applicants for equivalency may be registered for the exam pending review but should expect a separate letter regarding the outcome of the review. Applicants who do not receive an equivalency status letter within four weeks of submission of the application and equivalency request should contact The IIA.

How to Register and Apply for the CIA Exam

You must complete a Certified Internal Auditor Program Registration/Application Form for entrance into the CIA program. The application form is available for download or automatic transfer at www.theiia.org. All documents and fees must be filed to arrive at The Institute on or before March 31 for the May examination and September 30 for the November examination. Submit the following items:

1.   A copy of your diploma, transcripts, or other proof of completion of a degree program. This must be submitted with the application form.
2.   A Character Reference Form (also available at The IIA's web site www.theiia.org)
3.   Verification of professional work experience (can be submitted later when the criteria have been met). Visit The IIA web site to obtain an experience verification form (www.theiia.org).

The candidate must sign the registration form agreeing to abide by The IIA Code of Ethics. Each registrant is responsible for making timely delivery of the required fees and forms. **The Institute cannot guarantee a candidate's right to sit for the examination if procedures are not followed.** If sending via mail, the application should be mailed to the IIA's Atlanta address as shown on the application.

Candidates must reapply each exam cycle for any remaining parts. A candidate may initially take one, two, three, or all four parts of the examination. A candidate may reapply to repeat any parts failed by submitting the registration form that accompanies the grade letter by using the reapplication form on The IIA web site (www.theiia.org), or by contacting The IIA's Customer Service Center -- e-mail: custserv@theiia.org, fax: (407) 937-1101, or telephone: (407) 937-1111. The candidate must also pay the appropriate examination fee. A candidate may take as few as one part at subsequent sittings during the two-year eligibility period.

Each person enrolled in the CIA program is responsible for providing timely written notice of any change of address to the IIA Customer Service Center.

Eligibility Period for the Exam

A candidate has an initial eligibility period of two years (five examinations) after his/her first registration is approved. The eligibility period is subsequently extended for two years each time a candidate sits for a part. A candidate's eligibility will expire only if the candidate does not take a single exam part within any two-year period. If eligibility expires, the candidate loses credit for any part or parts previously passed and must reregister for consideration as a candidate for future examinations.

Professional Recognition Credit for Part IV

The IIA offers a Part IV Professional Recognition Credit for qualified professional certifications. Registered candidates and new CIA candidates who have successfully completed the examination requirements for many designations are eligible to receive credit for Part IV of the CIA exam. Please visit The IIA's website (www.theiia.org) for a complete list of certifications approved for credit. Hence, candidates who attain the credit for Part IV and pass Parts I, II, and III satisfy the examination requirement for the CIA designation.

The CIA exam is a **nondisclosed** exam.   **Nondisclosed** means that exam questions and solutions are NOT released after each examination. In order to keep our books and software up-to-date and relevant to CIA candidates, we request feedback on our books and software after each CIA exam. We need to know what topics need to be added or enhanced. Note that we are not asking for information about CIA questions, per se. Rather, we are asking for feedback on our books and software. This approach has been approved by The IIA.

Special Student Examination Fee

The registration fee is the charge for enrolling candidates in the CIA program. The CIA examination is available to full-time students at reduced fees (half price). For them, the member registration fee is $30 (instead of $60), plus a fee of $35 (instead of $70) per part. Students may sit only one time for each part at this special rate.

1.   To be eligible for the reduced rate, the student must

   a.   Be a full-time student as defined by the institution in which the student is enrolled (a minimum of 12 semester hours or its equivalent for undergraduate students and 9 semester hours for graduate students).
   b.   Register for and take the CIA exam while enrolled in school.
   c.   Be enrolled as a senior in an undergraduate program or as a graduate student.

2.   In addition to the requirements above, the following items should be submitted to the Certification Department of The Institute of Internal Auditors while the student is still enrolled in school:

   a.   A Certified Internal Auditor Examination Registration/Application Form *(with school address substituted for business address)*
   b.   A completed and signed Full-Time Student Status Form in lieu of a transcript
   c.   A completed and signed Character Reference Form
   d.   Payment for the $30 registration fee and the $35 examination fee for each part

Fees for Full-Time Educators

Educators are invited to take the examination free of charge. Along with the required CIA Examination Application Form, educators should include a letter attesting to their college- or university-level teaching. These are submitted for approval of The IIA's Academic Relations Committee. Letters must

1.   Be printed on the university's letterhead
2.   Specify the courses taught during each semester or quarter
3.   Verify that the candidate had a full-time appointment for each academic year submitted
4.   Be signed by the dean of the college of business administration

IIA Refund and Deferral Policy

The registration fee is neither refundable nor transferable. The examination fee is refundable with a written request. A $25 processing fee will be charged. Candidates must notify The IIA in writing (via mail, fax, or e-mail) in order to make changes to their registration, such as changing examination sites, changing the examination parts being taken, deferring to sit at a later examination, or canceling the registration. Payment of any required fees is due at the time the change is made.

Deferrals or changes may be made at no cost if written notice is received by the registration deadline (March 31 and September 30). A $25 fee will be charged for deferrals, changes, or cancelations received after the deadline. This fee increases to $70 on the Wednesday of the week before the examination.

If no written notice or deferral of cancelation is given prior to the exam and the candidate fails to appear, (s)he is classified as a no-show, and a penalty fee of $70 will be deducted from fees paid. Any remainder will be held in the candidate's account pending further instructions. Monies left in the account after a candidate's eligibility period expires are subject to forfeiture.

CIA Exam Administration

About three weeks before the exam, candidates will receive an authorization letter with a candidate number, the exam site number and address, the date and time to report to the site, and the time the exam will begin and end (see example on the opposite page). Any errors in the authorization letter should be reported to The IIA's Certification Department at (407) 937-1323, or e-mail: certification@theiia.org. When contacting The IIA, have the candidate ID number available. If you have not received your authorization letter within two weeks before the exam or you have lost your letter, then you should contact The IIA immediately.

The following items are **required** to be admitted to the exam site:

1. Authorization letter
2. Valid photo identification

CIA Candidate
«Address»
«CityStateZip»
«Country»

                                                                        Candidate/ID#

Dear Candidate:

This letter is your authorization to sit for the November 2004 CIA examination. You must present it along with a photo identification to gain admittance to the exam room. Arrive 30 minutes prior to start time.

Your requested language is: _____.

Your exam site is:

  «SiteNo» - «SiteName»
  «SiteAddr1»
  «SiteAddr2»
  «SiteAddr3»
  «SiteCityStateZip»
  «SiteCountry»

You are scheduled to take part(s):

For additional directions, contact (name and phone number of local contact).

The IIA Instructions to Candidates

The IIA instructions to candidates from a recent exam are reproduced below and on the next page to give you further insight into actual exam procedures.

Instructions to CIA Candidates

EXAMINATION SUPERVISORS ARE TO READ THESE INSTRUCTIONS VERBATIM TO THE CANDIDATES APPROXIMATELY FIVE MINUTES BEFORE START OF THE EXAMINATION. DO NOT EXTEMPORIZE.

(Extra copies for late arrivals, per IV.F of the "instructions.")

Do **not** open your booklet or write on the accompanying materials until instructed to do so.

As a courtesy to others, please turn off all cellular phones, beepers, etc., for the duration of the exam.

A No. 2 soft lead pencil must be used to complete the multiple-choice answer sheet. Darken only the appropriate blocks, as shown in the instructions on the multiple-choice answer sheet. **Marks outside the blocks could adversely affect the score you receive.**

At this time, please remove the white multiple-choice answer sheet and the colored control sheet from inside the exam booklet, and close the exam booklet.

On the multiple-choice answer sheet, write the exam language code (the language of your exam), exam site number and your candidate identification number in the blanks provided, and darken the appropriate boxes below each number. If your identification or ID number has fewer than 7 digits, please add any necessary zeroes to the **left** of your ID number so that the last digit of your ID number is in the space to the far right.

Locate the exam serial number on the upper left-hand corner of your exam booklet's cover, and copy this number in the space provided on the multiple-choice answer sheet.

Next, complete the control sheet, **making sure to read and sign the nondisclosure agreement**.

The specific restrictive rules that will be in effect during the examination are:

1.   No reference material, templates, or other aids may be used, except for battery- or solar-powered, nonprinting, nonprogrammable, six-function calculators with only addition, subtraction, multiplication, division, square root, and percentage functions.

2.   All answers submitted must be your own.

3.   If you must be excused from the room, notify a monitor. You will be on the honor system during your absence. Only **one** candidate may leave the room at a time.

4.   You may not talk during the examination.

5.   You may not walk about the room during the examination.

6.   No other act that appears to violate examination ethics will be permitted.

Breaking any of these rules could result in losing the privilege of sitting for this (or a future) CIA examination under Article 1 of The Institute of Internal Auditors' Code of Ethics.

You will have three and one-half hours in which to complete the examination. If you finish before the full time has elapsed, please turn in your materials and leave the room quietly.

Your examination booklet, all scratch paper and notes are to be turned in with your answers. You are not to discuss the examination with anyone.

I will announce when 30 minutes remain, when five minutes remain, and when time has expired. Please do **not** ask me or the other proctors to interpret any questions, as we are not permitted to discuss the content of the examination.

-- (continued) --

CANDIDATES WHO HAVE CONCERNS REGARDING EXAM QUESTIONS or the testing experience should submit their comments by fax (+1-407-937-1313) or by e-mail to certification@theiia.org. These comments must be received within 96 hours of completion of the exam so that they will be available to the Board of Regents for review before grading begins. Comments on exam questions must identify the general content of the question and briefly outline any perceived flaw. Candidate input will be gratefully acknowledged and considered in the evaluation of the exam and the testing program. If you prefer, I can collect specific comments and forward them to The IIA Certification Department.

Before beginning work on the exam, read carefully all the instructions on the exam booklet's cover and opening page.

Upon opening your exam booklet, check the page numbers to ensure no pages are missing. After the last question (Question #80), the phrase "End of Part" should appear.

Are there any questions?

You may now open your exam booklet and begin work.

Grading the CIA Exam and Grade Reporting

The examination proctors return the CIA examinations to The IIA offices by registered mail, Federal Express, or other means to guarantee the safety and security of the examination. The week following the examination, the exams are received and checked against shipping control lists prepared by the proctors. Individual candidate numbers are checked on each answer sheet of every candidate's exam. The highest priority is given to assuring that no candidate papers are misplaced or lost.

The grading process includes both a review of the suggested responses before the exam is given and a post-exam review of all questions that perform poorly in terms of difficulty and reliability. After this review, the Board may choose to accept more than one response as correct on certain questions that did not perform as well as expected.

The multiple-choice question answer sheets are graded using an optical scanner, and all irregularities are researched. If the difficulty of an exam part is higher than expected, a difficulty adjustment may be added to all candidates' scores before exam results are finalized. Statistical information from pre-tested questions is used to maintain comparable difficulty from one CIA exam to the next. Because the exact number of questions required to pass the exam may be slightly different from one exam to another, all raw scores are converted onto a reporting scale of 250 to 750 points, in order to ensure a common standard. A scaled score of 600 points or higher is required to pass the CIA exam. (A scaled score of 600 would be the equivalent of achieving 75 percent correct on an exam of appropriate difficulty.)

Examination results are mailed by July 15 for May exams and January 15 for November exams. If you earn a passing score, you are notified of passing and no specific grade is released. If you earn a score below the passing mark, it is reported to you along with a brief analysis of your exam performance by topic so you can see how much additional effort is required (see sample grade release letter below). Plan on receiving good news soon!

DATE

CIA CANDIDATE
ADDRESS
CITYSTATEZIP
COUNTRY

Dear NAME: I.D. No. #####

Thank you for taking the November 2003 Certified Internal Auditor examination. Your results are listed below.
CIA exam scores are now reported on a scale of 250 to 750 points (see insert), and a scaled score of 600 points
or higher is required for successful completion of each part of the exam. No scores are released for parts passed.

PART I	PART II	PART III	PART IV*
PREVIOUSLY PASSED	PREVIOUSLY PASSED	485	PASSED

 *If you have now passed Parts I, II, and III and plan to apply for Professional Recognition Credit for Part IV,
please provide the necessary documents and payment by DATE in order to ensure prompt processing of your
request. Instructions and a list of approved certifications are available on The IIA's web site (www.theiia.org)
under Certifications/CIA.

All scores are considered final. In order to help guide your future study, an analysis of the strengths and
weaknesses of your exam performance is provided below for any part on which you received a non-passing
score. The analysis includes (1) the main topic areas for the exam part (see IIA web site for detailed outline), (2)
the percentage of questions tested in each topic area, and (3) an assessment of improvement needed based on
your performance on the November 2003 exam.

Performance Assessment For Part III

Business Processes (15-25%): You need a moderate amount of improvement in this area.

Financial Accounting and Finance (15-25%): You performed competently in this area but should review it during
study.

Managerial Accounting (10-20%): You performed competently in this area but should review it during study.

Regulatory, Legal, and Economics (5-15%): You performed competently in this area but should review it during
study.

Information Technology (IT) (30-40%): You need a large amount of improvement in this area.

We wish you the best in your pursuit of the Certified Internal Auditor designation.

The IIA Certification Department

Maintaining Your CIA Designation

    After certification, CIAs are required to maintain and update their knowledge and skills.
Practicing CIAs must complete and report 80 hours of Continuing Professional Education (CPE)
every two years. Every February, CIAs who are required to report in the current year will receive
reporting forms and instructions from The IIA. Completed forms should be filed with The IIA by
May 31 of the required reporting year. Each July, participants in the current year's CPE program
will receive a status report acknowledging acceptance of the number of hours reported.
Even-numbered certificates report in even years and odd-numbered certificates in odd years.

PREPARING TO PASS THE CIA EXAM

Control: How To

You have to be in control to be successful during exam preparation and execution. Control can also contribute greatly to your personal and other professional goals. The objective is to be confident that the best possible performance is being generated. Control is a process whereby you

1. Develop expectations, standards, budgets, and plans.
2. Undertake activity, production, study, and learning.
3. Measure the activity, production, output, and knowledge.
4. Compare actual activity with expected and budgeted activity.
5. Modify the activity, behavior, or study to better achieve the desired outcome.
6. Revise expectations and standards in light of actual experience.
7. Continue the process or restart the process in the future.

Every day you rely on control systems implicitly. For example, when you groom your hair, you use a control system. You have expectations about the desired appearance of your hair and the time required to style it. You monitor your progress and make adjustments as appropriate. The control process, however, is applicable to all of your endeavors, both professional and personal. You should refine your personal control processes specifically toward passing the CIA exam.

In this book, we suggest explicit control systems for

1. Preparing to take the CIA exam
2. Studying an individual Gleim study unit
3. Answering individual multiple-choice questions

Most endeavors will improve with explicit control. This is particularly true of the CIA examination.

1. Develop an explicit control system over your study process.

2. Practice your question answering techniques (and develop control) as you prepare solutions to recent CIA questions during your study program.

3. Prepare a detailed plan of steps you will take at the CIA exam.

How Many Parts to Take

The CIA examination consists of four parts; however, according to The IIA, you may choose to take only one part at each sitting.

Our recommendation is to take and pass all four parts the first time. Some candidates, however, will not be able to follow this approach for a variety of reasons. Parts I and II cover internal auditing subject matter, whereas Part III, Business Analysis and Information Technology, and Part IV, Business Management Skills, cover a wide variety of material. Thus, most candidates planning to sit for only two parts of the initial exam will choose Parts I and II because of the efficiencies involved. Part III is the least related to traditional accounting. Part IV tests material more familiar to accounting majors.

Candidates have an initial eligibility period of 2 years from the first exam after their registration is approved. In addition, each time a candidate sits for an exam part, the candidate's eligibility period is extended 2 years from the date of the last exam part taken. A candidate's eligibility expires only if the candidate does not take a single exam part within any 2-year period. If a candidate's eligibility expires, the candidate loses credit for any part or parts passed and must submit a new CIA Exam Application Form and appropriate fees in order to take future examinations.

Study Plan, Time Budget, and Calendar

Complete one *CIA Review* study unit at a time. Initially, budget 3 to 4 hours per study unit (1 to 2 hours studying the outline and 1 to 2 minutes each on all the multiple-choice questions). Depending on your background, you may need significantly more time to prepare.

This Introduction	2
10 study units at 3.5 hours each	35
General review	3
Total Hours	40

Each week you should evaluate your progress and review your preparation plans for the time remaining prior to the exam. Use a calendar to note the exam dates and the weeks to go before the exam. Marking a calendar will facilitate your planning. Review your commitments, e.g., out-of-town assignments, personal responsibilities, etc., and note them on your calendar to assist you in keeping to your schedule.

How to Study a Study Unit (books only*)

1. Gain an overview of the study unit -- familiarity with the topic, number of pages of outline, number of multiple-choice questions -- and estimate the time you will invest.

2. Answer five to ten multiple-choice questions. Choose one or two questions from each subunit.

3. The purpose of answering multiple-choice questions before working through the study outline is to understand the standards to which you will be held. This will motivate you to concentrate on the study outline.

4. Work through the study outline. Learn and understand the concepts. Remember, you are aiming toward the analysis, synthesis, and evaluation levels of knowledge, not rote memorization. Study the outlines with the objective of being able to explain the subject matter to third parties.

* We recommend using *CIA Test Prep* software as discussed on the next page. It will give you a definite advantage.

5. After you are comfortable with the study outlines, apply your multiple-choice question answering technique (see page 18) to answer all of the multiple-choice questions by marking the correct answer before consulting the answer and answer explanation. It is essential to mark your answer choice before looking at the answer. Use the bookmark at the back of each Gleim *CIA Review* book to cover the answers.

6. Develop a 75%+ proficiency level within each study unit. You will achieve this proficiency level by studying the outlines and answering multiple-choice questions.

Learning from questions you answer incorrectly is very important. Each question you answer incorrectly is an <u>opportunity</u> to avoid missing actual test questions on your CIA exam. Thus, you should carefully study the answer explanations provided until you understand why the original answer you chose is wrong, as well as why the correct answer indicated is correct. This study technique may prove to be the difference between passing and failing for many CIA candidates.

You **must** determine why you answered questions incorrectly and learn how to avoid the same error in the future. Reasons for missing questions include:

    a.   Misreading the requirement (stem)
    b.   Failing to understand what is required
    c.   Making a math error
    d.   Applying the wrong rule or concept
    e.   Being distracted by one or more of the answers
    f.   Incorrectly eliminating answers from consideration
    g.   Lacking any knowledge of the topic tested
    h.   Employing bad intuition (Why?) when guessing

7.   Gleim *CIA Test Prep* software will significantly benefit your study efforts, especially when using the 20-question test routine discussed next.

Adding CIA Test Prep Software

Using *CIA Test Prep* really works! The software forces you to commit to your answer choice before looking at answer explanations. It also keeps track of your time and the results of your effort. Each study session and each test session are kept in the performance history and are viewable in either a table or a graphical format.

Each Test Prep disk covers a different part of the CIA exam, includes over 1,000 questions, and contains a Windows™ version of the program. All questions have been updated to reflect the current subject matter.

Read and study the following six steps regarding how to use the software with the books. Using *CIA Test Prep* will greatly facilitate your study and success on the CIA exam! DO NOT neglect diagnosing the reasons for answering questions incorrectly; i.e., learn from your mistakes while studying so you avoid making mistakes on the CIA exam.

Avoid studying Gleim questions to learn the correct answers. Use Gleim questions to help you learn how to answer CIA questions under exam conditions. Expect the unexpected and be prepared to deal with the unexpected. Always take one 20-question test in test mode *before* studying the material in each study unit. These test sessions will allow you to practice answering questions you have not seen before. Become an educated guesser when you encounter questions in doubt; you will outperform the inexperienced exam taker.

The best way to prepare to PASS:

1 In test mode, answer a 20-question test from each study unit before studying the study unit.

2 Study the knowledge transfer outline for the study unit in your Gleim book.

3 Take two or three 20-question tests in test mode after studying knowledge transfer outlines.

4 After EACH test session, immediately switch to study mode and select questions "missed on last session" so you can reanswer these questions AND analyze why you answered each question incorrectly.

5 Continue the process until you approach a 75% proficiency level.

6 Modify the process to suit your individual learning process.

It is imperative that you complete at least one or two study units a week so you can review your progress and realize how attainable a comprehensive CIA review program is when using Gleim books and software. Remember to get ahead of your schedule to give yourself confidence.

> After you complete each 20-question test, ALWAYS do a study session of questions you missed. FOCUS on why you selected the incorrect answer, NOT the correct answer. You want to learn from your mistakes during study so you avoid mistakes on the exam.

If You Failed One or More Parts

The pass rate on each part of the CIA exam averages about 45%. Thus, you may not pass all parts attempted. If you failed one or more parts, you should retake them the next time the CIA exam is offered.

1. Once you have put the reaction to the bad news behind you, you should regroup and begin implementing the suggestions in this introduction. The Gleim system really works! Avoid thinking "I knew that" or "I don't have to study that again." What you knew and how you took the exam last time did NOT work. Develop new and improved perspectives.

2. Avoid failure on the next exam by **identifying**, **correcting**, and **understanding** your mistakes as you practice answering multiple-choice questions during your study sessions. Use *CIA Test Prep* software as described above. This methodology applies to all CIA candidates. Understand your mistakes while you study so you can avoid mistakes on the exam.

As you practice answering multiple-choice questions under exam conditions, it is imperative that you restudy each question you answer incorrectly.

Multiple-Choice Question Answering Technique

The following suggestions are to assist you in maximizing your score on each part of the CIA exam. Remember, knowing how to take the exam and how to answer individual questions is as important as studying/reviewing the subject matter tested on the exam.

1. **Budget your time**. We make this point with emphasis. Just as you would fill up your gas tank prior to reaching empty, so too should you finish your exam before time expires.

    a. You will have 210 minutes to answer 125 multiple-choice questions.

    b. As you work through individual multiple-choice items, monitor your time. Your goal is to answer all of the items and achieve the maximum score possible.

2. **Answer the items in numerical order**.

    a. Do **not** agonize over any one item. Stay within your time budget.

    b. Mark any items you are unsure of with a big "?" and return to them later if time allows.

    c. Plan on going back to all questions marked with a "?."

    d. Never leave a multiple-choice item unanswered on your answer sheet. Your score is based on the number of correct responses. You will not be penalized for guessing incorrectly.

3. **For each multiple-choice item:**

    a. **Cover up the answer choices** with your hand or a piece of scratch paper. Do not allow the answer choices to affect your reading of the item stem.

        1) If four answer choices are presented, three of them are incorrect. These incorrect answers are called **distractors**. Often, distractors are written to appear correct at first glance until further analysis.

        2) In computational items, distractors are often the result of making common mistakes.

    b. **Read the item** stem carefully (the part of the question that precedes the answer choices) to determine the precise requirement.

        1) You may wish to underline or circle key language or data used in the stem.

        2) Focusing on what is required enables you to ignore extraneous information and to proceed directly to determining the correct answer.

            a) Be especially careful to note when the requirement is an **exception**; e.g., "Which of the following is **not** an indication of fraud?"

    c. **Determine the correct answer** before looking at the answer choices.

        1) By adhering to these steps, you know what is required and which are the relevant facts.

        2) However, some multiple-choice items are structured so that the answer cannot be determined from the stem alone.

    d.   **Read the answer choices** carefully.

       1)   Even if answer (A) appears to be the correct choice, review the remaining answer choices. You may discover that answer (B), (C), or (D) is a better choice.

       2)   Treat each answer choice as a true-false question. Consider marking a "T" or an "F" next to each answer choice as you analyze it.

    e.   **Select the best answer**. Circle the most likely or best answer choice on the question booklet. If you are uncertain, guess intelligently to improve on your 25% chance of getting the correct answer.

       1)   For many of the multiple-choice questions, two answer choices can be eliminated with minimal effort. Eliminating them can reduce the risk of random guessing and increase your chances of success.

4.   After completing your first pass through all 125 questions, return to the questions that you marked with a "?."

5.   While answering questions, make sure you are within your time budget so you will have enough time to transfer your answers in an unhurried manner. Do not wait until the very end of the exam session to transfer answers because you may run out of time.

6.   After you have answered all 125 questions, **transfer your answers to the objective answer sheet**.

    a.   Double-check that you have transferred the answers correctly; e.g., recheck every fifth or tenth answer from your question booklet to your answer sheet to ensure that you have not fallen out of sequence.

If You Don't Know the Answer

Guess, but make it an educated guess, which means select the best possible answer. First, rule out answers that you feel are obviously incorrect. Second, speculate on The IIA's purpose and/or the rationale behind the question. These steps may lead you to the correct answer. Third, select the best answer, or guess between equally appealing answers. Mark the question with a "?" in case you have time to return to it for further analysis. However, unless you made an obvious mistake or computational error, try to avoid changing answers at the last minute. Your first guess is usually the most intuitive.

If you cannot make an educated guess, read the item and each answer and pick the best or most intuitive answer. Never leave a question unanswered.

Do **not** look at the previous answer to try to detect an answer. The answers are random, but it is possible to have four or more consecutive questions with the same answer letter, e.g., answer B.

NOTE: Do not waste time beyond the amount budgeted. Move ahead and stay on or ahead of schedule.

TAKING THE CIA EXAM

CIA Examination Preparation Checklist

1. **Register** for the exam program (see pages 6 and 7) by March 31 for the May exam dates or September 30 for the November exam dates.

2. **Apply** to take the desired parts on the same application form (for the initial registration and application), or file the reapplication form.

    a. As soon as your examination location is confirmed by The IIA, make travel and lodging reservations.

3. Acquire your study materials. Rely on *CIA Review* and *CIA Test Prep* as your primary study source.

4. Plan your study program.

5. Locate a suitable place to study.

6. Implement your study program.

7. Periodically review, reassess, and revise your study program as needed.

8. Recognize that an orderly, controlled study program builds confidence, reduces anxiety, and produces success!

9. **Pass the examination!**

Exam Psychology

Plan ahead for the exam and systematically prepare for it. Go to the exam and give it your best. Neither you nor anyone else can expect more. If you have undertaken a systematic preparation program, you will do well.

Maintain a positive attitude and do not become depressed if you encounter difficulties before or during the exam. An optimist will usually do better than an equally well-prepared pessimist. Remember, you are not in a position to be objective about your results during the exam. Many well-prepared examination candidates have been pleasantly surprised by their scores. Indeed, you should be confident because you are competing with many less-qualified persons who have not prepared as well as you. Optimism and a fighting spirit are worth points on every exam, and fear or depression tends to impair performance.

Logistical and Health Concerns

As soon as The IIA notifies you of your examination site, find suitable quarters at a hotel within walking distance of both the exam site and restaurants, if possible. Try to avoid being dependent on a car, parking spaces, etc., during the exam.

Some CIA examination sites are on university campuses. Begin by calling the student union to inquire about accommodations. Call the university's general number and ask for room reservations at the student union. If rooms are not available at the student union, ask for the office in charge of meetings, which should be able to recommend a convenient hotel.

Even if the exam is being given within driving distance of your home, consider staying by yourself at a hotel on Tuesday and Wednesday evenings to be assured of avoiding distractions. The hotel should be quiet and have a comfortable bed and desk suitable for study. If possible, stay at a hotel with recreational facilities that you normally use, e.g., a pool, exercise room, etc.

Plan to arrive at your hotel early Tuesday. To avoid any surprises, visit the examination site Tuesday afternoon or evening (remember, starting time is 8:30 a.m. Wednesday). Make sure you know where it is and how to get there. Decide where you want to sit so you have everything settled before Wednesday morning. You should locate the restroom to avoid confusion if you need to use it during the exam. Also, check on the availability of vending machines close to the exam room (for a quick soda, coffee, snack, etc., during the exam).

On Tuesday and Wednesday evenings, confine your study to a brief review of the major points covered in the next day's exam sessions. Concentrate on the sideheadings and key terms in *CIA Review*. For most CIA candidates, the best advice is to relax the evening before and to get a good night's rest. Sleep disturbance is less likely if you follow your normal routines. However, individual tastes vary, and you should do what you know has led to exam success in the past.

Proper exercise, diet, and rest during the weeks before the exam are very important. High energy levels, reduced tension, and a positive attitude are among the benefits. A good aerobic fitness program, a nutritious and well-balanced diet, and a regular sleep pattern will promote your long-term emotional and physical well-being as well as contribute significantly to a favorable exam result. Of course, the use of health-undermining substances should be avoided.

Pencils, Calculators, and Other Materials

The IIA specifically requires a No. 2 or soft-lead pencil for the multiple-choice answer sheet because it has a machine-gradable format. Nonprinting, nonprogrammable, battery- or solar-powered, six-function hand-held calculators are permitted during the CIA exam. You must supply your own pencils and calculator.

Although the instructions to proctors indicate that no food or beverages are allowed in the exam room, you should probably bring a thermos that you can take outside (if the proctors do not relent) to have a quick cup of tea, coffee, etc. Alternatively, there may be vending machines near the examination room.

Examination Tactics

1. Arrive at the site in time to have a margin of safety. Remember to bring your authorization letter and photo ID. Check in and select a seat. One advantage of being early is that you will have your choice of seats.

2. Dressing for exam success means emphasizing comfort, not appearance. Be prepared to adjust for changes in temperature, e.g., remove a sweater or put on a coat. Do not bring notes, this text, other books, etc., to the exam. You will only make yourself nervous and confused by trying to cram during the last 5 minutes before the exam. Books are not allowed in the exam room anyway. You should, however, bring an adequate supply of authorized items, e.g., pencils, erasers, a timepiece, and an appropriate calculator (nonprinting, nonprogrammable, battery- or solar-powered, six-function hand-held).

3. Use a clear plastic bag to carry your exam supplies. A larger size is more appropriate for storing pencils, an eraser, a calculator, breath mints, chewing gum, candy, etc.

4. Read the exam instructions carefully.

5. Answer the 125 questions in chronological order, circle the correct (or best guess) answer to each question. You can and should write in your exam booklet. Mark questions that you are leaving for later or you wish to review with big question marks.

6. You have 210 minutes (3.5 hours) to answer 125 questions. If you allocate 1.4 minutes per question, you will use only 175 minutes, leaving 35 minutes to review your answers and transfer your answers to the machine readable answer sheet. If you pace yourself during the exam, you will have adequate time to complete each part.

7. After you worked through all 125 questions, you should return to the questions you have marked with question marks and select the best answer.

8. After you have answered all 125 questions, review each question carefully. If you made an obvious mistake, e.g., misread the question, make the correction. DO NOT, however, begin changing answers and second guessing yourself. Your first answer to each question should be based on the systematic question answering technique that you have practiced throughout your preparation program.

9. As a final step, transfer all of your answers from your exam booklet to your machine readable answer sheet carefully and deliberately. Darken the correct answer with a number 2 pencil. Recheck your sequence; the question number in your exam booklet should correspond with the question number on your answer sheet (a sure way to fail is to transfer your answers incorrectly).

10. Do not discuss the examination and your solutions with other candidates at the noon breaks or on Wednesday evening. This will only make you nervous and reduce your confidence. Obviously such discussions cannot affect your grade. Remember that you are as competent as other candidates and were well-prepared for the exam.

11. As soon as you complete the exam, we would like you to e-mail, fax, or write to us with your comments on our books and software. We are particularly interested in which topics need to be added or expanded. We are NOT asking about specific CIA questions. Rather, we are asking for feedback on our books and software. Use the last two pages in each Gleim book to send us your comments. This approach is approved by The IIA.

STUDY UNIT ONE
INTRODUCTION TO INTERNAL AUDITING

(13 pages of outline)

This study unit describes the development of internal auditing and the responsibilities of internal auditors. The relevant mandatory pronouncements of The IIA -- the **International Standards for the Professional Practice of Internal Auditing (Standards)** -- are also reproduced, including a listing of useful terms. The Standards will also be integrated throughout this volume with nonmandatory guidance provided by The IIA and other outline material.

1.1 DEVELOPMENT OF INTERNAL AUDITING

1. Internal auditing is a management-oriented discipline that has evolved rapidly since World War II. Once a function primarily concerned with financial and accounting matters, internal auditing now addresses the entire range of operating activities and performs a correspondingly wide variety of assurance and consulting services. The development of internal auditing was fostered by the increased size and decentralization of organizations, the greater complexity and technological sophistication of their operations, and the resulting need for an independent, objective means of evaluating and improving their risk management, control, and governance processes. Accordingly, The IIA's **definition of internal auditing** is as follows:

    Internal auditing is an independent, objective assurance and consulting activity designed to add value and improve an organization's operations. It helps an organization accomplish its objectives by bringing a systematic, disciplined approach to evaluate and improve the effectiveness of risk management, control, and governance processes.

2. Public policy considerations have also contributed to the improved status and broadened scope of internal auditing. Organizations are expected to maintain reasonably detailed and accurate accounting records and a reasonably effective system of internal accounting control, and public companies should have an internal audit activity and an audit committee composed of nonmanagement directors.

3. A factor that was both the result of, and a contributor to, the professionalization of internal auditing was the founding of The Institute of Internal Auditors.

    a. The articles of incorporation of The IIA state its purposes:

        To cultivate, promote, and disseminate knowledge and information concerning internal auditing and subjects related thereto; to establish and maintain high standards of integrity, honor, and character among internal auditors; to furnish information regarding internal auditing and the practice and methods thereof to its members, and to other persons interested therein, and to the general public; to cause the publication of articles relating to internal auditing and practices and methods thereof; to establish and maintain a library and reading rooms, meeting rooms and social rooms for the use of its members; to promote social intercourse among its members; and to do any and all things which shall be lawful and appropriate in furtherance of any of the purposes hereinbefore expressed.

b. The following is the official statement of The IIA Board of Directors regarding the CIA program:

1) ***Professional Qualifications***

To assist in achieving the goals and objectives of The Institute, the Certified Internal Auditor (CIA) Program was established. The Board of Directors will develop, approve and modify as necessary, such policies and procedures as may be required to stimulate and encourage this program.

While "Certified Internal Auditor" is intended to be the worldwide designation of qualified internal audit professionals, it is recognized for various reasons other professional organizations of internal auditors may develop similar designations. The Board of Directors will develop, approve and modify as necessary, such procedures as may be deemed desirable to recognize those designations.

The Board may also approve additional certifications as appropriate.

c. The IIA has promoted the professionalization of internal auditing primarily through

1) Adopting a common body of knowledge listing the disciplines related to internal auditing and the competencies that internal auditors must develop within each discipline

2) Establishing a certification program, including an examination that is a prerequisite to receipt of the Certified Internal Auditor designation

3) Administering a continuing professional education (CPE) program

4) Publishing a technical journal, *The Internal Auditor*

5) Establishing a Professional Practices Framework that includes the definition of internal auditing, The IIA *Code of Ethics*, the Standards, Practice Advisories, and Development & Practices Aids.

4. The pace of change in the profession is accelerating. In June 1999, The IIA approved a new definition of internal auditing and a new **Professional Practices Framework**. In June 2000, a new **Code of Ethics** was adopted.

a. In February 2001, the revised Standards were issued. They included **Attribute Standards** and **Performance Standards** that apply to all services provided by internal auditors. They also included **Implementation Standards** that apply to **assurance services**. These new Standards were effective January 1, 2002.

1) **Implementation Standards** relevant to **consulting** services became effective on July 1, 2002.

5. Currently, The IIA has proposed new and replacement standards and editorial changes, including changes in Glossary items. These proposals are available on The IIA's website (www.theiia.org).

6. Stop and review! You have completed the outline for this subunit. Study multiple-choice questions 1 through 9 beginning on page 35.

1.2 STANDARDS AND GLOSSARY

1. The environments and organizations in which internal audit activities are performed throughout the world are highly diverse. Moreover, these activities may be insourced or outsourced. This diversity affects the practice of internal auditing in each environment and organization. Nevertheless, compliance with the Standards is mandatory for individuals and entities providing internal auditing services. However, to accommodate the diversity of practice, the language of the Standards is broadly inclusive, and more specific guidance is left to other pronouncements.

    a. Internal audit activities may involve both assurance and consulting services.

2. According to The IIA, the Standards are intended to

    a. State basic principles for the practice of internal auditing.
    b. Provide a framework for performing and promoting value-added internal audit activities.
    c. Establish the basis for evaluating internal auditing performance.
    d. Improve organizational processes and operations.

3. The Standards consist of Attribute Standards (currently 1000-1340), Performance Standards (currently 2000-2600), and Implementation Standards (integrated with the other Standards). Attribute Standards concern the traits of entities and individuals providing internal auditing services. Performance Standards describe internal audit activities and criteria for evaluation of their performance. Attribute and Performance Standards furnish guidance for all internal auditing services (assurance, consulting, and other).

    a. Implementation Standards apply the other Standards to specific engagements. Thus, different groups of Implementation Standards may be promulgated for the major categories of internal audit activities. For example, final Implementation Standards have been issued for assurance services (e.g., 1110.A1) and consulting services (e.g., 1000.C1).

4. The Glossary appended to the Standards contains crucially important terminology. For example, "internal audit activity" and "chief audit executive" have replaced "internal auditing department" and "internal auditing director," respectively. These changes follow from the reality that the internal auditing function is often outsourced. Furthermore, the term "internal audit activity" is stated in terms of the definition of internal auditing. Other key definitions include those related to the nature of the work of the internal audit activity ("risk," "control," and "governance") and the kinds of engagements performed ("assurance services" and "consulting services").

5. The Standards are included in full here as a convenient reference for the examination candidate. However, they will be repeated in other Study Units and subunits as appropriate.

ATTRIBUTE STANDARDS

1000   ***Purpose, Authority, and Responsibility*** — *The purpose, authority, and responsibility of the internal audit activity should be formally defined in a charter, consistent with the Standards, and approved by the board.*

> *1000.A1 - The nature of assurance services provided to the organization should be defined in the audit charter. If assurance services are to be provided to parties outside the organization, the nature of these assurances should also be defined in the charter.*

> *1000.C1 - The nature of consulting services should be defined in the audit charter.*

1100   Independence and Objectivity — *The internal audit activity should be independent, and internal auditors should be objective in performing their work.*

1110   Organizational Independence — *The chief audit executive should report to a level within the organization that allows the internal audit activity to fulfill its responsibilities.*

1110.A1 - The internal audit activity should be free from interference in determining the scope of internal auditing, performing work, and communicating results.

1120   Individual Objectivity — *Internal auditors should have an impartial, unbiased attitude and avoid conflicts of interest.*

1130   Impairments to Independence or Objectivity — *If independence or objectivity is impaired in fact or appearance, the details of the impairment should be disclosed to appropriate parties. The nature of the disclosure will depend upon the impairment.*

1130.A1 - Internal auditors should refrain from assessing specific operations for which they were previously responsible. Objectivity is presumed to be impaired if an auditor provides assurance services for an activity for which the auditor had responsibility within the previous year.

1130.A2 - Assurance engagements for functions over which the chief audit executive has responsibility should be overseen by a party outside the internal audit activity.

1130.C1 - Internal auditors may provide consulting services relating to operations for which they had previous responsibilities.

1130.C2 - If internal auditors have potential impairments to independence or objectivity relating to proposed consulting services, disclosure should be made to the engagement client prior to accepting the engagement.

1200   Proficiency and Due Professional Care — *Engagements should be performed with proficiency and due professional care.*

1210   Proficiency — *Internal auditors should possess the knowledge, skills, and other competencies needed to perform their individual responsibilities. The internal audit activity collectively should possess or obtain the knowledge, skills, and other competencies needed to perform its responsibilities.*

1210.A1 - The chief audit executive should obtain competent advice and assistance if the internal audit staff lacks the knowledge, skills, or other competencies needed to perform all or part of the engagement.

1210.A2 - The internal auditor should have sufficient knowledge to identify the indicators of fraud but is not expected to have the expertise of a person whose primary responsibility is detecting and investigating fraud.

1210.C1 - The chief audit executive should decline the consulting engagement or obtain competent advice and assistance if the internal audit staff lacks the knowledge, skills, or other competencies needed to perform all or part of the engagement.

1220 **<u>Due Professional Care</u>** — *Internal auditors should apply the care and skill expected of a reasonably prudent and competent internal auditor. Due professional care does not imply infallibility.*

1220.A1 - The internal auditor should exercise due professional care by considering the:

- *Extent of work needed to achieve the engagement's objectives.*
- *Relative complexity, materiality, or significance of matters to which assurance procedures are applied.*
- *Adequacy and effectiveness of risk management, control, and governance processes.*
- *Probability of significant errors, irregularities, or noncompliance.*
- *Cost of assurance in relation to potential benefits.*

1220.A2 - The internal auditor should be alert to the significant risks that might affect objectives, operations, or resources. However, assurance procedures alone, even when performed with due professional care, do not guarantee that all significant risks will be identified.

1220.C1 - The internal auditor should exercise due professional care during a consulting engagement by considering the:

- *Needs and expectations of engagement clients, including the nature, timing, and communication of engagement results.*
- *Relative complexity and extent of work needed to achieve the engagement's objectives.*
- *Cost of the consulting engagement in relation to potential benefits.*

1230 **<u>Continuing Professional Development</u>** — *Internal auditors should enhance their knowledge, skills, and other competencies through continuing professional development.*

1300 **<u>Quality Assurance and Improvement Program</u>** — *The chief audit executive should develop and maintain a quality assurance and improvement program that covers all aspects of the internal audit activity and continuously monitors its effectiveness. The program should be designed to help the internal auditing activity add value and improve the organization's operations and to provide assurance that the internal audit activity is in conformity with the Standards and the Code of Ethics.*

1310 **<u>Quality Program Assessments</u>** — *The internal audit activity should adopt a process to monitor and assess the overall effectiveness of the quality program. The process should include both internal and external assessments.*

1311 **<u>Internal Assessments</u>** — *Internal assessments should include:*

- *Ongoing reviews of the performance of the internal audit activity; and*
- *Periodic reviews performed through self-assessment or by other persons within the organization with knowledge of internal auditing practices and the Standards.*

1312 **<u>External Assessments</u>** — *External assessments, such as quality assurance reviews, should be conducted at least once every five years by a qualified, independent reviewer or review team from outside the organization.*

1320   <u>**Reporting on the Quality Program**</u> — *The chief audit executive should communicate the results of external assessments to the board.*

1330   <u>**Use of "Conducted in Accordance with the Standards"**</u> — *Internal auditors are encouraged to report that their activities are "conducted in accordance with the Standards for the Professional Practice of Internal Auditing." However, internal auditors may use the statement only if assessments of the quality improvement program demonstrate that the internal audit activity is in compliance with the Standards.*

1340   <u>**Disclosure of Noncompliance**</u> — *Although the internal audit activity should achieve full compliance with the Standards and internal auditors with the Code of Ethics, there may be instances in which full compliance is not achieved. When noncompliance impacts the overall scope or operation of the internal audit activity, disclosure should be made to senior management and the board.*

<u>PERFORMANCE STANDARDS</u>

2000   <u>**Managing the Internal Audit Activity**</u> — *The chief audit executive should effectively manage the internal audit activity to ensure it adds value to the organization.*

    2010   <u>**Planning**</u> — *The chief audit executive should establish risk-based plans to determine the priorities of the internal audit activity, consistent with the organization's goals.*

        2010.A1 - The internal audit activity's plan of engagements should be based on a risk assessment, undertaken at least annually. The input of senior management and the board should be considered in this process.

        2010.C1 - The chief audit executive should consider accepting proposed consulting engagements based on the engagement's potential to improve management of risks, add value, and improve the organization's operations. Those engagements that have been accepted should be included in the plan.

    2020   <u>**Communication and Approval**</u> — *The chief audit executive should communicate the internal audit activity's plans and resource requirements, including significant interim changes, to senior management and to the board for review and approval. The chief audit executive should also communicate the impact of resource limitations.*

    2030   <u>**Resource Management**</u> — *The chief audit executive should ensure that internal audit resources are appropriate, sufficient, and effectively deployed to achieve the approved plan.*

    2040   <u>**Policies and Procedures**</u> — *The chief audit executive should establish policies and procedures to guide the internal audit activity.*

    2050   <u>**Coordination**</u> — *The chief audit executive should share information and coordinate activities with other internal and external providers of relevant assurance and consulting services to ensure proper coverage and minimize duplication of efforts.*

    2060   <u>**Reporting to the Board and Senior Management**</u> — *The chief audit executive should report periodically to the board and senior management on the internal audit activity's purpose, authority, responsibility, and performance relative to its plan. Reporting should also include significant risk exposures and control issues, corporate governance issues, and other matters needed or requested by the board and senior management.*

2100   ***Nature of Work*** *— The internal audit activity evaluates and contributes to the improvement of risk management, control, and governance systems.*

    2110   ***Risk Management*** *— The internal audit activity should assist the organization by identifying and evaluating significant exposures to risk and contributing to the improvement of risk management and control systems.*

        2110.A1 - The internal audit activity should monitor and evaluate the effectiveness of the organization's risk management system.

        2110.A2 - The internal audit activity should evaluate risk exposures relating to the organization's governance, operations, and information systems regarding the

- *Reliability and integrity of financial and operational information.*
- *Effectiveness and efficiency of operations.*
- *Safeguarding of assets.*
- *Compliance with laws, regulations, and contracts.*

        2110.C1 - During consulting engagements, internal auditors should address risk consistent with the engagement's objectives and should be alert to the existence of other significant risks.

        2110.C2 - Internal auditors should incorporate knowledge of risks gained from consulting engagements into the process of identifying and evaluating significant risk exposures of the organization.

    2120   ***Control*** *— The internal audit activity should assist the organization in maintaining effective controls by evaluating their effectiveness and efficiency and by promoting continuous improvement.*

        2120.A1 - Based on the results of the risk assessment, the internal audit activity should evaluate the adequacy and effectiveness of controls encompassing the organization's governance, operations, and information systems. This should include:

- *Reliability and integrity of financial and operational information.*
- *Effectiveness and efficiency of operations.*
- *Safeguarding of assets.*
- *Compliance with laws, regulations, and contracts.*

        2120.A2 - Internal auditors should ascertain the extent to which operating and program goals and objectives have been established and conform to those of the organization.

        2120.A3 - Internal auditors should review operations and programs to ascertain the extent to which results are consistent with established goals and objectives to determine whether operations and programs are being implemented or performed as intended.

        2120.A4 - Adequate criteria are needed to evaluate controls. Internal auditors should ascertain the extent to which management has established adequate criteria to determine whether objectives and goals have been accomplished. If adequate, internal auditors should use such criteria in their evaluation. If inadequate, internal auditors should work with management to develop appropriate evaluation criteria.

2120.C1 - During consulting engagements, internal auditors should address controls consistent with the engagement's objectives and should be alert to the existence of any significant control weaknesses.

2120.C2 - Internal auditors should incorporate knowledge of controls gained from consulting engagements into the process of identifying and evaluating significant risk exposures of the organization.

2130   **Governance** *— The internal audit activity should contribute to the organization's governance process by evaluating and improving the process through which (1) values and goals are established and communicated, (2) the accomplishment of goals is monitored, (3) accountability is ensured, and (4) values are preserved.*

2130.A1 - Internal auditors should review operations and programs to ensure consistency with organizational values.

2130.C1 - Consulting engagement objectives should be consistent with the overall values and goals of the organization.

2200   **Engagement Planning** *— Internal auditors should develop and record a plan for each engagement.*

2201   **Planning Considerations** *— In planning the engagement, internal auditors should consider:*

- *The objectives of the activity being reviewed and the means by which the activity controls its performance.*
- *The significant risks to the activity, its objectives, resources, and operations and the means by which the potential impact of risk is kept to an acceptable level.*
- *The adequacy and effectiveness of the activity's risk management and control systems compared to a relevant control framework or model.*
- *The opportunities for making significant improvements to the activity's risk management and control systems.*

2201.C1 - Internal auditors should establish an understanding with consulting engagement clients about objectives, scope, respective responsibilities, and other client expectations. For significant engagements, this understanding should be documented.

2210   **Engagement Objectives** *— The engagement's objectives should address the risks, controls, and governance processes associated with the activities under review.*

2210.A1 - When planning the engagement, the internal auditor should identify and assess risks relevant to the activity under review. The engagement objectives should reflect the results of the risk assessment.

2210.A2 - The internal auditor should consider the probability of significant errors, irregularities, noncompliance, and other exposures when developing the engagement objectives.

2210.C1 - Consulting engagement objectives should address risks, controls, and governance processes to the extent agreed upon with the client.

2220 <u>**Engagement Scope**</u> — *The established scope should be sufficient to satisfy the objectives of the engagement.*

> *2220.A1 - The scope of the engagement should include consideration of relevant systems, records, personnel, and physical properties, including those under the control of third parties.*

> *2220.C1 - In performing consulting engagements, internal auditors should ensure that the scope of the engagement is sufficient to address the agreed-upon objectives. If internal auditors develop reservations about the scope during the engagement, these reservations should be discussed with the client to determine whether to continue with the engagement.*

2230 <u>**Engagement Resource Allocation**</u> — *Internal auditors should determine appropriate resources to achieve engagement objectives. Staffing should be based on an evaluation of the nature and complexity of each engagement, time constraints, and available resources.*

2240 <u>**Engagement Work Program**</u> — *Internal auditors should develop work programs that achieve the engagement objectives. These work programs should be recorded.*

> *2240.A1 - Work programs should establish the procedures for identifying, analyzing, evaluating, and recording information during the engagement. The work program should be approved prior to the commencement of work, and any adjustments approved promptly.*

> *2240.C1 - Work programs for consulting engagements may vary in form and content depending upon the nature of the engagement.*

2300 <u>**Performing the Engagement**</u> — *Internal auditors should identify, analyze, evaluate, and record sufficient information to achieve the engagement's objectives.*

2310 <u>**Identifying Information**</u> — *Internal auditors should identify sufficient, reliable, relevant, and useful information to achieve the engagement's objectives.*

2320 <u>**Analysis and Evaluation**</u> — *Internal auditors should base conclusions and engagement results on appropriate analyses and evaluations.*

2330 <u>**Recording Information**</u> — *Internal auditors should record relevant information to support the conclusions and engagement results.*

> *2330.A1 - The chief audit executive should control access to engagement records. The chief audit executive should obtain the approval of senior management and/or legal counsel prior to releasing such records to external parties, as appropriate.*

> *2330.A2 - The chief audit executive should develop retention requirements for engagement records. These retention requirements should be consistent with the organization's guidelines and any pertinent regulatory or other requirements.*

> *2330.C1 - The chief audit executive should develop policies governing the custody and retention of engagement records, as well as their release to internal and external parties. These policies should be consistent with the organization's guidelines and any pertinent regulatory or other requirements.*

2340 <u>**Engagement Supervision**</u> — *Engagements should be properly supervised to ensure objectives are achieved, quality is assured, and staff is developed.*

2400   ***Communicating Results*** — *Internal auditors should communicate the engagement results promptly.*

> **2410**   ***Criteria for Communicating*** — *Communications should include the engagement's objectives and scope as well as applicable conclusions, recommendations, and action plans.*
>
> > *2410.A1 - The final communication of results should, where appropriate, contain the internal auditor's overall opinion.*
> >
> > *2410.A2 - Engagement communications should acknowledge satisfactory performance.*
> >
> > *2410.C1 - Communication of the progress and results of consulting engagements will vary in form and content depending upon the nature of the engagement and the needs of the client.*
>
> **2420**   ***Quality of Communications*** — *Communications should be accurate, objective, clear, concise, constructive, complete, and timely.*
>
> > **2421 *Errors and Omissions*** — *If a final communication contains a significant error or omission, the chief audit executive should communicate corrected information to all individuals who received the original communication.*
>
> **2430**   ***Engagement Disclosure of Noncompliance with the Standards*** — *When noncompliance with the Standards impacts a specific engagement, communication of the results should disclose the:*
>
> > - *Standard(s) with which full compliance was not achieved,*
> > - *Reason(s) for noncompliance, and*
> > - *Impact of noncompliance on the engagement.*
>
> **2440**   ***Disseminating Results*** — *The chief audit executive should disseminate results to the appropriate individuals.*
>
> > *2440.A1 - The chief audit executive is responsible for communicating the final results to individuals who can ensure that the results are given due consideration.*
> >
> > *2440.C1 - The chief audit executive is responsible for communicating the final results of consulting engagements to clients.*
> >
> > *2440.C2 - During consulting engagements, risk management, control, and governance issues may be identified. Whenever these issues are significant to the organization, they should be communicated to senior management and the board.*

2500   ***Monitoring Progress*** — *The chief audit executive should establish and maintain a system to monitor the disposition of results communicated to management.*

> *2500.A1 - The chief audit executive should establish a follow-up process to monitor and ensure that management actions have been effectively implemented or that senior management has accepted the risk of not taking action.*
>
> *2500.C1 - The internal audit activity should monitor the disposition of results of consulting engagements to the extent agreed upon with the client.*

2600 <u>**Management's Acceptance of Risks**</u> — *When the chief audit executive believes that senior management has accepted a level of residual risk that is unacceptable to the organization, the chief audit executive should discuss the matter with senior management. If the decision regarding residual risk is not resolved, the chief audit executive and senior management should report the matter to the board for resolution.*

Glossary

Add Value - *Organizations exist to create value or benefit to their owners, other stakeholders, customers, and clients. This concept provides purpose for their existence. Value is provided through their development of products and services and their use of resources to promote those products and services. In the process of gathering data to understand and assess risk, internal auditors develop significant insight into operations and opportunities for improvement that can be extremely beneficial to their organization. This valuable information can be in the form of consultation, advice, written communications, or through other products all of which should be properly communicated to the appropriate management or operating personnel.*

Adequate Control - *Present if management has planned and organized (designed) in a manner that provides reasonable assurance that the organization's risks have been managed effectively and that the organization's goals and objectives will be achieved efficiently and economically.*

Assurance Services - *An objective examination of evidence for the purpose of providing an independent assessment on risk management, control, or governance processes for the organization. Examples may include financial, performance, compliance, system security, and due diligence engagements.*

Board - *A board of directors, audit committee of such boards, head of an agency or legislative body to whom internal auditors report, board of governors or trustees of a nonprofit organization, or any other designated governing body of an organization.*

Charter - *The charter of the internal audit activity is a formal written document that defines the activity's purpose, authority, and responsibility. The charter should (a) establish the internal audit activity's position within the organization; (b) authorize access to records, personnel, and physical properties relevant to the performance of engagements; and (c) define the scope of internal audit activities.*

Chief Audit Executive - *Top position within the organization responsible for internal audit activities. In a traditional internal audit activity, this would be the internal audit director. In the case where internal audit activities are obtained from outside service providers, the chief audit executive is the person responsible for overseeing the service contract and the overall quality assurance of these activities, reporting to senior management and the board regarding internal audit activities, and follow-up of engagement results. The term also includes such titles as general auditor, chief internal auditor, and inspector general.*

Code of Ethics - *The purpose of the Code of Ethics of The Institute of Internal Auditors (IIA) is to promote an ethical culture in the global profession of internal auditing. A code of ethics is necessary and appropriate for the profession of internal auditing, founded as it is on the trust placed in its objective assurance about risk, control, and governance. The Code of Ethics applies to both individuals and entities that provide internal audit services.*

Compliance - *The ability to reasonably ensure conformity and adherence to organization policies, plans, procedures, laws, regulations, and contracts.*

Conflict of Interest - *Any relationship that is or appears to be not in the best interest of the organization. A conflict of interest would prejudice an individual's ability to perform his or her duties and responsibilities objectively.*

Consulting Services - Advisory and related client service activities, the nature and scope of which are agreed upon with the client and are intended to add value and improve an organization's operations. Examples include counsel, advice, facilitation, process design, and training.

Control - Any action taken by management, the board, and other parties to enhance risk management and increase the likelihood that established objectives and goals will be achieved. Management plans, organizes, and directs the performance of sufficient actions to provide reasonable assurance that objectives and goals will be achieved.

Control Environment - The attitude and actions of the board and management regarding the significance of control within the organization. The control environment provides the discipline and structure for the achievement of the primary objectives of the system of internal control. The control environment includes the following elements:

- Integrity and ethical values.
- Management's philosophy and operating style.
- Organizational structure.
- Assignment of authority and responsibility.
- Human resource policies and practices.
- Competence of personnel.

Control Processes - The policies, procedures, and activities that are part of a control framework, designed to ensure that risks are contained within the risk tolerances established by the risk management process.

Engagement - A specific internal audit assignment, task, or review activity, such as an internal audit, Control Self-Assessment review, fraud examination, or consultancy. An engagement may include multiple tasks or activities designed to accomplish a specific set of related objectives.

Engagement Objectives - Broad statements developed by internal auditors that define intended engagement accomplishments.

Engagement Work Program - A document that lists the procedures to be followed during an engagement, designed to achieve the engagement plan.

External Service Provider - A person or firm, independent of the organization, who has special knowledge, skill, and experience in a particular discipline. Outside service providers include, among others, actuaries, accountants, appraisers, environmental specialists, fraud investigators, lawyers, engineers, geologists, security specialists, statisticians, information technology specialists, external auditors, and other auditing organizations. The board, senior management, or the chief audit executive may engage an outside service provider.

Fraud - Any illegal acts characterized by deceit, concealment or violation of trust. These acts are not dependent upon the application of threat of violence or of physical force. Frauds are perpetrated by individuals and organizations to obtain money, property or services; to avoid payment or loss of services; or to secure personal or business advantage.

Governance Process - The procedures utilized by the representatives of the organization's stakeholders (e.g., shareholders, etc.) to provide oversight of risk and control processes administered by management.

Impairments - Impairments to individual objectivity and organizational independence may include personal conflicts of interest; scope limitations; restrictions on access to records, personnel, and properties; and resource limitations (funding).

Internal Audit Activity - A department, division, team of consultants, or other practitioner(s) that provides independent, objective assurance and consulting services designed to add value and improve an organization's operations. The internal audit activity helps an organization accomplish its objectives by bringing a systematic, disciplined approach to evaluate and improve the effectiveness of risk management, control, and governance processes.

Objectivity - An unbiased mental attitude that requires internal auditors to perform engagements in such a manner that they have an honest belief in their work product and that no significant quality compromises are made. Objectivity requires internal auditors not to subordinate their judgment on audit matters to that of others.

Risk - The uncertainty of an event occurring that could have an impact on the achievement of objectives. Risk is measured in terms of consequences and likelihood.

6. Stop and review! You have completed the outline for this subunit. Study multiple-choice questions 10 through 23 beginning on page 38.

QUESTIONS

1.1 Development of Internal Auditing

1. From a modern internal auditing perspective, which one of the following statements represents the most important benefit of an internal auditing activity to management?

A. Assurance that published financial statements are correct.

B. Assurance that fraudulent activities will be detected.

C. Assurance that the organization is complying with legal requirements.

D. Assurance that there is reasonable control over day-to-day operations.

Answer (D) is correct. *(CMA, adapted)*
REQUIRED: The most important benefit of an IAA.
DISCUSSION: According to the definition of internal auditing, "Internal auditing is an independent, objective assurance and consulting activity designed to add value and improve an organization's operations. It helps an organization accomplish its objectives by bringing a systematic, disciplined approach to evaluate and improve the effectiveness of risk management, control, and governance processes." Thus, it helps the organization to maintain effective controls by evaluating their effectiveness and efficiency and by promoting continuous improvement (Standard 2120).
Answer (A) is incorrect because published financial statements are only required to be fairly presented. Internal audit activities cannot assure correctness. Answer (B) is incorrect because internal auditing's responsibility with respect to fraud detection is to examine and evaluate the adequacy and effectiveness of internal control. Answer (C) is incorrect because internal auditing evaluates and contributes to the improvement of risk management, control, and governance processes, but it cannot assure compliance with legal requirements.

2. Of the following, which is the major objective of The Institute of Internal Auditors (IIA)?

A. Cultivate, promote, and disseminate information concerning internal auditing and related subjects.

B. Oversee the activities of internal auditors.

C. Promulgate standards that must be followed by all businesses.

D. Investigate accusations that Certified Internal Auditors have violated The Institute of Internal Auditors *Code of Ethics*.

Answer (A) is correct. *(CIA, adapted)*
REQUIRED: The major objective of The IIA.
DISCUSSION: The articles of incorporation of The IIA state its purposes: "To cultivate, promote, and disseminate knowledge and information concerning internal auditing and subjects related thereto; to establish and maintain high standards of integrity, honor, and character among internal auditors; to furnish information regarding internal auditing and the practice and methods thereof to its members, and to other persons interested therein, and to the general public; to cause the publication of articles relating to internal auditing and practices and methods thereof; to establish and maintain a library and reading rooms, meeting rooms and social rooms for the use of its members; to promote social intercourse among its members; and to do any and all things which shall be lawful and appropriate in furtherance of any of the purposes hereinbefore expressed."
Answer (B) is incorrect because The IIA is not a regulatory agency. Answer (C) is incorrect because the Standards are mandatory guidance for individuals and entities that provide internal auditing services, not for businesses. Answer (D) is incorrect because investigating ethics violations is not a major objective.

3. Which of the following is not a part of The IIA's stated purpose?

    A. To cultivate, promote, and disseminate knowledge and information concerning internal auditing and related subjects.

    B. To establish and maintain high standards of integrity, honor, and character among internal auditors.

    C. To adopt a common body of knowledge listing and disciplines related to internal auditing and the competencies that internal auditors must develop within each discipline.

    D. To cause the publication of articles relating to internal auditing and practices and methods thereof.

Answer (C) is correct. *(Publisher)*
    REQUIRED: The item that is not a part of The IIA's stated purposes.
    DISCUSSION: According to the articles of incorporation of The IIA, its purposes are: to cultivate, promote, and disseminate knowledge and information concerning internal auditing and related subjects; to establish and maintain high standards of integrity, honor, and character among internal auditors; to furnish information regarding internal auditing and its practice and methods to its members, and to other interested persons, and to the general public; to cause the publication of articles relating to internal auditing and its practices and methods; to establish and maintain a library and reading rooms, meeting rooms and social rooms for the use of its members; to promote social intercourse among its members; and to do any and all things that are lawful and appropriate in furtherance of any of these purposes. Answer (C) is not a part of the IIA's stated purpose, although it is a way that The IIA has promoted the professionalism of internal auditing.

4. The internal auditing profession is believed to have advanced primarily as a consequence of

    A. Increased interest by graduating students and experienced auditors.

    B. The limitation of the external audit's scope.

    C. Job qualification specifications that include added emphasis on background knowledge and skills.

    D. Increased complexity and sophistication of business operations.

Answer (D) is correct. *(CIA, adapted)*
    REQUIRED: The reason for the internal auditing profession's increasing importance.
    DISCUSSION: The increased complexity and sophistication of business operations have required management to rely on an internal audit activity that adds value by evaluating and contributing to the improvement of risk management, control, and governance systems.
    Answer (A) is incorrect because increased interest by graduating students and experienced auditors is not the primary reason for the advancement of the internal auditing profession, but it contributes to, or results from, such advancement. Answer (B) is incorrect because a limitation on the external audit's scope does not contribute to the profession's advancement. Answer (C) is incorrect because improved qualifications of internal auditors are a result of increased complexity and sophistication of business operations.

5. What kind of considerations have contributed most significantly to the improved status and broadened scope of internal auditing?

    A. Economic considerations.

    B. Public policy considerations.

    C. Market considerations.

    D. Management considerations.

Answer (B) is correct. *(Publisher)*
    REQUIRED: The considerations that have contributed to the improved status and broadened scope of internal auditing.
    DISCUSSION: Public policy considerations have contributed to the improved status and broadened scope of internal auditing. Organizations are expected to maintain reasonably detailed and accurate accounting records and a reasonably effective system of internal accounting control, and public companies should have an internal audit activity and an audit committee composed on nonmanagement directors.

6. The proper organizational role of internal auditing is to

    A. Assist the external auditor in order to reduce external audit fees.

    B. Perform studies to assist in the attainment of more efficient operations.

    C. Serve as the investigative arm of the board.

    D. Serve as an independent, objective assurance and consulting activity that adds value to operations.

Answer (D) is correct. *(CIA, adapted)*
    REQUIRED: The role of internal auditing.
    DISCUSSION: According to the definition of internal auditing, "Internal auditing is an independent, objective assurance and consulting activity designed to add value and improve an organization's operations. It helps an organization accomplish its objectives by bringing a systematic, disciplined approach to evaluate and improve the effectiveness of risk management, control, and governance processes."
    Answer (A) is incorrect because reducing external audit fees may be a direct result of internal audit work, but it is not a reason for staffing an internal audit activity. Answer (B) is incorrect because the primary role of internal auditing includes but is not limited to assessing the efficiency of operations. Answer (C) is incorrect because internal auditors serve management as well as the board.

7. A major reason for establishing an internal audit activity is to

  A. Relieve overburdened management of the responsibility for establishing effective controls.

  B. Safeguard resources entrusted to the organization.

  C. Ensure the reliability and integrity of financial and operational information.

  D. Evaluate and improve the effectiveness of control processes.

Answer (D) is correct. *(CIA, adapted)*

REQUIRED: The major reason for establishing an internal audit activity.

DISCUSSION: According to the Glossary, control processes are defined as "The policies, procedures, and activities that are part of a control framework, designed to ensure that risks are contained within the risk tolerances established by the risk management process." Hence, they have a prominent role in internal auditing, which "helps an organization accomplish its objectives by bringing a systematic, disciplined approach to evaluate and improve the effectiveness of risk management, control, and governance processes."

Answer (A) is incorrect because management is responsible for the establishment of internal control. Answer (B) is incorrect because risk management, control, and governance processes ultimately serve to safeguard the organization's resources. Answer (C) is incorrect because the IAA cannot ensure the reliability and integrity of financial and operational information. Its responsibility is to evaluate risk exposures relating to governance, operations, and information systems regarding the reliability and integrity of financial and operational information (Standard 2110.A2). Based on the risk assessment, it then evaluates the adequacy and effectiveness of controls (Standard 2120.A1).

8. What is a role of The IIA Board of Directors?

  A. To publish *The Internal Auditor*.

  B. To administer a continuing education program for internal auditors.

  C. To establish a certification program, including an examination that is a prerequisite to receipt of the Certified Internal Auditor designation.

  D. To develop procedures required to stimulate and encourage the Certified Internal Auditor Program.

Answer (D) is correct. *(Publisher)*

REQUIRED: The item that is a role of The IIA Board of Directors.

DISCUSSION: In the official statement of the IIA Board of Directors regarding the CIA program they stated "The Board of Directors will develop, approve, and modify as necessary, such procedures as may be required to stimulate and encourage the Certified Internal Auditor Program." The board also stated it would develop, approve, and modify as necessary, such procedures as may be deemed desirable to make the "Certified Internal Auditor" a worldwide designation of qualified internal audit professionals.

9. The Attribute Standards and Performance Standards that apply to all services provided by internal auditors were effective as of what date?

  A. June 1999.

  B. January 1, 2001.

  C. July 1, 2002.

  D. February 2001.

Answer (B) is correct. *(Publisher)*

REQUIRED: The date that the Attribute and Performance Standards became effective.

DISCUSSION: In February 2001, the revised Standards were issued. They include Attribute Standards and Performance Standards that apply to all services provided by internal auditors and Implementation Standards that apply to assurance services. These new Standards were effective January 1, 2002.

Answer (A) is incorrect because June 1999 is when the IIA approved the new definition of internal auditing and a new Professional Practices Framework. Answer (C) is incorrect because July 1, 2002 is the date that Implementation Standards relevant to consulting activities became effective. Answer (D) is incorrect because February 2001 is the date the revised Standards were issued.

1.2 Standards and Glossary

10. One of the purposes of the Standards for the Professional Practice of Internal Auditing as stated in the Introduction to the current version of the Standards is to

   A. Encourage the professionalization of internal auditing.

   B. Establish the independence of the internal audit activity and emphasize the objectivity of internal auditing.

   C. Encourage external auditors to make more extensive use of the work of internal auditors.

   D. Establish the basis for evaluating internal auditing performance.

Answer (D) is correct.   *(CIA, adapted)*
REQUIRED: The purpose of the Standards.
DISCUSSION: The Introduction states the following purposes of the current version of the Standards:

1. Delineate basic principles that represent the practice of internal auditing as it should be.

2. Provide a framework for performing and promoting a broad range of value-added internal audit activities.

3. Establish the basis for evaluating internal auditing performance.

4. Foster improved organizational processes and operations.

Answer (A) is incorrect because the professionalization of internal auditing is important but is not a purpose of the Standards. Answer (B) is incorrect because independence and objectivity are but two aspects of the practice of internal auditing as it should be. Answer (C) is incorrect because the Standards do not formally encourage external auditors to make more extensive use of the work of internal auditors.

11. Internal audit activities may involve which of the following?

   A. Assurance services.

   B. Consulting services.

   C. Both assurance and consulting services.

   D. Neither assurance nor consulting services.

Answer (C) is correct.   *(Publisher)*
REQUIRED: The services that may be included in internal audit activities.
DISCUSSION: Internal audit activities may involve both assurance and consulting services. Assurance services are objective examinations of evidence for the purpose of providing an independent assessment on risk management, control, or governance processes for the organization. Consulting services are advisory and related client service activities, the nature and scope of which are agreed upon with the client and are intended to add value and improve an organization's operations.

12. The most accurate term for the procedures used by the representatives of the organization's stakeholders to provide oversight of processes administered by management is

   A. Governance.

   B. Control.

   C. Risk management.

   D. Monitoring.

Answer (A) is correct.   *(Publisher)*
REQUIRED: The most accurate term for the means of providing oversight of processes administered by management.
DISCUSSION: A governance process consists of the procedures used by the representatives of the organization's stakeholders to provide oversight of processes administered by management ... (Glossary).
Answer (B) is incorrect because control is any action taken by management, the board, and other parties to enhance risk management and increase the likelihood that established objectives and goals will be achieved. Management plans, organizes, and directs the performance of sufficient actions to provide reasonable assurance that objectives and goals will be achieved. Answer (C) is incorrect because risk management includes the organizational actions taken to optimize the consequences of uncertain events that could have an effect on the achievement of organizational objectives. It is not currently defined in the Standards or Glossary. Answer (D) is incorrect because monitoring consists of actions taken by management and others to assess the quality of internal control system performance over time. It is not currently defined in the Standards and Glossary.

13. The Standards consist of three types of standards. Which type of standards concerns the traits of entities and individuals providing internal auditing services?

A. Implementation Standards.

B. Performance Standards.

C. Attribute Standards.

D. Independence Standards.

Answer (C) is correct. *(Publisher)*

REQUIRED: The type of standards that concerns the traits of entities and individuals providing internal auditing services.

DISCUSSION: The Standards consist of Attribute Standards, Performance Standards, and Implementation Standards. Attribute Standards concern the traits of entities and individuals providing internal auditing services. Performance Standards describe internal audit activities and criteria for evaluation of their performance. Attribute and Performance Standards furnish guidance for all internal auditing services (assurance, consulting, and other).

Answer (A) is incorrect because Implementation Standards apply the other standards to specific engagements. Answer (B) is incorrect because Performance Standards describe internal audit activities and criteria for evaluation of their performance. Answer (D) is incorrect because Independence Standards are not one of the three types of standards in the Standards.

14. Jan is trying to locate a standard identifying the criteria for evaluating an internal audit activity. How can Jan quickly determine which standards supply this information?

A. Read the title of each Standard.

B. Look at the Standard numbers.

C. Read the first sentence of each Standard.

D. Read the title and first sentence of each Standard.

Answer (B) is correct. *(Publisher)*

REQUIRED: The best method for locating a certain type of standard.

DISCUSSION: Jan is trying to locate a standard identifying the criteria for evaluating an internal audit activity. The kind of standard Jan is looking for is a Performance Standard. Performance Standards describe internal audit activities and criteria for evaluation of their performance. Performance Standards are currently numbered (2000-2600). By quickly scanning the numbers of the standards, Jan can locate the standards that may supply the information needed.

Answer (A) is incorrect because reading the title of the standards will take longer than scanning the Standard numbers and quickly turning to the correct set of standards. Once Jan is in the correct set of standards, identified by their number, then reading the titles may help Jan locate the specific information she is looking for. Answer (C) is incorrect because reading the first sentence of each standard will be time consuming and may not help Jan determine which standards will supply her with the information that she needs. Answer (D) is incorrect because reading the title and first sentence of each standard will be very time consuming and of no help to Jan unless she is reading within the correct set of standards.

15. Internal auditing is an assurance and consulting activity. An example of an assurance service is a

A. Process design engagement.

B. Facilitation engagement.

C. Training engagement.

D. Compliance engagement.

Answer (D) is correct. *(Publisher)*

REQUIRED: The example of an assurance service.

DISCUSSION: According to the Glossary, an assurance service is "an objective examination of evidence for the purpose of providing an independent assessment on risk management, control, or governance processes for the organization. Examples may include financial, performance, compliance, system security, and due diligence engagements." Consulting services include "advisory and related client service activities, the nature and scope of which are agreed upon with the client and are intended to add value and improve an organization's operations. Examples include counsel, advice, facilitation, process design, and training."

3/3
11/15

16. George is the new internal auditor for XYZ Corporation. George was in charge of payroll for XYZ just 10 months ago. What activity in regard to payroll would be considered an impairment of independence or objectivity if performed by George?

A. Providing consulting services.

B. Providing assurance services.

C. Providing assurance or consulting services.

D. Neither assurance nor consulting services.

Answer (B) is correct. *(Publisher)*
REQUIRED: The activity that will impair independence or objectivity.
DISCUSSION: Internal auditors should refrain from assessing specific operations for which they were previously responsible. Objectivity is presumed to be impaired if an auditor provides assurance services for an activity for which the auditor had responsibility within the previous year (Standard 1130.A1). Therefore, if George provides assurance services for payroll, his objectivity is presumed to be impaired. Internal auditors may provide consulting services relating to operations for which they had previous responsibilities (Standard 1130.C1).
Answer (A) is incorrect because providing consulting services to payroll will not impair the independence of objectivity of George (Standard 1130.C1). Answer (C) is incorrect because providing consulting services to payroll will not impair the independence or objectivity of George. Answer (D) is incorrect because providing assurance services to payroll will impair the objectivity of George (Standard 1130.A1).

17. The work of the internal audit activity includes evaluating and contributing to the improvement of risk management systems. Risk is

I.   The negative effect of events certain to occur
II. Measured in terms of consequences
III. Measured in terms of likelihood

A. I only.

B. I and II only.

C. II and III only.

D. I, II, and III.

Answer (C) is correct. *(Publisher)*
REQUIRED: The nature of risk.
DISCUSSION: The IAA should assist the organization by identifying and evaluating significant exposures to risk and contributing to the improvement of risk management and control systems (Standard 2110). Risk is the uncertainty of an event the occurrence of which could have an effect on the achievement of organizational objectives. It is measured in terms of consequences and likelihood (Glossary).

18. The chief audit executive is best defined as the

A. Inspector general.

B. Person responsible for the internal audit function.

C. Outside provider of internal audit services.

D. Person responsible for overseeing the contract with the outside provider of internal audit services.

Answer (B) is correct. *(Publisher)*
REQUIRED: The best definition of the chief audit executive.
DISCUSSION: The chief audit executive is the "top position within the organization responsible for internal audit activities." In a traditional internal audit activity, this person is the internal audit director. When internal auditing services are obtained from outside service providers, the CAE is the person responsible for overseeing the service contract and overall quality assurance, reporting to senior management and the board regarding internal audit activities, and follow-up of engagement results. The term also includes such titles as general auditor, chief internal auditor, and inspector general (Glossary).

19. What action should the chief audit executive take when (s)he believes that senior management has accepted a level of residual risk that is unacceptable to the organization?

A. Report the matter to the board for resolution.

B. Report the matter to an external authority.

C. Discuss the matter with external auditors.

D. Discuss the matter with senior management.

Answer (D) is correct. *(Publisher)*
REQUIRED: The action that the CAE should take when (s)he believes that senior management has accepted a level of residual risk that is unacceptable to the organization.
DISCUSSION: When the CAE believes that senior management has accepted a level of residual risk that is unacceptable to the organization, the chief audit executive should discuss the matter with senior management. If the decision regarding residual risk is not resolved, the chief audit executive and senior management should report the matter to the board for resolution (Standard 2600).
Answer (A) is incorrect because the CAE should report the matter to the board for resolution when a decision is not resolved after a discussion with senior management. Answer (B) is incorrect because the matter should be discussed with senior management. Answer (C) is incorrect because the CAE would not discuss the matter with senior management.

20. Which of the following is the most accurate term for the attitudes and actions of the board and management regarding the significance of control within the organization?

   A. Control processes.

   B. Control environment.

   C. Governance process.

   D. Management's philosophy and operating style.

Answer (B) is correct. *(Publisher)*
   REQUIRED: The term for the attitudes and actions of the board and management regarding control.
   DISCUSSION: According to the Glossary, the control environment encompasses the attitude and actions of the board and management regarding the significance of control within the organization. The control environment provides the discipline and structure for the achievement of the primary objectives of the system of internal control. The control environment includes the following elements:

- Integrity and ethical values
- Management's philosophy and operating style
- Organizational structure
- Assignment of authority and responsibility
- Human resource policies and practices
- Competence of personnel

   Answer (A) is incorrect because control processes are the policies, procedures, and activities that are part of a control framework, designed to ensure that risks are contained within the risk tolerances established by the risk management process. Answer (C) is incorrect because the governance process consists of the procedures used by the representatives of the organization's stakeholders (e.g., shareholders, etc.) to provide oversight of risk and control processes administered by management. Answer (D) is incorrect because management's philosophy and operating style is just one element of the control environment.

21. In exercising due professional care, an internal auditor should consider which of the following?

I. The relative complexity, materiality, or significance of matters to which assurance procedures are applied.

II. The extent of assurance procedures necessary to ensure that all significant risks will be identified.

III. The probability of significant errors, irregularities, or noncompliance.

   A. I and II.

   B. II and III.

   C. I and III.

   D. I, II, and III.

Answer (C) is correct. *(Publisher)*
   REQUIRED: The items that should be considered by an internal auditor when exercising due professional care.
   DISCUSSION: According to Standard 1220.A1, the internal auditor should exercise due professional care by considering the:

- Extent of work needed to achieve the engagement's objectives.
- Relative complexity, materiality, or significance of matters to which assurance procedures are applied.
- Adequacy and effectiveness of risk management, control, and governance processes.
- Probability of significant errors, irregularities, or noncompliance.
- Cost of assurance in relation to potential benefits.

Assurance procedures alone, even when performed with due professional care, do not guarantee that all significant risks will be identified (Standard 1220.A2).
   Answer (A) is incorrect because (II) the extent of assurance procedures necessary to ensure that all significant risks will be identified, is not something that the internal auditor should consider when exercising due professional care. Answer (B) is incorrect because (II) the extent of assurance procedures necessary to ensure that all significant risks will be identified, is not something that the internal auditor should consider when exercising due professional care. Answer (D) is incorrect because (II) the extent of assurance procedures necessary to ensure that all significant risks will be identified, is not something that the internal auditor should consider when exercising due professional care.

22. Engagement objectives are stated in

I.   The engagement program
II. Engagement communications
III. The statement of the engagement scope

    A. I and III only.

    B. I and II only.

    C. II and III only.

    D. I, II, and III.

Answer (D) is correct. *(Publisher)*
    REQUIRED: The source(s) of engagement objectives.
    DISCUSSION: Engagement objectives are broad statements developed by internal auditors that define intended engagement accomplishments (Glossary). The engagement work program is a document that lists the procedures to be followed during an engagement that are designed to achieve the engagement objectives (Standard 2240). The engagement work program also states the objectives of the engagement. An engagement communication includes the engagement's objectives and scope as well as applicable conclusions, recommendations, and action plans (Standard 2410). The engagement purpose, which is included in the communication, describes the engagement objectives and may explain why the engagement was conducted and what it was expected to achieve.

23. The actions taken to enhance risk management and increase the likelihood that established objectives and goals will be achieved are best described as

    A. Supervision.

    B. Quality assurance.

    C. Control.

    D. Compliance.

Answer (C) is correct. *(Publisher)*
    REQUIRED: The term for actions taken to enhance risk management and increase the likelihood that established objectives and goals will be achieved.
    DISCUSSION: Control is any action taken by management, the board, and other parties to enhance risk management and increase the likelihood that established objectives and goals will be achieved. Management plans, organizes, and directs the performance of sufficient actions to provide reasonable assurance that objectives and goals will be achieved.
    Answer (A) is incorrect because supervision is just one means of achieving control. Answer (B) is incorrect because quality assurance relates to just one set of objectives and goals. It does not pertain to achievement of all established organizational objectives and goals. Answer (D) is incorrect because compliance is the ability to reasonably ensure conformity and adherence to organization policies, plans, procedures, laws, regulations, and contracts.

Use Gleim's ***CIA Test Prep*** for interactive testing with over 2,000 additional multiple-choice questions!

2/2

19/23 = 83%

STUDY UNIT TWO
CHARTER, INDEPENDENCE, AND OBJECTIVITY

(17 pages of outline)

The purpose, authority, and responsibility of internal auditing should be adequate to enable the internal audit activity to accomplish its objectives. For that reason, the purpose, authority, and responsibility should be stated in a written charter and periodically reassessed.

Internal auditing is an independent, objective assurance and consulting activity designed to add value and improve an organization's operations. Accordingly, the SPPIA require the internal audit activity to be independent and the internal auditors to be objective in performing their work. Thus, independence is an attribute of an organizational unit, and objectivity is an attribute of individuals. In this context, independence means that internal auditors can carry out their duties freely and objectively, and objectivity is an independence in mental attitude.

2.1 PURPOSE, AUTHORITY, AND RESPONSIBILITY

1.   This subunit concerns the content of the charter of the internal audit activity. One General Attribute Standard, an Assurance Implementation Standard, a Consulting Implementation Standard, and three Practice Advisories currently address this topic.

1000   ***Purpose, Authority, and Responsibility*** *– The purpose, authority, and responsibility of the internal audit activity should be formally defined in a charter, consistent with the Standards, and approved by the board.**

*The term "board" here and elsewhere in pronouncements of The IIA includes "a board of directors, audit committee of such boards, head of an agency or legislative body to whom internal auditors report, board of governors or trustees of a nonprofit organization, or any other designated governing body of an organization."

Practice Advisory 1000-1: Internal Audit Charter

1.   *The purpose, authority, and responsibility of the internal audit activity should be defined in a charter. The chief audit executive should seek approval of the charter by senior management as well as acceptance by the board, audit committee, or appropriate governing authority. The charter should (a) establish the internal audit activity's position within the organization; (b) authorize access to records, personnel, and physical properties relevant to the performance of engagements; and (c) define the scope of internal audit activities.*

2.   *The internal audit activity's charter should be in writing. A written statement provides formal communication for review and approval by management and for acceptance by the board. It also facilitates a periodic assessment of the adequacy of the internal audit activity's purpose, authority, and responsibility. Providing a formal, written document containing the charter of the internal audit activity is critical in managing the auditing function within the organization. The purpose, authority, and responsibility should be defined and communicated to establish the role of the internal audit activity and to provide a basis for management and the board to use in evaluating the operations of the function. If a question should arise, the charter also provides a formal, written agreement with management and the board about the role and responsibilities of the internal audit activity within the organization.*

3.   The chief audit executive should periodically assess whether the purpose, authority, and responsibility, as defined in the charter, continue to be adequate to enable the internal audit activity to accomplish its objectives. The result of this periodic assessment should be communicated to senior management and the board.

> **1000.A1 –**   The nature of assurance services provided to the organization should be defined in the audit charter. If assurances are to be provided to parties outside the organization, the nature of these assurances should also be defined in the charter.
>
> **1000.C1 –**   The nature of consulting services should be defined in the audit charter.

Practice Advisory 1000.C1-1: Principles Guiding the Performance of Consulting Activities of Internal Auditors

1.   **Value Proposition –** The value proposition of the internal audit activity is realized within every organization that employs internal auditors in a manner that suits the culture and resources of that organization. That value proposition is captured in the definition of internal auditing and includes assurance and consulting activities designed to add value to the organization by bringing a systematic, disciplined approach to the areas of governance, risk, and control.

2.   **Consistency with Internal Audit Definition –** A disciplined, systematic evaluation methodology is incorporated in each internal audit activity. The list of services can generally be incorporated into the broad categories of assurance and consulting. However, the services may also include evolving forms of value-adding services that are consistent with the broad definition of internal auditing.

3.   **Audit Activities Beyond Assurance and Consulting –** There are multiple internal auditing services. Assurance and consulting are not mutually exclusive and do not preclude other auditing services such as investigations and nonauditing roles. Many audit services will have both an assurance and consultative (advising) role.

4.   **Interrelationship between Assurance and Consulting –** Internal audit consulting enriches value-adding internal auditing. While consulting is often the direct result of assurance services, it should also be recognized that assurance could also be generated from consulting engagements.

5.   **Empower Consulting Through the Internal Audit Charter –** Internal auditors have traditionally performed many types of consulting services, including the analysis of controls built into developing systems, analysis of security products, serving on task forces to analyze operations and make recommendations, and so forth. The board (or audit committee) should empower the internal audit activity to perform additional services if they do not represent a conflict of interest or detract from its obligations to the committee. That empowerment should be reflected in the internal audit charter.

6.   **Objectivity –** Consulting services may enhance the auditor's understanding of business processes or issues related to an assurance engagement and do not necessarily impair the auditor's or the internal audit activity's objectivity. Internal auditing is not a management decision-making function. Decisions to adopt or implement recommendations made as a result of an internal auditing advisory service should be made by management. Therefore, internal auditing objectivity should not be impaired by the decisions made by management.

7. **Internal Audit Foundation for Consulting Services** – *Much of consulting is a natural extension of assurance and investigative services and may represent informal or formal advice, analysis, or assessments. The internal audit activity is uniquely positioned to perform this type of consulting work based on (a) its adherence to the highest standards of objectivity and (b) its breadth of knowledge about organizational processes, risk, and strategies.*

8. **Communication of Fundamental Information** – *A primary internal auditing value is to provide assurance to senior management and audit committee directors. Consulting engagements cannot be rendered in a manner that masks information that in the judgment of the chief audit executive (CAE) should be presented to senior executives and board members. All consulting is to be understood in that context.*

9. **Principles of Consulting Understood by the Organization** – *Organizations must have ground rules for the performance of consulting services that are understood by all members of an organization, and these rules should be codified in the audit charter approved by the audit committee and promulgated in the organization.*

10. **Formal Consulting Engagements** – *Management often engages outside consultants for formal consulting engagements that last a significant period of time. However, an organization may find that the internal audit activity is uniquely qualified for some formal consulting tasks. If an internal audit activity undertakes to perform a formal consulting engagement, the internal audit group should bring a systematic, disciplined approach to the conduct of the engagement.*

11. **CAE Responsibilities** – *Consulting services permit the CAE to enter into dialogue with management to address specific managerial issues. In this dialogue, the breadth of the engagement and timeframes are made responsive to management needs. However, the CAE retains the prerogative of setting the audit techniques and the right of reporting to senior executives and audit committee members when the nature and materiality of results pose significant risks to the organization.*

12. **Criteria for Resolving Conflicts or Evolving Issues** – *An internal auditor is first and foremost an internal auditor. Thus, in the performance of all services the internal auditor is guided by The IIA Code of Ethics and the Attribute and Performance Standards of the Standards for the Professional Practice of Internal Auditing. The resolution of any unforeseen conflicts or activities should be consistent with the Code of Ethics and Standards.*

Practice Advisory 1000.C1-2: Additional Considerations for Formal Consulting Engagements

The following is the portion of this omnibus Practice Advisory relevant to
  Standard 1000.C1:

Definition of Consulting Services

1. *The Glossary in the **Standards** defines "consulting services" as follows: "Advisory and related client service activities, the nature and scope of which are agreed upon with the client and which are intended to add value and improve an organization's operations. Examples include counsel, advice, facilitation, process design, and training."*

2. *The chief audit executive should determine the methodology to use for classifying engagements within the organization. In some circumstances, it may be appropriate to conduct a "blended" engagement that incorporates elements of both consulting and assurance activities into one consolidated approach. In other cases, it may be appropriate to distinguish between the assurance and consulting components of the engagement.*

3.   *Internal auditors may conduct consulting services as part of their normal or routine activities as well as in response to requests by management. Each organization should consider the type of consulting activities to be offered and determine if specific policies or procedures should be developed for each type of activity. Possible categories could include:*

- *Formal consulting engagements – planned and subject to written agreement.*
- *Informal consulting engagements – routine activities, such as, participation on standing committees, limited-life projects, ad-hoc meetings, and routine information exchange.*
- *Special consulting engagements – participation on a merger and acquisition team or system conversion team.*
- *Emergency consulting engagements – participation on a team established for recovery or maintenance of operations after a disaster or other extraordinary business event or a team assembled to supply temporary help to meet a special request or unusual deadline.*

4.   *Auditors generally should not agree to conduct a consulting engagement simply to circumvent, or to allow others to circumvent, requirements that would normally apply to an assurance engagement if the service in question is more appropriately conducted as an assurance engagement. This does not preclude adjusting methodologies where services once conducted as assurance engagements are deemed more suitable to being performed as a consulting engagement.*

2.   The following example of a **charter** is from The IIA.

MISSION AND SCOPE OF WORK

The mission of the internal audit department is to provide independent, objective assurance and consulting services designed to add value and improve the organization's operations. It helps the organization accomplish its objectives by bringing a systematic, disciplined approach to evaluate and improve the effectiveness of risk management, control, and governance processes.

The scope of work of the internal audit department is to determine whether the organization's network of risk management, control, and governance processes, as designed and represented by management, is adequate and functioning in a manner to ensure:

- *Risks are appropriately identified and managed.*
- *Interaction with the various governance groups occurs as needed.*
- *Significant financial, managerial, and operating information is accurate, reliable, and timely.*
- *Employees' actions are in compliance with policies, standards, procedures, and applicable laws and regulations.*
- *Resources are acquired economically, used efficiently, and adequately protected.*
- *Programs, plans, and objectives are achieved.*
- *Quality and continuous improvement are fostered in the organization's control process.*
- *Significant legislative or regulatory issues impacting the organization are recognized and addressed appropriately.*

Opportunities for improving management control, profitability, and the organization's image may be identified during audits. They will be communicated to the appropriate level of management.

ACCOUNTABILITY

The chief audit executive, in the discharge of his/her duties, shall be accountable to management and the audit committee to:

- *Provide annually an assessment on the adequacy and effectiveness of the organization's processes for controlling its activities and managing its risks in the areas set forth under the mission and scope of work.*

- *Report significant issues related to the processes for controlling the activities of the organization and its affiliates, including potential improvements to those processes, and provide information concerning such issues through resolution.*

- *Periodically provide information on the status and results of the annual audit plan and the sufficiency of department resources.*

- *Coordinate with and provide oversight of other control and monitoring functions (risk management, compliance, security, legal, ethics, environmental, external audit).*

INDEPENDENCE

To provide for the independence of the internal auditing department, its personnel report to the chief audit executive, who reports functionally to the audit committee and administratively to the chief executive officer in a manner outlined in the above section on Accountability. It will include as part of its reports to the audit committee a regular report on internal audit personnel.

RESPONSIBILITY

The chief audit executive and staff of the internal audit department have responsibility to:

- *Develop a flexible annual audit plan using an appropriate risk-based methodology, including any risks or control concerns identified by management, and submit that plan to the audit committee for review and approval as well as periodic updates.*

- *Implement the annual audit plan, as approved, including as appropriate any special tasks or projects requested by management and the audit committee.*

- *Maintain a professional audit staff with sufficient knowledge, skills, experience, and professional certifications to meet the requirements of this Charter.*

- *Evaluate and assess significant merging/consolidating functions and new or changing services, processes, operations, and control processes coincident with their development, implementation, and/or expansion.*

- *Issue periodic reports to the audit committee and management summarizing results of audit activities.*

- *Keep the audit committee informed of emerging trends and successful practices in internal auditing.*

- *Provide a list of significant measurement goals and results to the audit committee.*

- *Assist in the investigation of significant suspected fraudulent activities within the organization and notify management and the audit committee of the results.*

- *Consider the scope of work of the external auditors and regulators, as appropriate, for the purpose of providing optimal audit coverage to the organization at a reasonable overall cost.*

AUTHORITY

The chief audit executive and staff of the internal audit department are authorized to:

- *Have unrestricted access to all functions, records, property, and personnel.*
- *Have full and free access to the audit committee.*
- *Allocate resources, set frequencies, select subjects, determine scopes of work, and apply the techniques required to accomplish audit objectives.*
- *Obtain the necessary assistance of personnel in units of the organization where they perform audits, as well as other specialized services from within or outside the organization.*

The chief audit executive and staff of the internal audit department are not authorized to:

- *Perform any operational duties for the organization or its affiliates.*
- *Initiate or approve accounting transactions external to the internal auditing department.*
- *Direct the activities of any organization employee not employed by the internal auditing department, except to the extent such employees have been appropriately assigned to auditing teams or to otherwise assist the internal auditors.*

STANDARDS OF AUDIT PRACTICE

*The internal audit department will meet or exceed the **Standards for the Professional Practice of Internal Auditing** of The Institute of Internal Auditors.*

_____
Chief Audit Executive

_____
Chief Executive Officer

_____
Audit Committee Chair

*Dated*_____

3. The charter helps to establish the organizational status of the internal audit activity by defining its purpose, authority, and responsibility.

   a. The reporting level of the internal audit activity should be sufficient to enable the internal audit activity to fulfill its responsibilities.

   b. In some organizations, that reporting level is the board of directors. Many internal audit activities currently report to lower levels, but the trend is toward reporting to upper levels.

   c. The CAE should also have regular communication with the board, audit committee, or other appropriate governing authority.

      1) Regular communication with the board helps assure independence and promote broad engagement coverage, adequate consideration of engagement communications, and appropriate action on engagement recommendations.

      2) The audit committee should be composed only of external members of the board or its equivalent in order to enhance the independence of both the internal and external auditing functions.

    d.   In some organizations, the CAE is present at executive committee meetings in an advisory capacity similar to that of the organization's counsel.

    e.   The status of the internal audit activity is enhanced by a conscious effort to promote its services within the organization through

        1)   Providing an excellent product conveyed through professionally prepared engagement communications

        2)   Avoiding preoccupation with matters of little significance

        3)   Extending the internal audit function to all the sectors of the organization

        4)   Emphasizing internal auditors' proficiency and professionalism

            a)   Internal auditors should engage only in those services for which they have the necessary knowledge, skills, and other competencies.

        5)   Offering assistance in the solution of management problems

        6)   Viewing all recommendations for correction or improvement through the eyes of senior management

        7)   Remaining abreast of modern management techniques so as to provide better assistance to management

4.   An alternative to staffing an internal audit activity is to outsource internal auditing functions.

    a.   To a large organization, the primary advantage of **outsourcing** is that large outside service providers ordinarily have offices in various locations; therefore, engagement requirements in distant locations are more easily accommodated.

    b.   The disadvantages are that internal auditors tend to be more familiar with the organization, and they are more readily available to the organization because they are unaffected by other priorities, such as other clients.

        1)   Another disadvantage is that legal requirements may prevent the external audit firm from providing internal audit services.

    c.   **Cosourcing** is an approach in which the internal audit activity obtains external aid in performing certain activities.

5.   Stop and review! You have completed the outline for this subunit. Study multiple-choice questions 1 through 16 beginning on page 59.

2.2 INDEPENDENCE AND OBJECTIVITY

1.   This subunit addresses the independence attribute of the internal audit activity and the objectivity attribute of the individual internal auditors. It describes the appropriate reporting level of the internal audit activity and the desirability of its freedom from interference. It also defines objectivity and the required disclosures when independence or objectivity has been impaired. Other issues addressed include the effects of the internal auditors' responsibility for operations. These subjects are covered in one General Attribute Standard, three Specific Attribute Standards, three Assurance Implementation Standards, two Consulting Implementation Standards, and nine Practice Advisories.

1100   ***Independence and Objectivity*** *– The internal audit activity should be independent, and internal auditors should be objective in performing their work.*

Practice Advisory 1100-1: Independence and Objectivity

1.   Internal auditors are independent when they can carry out their work freely and objectively. Independence permits internal auditors to render the impartial and unbiased judgments essential to the proper conduct of engagements. It is achieved through organizational status and objectivity.

1110   **Organizational Independence** – The chief audit executive should report to a level within the organization that allows the internal audit activity to fulfill its responsibilities.

Practice Advisory 1110-1: Organizational Independence

1.   Internal auditors should have the support of senior management and of the board so that they can gain the cooperation of engagement clients and perform their work free from interference.

2.   The chief audit executive should be responsible to an individual in the organization with sufficient authority to promote independence and to ensure broad engagement coverage, adequate consideration of engagement communications, and appropriate action on engagement recommendations.

3.   Ideally, the chief audit executive should report functionally to the audit committee, board of directors, or other appropriate governing authority, and administratively to the chief executive officer of the organization.

4.   The chief audit executive should have direct communication with the board, audit committee, or other appropriate governing authority. Regular communication with the board helps assure independence and provides a means for the board and the chief audit executive to keep each other informed on matters of mutual interest.

5.   Direct communication occurs when the chief audit executive regularly attends and participates in meetings of the board, audit committee, or other appropriate governing authority which relate to its oversight responsibilities for auditing, financial reporting, organizational governance, and control. The chief audit executive's attendance and participation at these meetings provide an opportunity to exchange information concerning the plans and activities of the internal audit activity. The chief audit executive should meet privately with the board, audit committee, or other appropriate governing authority at least annually.

6.   Independence is enhanced when the board concurs in the appointment or removal of the chief audit executive.

Practice Advisory 1110-2: Chief Audit Executive (CAE) Reporting Lines

1. The IIA's **Standards for the Professional Practice of Internal Auditing (Standards)** require that the chief audit executive (CAE) report to a level within the organization that allows the internal audit activity to fulfill its responsibilities. The Institute believes strongly that to achieve necessary independence, the CAE should report functionally to the audit committee or its equivalent. For administrative purposes, in most circumstances, the CAE should report directly to the chief executive officer of the organization. The following descriptions of what The IIA considers "functional reporting" and "administrative reporting" are provided to help focus the discussion in this practice advisory.

- Functional Reporting - The functional reporting line for the internal audit function is the ultimate source of its independence and authority. As such, The IIA recommends that the CAE report functionally to the audit committee, board of directors, or other appropriate governing authority. In this context, report functionally means that the governing authority would

  - approve the overall charter of the internal audit function.
  - approve the internal audit risk assessment and related audit plan.
  - receive communications from the CAE on the results of the internal audit activities or other matters that the CAE determines are necessary, including private meetings with the CAE without management present.
  - approve all decisions regarding the appointment or removal of the CAE.
  - approve the annual compensation and salary adjustment of the CAE.
  - make appropriate inquiries of management and the CAE to determine whether there are scope or budgetary limitations that impede the ability of the internal audit function to execute its responsibilities.

- Administrative Reporting - Administrative Reporting is the reporting relationship within the organization's management structure that facilitates the day-to-day operations of the internal audit function. Administrative reporting typically includes:

  - budgeting and management accounting.
  - human resource administration including personnel evaluations and compensation.
  - internal communications and information flows.
  - administration of the organization's internal policies and procedures.

2. This advisory focuses on considerations in establishing or evaluating CAE reporting lines. Appropriate reporting lines are critical to achieve the independence, objectivity, and organizational stature for an internal audit function necessary to effectively fulfill its obligations. CAE reporting lines are also critical to ensuring the appropriate flow of information and access to key executives and managers that are the foundations of risk assessment and reporting of results of audit activities. Conversely, any reporting relationship that impedes the independence and effective operations of the internal audit function should be viewed by the CAE as a serious scope limitation, which should be brought to the attention of the audit committee or its equivalent.

3.   This advisory also recognizes that CAE reporting lines are affected by the nature of the organization (public or private as well as relative size); common practices of each country; growing complexity of organizations (joint ventures, multinational corporations with subsidiaries); and the trend towards internal audit groups providing value-added services with increased collaboration on priorities and scope with their clients. Accordingly, while The IIA believes that there is an ideal reporting structure with functional reporting to the Audit Committee and administrative reporting to the CEO, other relationships can be effective if there are clear distinctions between the functional and administrative reporting lines and appropriate activities are in each line to ensure that the independence and scope of activities is maintained. Internal auditors are expected to use professional judgment to determine the extent to which the guidance provided in this advisory should be applied in each given situation.

4.   The **Standards** stress the importance of the chief audit executive reporting to an individual with sufficient authority to promote independence and to ensure broad audit coverage. The **Standards** are purposely somewhat generic about reporting relationships, however, because they are designed to be applicable at all organizations regardless of size or any other factors. Factors that make "one size fits all" unattainable include organization size, and type of organization (private, governmental, corporate). Accordingly, the CAE should consider the following attributes in evaluating the appropriateness of the administrative reporting line.

- Does the individual have sufficient authority and stature to ensure the effectiveness of the function?
- Does the individual have an appropriate control and governance mindset to assist the CAE in their role?
- Does the individual have the time and interest to actively support the CAE on audit issues?
- Does the individual understand the functional reporting relationship and support it?

5.   The CAE should also ensure that appropriate independence is maintained if the individual responsible for the administrative reporting line is also responsible for other activities in the organization, which are subject to internal audit. For example, some CAEs report administratively to the Chief Financial Officer, who is also responsible for the organization's accounting functions. The internal audit function should be free to audit and report on any activity that also reports to its administrative head if it deems that coverage appropriate for its audit plan. Any limitation in scope or reporting of results of these activities should be brought to the attention of the audit committee.

6.   Under the recent move to a stricter legislative and regulatory climate regarding financial reporting around the globe, the CAE's reporting lines should be appropriate to enable the internal audit activity to meet any increased needs of the audit committee or other significant stakeholders. Increasingly, the CAE is being asked to take a more significant role in the organization's governance and risk management activities. The reporting lines of the CAE should facilitate the ability of the internal audit activity to meet these expectations.

7.   Regardless of which reporting relationship the organization chooses, several key actions can help assure that the reporting lines support and enable the effectiveness and independence of the internal auditing activity.

- Functional Reporting:

  - The functional reporting line should go directly to the Audit Committee or its equivalent to ensure the appropriate level of independence and communication.

  - The CAE should meet privately with the audit committee or its equivalent, without management present, to reinforce the independence and nature of this reporting relationship.

  - The audit committee should have the final authority to review and approve the annual audit plan and all major changes to the plan.

  - At all times, the CAE should have open and direct access to the chair of the audit committee and its members; or the chair of the board or full board if appropriate.

  - At least once a year, the audit committee should review the performance of the CAE and approve the annual compensation and salary adjustment.

  - The charter for the internal audit function should clearly articulate both the functional and administrative reporting lines for the function as well as the principle activities directed up each line.

- Administrative Reporting:

  - The administrative reporting line of the CAE should be to the CEO or another executive with sufficient authority to afford it appropriate support to accomplish its day-to-day activities. This support should include positioning the function and the CAE in the organization's structure in a manner that affords appropriate stature for the function within the organization. Reporting too low in an organization can negatively impact the stature and effectiveness of the internal audit function.

  - The administrative reporting line should not have ultimate authority over the scope or reporting of results of the internal audit activity.

  - The administrative reporting line should facilitate open and direct communications with executive and line management. The CAE should be able to communicate directly with any level of management including the CEO.

  - The administrative reporting line should enable adequate communications and information flow such that the CAE and the internal audit function have an adequate and timely flow of information concerning the activities, plans and business initiatives of the organization.

  - Budgetary controls and considerations imposed by the administrative reporting line should not impede the ability of the internal audit function to accomplish its mission.

8. CAEs should also consider their relationships with other control and monitoring functions (risk management, compliance, security, legal, ethics, environmental, external audit) and facilitate the reporting of material risk and control issues to the audit committee.

> **1110.A1 –**   The internal audit activity should be free from interference in determining the scope of internal auditing, performing work, and communicating results.

Practice Advisory 1110.A1-1: Disclosing Reasons for Information Requests

1. At times, an internal auditor may be asked by the engagement client or other parties to explain why a document that has been requested is relevant to an engagement. Disclosure or nondisclosure during the engagement of the reasons documents are needed should be determined based on the circumstances. Significant irregularities may dictate a less open environment than would normally be conducive to a cooperative engagement. However, that is a judgment that should be made by the chief audit executive in light of the specific circumstances.

1120   **Individual Objectivity** – Internal auditors should have an impartial, unbiased attitude and avoid conflicts of interest.

Practice Advisory 1120-1: Individual Objectivity

1. Objectivity is an independent mental attitude that internal auditors should maintain in performing engagements. Internal auditors are not to subordinate their judgment on engagement matters to that of others.

2. Objectivity requires internal auditors to perform engagements in such a manner that they have an honest belief in their work product and that no significant quality compromises are made. Internal auditors are not to be placed in situations in which they feel unable to make objective professional judgments.

3. Staff assignments should be made so that potential and actual conflicts of interest and bias are avoided. The chief audit executive should periodically obtain from the internal auditing staff information concerning potential conflicts of interest and bias. Staff assignments of internal auditors should be rotated periodically whenever it is practicable to do so.

4. The results of internal auditing work should be reviewed before the related engagement communications are released to provide reasonable assurance that the work was performed objectively.

5. It is unethical for an internal auditor to accept a fee or gift from an employee, client, customer, supplier, or business associate. Accepting a fee or gift may create an appearance that the auditor's objectivity has been impaired. The appearance that objectivity has been impaired may apply to current and future engagements conducted by the auditor. The status of engagements should not be considered as justification for receiving fees or gifts. The receipt of promotional items (such as pens, calendars, or samples) that are available to the general public and have minimal value should not hinder internal auditors' professional judgments. Internal auditors should report the offer of all material fees or gifts immediately to their supervisors.

1130 <u>*Impairments to Independence or Objectivity*</u> – *If independence or objectivity is impaired in fact or appearance, the details of the impairment should be disclosed to appropriate parties. The nature of the disclosure will depend upon the impairment.*

Practice Advisory 1130-1: Impairments to Independence or Objectivity

1. *Internal auditors should report to the chief audit executive any situations in which a conflict of interest or bias is present or may reasonably be inferred. The chief audit executive should then reassign such auditors.*

2. *A scope limitation is a restriction placed upon the internal audit activity that precludes the audit activity from accomplishing its objectives and plans. Among other things, a scope limitation may restrict the:*

   - *Scope defined in the charter.*
   - *Internal audit activity's access to records, personnel, and physical properties relevant to the performance of engagements.*
   - *Approved engagement work schedule.*
   - *Performance of necessary engagement procedures.*
   - *Approved staffing plan and financial budget.*

3. *A scope limitation along with its potential effect should be communicated, preferably in writing, to the board, audit committee, or other appropriate governing authority.*

4. *The chief audit executive should consider whether it is appropriate to inform the board, audit committee, or other appropriate governing authority regarding scope limitations that were previously communicated to and accepted by the board, audit committee, or other appropriate governing authority. This may be necessary, particularly when there have been organization, board, senior management, or other changes.*

   1130.A1 – *Internal auditors should refrain from assessing specific operations for which they were previously responsible. Objectivity is presumed to be impaired if an auditor provides assurance services for an activity for which the auditor had responsibility within the previous year.*

Practice Advisory 1130.A1-1: Assessing Operations for Which Internal Auditors Were Previously Responsible

1. *Internal auditors should not assume operating responsibilities. If senior management directs internal auditors to perform nonaudit work, it should be understood that they are not functioning as internal auditors. Moreover, objectivity is presumed to be impaired when internal auditors perform an assurance review of any activity for which they had authority or responsibility within the past year. This impairment should be considered when communicating audit engagement results.*

   - *If internal auditors are directed to perform nonaudit duties that may impair objectivity, such as preparation of bank reconciliations, the chief audit executive should inform senior management and the board that this activity is not an assurance audit activity; and, therefore, audit-related conclusions should not be drawn.*

- *In addition, when operating responsibilities are assigned to the internal audit activity, special attention must be given to ensure objectivity when a subsequent assurance engagement in the related operating area is undertaken. Objectivity is presumed to be impaired when internal auditors audit any activity for which they had authority or responsibility within the past year. These facts should be clearly stated when communicating the results of an audit engagement relating to an area where an auditor had operating responsibilities.*

2. *At any point that assigned activities involve the assumption of operating authority, audit objectivity would be presumed to be impaired with respect to that activity.*

3. *Persons transferred to or temporarily engaged by the internal audit activity should not be assigned to audit those activities they previously performed until a reasonable period of time (at least one year) has elapsed. Such assignments are presumed to impair objectivity, and additional consideration should be exercised when supervising the engagement work and communicating engagement results.*

4. *The internal auditor's objectivity is not adversely affected when the auditor recommends standards of control for systems or reviews procedures before they are implemented. The auditor's objectivity is considered to be impaired if the auditor designs, installs, drafts procedures for, or operates such systems.*

5. *The occasional performance of nonaudit work by the internal auditor, with full disclosure in the reporting process, would not necessarily impair independence. However, it would require careful consideration by management and the internal auditor to avoid adversely affecting the internal auditor's objectivity.*

Practice Advisory 1130.A1-2: Internal Audit Responsibility for Other (Non-Audit) Functions

1. *Some internal auditors have been assigned or accepted non-audit duties because of a variety of business reasons that make sense to management of the organization. Internal auditors are more frequently being asked to perform roles and responsibilities that may impair independence or objectivity. Given the increasing demand on organizations, both public and private, to develop more efficient and effective operations and to do so with fewer resources, some internal audit activities are being directed by their organization's management to assume responsibility for operations that are subject to periodic internal auditing assessments.*

2. *When the internal audit activity or individual internal auditor is responsible for, or management is considering assigning, an operation that it might audit, the internal auditor's independence and objectivity may be impaired. The internal auditor should consider the following factors in assessing the impact on independence and objectivity:*

   - *The requirements of The IIA Code of Ethics and Standards for the Professional Practice of Internal Auditing (Standards);*
   - *Expectations of stakeholders that may include the shareholders, board of directors, audit committee, management, legislative bodies, public entities, regulatory bodies, and public interest groups;*
   - *Allowances and/or restrictions contained in the internal audit activity charter;*
   - *Disclosures required by the Standards; and*
   - *Subsequent audit coverage of the activities or responsibilities accepted by the internal auditor.*

3. *Internal auditors should consider the following factors to determine an appropriate course of action when presented with the opportunity of accepting responsibility for a nonaudit function:*

- *The IIA Code of Ethics and Standards require the internal audit activity to be independent, and internal auditors to be objective in performing their work.*

  - *If possible, internal auditors should avoid accepting responsibility for non-audit functions or duties that are subject to periodic internal auditing assessments. If this is not possible, then;*
  - *Impairment to independence and objectivity are required to be disclosed to appropriate parties, and the nature of the disclosure depends upon the impairment.*
  - *Objectivity is presumed to be impaired if an auditor provides assurance services for an activity for which the auditor had responsibility within the previous year.*
  - *If on occasion management directs internal auditors to perform non-audit work, it should be understood that they are not functioning as internal auditors.*

- *Expectations of stakeholders, including regulatory or legal requirements, should be evaluated and assessed in relation to the potential impairment.*

- *If the internal audit activity charter contains specific restrictions or limiting language regarding the assignment of non-audit functions to the internal auditor, then these restrictions should be disclosed and discussed with management. If management insists on such an assignment, the auditor should disclose and discuss this matter with the audit committee or appropriate governing body. If the charter is silent on this matter, the guidance noted in the following points should be considered. All the points noted below are subordinated to the language of the charter.*

- *Assessment – The results of the assessment should be discussed with management, the audit committee, and/or other appropriate stakeholders. A determination should be made regarding a number of issues, some of which affect one another:*

  - *The significance of the operational function to the organization (in terms of revenue, expenses, reputation, and influence) should be evaluated.*
  - *The length or duration of the assignment and scope of responsibility should be evaluated.*
  - *Adequacy of separation of duties should be evaluated.*
  - *The potential impairment to objectivity or independence or the appearance of such impairment should be considered when reporting audit results.*

- *Audit of the Function and Disclosure – Given that the internal audit activity has operational responsibilities and that operation is part of the audit plan, there are several avenues for the auditor to consider.*
  - *The audit may be performed by a contracted, third party entity, by external auditors, or by the internal audit function. In the first two situations, impairment of objectivity is minimized by the use of auditors outside of the organization. In the latter case, objectivity would be impaired.*
  - *Individual auditors with operational responsibility should not participate in the audit of the operation. If possible, auditors conducting the assessment should be supervised by, and report the results of the assessment to, those whose independence or objectivity is not impaired.*
  - *Disclosure should be made regarding the operational responsibilities of the auditor for the function, the significance of the operation to the organization (in terms of revenue, expenses, or other pertinent information), and the relationship of those who audited the function to the auditor.*
  - *Disclosure of the internal auditor's operational responsibilities should be made in the related engagement communication and in the auditor's standard communication to the audit committee or other governing body.*

1130.A2 –   *Assurance engagements for functions over which the chief audit executive has responsibility should be overseen by a party outside the internal audit activity.*

1130.C1 –   *Internal auditors may provide consulting services relating to operations for which they had previous responsibilities.*

1130.C2 –   *If internal auditors have potential impairments to independence or objectivity relating to proposed consulting services, disclosure should be made to the engagement client prior to accepting the engagement.*

Practice Advisory 1000.C1-2: Additional Considerations for Formal Consulting Engagements

The following is the portion of this omnibus Practice Advisory relevant to Standards 1130.C1 and 1130.C2:

Independence and Objectivity in Consulting Engagements

5.   *Internal auditors are sometimes requested to provide consulting services relating to operations for which they had previous responsibilities or had conducted assurance services. Prior to offering consulting services, the Chief Audit Executive should confirm that the board understands and approves the concept of providing consulting services. Once approved, the internal audit charter should be amended to include authority and responsibilities for consulting activities, and the internal audit activity should develop appropriate policies and procedures for conducting such engagements.*

6.   Internal auditors should maintain their objectivity when drawing conclusions and offering advice to management. If impairments to independence or objectivity exist prior to commencement of the consulting engagement, or subsequently develop during the engagement, disclosure should be made immediately to management.

7.   Independence and objectivity may be impaired if assurance services are provided within one year after a formal consulting engagement. Steps can be taken to minimize the effects of impairment by assigning different auditors to perform each of the services, establishing independent management and supervision, defining separate accountability for the results of the projects, and disclosing the presumed impairment. Management should be responsible for accepting and implementing recommendations.

8.   Care should be taken, particularly involving consulting engagements that are ongoing or continuous in nature, so that internal auditors do not inappropriately or unintentionally assume management responsibilities that were not intended in the original objectives and scope of the engagement.

2.   Stop and review! You have completed the outline for this subunit. Study multiple-choice questions 17 through 45 beginning on page 64.

QUESTIONS
2.1 Purpose, Authority, and Responsibility

1. During an engagement to evaluate the organization's accounts payable function, an internal auditor plans to confirm balances with suppliers. What is the source of authority for such contacts with units outside the organization?

A. Internal audit activity policies and procedures.

B. The Standards.

C. The Code of Ethics.

D. The internal audit activity's charter.

Answer (D) is correct. *(CIA, adapted)*
    REQUIRED: The source of authority for an internal auditor to contact units outside the organization.
    DISCUSSION: The purpose, authority, and responsibility of the internal audit activity should be formally defined in a charter, consistent with the Standards, and approved by the board (Standard 1000). The charter should establish the internal audit activity's position within the organization; authorize access to records, personnel, and physical properties relevant to the performance of engagements; and define the scope of internal audit activities (PA 1000-1). Thus, the charter should prescribe the internal audit activity's relationships with other units within the organization and with those outside.
    Answer (A) is incorrect because policies and procedures guide the internal auditors in their consistent compliance with the internal audit activity's standards of performance. Answer (B) is incorrect because the IAA's authority is defined in a charter approved by the board. Answer (C) is incorrect because the purpose of the Code of Ethics is to promote an ethical culture in the profession of internal auditing.

2. An element of authority that should be included in the charter of the internal audit activity is

A. Identification of the organizational units where engagements are to be performed.

B. Identification of the types of disclosures that should be made to the audit committee.

C. Access to records, personnel, and physical properties relevant to the performance of engagements.

D. Access to the external auditor's engagement records.

Answer (C) is correct. *(CIA, adapted)*
    REQUIRED: The element of authority that should be included in the charter of the internal audit activity.
    DISCUSSION: The purpose, authority, and responsibility of the internal audit activity should be defined in a charter, consistent with the Standards, and approved by the board (Standard 1000). The charter should establish the internal audit activity's position within the organization; authorize access to records, personnel, and physical properties relevant to the performance of engagements; and define the scope of internal audit activities (PA 1000-1).
    Answer (A) is incorrect because the charter should not specifically identify the subjects of engagements. Answer (B) is incorrect because disclosure to the audit committee is an obligation, not an element of authority. Answer (D) is incorrect because access to the external auditor's engagement records cannot be guaranteed.

2/2.

3. To avoid being the apparent cause of conflict between an organization's senior management and the audit committee, the chief audit executive should

- A. Communicate all engagement results to both senior management and the audit committee.
- B. Strengthen the independence of the internal audit activity through organizational status.
- C. Discuss all reports to senior management with the audit committee first.
- D. Request board approval of policies that include internal audit activity relationships with the audit committee.

Answer (D) is correct. *(CIA, adapted)*
REQUIRED: The step taken to prevent the internal audit activity from being the apparent cause of conflict.
DISCUSSION: The purpose, authority, and responsibility of the internal audit activity should be formally defined in a charter, consistent with the Standards, and approved by the board (Standard 1000). The charter should establish the internal audit activity's position within the organization; authorize access to records, personnel, and physical properties relevant to the performance of engagements; and define the scope of internal audit activities (PA 1000-1).
Answer (A) is incorrect because receipt of all engagement results by senior management and the audit committee is unnecessary and inefficient. Answer (B) is incorrect because organizational status helps the internal audit activity to achieve independence but is not, by itself, enough to avoid conflict. Answer (C) is incorrect because the audit committee essentially has an oversight rather than an operational role.

4. The audit committee of an organization has charged the chief audit executive (CAE) with upgrading the internal audit activity. The CAE's first task is to develop a charter. What item should be included in the statement of objectives?

- A. Report all engagement results to the audit committee every quarter.
- B. Notify governmental regulatory agencies of unethical business practices by organization management.
- C. Evaluate the adequacy and effectiveness of the organization's controls.
- D. Submit budget variance reports to management every month.

Answer (C) is correct. *(CIA, adapted)*
REQUIRED: The item included in the statement of objectives of the charter.
DISCUSSION: The purpose, authority, and responsibility of the internal audit activity should be formally defined in a charter, consistent with the Standards, and approved by the board (Standard 1000). The charter should establish the internal audit activity's position within the organization; authorize access to records, personnel, and physical properties relevant to the performance of engagements; and define the scope of internal audit activities (PA 1000-1). According to Standard 2120, "The internal audit activity should assist the organization in maintaining effective controls by evaluating their effectiveness and efficiency and by promoting continuous improvement."
Answer (A) is incorrect because only significant engagement results should be discussed with the audit committee.
Answer (B) is incorrect because internal auditors ordinarily are not required to report deficiencies in regulatory compliance to the appropriate agencies. However, they must observe the law and make disclosures expected by the law and profession (Rule of Conduct 1.2). Answer (D) is incorrect because submission of budgetary variance reports is not a primary objective of internal auditing. It is a budgetary control that management may require on a periodic basis.

5. The authority of the internal audit activity is limited to that granted by

- A. The board and the controller.
- B. Senior management and the Standards.
- C. Management and the board.
- D. The audit committee and the chief financial officer.

Answer (C) is correct. *(CIA, adapted)*
REQUIRED: The source of authority of the internal audit activity.
DISCUSSION: The purpose, authority, and responsibility of the internal audit activity should be formally defined in a charter, consistent with the Standards, and approved by the board (Standard 1000). Furthermore, PA 1000-1 states that the CAE should seek approval of the charter by senior management. The charter should establish the internal audit activity's position within the organization; authorize access to records, personnel, and physical properties relevant to the performance of engagements; and define the scope of internal audit activities.
Answer (A) is incorrect because the controller is not the only member of management. Answer (B) is incorrect because the Standards provide no actual authority to the IAA. Answer (D) is incorrect because management and the board, not a committee of the board and a particular manager, endow the IAA with its authority.

2/3
4/5

6. Is it appropriate for an internal auditor to conduct an engagement that incorporates elements of both consulting and assurance activities into one consolidated approach?

    A. Yes, this is always appropriate.

    B. Yes, in some circumstances.

    C. No, unless the audit committee gives permission.

    D. No, this is never appropriate.

Answer (B) is correct. *(Publisher)*

REQUIRED: The propriety of conducting an engagement that incorporates elements of both consulting and assurance activities into one consolidated approach.

DISCUSSION: According to PA 1000.C1-2, in some circumstances, it may be appropriate to conduct an engagement that incorporates elements of both consulting and assurance activities into one consolidated approach. These engagements are referred to as "blended engagements." In other cases, it may be appropriate to distinguish between the assurance and consulting components of the engagement.

Answer (A) is incorrect because it may be appropriate to distinguish between the assurance and consulting components of an engagement in some circumstances. Answer (C) is incorrect because it is appropriate to incorporate elements of both consulting and assurance activities into one consolidated approach in some circumstances, but permission of the audit committee is not necessarily required. Answer (D) is incorrect because the consolidation is appropriate in some circumstances.

7. Participation on a system conversion team falls into which possible category of consulting engagements?

    A. Formal consulting engagements.

    B. Special consulting engagements.

    C. Informal consulting engagements.

    D. Emergency consulting engagements.

Answer (B) is correct. *(Publisher)*

REQUIRED: The category of consulting engagement that best encompasses participation on a system conversion team.

DISCUSSION: Each organization should consider the type of consulting activities to be offered and determine if specific policies and procedures should be developed for each type of activity. PA 1000.C1-2 lists four possible categories for consulting engagements. These categories are Formal, Informal, Special, and Emergency. Special consulting engagements include activities such as participation on a merger and acquisition team or system conversion team.

Answer (A) is incorrect because formal consulting engagements are planned and subject to written agreement. Answer (C) is incorrect because informal consulting engagements include routine activities, such as participation on standing committees, limited-life projects, ad-hoc meetings, and routine information exchange. Answer (D) is incorrect because emergency consulting engagements encompass activities like participation on a team established for recovery or maintenance of operations after a disaster or other extraordinary business event, or a team assembled to supply temporary help to meet a special request or unusual deadline.

8. A charter is one of the more important factors positively affecting the internal audit activity's independence. Which of the following is least likely to be part of the charter?

    A. Access to records within the organization.

    B. The scope of internal audit activities.

    C. The length of tenure of the chief audit executive.

    D. Access to personnel within the organization.

Answer (C) is correct. *(CIA, adapted)*

REQUIRED: The item not included in the IAA's charter.

DISCUSSION: The independence of the IAA is enhanced when the board concurs in the appointment or removal of the CAE (PA 1110-1), but the length of the CAE's employment is less significant than defining the purpose, authority, and responsibility of the IAA (Standard 1000). The charter establishes the IAA's position within the organization; authorizes access to records, personnel, and physical properties; and defines the scope of internal audit activities (PA 1000-1).

9. Internal auditing has planned an engagement to evaluate the effectiveness of the quality assurance function as it affects the receipt of goods, the transfer of the goods into production, and the scrap costs related to defective items. The engagement client argues that such an engagement is not within the scope of the internal audit activity and should come under the purview of the quality assurance department only. What is the most appropriate response?

A. Refer to the internal audit activity's charter and the approved engagement plan that includes the area designated for evaluation in the current time period.

B. Because quality assurance is a new function, seek the approval of management as a mediator to set the scope of the engagement.

C. Indicate that the engagement will evaluate the function only in accordance with the standards set by, and approved by, the quality assurance function before beginning the engagement.

D. Terminate the engagement because it will not be productive without the client's cooperation.

Answer (A) is correct. *(CIA, adapted)*
REQUIRED: The most appropriate response to an assertion that an engagement to evaluate the effectiveness of the quality assurance function is beyond the scope of the IAA.
DISCUSSION: The charter should define the purpose, authority, and responsibility of the IAA (Standard 1000). Among other matters, it should define the scope of internal audit activities. Furthermore, the CAE should submit annually to senior management for approval, and to the board for its information, a summary of the IAA's work schedule, staffing plan, and financial budget (PA 2020-1).
Answer (B) is incorrect because the engagement client does not determine the scope of this type of assurance engagement. A scope limitation imposed by the client might prevent the IAA from achieving its objectives. Answer (C) is incorrect because other objectives may be established by management and the internal auditors. The engagement should not be limited to the specific standards set by the quality assurance department, but it should consider such standards in the development of the engagement program. Answer (D) is incorrect because the internal auditors should conduct the engagement and communicate any scope limitations to management and the board.

10. The chief audit executive has assigned an internal auditor to perform a year-end engagement to evaluate payroll records. The internal auditor has contacted the director of compensation and has been refused access to necessary documents. To avoid this problem,

A. Access to records relevant to performance of engagements should be specified in the internal audit activity's charter.

B. Internal auditing should be required to report to the CEO of the organization.

C. By following the long-range planning process, access to all relevant records should be guaranteed.

D. Audit committee approval should be required for all scope limitations.

Answer (A) is correct. *(CIA, adapted)*
REQUIRED: The means of avoiding an engagement client's refusal to permit access to necessary documents.
DISCUSSION: The IAA should have the support of management and the board in gaining cooperation from all engagement clients (PA 1110-1). Specific guidelines should be written in its charter authorizing access to records, personnel, and physical properties relevant to the performance of engagements (PA 1000-1). Such provisions reduce the likelihood of scope limitations.
Answer (B) is incorrect because the IAA need not report to a specific individual in the organization, although reporting administratively to the CEO is desirable. Answer (C) is incorrect because following the long-range planning process provides no guarantee of access. Answer (D) is incorrect because the IAA should inform the board of any scope limitations, but its approval is not required.

11. A charter is being drafted for a newly formed internal audit activity. Which of the following best describes the appropriate organizational status that should be incorporated into the charter?

A. The chief audit executive should report to the chief executive officer but have access to the board of directors.

B. The chief audit executive should be a member of the audit committee of the board of directors.

C. The chief audit executive should be a staff officer reporting to the chief financial officer.

D. The chief audit executive should report to an administrative vice president.

Answer (A) is correct. *(CIA, adapted)*
REQUIRED: The appropriate organizational status that should be incorporated into the charter.
DISCUSSION: The CAE should be responsible to an individual in the organization with sufficient authority to promote independence and to ensure broad engagement coverage, adequate consideration of engagement communications, and appropriate action on engagement recommendations. The higher the level to which the IAA reports, the more likely that independence will be assured. Ideally, the CAE should report functionally to the audit committee, board of directors, or other appropriate governing authority and administratively to the CEO (PA 1110-1).

12. A written charter approved by the board that formally defines the internal audit activity's purpose, authority, and responsibility enhances its

A. Exercise of due professional care.

B. Proficiency.

C. Relationship with management.

D. Independence.

Answer (D) is correct. *(CIA, adapted)*
REQUIRED: The purpose of a charter.
DISCUSSION: The charter should (a) establish the IAA's position within the organization; (b) authorize access to records, personnel, and physical properties relevant to the performance of engagements; and (c) define the scope of internal audit activities (PA 1000-1). Thus, the charter helps establish the IAA's organizational status. Objectivity and organizational status are the means of achieving independence (PA 1100-1).
Answer (A) is incorrect because due professional care is an attribute of work performed. Answer (B) is incorrect because proficiency is an attribute of the knowledge, skills, and other competencies possessed by internal auditors. Answer (C) is incorrect because the IAA's relationship with management is a function of professionalism. The charter establishes independence, not a working relationship.

13. The status of the internal audit activity should be free from the effects of irresponsible policy changes by management. The most effective way to assure that freedom is to

A. Have the internal audit charter approved by the board.

B. Adopt policies for the functioning of the internal audit activity.

C. Establish an audit committee within the board.

D. Develop written policies and procedures to serve as standards of performance for the internal audit activity.

Answer (A) is correct. *(CIA, adapted)*
REQUIRED: The most effective way to assure that internal auditing is free from irresponsible policy changes.
DISCUSSION: The purpose, authority, and responsibility of the internal audit activity should be formally defined in a charter, consistent with the Standards, and approved by the board (Standard 1000). The charter should establish the IAA's position within the organization; authorize access to records, personnel, and physical properties relevant to the performance of engagements; and define the scope of internal audit activities (PA 1000-1). Approval of the charter by the board protects the IAA from management actions that could weaken its status.
Answer (B) is incorrect because adoption of policies for the functioning of the IAA does not protect its status. Answer (C) is incorrect because the establishment of an audit committee does not ensure the status of the IAA without its involvement in matters such as acceptance of the charter. Answer (D) is incorrect because written policies and procedures serve to guide the internal auditing staff but have little effect on management.

14. In some organizations, internal auditing functions are outsourced. Management in a large organization should recognize that the external auditor may have an advantage, compared with the internal auditor, because of the external auditor's

A. Familiarity with the organization. Its annual audits provide an in-depth knowledge of the organization.

B. Size. It can hire experienced, knowledgeable, and certified staff.

C. Size. It is able to offer continuous availability of staff unaffected by other priorities.

D. Structure. It may more easily accommodate engagement requirements in distant locations.

Answer (D) is correct. *(CIA, adapted)*
REQUIRED: The advantage of outsourcing internal auditing functions.
DISCUSSION: Large organizations that are geographically dispersed may find outsourcing internal auditing functions to external auditors to be effective. A major public accounting firm ordinarily has operations that are national or worldwide in scope.
Answer (A) is incorrect because the internal auditing staff is likely to be more familiar with the organization than the external auditor given the continuous nature of its responsibilities. Answer (B) is incorrect because the internal auditor can also hire experienced, knowledgeable, and certified staff. Answer (C) is incorrect because the internal auditing staff is more likely to be continuously available. The external auditor has responsibilities to many other clients.

15. Internal auditors may provide consulting services that add value and improve an organization's operations. The performance of these services

    A. Impairs internal auditors' objectivity with respect to an assurance service involving the same engagement client.

    B. Precludes generation of assurance from a consulting engagement.

    C. Should be consistent with the internal audit activity's empowerment reflected in the charter.

    D. Imposes no responsibility to communicate information other than to the engagement client.

Answer (C) is correct. *(Publisher)*
    REQUIRED: The internal auditors' responsibility regarding consulting services.
    DISCUSSION: According to Standard 1000.C1, the nature of consulting services should be defined in the charter. Internal auditors have traditionally performed many types of consulting services, including the analysis of controls built into developing systems, analysis of security products, serving on task forces to analyze operations and make recommendations, and so forth. The board (or audit committee) should empower the internal audit activity to perform additional services if they do not represent a conflict of interest or detract from its obligations to the committee. That empowerment should be reflected in the internal audit charter (PA 1000.C1-1).
    Answer (A) is incorrect because consulting services do not necessarily impair objectivity. Decisions to implement recommendations made as a result of a consulting service should be made by management. Thus, decision-making by management does not impair the internal auditors' objectivity. Answer (B) is incorrect because assurance and consulting services are not mutually exclusive. One type of service may be generated from the other. Answer (D) is incorrect because a primary internal auditing value is to provide assurance to senior management and audit committee directors. Consulting engagements cannot be rendered in a manner that masks information that in the judgment of the chief audit executive (CAE) should be presented to senior executives and board members (PA 1000.C1-1).

16. An approach in which the internal audit activity obtains external aid in performing certain activities is referred to as which of the following?

    A. Consourcing.

    B. Outsourcing.

    C. Joint Venture.

    D. Informal consulting.

Answer (A) is correct. *(Publisher)*
    REQUIRED: The term that best describes an approach in which the internal audit activity obtains external aid in performing certain activities.
    DISCUSSION: Consourcing is an approach in which the internal audit activity obtains external aid in performing certain activities. It allows an organization to obtain the benefits of both an internal audit activity and the benefits of outsourcing.
    Answer (B) is incorrect because outsourcing is an alternative to staffing an internal audit activity. Answer (C) is incorrect because a joint venture is a partnership or conglomerate, usually between organizations. Answer (D) is incorrect because informal consulting is a form of engagement that includes routine activities, such as participation on standing committees; limited-life projects; ad-hoc meetings; and routine information exchange.

2.2 Independence and Objectivity

17. Independence is most likely impaired by an internal auditor's

    A. Continuation on an engagement at a division for which (s)he will soon be responsible as the result of a promotion.

    B. Reduction of the scope of an engagement due to budget restrictions.

    C. Participation on a task force that recommends standards for control of a new distribution system.

    D. Review of a purchasing agent's contract drafts prior to their execution.

Answer (A) is correct. *(CIA, adapted)*
    REQUIRED: The action most likely impairing independence.
    DISCUSSION: When the IAA or an individual internal auditor is responsible for, or management is considering assigning, an operation that might be the subject of an engagement, independence and objectivity may be impaired. The internal auditor should consider the following factors in assessing the effect on independence and objectivity: The IIA Code of Ethics, the SPPIA, the expectations of the stakeholders, the IAA's charter, required disclosures, and subsequent coverage of the activities or responsibilities accepted (PA 1130.A1-2).
    Answer (B) is incorrect because budget restrictions do not constitute an impairment of independence. Answer (C) is incorrect because an internal auditor may recommend standards of control. However, designing, installing, drafting procedures for, or operating systems might impair objectivity (PA 1130.A1-1). Answer (D) is incorrect because an internal auditor may review contracts prior to their execution.

18. In which of the following situations does an internal auditor potentially lack objectivity?

A. An internal auditor reviews the procedures for a new electronic data interchange (EDI) connection to a major customer before it is implemented.

B. A former purchasing assistant performs a review of internal controls over purchasing 4 months after being transferred to the internal auditing department.

C. An internal auditor recommends standards of control and performance measures for a contract with a service organization for the processing of payroll and employee benefits.

D. A payroll accounting employee assists an internal auditor in verifying the physical inventory of small motors.

Answer (B) is correct. *(CIA, adapted)*
REQUIRED: The situation in which the internal auditor may lack objectivity.
DISCUSSION: Persons transferred to or temporarily engaged by the internal audit activity should not be assigned to engagements involving those activities they previously performed until a reasonable period of time (at least one year) has elapsed. Such assignments are presumed to impair objectivity. Additional consideration is required when such persons are supervising the engagement work and communicating engagement results (PA 1130.A1-1). However, internal auditors may provide consulting services relating to operations for which they had previous responsibilities (Standard 1130.C1), provided that prior disclosure is made to the client of any potential impairments of independence or objectivity (Standard 1130.C2). Objectivity is not adversely affected when the internal auditor recommends standards of control for systems or reviews procedures before they are implemented. Designing, installing, drafting procedures for, or operating systems is presumed to impair objectivity. Use of staff from other areas to assist the internal auditor does not impair objectivity, especially when the staff is from outside of the area where the engagement is being performed.

19. Which of the following activities is not presumed to impair the objectivity of an internal auditor?

I. Recommending standards of control for a new information system application

II. Drafting procedures for running a new computer application to ensure that proper controls are installed

III. Performing reviews of procedures for a new computer application before it is installed

A. I only.

B. II only.

C. III only.

D. I and III.

Answer (D) is correct. *(CIA, adapted)*
REQUIRED: The activity(ies) not presumed to impair objectivity.
DISCUSSION: The internal auditor's objectivity is not adversely affected when (s)he recommends standards of control for systems or reviews procedures before they are implemented. Designing, installing, drafting procedures for, or operating systems is presumed to impair objectivity (PA 1130.A1-1).

20. Internal auditors must be objective in performing their work. Assume that the chief audit executive received an annual bonus as part of that individual's compensation package. The bonus may impair the CAE's objectivity if

A. The bonus is administered by the board of directors or its salary administration committee.

B. The bonus is based on monetary amounts recovered or recommended future savings as a result of engagements.

C. The scope of internal auditing work is evaluating control rather than account balances.

D. All of the answers are correct.

Answer (B) is correct. *(CIA, adapted)*
REQUIRED: The conditions under which a bonus may impair the CAE's objectivity.
DISCUSSION: Objectivity may be impaired if the bonus is based on monetary amounts recovered or recommended future savings as a result of engagements. A bonus based on either of these criteria could unduly influence the type of engagements performed or the recommendations made.
Answer (A) is incorrect because the board of directors should determine the CAE's compensation. Answer (C) is incorrect because the IAA's scope of work includes evaluating and contributing to the improvement of risk management, control, and governance processes. Answer (D) is incorrect because objectivity is not impaired if the board determines the director's compensation or if the scope of work is evaluating control rather than account balances.

21. An internal auditor has recently received an offer from the manager of the marketing department of a weekend's free use of his beachfront condominium. No engagement is currently being conducted in the marketing department, and none is scheduled. The internal auditor

    A. Should reject the offer and report it to the appropriate supervisor.

    B. May accept the offer because its value is immaterial.

    C. May accept the offer because no engagement is being conducted or planned.

    D. May accept the offer if approved by the appropriate supervisor.

Answer (A) is correct. *(Publisher)*
REQUIRED: The true statement about the offer of a gift by a nonclient member of the organization.
DISCUSSION: It is unethical for an internal auditor to accept a fee or gift from an employee, client, customer, supplier, or business associate. Accepting a fee or gift may imply that the auditor's objectivity has been impaired. Even though an engagement is not being conducted in the applicable area at that time, a future engagement may result in the appearance of impairment of objectivity. Thus, no consideration should be given to the engagement status as justification for receiving fees or gifts. The receipt of promotional items (such as pens, calendars, or samples) that are available to the general public and have minimal value should not hinder internal auditors' professional judgments. Internal auditors should report the offer of all material fees or gifts immediately to their supervisors (PA 1120-1).
Answer (B) is incorrect because the value of a weekend vacation is not immaterial. Answer (C) is incorrect because the status of engagements should not be considered as justification for receiving fees or gifts. Answer (D) is incorrect because a supervisor may not approve unethical behavior.

22. Management has requested the internal audit activity to perform an engagement to recommend procedures and policies for improving management control over the telephone marketing operations of a major division. The chief audit executive should

    A. Not accept the engagement because recommending controls would impair future objectivity regarding this operation.

    B. Not accept the engagement because internal audit activities are presumed to have expertise regarding accounting controls, not marketing controls.

    C. Accept the engagement, but indicate to management that, because recommending controls impairs independence, future engagements in the area will be impaired.

    D. Accept the engagement because objectivity will not be impaired.

Answer (D) is correct. *(CIA, adapted)*
REQUIRED: The acceptability of an engagement to recommend standards of control.
DISCUSSION: The CAE should accept the engagement; assign staff with the knowledge, skills, and other competencies essential to its performance; and make appropriate recommendations. Recommending standards of control for systems or reviewing procedures prior to implementation does not impair objectivity (PA 1130.A1-1). Moreover, if this engagement is deemed to involve consulting services, objectivity is not required provided that any impairment thereof is disclosed to the client prior to acceptance of the engagement (Standard 1130.C2).
Answer (A) is incorrect because the CAE should accept the engagement. Recommending controls is not considered to impair independence or objectivity. Answer (B) is incorrect because the engagement should be accepted. The IAA should be able to evaluate the adequacy and effectiveness of controls encompassing the organization's governance, operations, and information systems (Standard 2120.A1). Answer (C) is incorrect because independence is not impaired by making control recommendations.

23. When faced with an imposed scope limitation, the chief audit executive should

    A. Refuse to perform the engagement until the scope limitation is removed.

    B. Communicate the potential effects of the scope limitation to the audit committee of the board of directors.

    C. Increase the frequency of engagements concerning the activity in question.

    D. Assign more experienced personnel to the engagement.

Answer (B) is correct. *(CIA, adapted)*
REQUIRED: The appropriate response to an imposed scope limitation.
DISCUSSION: A scope limitation is a restriction placed upon the IAA that precludes the accomplishment of its objectives and plans. Among other things, a scope limitation may restrict (a) the scope defined in the charter; (b) the IAA's access to records, personnel, and physical properties relevant to the performance of engagements; (c) the approved engagement work schedule; (d) necessary engagement procedures; and (e) the approved staffing plan and financial budget. A scope limitation along with its potential effect should be communicated, preferably in writing, to the board, audit committee, or other appropriate governing authority (PA 1130-1).
Answer (A) is incorrect because the engagement may be conducted under a scope limitation. Answer (C) is incorrect because a scope limitation does not necessarily require more frequent engagements. Answer (D) is incorrect because a scope limitation does not necessarily require more experienced personnel.

24. The internal auditors must be able to distinguish carefully between a scope limitation and other limitations. Which of the following is not considered a scope limitation?

A. The divisional management of an engagement client has indicated that the division is in the process of converting a major computer system and has indicated that the information systems portion of the planned engagement will have to be postponed until next year.

B. The audit committee reviews the engagement work schedule for the year and deletes an engagement that the chief audit executive thought was important to conduct.

C. The engagement client has indicated that certain customers cannot be contacted because the organization is in the process of negotiating a long-term contract with the customers and they do not want to upset the customers.

D. None of the answers are correct.

Answer (B) is correct. *(CIA, adapted)*
REQUIRED: The item that is not a scope limitation.
DISCUSSION: The audit committee's decision to delete an engagement from the annual engagement work schedule is not a scope limitation. Its responsibility is to review and approve the planned scope of activities for the year.
Answer (A) is incorrect because postponing the portion of an engagement concerning a major computer system is a scope limitation. This delay restricts the performance of the engagement. Scope limitations are reported to senior management and the board for their determination as to whether the limitations are justified. Answer (C) is incorrect because prohibiting contact with certain customers is a scope limitation. This prohibition restricts the performance of specific procedures. Answer (D) is incorrect because other answer choices state scope limitations.

Questions 25 and 26 are based on the following information. The internal audit activity (IAA) of an organization has been in existence for 10 years, but its charter has not yet been approved by the board. However, the board is chaired by the chief executive officer (CEO) and includes the controller and one outside board member. The chief audit executive (CAE) reports directly to the controller who approves the IAA's work schedule. Thus, the IAA has never felt the need to push for a formal approval of the charter. The organization is publicly held and has nine major divisions. The previous CAE was recently dismissed following a dispute between the CAE and a major engagement client. A new CAE with significant experience in both public accounting and internal auditing has just been hired. Within the first month, the new CAE encountered substantial resistance from an engagement client regarding the nature of the work and the IAA's access to records. Moreover, the CEO accused the CAE of not operating "in the best interests of the organization."

---

25. Which of the following combinations best illustrates a scope limitation and the appropriate response by the CAE?

	Nature of Limitation	Internal Auditing Action
A.	Engagement client limits scope based upon proprietary information.	Report only to the controller
B.	Engagement client will not provide access to records needed for approved work schedule.	Report to the board
C.	Engagement client requests that the engagement be delayed for 2 weeks to allow it to close its books.	Report directly to the CEO and controller
D.	Engagement client will not allow internal auditor to contact major customers as part of an engagement to evaluate the efficiency of operations.	No reporting needed because the operational engagement concerns operational efficiency

Answer (B) is correct. *(CIA, adapted)*
REQUIRED: The combination best illustrating a scope limitation.
DISCUSSION: A scope limitation is a restriction placed on the internal audit activity that precludes the IAA from accomplishing its objectives and plans. Among other things, a scope limitation may restrict the IAA's access to records, personnel, and physical properties relevant to the performance of engagements. A scope limitation and its potential effect should be communicated, preferably in writing, to the board, audit committee, or other appropriate governing authority (PA 1130-1).
Answer (A) is incorrect because a scope limitation should be reported to the board, audit committee, or other appropriate governing authority. Answer (C) is incorrect because merely delaying the engagement to permit closing the books is not usually considered a scope limitation. Answer (D) is incorrect because reporting is necessary.

26. From the perspective of the internal audit activity, which of the following facts, by themselves, could contribute to a lack of independence?

I. The CEO accused the new director of not operating "in the best interests of the organization."

II. The majority of audit committee members come from within the organization.

III. The IAA's charter has not been approved by the board.

    A. I only.

    B. II only.

    C. II and III only.

    D. I, II, and III.

Answer (D) is correct. *(CIA, adapted)*
REQUIRED: The factor(s) contributing to a lack of independence.
DISCUSSION: The CEO's statement suggests that the IAA lacks the support of management and the board. Furthermore, the lack of outside audit committee members may contribute to a loss of independence. The failure to approve the charter may have the same effect. The charter enhances the independence of the IAA because, by specifying the purpose, authority, and responsibility of the IAA, it establishes the position of the IAA in the organization (PA 1000-1). Independence is achieved through organizational status and objectivity (PA 1100-1).
Answer (A) is incorrect because lack of a charter and lack of outside directors weaken the IAA's position. Answer (B) is incorrect because lack of support by the CEO and lack of a charter weaken the IAA's position. Answer (C) is incorrect because lack of support by the CEO weakens the IAA's position.

27. Prior to performing consulting services, the Chief Audit Executive should get approval from whom?

    A. The audit committee.

    B. The board of directors.

    C. The chief executive officer.

    D. The external auditor.

Answer (B) is correct. *(Publisher)*
REQUIRED: The individual/group that the CAE should get approval from prior to performing consulting services.
DISCUSSION: Internal auditors are sometimes requested to provide consulting services relating to operations for which they had previous responsibilities or had conducted assurance services. Prior to offering consulting services, the Chief Audit Executive should confirm that the board understands and approves the concept of providing consulting services (PA 1000.C1-2).

28. During the course of an engagement, an internal auditor makes a preliminary determination that a major division has been inappropriately capitalizing research and development expense. The engagement is not yet completed, and the internal auditor has not documented the problem or determined that it really is a problem. However, the internal auditor is informed that the chief audit executive has received the following communication from the president of the organization:

> "The controller of Division B informs me that you have discovered a questionable account classification dealing with research and development expense. We are aware of the issue. You are directed to discontinue any further investigation of this matter until informed by me to proceed. Under the confidentiality standard of your profession, I also direct you not to communicate with the outside auditors regarding this issue."

Which of the following is an appropriate action for the CAE to take regarding the questionable item?

    A. Immediately report the communication to The Institute of Internal Auditors and ask for an ethical interpretation and guidance.

    B. Inform the president that this scope limitation will need to be reported to the board.

    C. Continue to investigate the area until all the facts are determined and document all the relevant facts in the engagement records.

    D. Immediately notify the external auditors of the problem to avoid aiding and abetting a potential crime by the organization.

Answer (B) is correct. *(CIA, adapted)*
REQUIRED: The action by the CAE after senior management imposes a scope limitation.
DISCUSSION: A scope limitation along with its potential effect should be communicated, preferably in writing, to the board, audit committee, or other appropriate governing authority (PA 1130-1).
Answer (A) is incorrect because The IIA has no authority in this matter. Answer (C) is incorrect because the CAE should first consult the board. The CAE adds value by serving the organization, and the board may, in fact, be fully aware of the problem and may not want to incur additional costs. Answer (D) is incorrect because the engagement work is preliminary, and the internal auditor has not yet formed a basis for an opinion. Thus, contacting the external auditors is premature. However, if an inquiry is made by the external auditors, the internal auditors should share the work done to date.

29. For control and monitoring functions that the CAE has a relationship with (risk management, compliance, security, legal, etc.) the CAE should do which of the following?

    A. Facilitate the reporting of material risk and control issues to the Chief Executive Officer.

    B. Facilitate the reporting of material risk and control issues to the external auditor.

    C. Facilitate the reporting of material risk and control issues to the audit committee.

    D. Facilitate the reporting of material risk and control issues to no one, since this is not a responsibility of the CAE.

Answer (C) is correct. *(Publisher)*
    REQUIRED: The individual/group that the CAE should facilitate the reporting of material risk and control issues to for control and monitoring functions that the CAE has a relationship with.
    DISCUSSION: CAEs should consider their relationships with other control and monitoring functions (risk management, compliance, security, legal, ethics, environmental, external audit) and facilitate the reporting of material risk and control issues to the audit committee (PA 1110-2).

30. An organization is in the process of establishing its new internal audit activity. The controller has no previous experience with internal auditors. Due to this lack of experience, the controller advised the applicants that the CAE will be reporting to the external auditors. However, the new chief audit executive will have free access to the controller to report anything important. The controller will then convey the CAE's concerns to the board of directors. The IAA will

    A. Be independent because the CAE has direct access to the board.

    B. Not be independent because the CAE reports to the external auditors.

    C. Not be independent because the controller has no experience with internal auditors.

    D. Not be independent because the organization did not specify that the applicants must be certified internal auditors.

Answer (B) is correct. *(CIA, adapted)*
    REQUIRED: The true statement about a requirement that the IAA report to the external auditors and the controller.
    DISCUSSION: The CAE should be responsible to an individual in the organization with sufficient authority to promote independence (PA 1110-1). External auditors are not individuals in the organization.
    Answer (A) is incorrect because the IAA will not have direct access to the board. The access is indirect via the controller. Answer (C) is incorrect because whether the controller has experience with internal auditors does not affect the IAA's independence. Answer (D) is incorrect because although desirable, the CIA designation is not mandatory for a person to become an internal auditor. A CIA should insist on IAA independence.

31. A medium-sized publicly owned organization operating in Country X has grown to a size that the governing authority believes warrants the establishment of an internal audit activity. Country X has legislated internal auditing requirements for government-owned organizations. The organization changed the bylaws to reflect the establishment of the internal audit activity. The governing authority decided that the chief audit executive (CAE) must be a certified internal auditor and will report directly to the newly established audit committee. Which of the items discussed above will contribute the most to the new CAE's independence?

    A. The establishment of the internal audit activity is documented in the bylaws.

    B. Country X has legislated internal auditing requirements.

    C. The CAE will report to the audit committee.

    D. The CAE is to be a certified internal auditor.

Answer (C) is correct. *(CIA, adapted)*
    REQUIRED: The item that contributes most to a CAE's independence.
    DISCUSSION: Independence is achieved through organizational status and objectivity. The CAE should be responsible to an individual with sufficient authority to promote independence (PA 1100-1 and PA 1110-1). The board (and by extension the audit committee) is the highest authority in the organization.
    Answer (A) is incorrect because documentation in the by-laws does little to promote independence. Answer (B) is incorrect because legislated internal auditing requirements in Country X do not promote independence. Answer (D) is incorrect because independence is achieved through organizational status and objectivity.

32. The governing authority (audit committee or board of directors) that the CAE should functionally report to is responsible for which of the following activities?

I.   Internal communication and information flows

II. Approval of the internal audit risk assessment and related audit plan

III. Approval of annual compensation and salary adjustment for the CAE

   A. I and II.

   B. II and III.

   C. I and III.

   D. I, II, and III.

Answer (B) is correct. *(Publisher)*
REQUIRED: The activities that the governing authority of the CAE is responsible for.
DISCUSSION: PA 1110-2 gives a description of what The IIA considers functional reporting. The IIA recommends that the CAE report functionally to the audit committee, board of directors, or other appropriate governing authority. In this context, report functionally means that the governing authority should

- Approve the overall charter of the internal audit function.
- Approve the internal audit risk assessment and related audit plan.
- Receive communications from the CAE on the results of the internal audit activities or other matters that the CAE determines are necessary, including private meetings with the CAE without management present.
- Approve all decisions regarding the appointment or removal of the CAE.
- Approve the annual compensation and salary adjustment of the CAE.
- Make appropriate inquiries of management and the CAE to determine whether there are scope or budgetary limitations that impede the ability of the internal audit function to execute its responsibilities.

Answer (A) is incorrect because internal communication and information flows are items that administrative reporting typically includes. Answer (C) is incorrect because internal communication and information flows are items that administrative reporting typically includes. Answer (D) is incorrect because internal communication and information flows are items that administrative reporting typically includes.

33. The reporting relationship within the organization's management structure that facilitates the day-to-day operations of the internal audit function is referred to as which of the following?

   A. Administrative reporting.

   B. Financial reporting.

   C. Management reporting.

   D. Functional reporting.

Answer (A) is correct. *(Publisher)*
REQUIRED: The type of reporting that facilitates the day-to-day operations of the internal audit function.
DISCUSSION: As stated in PA 1110-2, administrative reporting is the reporting relationship within the organization's management structure that facilitates the day-to-day operations of the internal audit function. Administrative reporting typically includes:

- Budgeting and management accounting.
- Human resource administration, including personnel evaluations and compensation.
- Internal communications and information flows.
- Administration of the organization's internal policies and procedures.

Answer (B) is incorrect because financial reporting focuses primarily on reporting information about an enterprise's performance provided by measures of earnings and its components. Answer (C) is incorrect because a form of management reporting is the financial statements, which report on the organization's performance to external parties. Answer (D) is incorrect because functional reporting deals with reporting to the audit committee or board of directors in order to achieve independence and authority.

34. An external quality assessment team was evaluating the independence of an internal audit activity. The internal audit activity performs engagements concerning all of the elements included in its scope. Which of the following reporting responsibilities is most likely to threaten the internal audit activity's independence? Reporting to the

A. President.

B. Treasurer.

C. Executive vice president.

D. Audit committee.

Answer (B) is correct. *(CIA, adapted)*
REQUIRED: The reporting responsibility that most likely threatens independence.
DISCUSSION: The CAE should report to an individual in the organization that has sufficient authority to promote independence and to ensure broad engagement coverage, adequate consideration of engagement communications, and appropriate action on engagement recommendations (PA 1110-1). The higher the level to which the IAA reports, the more likely that independence will be assured. The highest level to which it might report is the audit committee, which includes outside members of the board of directors. The next highest is the chief executive officer. Reporting to the treasurer limits the influence and independence of the IAA.
Answer (A) is incorrect because being responsible to the president helps preserve the IAA's independence by enhancing its status. Answer (C) is incorrect because the executive vice president is higher ranking than the treasurer. Answer (D) is incorrect because the audit committee is higher ranking than the treasurer.

35. Independence and objectivity may be impaired if assurance services are provided within one year after a formal consulting engagement. What steps can be taken to minimize the effects of this kind of impairment?

I. Assigning different auditors to perform each of the services.

II. Establishing independent management and supervision.

III. Defining separate accountability for the results of projects.

IV. Disclosing the presumed impairment.

A. I and III.

B. I, III, and IV.

C. II, III, and IV.

D. I, II, IIII, and IV.

Answer (D) is correct. *(Publisher)*
REQUIRED: The steps that can be taken to minimize the effects of impairment.
DISCUSSION: Independence and objectivity may be impaired if assurance services are provided within one year after a formal consulting engagement. Steps can be taken to minimize the effects of impairment by assigning different auditors to perform each of the services, establishing independent management and supervision, defining separate accountability for the results of the projects, and disclosing the presumed impairment. Management should be responsible for accepting and implementing recommendations (PA 1000.C1-2).

36. During the performance of an engagement to evaluate a division's controls over purchasing, the chief purchasing agent asked why the internal auditor had requested documents pertaining to transactions with a particular supplier. The internal auditor's proper response is to

A. Treat the inquiry as a scope limitation.

B. Explain the reasons for the information request to promote cooperation with the engagement client.

C. Refuse to explain the information request to preserve the integrity of the engagement process.

D. Consider the specific circumstances before deciding whether to disclose the reasons for the information request.

Answer (D) is correct. *(Publisher)*
REQUIRED: The internal auditor's proper response to an engagement client's information request.
DISCUSSION: At times, an internal auditor may be asked by the engagement client or other parties to explain why a document that has been requested is relevant to an engagement. Disclosure or nondisclosure during the engagement of the reasons documents are needed should be determined based on the circumstances. Significant irregularities may dictate a less open environment than would normally be conducive to a cooperative engagement. However, that is a judgment that should be made by the chief audit executive in light of the specific circumstances (PA 1110.A1-1).
Answer (A) is incorrect because a scope limitation is a restriction placed upon the IAA that precludes it from accomplishing its objectives and plans (PA 1130-1). Answer (B) is incorrect because the CAE should consider the specific circumstances before deciding whether to disclose the reasons for the information request. Answer (C) is incorrect because it is not always necessary or desirable to refuse to explain an information request.

37. Which of the following statements is an appropriate reason for the internal audit activity not to participate in the systems development process?

    A. Participation will affect independence, and the internal auditors will not be able to perform an objective evaluation after the system is implemented.

    B. Participation will delay implementation of the project.

    C. Participation will cause the internal auditors to be labeled as partial owners of the application, and they will then have to share the blame for any problems that remain in the system.

    D. None of the answers are correct.

Answer (D) is correct. *(CIA, adapted)*
    REQUIRED: The reason for the IAA not to participate in systems development.
    DISCUSSION: Objectivity is not adversely affected when the internal auditors recommend standards of control for systems or review procedures before they are implemented. Designing, installing, drafting procedures for, or operating systems is presumed to impair objectivity (PA 1130.A1-1). Moreover, if this engagement is deemed to involve consulting services, objectivity is not required provided that any impairment thereof is disclosed to the client prior to acceptance of the engagement (Standard 1130.C2).
    Answer (A) is incorrect because IAA independence should not be affected by recommending control standards or reviewing procedures before implementation. Answer (B) is incorrect because IAA participation will not delay the project unless needed controls were absent. Answer (C) is incorrect because the internal auditors should participate in systems development but should not draft procedures or design, install, or operate the system.

38. Independence permits internal auditors to render impartial and unbiased judgments. The best way to achieve independence is through

    A. Individual knowledge and skills.

    B. Organizational status and objectivity.

    C. Supervision within the organization.

    D. Organizational knowledge and skills.

Answer (B) is correct. *(CIA, adapted)*
    REQUIRED: The best way to achieve independence.
    DISCUSSION: The IAA should be independent (Standard 1100). Internal auditors are independent when they can carry out their work freely and objectively. Independence permits internal auditors to render the impartial and unbiased judgments essential to the proper conduct of engagements. It is achieved through organizational status and objectivity (PA 1100-1).
    Answer (A) is incorrect because individual knowledge and skills allow individual auditors to achieve professional proficiency. Answer (C) is incorrect because supervision ensures that engagement objectives are achieved, quality is assured, and staff is developed (Standard 2340). Answer (D) is incorrect because organizational knowledge and skills allow the IAA collectively to achieve professional proficiency.

39. The internal audit function should be free to audit and report on any activity that also reports to its administrative head if it deems that coverage appropriate for its audit plan. Any limitation in scope or reporting of results of these activities should be brought to the attention of whom?

    A. Chief Executive Officer.

    B. Chief Financial Officer.

    C. External Auditor.

    D. Audit Committee.

Answer (D) is correct. *(Publisher)*
    REQUIRED: The person/group that should be notified when a scope or reporting of results limitation for the internal audit function exists.
    DISCUSSION: The CAE should ensure that appropriate independence is maintained if the individual responsible for the administrative reporting line is also responsible for other activities in the organization, which are subject to internal audit. For example, some CAEs report administratively to the Chief Financial Officer, who is also responsible for the organization's accounting functions. The internal audit activity should be free to audit and report on any activity that also reports to its administrative head if it deems that coverage appropriate for its audit plan. Any limitation in scope or reporting of results of these activities should be brought to the attention of the audit committee (PA 1110-2).
    Answer (A) is incorrect because the CEO is not independent from the organization. Answer (B) is incorrect because the CFO is also responsible for the organization's accounting functions, such that when a scope or reporting limitation exists, the CFO may be responsible for it. Therefore, the CAE should report these limitations to the independent audit committee. Answer (C) is incorrect because the external auditor should not be notified unless the audit committee believes it is necessary.

40. When evaluating the independence of an internal audit activity, a quality assurance review team performing an external assessment considers several factors. Which of the following factors has the least amount of influence when judging an internal audit activity's independence?

A. Criteria used in making internal auditors' assignments.

B. The extent of internal auditor training in communications skills.

C. Relationship between engagement records and engagement communications.

D. Impartial and unbiased judgments.

Answer (B) is correct.   *(CIA, adapted)*
REQUIRED: The factor that least influences independence.
DISCUSSION: The IAA should be independent (Standard 1100). Internal auditors are independent when they can carry out their work freely and objectively. Independence permits internal auditors to render the impartial and unbiased judgments essential to the proper conduct of engagements. It is achieved through organizational status and objectivity (PA 1100-1). However, training in communication relates to the knowledge, skills, and other competencies needed to perform engagements, not to independence.
Answer (A) is incorrect because how individual internal auditors are assigned relates to independence. The auditor's personal relationships with operating personnel, work experience with the engagement client, etc., affect independence. Answer (C) is incorrect because, if significant engagement observations found in the engagement records are omitted from the engagement communications, independence is brought into question. Answer (D) is incorrect because unbiased judgment is an aspect of independence.

41. Regardless of which reporting relationship the organization chooses, several key actions can help assure that the reporting lines support and enable the effectiveness and independence of the internal auditing activity. Which key action will not achieve its functional reporting purpose?

A. The functional reporting line should go directly to the Audit Committee or its equivalent to ensure the appropriate level of independence and communication.

B. The CAE should meet with the audit committee or its equivalent, with management, to reinforce the independence and nature of this reporting relationship.

C. The audit committee should have the final authority to review and approve the annual audit plan and all major changes to the plan.

D. At all times, the CAE should have open and direct access to the chair of the audit committee and its members; or the chair of the board or full board if appropriate.

Answer (B) is correct.   *(Publisher)*
REQUIRED: The key action that will not achieve its functional reporting purpose.
DISCUSSION: The key actions for functional reporting are:

- The functional reporting line should go directly to the Audit Committee or its equivalent to ensure the appropriate level of independence and communication.
- The CAE should meet privately with the audit committee or its equivalent, without management present, to reinforce the independence and nature of this reporting relationship.
- The audit committee should have the final authority to review and approve the annual audit plan and all major changes to the plan.
- At all times, the CAE should have open and direct access to the chair of the audit committee and its members; or the chair of the board or full board if appropriate.
- At least once a year, the audit committee should review the performance of the CAE and approve the annual compensation and salary adjustment.
- The charter for the internal audit function should clearly articulate both the functional and administrative reporting lines for the function as well as the principle activities directed up each line (PA 1110-2).

The purpose of helping to assure that the reporting lines are effective and independent will not be achieved if management is present during all the CAE's meetings with the audit committee or its equivalent.

42. The administrative reporting line of the CAE should be to whom?

A. The audit committee.

B. Line management.

C. Board of directors.

D. CEO or equivalent.

Answer (D) is correct.   *(Publisher)*
REQUIRED: The individual/group that the CAE should administratively report to.
DISCUSSION: The administrative reporting line of the CAE should be to the CEO or another executive with sufficient authority to provide appropriate support to accomplish its day-to-day activities. This support should include positioning the function and the CAE in the organization's structure in a manner that affords appropriate stature for the function within the organization. Reporting too low in an organization can negatively impact the stature and effectiveness of the internal audit function.
Answer (A) is incorrect because the functional reporting line should go directly to the audit committee. Answer (B) is incorrect because the administrative reporting line should facilitate open and direct communications with line management. Answer (C) is incorrect because the board of directors is a group that the CAE should have open and direct communications with at all times for functional reporting issues.

43. An internal auditor who had been supervisor of the accounts payable section should not perform an assurance review of that section

- A. Because there is no way to measure a reasonable period of time in which to establish independence.
- B. Until a reasonable period of time has elapsed.
- C. Until after the next annual review by the external auditors.
- D. Until it is clear that the new supervisor has assumed the responsibilities.

Answer (B) is correct. *(CIA, adapted)*
REQUIRED: The appropriate time for an internal auditor to review an operating activity for which (s)he had responsibility.
DISCUSSION: Persons transferred to, or temporarily engaged by, the internal audit activity should not be assigned to engagements involving assurance reviews of activities they previously performed until a reasonable period of time (at least 1 year) has elapsed. Such assignments are presumed to impair objectivity (PA 1130.A1-1).
Answer (A) is incorrect because a "reasonable period" is ordinarily determinable. Answer (C) is incorrect because the external review does not bear any relation to restoring the internal auditor's objectivity. Answer (D) is incorrect because the new supervisor presumably would have assumed his/her responsibilities immediately. Hence, a reasonable time could not have elapsed.

44. Independence permits internal auditors to render the impartial and unbiased judgments essential to the proper conduct of engagements. Which of the following best promotes independence?

- A. A policy that requires internal auditors to report to the chief audit executive any situations in which a conflict of interest or bias on the part of the individual internal auditor is present or may reasonably be inferred.
- B. A policy that prevents the internal audit activity from recommending standards of control for systems that it evaluates.
- C. An organizational policy that allows engagements concerning sensitive operations to be outsourced.
- D. An organizational policy that prevents personnel transfers from operating activities to the internal audit activity.

Answer (A) is correct. *(CIA, adapted)*
REQUIRED: The policy best promoting independence.
DISCUSSION: Staff assignments should be made so that potential and actual conflicts of interest and bias are avoided. Moreover, staff assignments of internal auditors should be rotated periodically whenever it is practicable to do so. The CAE should periodically obtain from the internal auditing staff information concerning potential conflicts of interest and bias, and internal auditors should report to the CAE any situations in which a conflict of interest or bias is present or may reasonably be inferred. The CAE should then reassign such auditors (PA 1120-1 and PA 1130-1).
Answer (B) is incorrect because internal auditing may recommend standards of control for systems that it evaluates. Answer (C) is incorrect because outsourcing certain engagements does not promote the independence of the IAA. Answer (D) is incorrect because transfers from operating activities to the IAA usually are permitted. However, transferees should not be assigned to engagements concerning activities they previously performed until a reasonable period of time has elapsed.

45. Assuming that the internal auditing staff possesses the necessary experience and training, which of the following services is most appropriate for a staff internal auditor to undertake?

- A. Substitute for the accounts payable supervisor while (s)he is on sick leave.
- B. Determine the profitability of alternative investment acquisitions and select the best alternative.
- C. As part of an evaluation team, review vendor accounting software internal controls and rank according to exposures.
- D. Participate in an internal audit of the accounting department shortly after transferring from the accounting department.

Answer (C) is correct. *(CIA, adapted)*
REQUIRED: The service most appropriate for an internal auditor to undertake.
DISCUSSION: An internal auditor's objectivity is not impaired when (s)he recommends standards of control for systems or reviews procedures before they are implemented (PA 1130.A1-1). Moreover, if this engagement is deemed to involve consulting services, objectivity is not required provided that any impairment thereof is disclosed to the client prior to acceptance of the engagement (Standard 1130.C2).
Answer (A) is incorrect because an internal auditor's objectivity is presumed to be impaired for a reasonable period of time with respect to activities (s)he previously performed. Answer (B) is incorrect because investment decisions are the prerogative of management. Answer (D) is incorrect because an internal auditor should not be assigned to engagements concerning activities (s)he previously performed until a reasonable time has elapsed.

STUDY UNIT THREE
STANDARDS AND PROFICIENCY

(9 pages of outline)

Maintenance of a high degree of competence in the performance of work is a characteristic of a profession. Accordingly, The IIA issues pronouncements to impart an understanding of the roles and responsibilities of internal auditing to its constituencies, to establish the basis for the guidance and measurement of internal auditing performance, and to improve the practice of internal auditing.

Professional proficiency is also an ethical obligation of entities and individuals that provide internal auditing services. The Principles and Rules of Conduct from The IIA *Code of Ethics* are pertinent to this aspect of proficiency. Thus, internal auditors

1.1   *Shall perform their work with honesty, diligence, and responsibility.*

4.1   *Shall engage only in those services for which they have the necessary knowledge, skills, and experience.*

4.2   *Shall perform internal auditing services in accordance with the Standards for the Professional Practice of Internal Auditing.*

4.3   *Shall continually improve their proficiency and the effectiveness and quality of their services.*

3.1 PROFESSIONAL PRACTICES FRAMEWORK

1. The **Internal Auditing Standards Board (IASB)** is the official body charged by The IIA with developing professional standards for internal auditing. Its primary responsibility is to provide guidance to practitioners.

2. The **International Ethics Committee** considers needed changes in the *Code of Ethics* and investigates complaints against members of The IIA and CIAs.

    a. A recent change in The IIA's content specification outline for Part I added a topic about compliance (and promoting compliance) with The IIA Code of Ethics. Thus, candidates preparing for Part I should review our Study Unit 9, Ethics, in Part II of CIA Examination Review.

3. Administrative Directives (ADs) are submitted by the appropriate committees to the **Executive Committee** for approval.

4. The **Board of Regents** establishes requirements for the CIA designation and continuing professional education (CPE) for CIAs.

5. The following is a tabular presentation of the elements of the **Professional Practices Framework**:

Content	Process	Final Approval	Compliance Requirement
Definition of Internal Auditing	Developed and updated by the Board of Directors with assistance, as appropriate, from the Guidance Planning Committee. Exposure drafts distributed to members, stakeholders, and other professionals. IIA staff will respond to informal inquiries and provide clarification.	Board of Directors	The definition applies to organizations and individuals that identify with the Professional Practice of Internal Auditing. The definition is the umbrella under which the framework of ethics, standards, and guidance is developed.
Code of Ethics	Developed and updated by Board of Directors with assistance, as appropriate, from the Ethics Committee. Exposure drafts distributed to members, stakeholders, and other professionals. IIA staff will respond to informal inquiries and provide clarification.	Board of Directors	Applies to Internal Auditors performing internal auditing services. Also, applicable to IIA members and CIAs in all circumstances.
Standards for the Professional Practice of Internal Auditing - Attribute Standards	Developed and updated by the Internal Auditing Standards Board with assistance, as appropriate, from other IIA Committees and appointed task forces. Exposure drafts distributed to members, stakeholders, and other professionals. IIA staff will respond to informal inquiries and provide clarification.	Internal Auditing Standards Board	Applies to Standards for Attributes of organizations and individuals performing internal auditing services.
Standards for the Professional Practice of Internal Auditing - Performance Standards	Developed and updated by the Internal Auditing Standards Board with assistance, as appropriate, from other IIA Committees and appointed task forces. Exposure drafts distributed to members, stakeholders, and other professionals. IIA staff will respond to informal inquiries and provide clarification.	Internal Auditing Standards Board	Applies to Standards for Performance of organizations and individuals performing internal auditing services.
Standards for the Professional Practice of Internal Auditing - Implementation Standards	Developed and updated by the Internal Auditing Standards Board with assistance, as appropriate, from other IIA Committees and appointed task forces. Exposure drafts distributed to members, stakeholders, and other professionals. IIA staff will respond to informal inquiries and provide clarification.	Internal Auditing Standards Board	Applies to organizations and individuals performing the specific internal auditing services and procedures delineated by these Standards. Broad categories are assurance services and consulting services Implementation Standards.
Guidance - Practice Advisories	Developed and updated by the Professional Issues Committee or other group designated by the Guidance Planning Committee. Exposure drafts distributed as appropriate, but not mandatory. IIA staff will respond to informal inquiries and provide clarification.	Reviewed and released by the Professional Issues Committee	Not mandatory but represent best practices endorsed by The IIA as means of implementing the SPPIA.
Guidance - Development and Practice Aids	IIA Staff would direct practitioner to this type of guidance. Examples are educational products, research studies, seminars, and conferences.	Not necessary	Compliance not required. Provided to assist organizations and individuals to which this guidance is relevant.

a. The IIA *Code of Ethics* is in *CIA Review* Part II.

b. The full text of the SPPIA is in Study Unit 1, but individual sections also appear in the appropriate study units in *CIA Review* Parts I and II.

c. Practice Advisories are presented with the related sections of the SPPIA. They are nonmandatory interpretations of the SPPIA or their application in specific situations. Much of the material in the Practice Advisories was formerly included in the Codification of Internal Auditing Standards (the Red Book) as Guidelines (initially issued as Statements of Internal Auditing Standards). Practice Advisories also contain some guidance previously included in the Professional Standards Practice Releases (PSPRs), which provided nonmandatory interpretations of the Standards in Q&A format. The 39 PSPRs were released in 1996 and 1997.

d. ADs specify the process and related procedures to be followed by The IIA and the IASB in administering the Standards, the related pronouncements, and the programs and activities included in the IASB's mission statement. However, ADs are not tested directly on the exam.

6. Stop and review! You have completed the outline for this subunit. Study multiple-choice questions 1 through 4 beginning on page 83.

3.2 PROFESSIONAL PROFICIENCY

1. This subunit describes the attributes of individual internal auditors and of the internal audit activity that permit the rendition of services with professional proficiency. It also defines due professional care and presents the continuing professional development requirements. These matters are covered in one General Attribute Standard, three Specific Attribute Standards, four Assurance Implementation Standards, two Consulting Implementation Standards, and six Practice Advisories. A proposed Practice Advisory relating to consulting engagements and partly applicable to this subunit is also available (Study Unit 1).

1200 *Proficiency and Due Professional Care* – *Engagements should be performed with proficiency and due professional care.*

Practice Advisory 1200-1: Proficiency and Due Professional Care

1. *Professional proficiency is the responsibility of the chief audit executive and each internal auditor. The chief audit executive should ensure that persons assigned to each engagement collectively possess the necessary knowledge, skills, and other competencies to conduct the engagement properly.*

2. *Internal auditors should comply with professional standards of conduct. The Institute of Internal Auditors' Code of Ethics extends beyond the definition of internal auditing to include two essential components:*

    - *Principles that are relevant to the profession and practice of internal auditing -- specifically, integrity, objectivity, confidentiality, and competency; and*
    - *Rules of Conduct that describe behavior norms expected of internal auditors. These rules are an aid to interpreting the Principles into practical applications and are intended to guide the ethical conduct of internal auditors.*

1210 *Proficiency* – *Internal auditors should possess the knowledge, skills, and other competencies needed to perform their individual responsibilities. The internal audit activity collectively should possess or obtain the knowledge, skills, and other competencies needed to perform its responsibilities.*

Practice Advisory 1210-1: Proficiency

1. *Each internal auditor should possess certain knowledge, skills, and other competencies:*

    - *Proficiency in applying internal auditing standards, procedures, and techniques is required in performing engagements. Proficiency means the ability to apply knowledge to situations likely to be encountered and to deal with them without extensive recourse to technical research and assistance.*
    - *Proficiency in accounting principles and techniques is required of auditors who work extensively with financial records and reports.*

- *An understanding of management principles is required to recognize and evaluate the materiality and significance of deviations from good business practices. An understanding means the ability to apply broad knowledge to situations likely to be encountered, to recognize significant deviations, and to be able to carry out the research necessary to arrive at reasonable solutions.*

- *An appreciation is required of the fundamentals of subjects such as accounting, economics, commercial law, taxation, finance, quantitative methods, and information technology. An appreciation means the ability to recognize the existence of problems or potential problems and to determine the further research to be undertaken or the assistance to be obtained.*

2. *Internal auditors should be skilled in dealing with people and in communicating effectively. Internal auditors should understand human relations and maintain satisfactory relationships with engagement clients.*

3. *Internal auditors should be skilled in oral and written communications so that they can clearly and effectively convey such matters as engagement objectives, evaluations, conclusions, and recommendations.*

4. *The chief audit executive should establish suitable criteria of education and experience for filling internal auditing positions, giving due consideration to scope of work and level of responsibility. Reasonable assurance should be obtained as to each prospective auditor's qualifications and proficiency.*

5. *The internal auditing staff should collectively possess the knowledge and skills essential to the practice of the profession within the organization.*

1210.A1 - *The chief audit executive should obtain competent advice and assistance if the internal audit staff lacks the knowledge, skills, or other competencies needed to perform all or part of the engagement.*

Practice Advisory 1210.A1-1: Obtaining Services to Support or Complement the Internal Audit Activity

1. *The internal audit activity should have employees or use outside service providers who are qualified in disciplines such as accounting, auditing, economics, finance, statistics, information technology, engineering, taxation, law, environmental affairs, and such other areas as needed to meet the internal audit activity's responsibilities. Each member of the internal audit activity, however, need not be qualified in all disciplines.*

2. *An outside service provider is a person or firm, independent of the organization, who has special knowledge, skill, and experience in a particular discipline. Outside service providers include, among others, actuaries, accountants, appraisers, environmental specialists, fraud investigators, lawyers, engineers, geologists, security specialists, statisticians, information technology specialists, the organization's external auditors, and other auditing organizations. An outside service provider may be engaged by the board, senior management, or the chief audit executive.*

3. *Outside service providers may be used by the internal audit activity in connection with, among other things:*

- *Auditing activities for which a specialized skill and knowledge are required, such as information technology, statistics, taxes, language translations, or to achieve the objectives in the engagement work schedule.*

- *Valuations of assets such as land and buildings, works of art, precious gems, investments, and complex financial instruments.*

- Determination of quantities or physical condition of certain assets such as mineral and petroleum reserves.
- Measuring the work completed and to be completed on contracts in progress.
- Fraud and security investigations.
- Determination of amounts by using specialized methods such as actuarial determinations of employee benefit obligations.
- Interpretation of legal, technical, and regulatory requirements.
- Evaluating the internal audit activity's quality improvement program in accordance with Section 1300 of the Standards.
- Mergers and acquisitions.

4. When the chief audit executive intends to use and rely on the work of an outside service provider, the chief audit executive should assess the competency, independence, and objectivity of the outside service provider as it relates to the particular assignment to be performed. This assessment should also be made when the outside service provider is selected by senior management or the board, and the chief audit executive intends to use and rely on the outside service provider's work. When the selection is made by others and the chief audit executive's assessment determines that he or she should not use and rely on the work of an outside service provider, the results of the assessment should be communicated to senior management or the board, as appropriate.

5. The chief audit executive should determine that the outside service provider possesses the necessary knowledge, skills, and other competencies to perform the engagement. When assessing competency, the chief audit executive should consider the following:

- Professional certification, license, or other recognition of the outside service provider's competency in the relevant discipline.
- Membership of the outside service provider in an appropriate professional organization and adherence to that organization's code of ethics.
- The reputation of the outside service provider. This may include contacting others familiar with the outside service provider's work.
- The outside service provider's experience in the type of work being considered.
- The extent of education and training received by the outside service provider in disciplines that pertain to the particular engagement.
- The outside service provider's knowledge and experience in the industry in which the organization operates.

6. The chief audit executive should assess the relationship of the outside service provider to the organization and to the internal audit activity to ensure that independence and objectivity are maintained throughout the engagement. In performing the assessment, the chief audit executive should determine that there are no financial, organizational, or personal relationships that will prevent the outside service provider from rendering impartial and unbiased judgments and opinions when performing or reporting on the engagement.

7. In assessing the independence and objectivity of the outside service provider, the chief audit executive should consider:

- The financial interest the provider may have in the organization.
- The personal or professional affiliation the provider may have with the board, senior management, or others within the organization.

- The relationship the provider may have had with the organization or the activities being reviewed.
- The extent of other ongoing services the provider may be performing for the organization.
- Compensation or other incentives that the provider may have.

8.   If the outside service provider is also the organization's external auditor and the nature of the engagement is extended audit services, the chief audit executive should ascertain that work performed does not impair the external auditor's independence. Extended audit services refers to those services beyond the requirements of auditing standards generally accepted by external auditors. If the organization's external auditors act or appear to act as members of senior management, management, or as employees of the organization, then their independence is impaired. Additionally, external auditors may provide the organization with other services such as tax and consulting. Independence, however, should be assessed in relation to the full range of services provided to the organization.

9.   The chief audit executive should obtain sufficient information regarding the scope of the outside service provider's work. This is necessary in order to ascertain that the scope of work is adequate for the purposes of the internal auditing activity. It may be prudent to have these and other matters documented in an engagement letter or contract. The chief audit executive should review with the outside service provider:

- Objectives and scope of work.
- Specific matters expected to be covered in the engagement communications.
- Access to relevant records, personnel, and physical properties.
- Information regarding assumptions and procedures to be employed.
- Ownership and custody of engagement working papers, if applicable.
- Confidentiality and restrictions on information obtained during the engagement.

10. When the outside service provider performs internal auditing activities, the chief audit executive should specify and ensure that the work complies with the Standards for the Professional Practice of Internal Auditing. In reviewing the work of an outside service provider, the chief audit executive should evaluate the adequacy of work performed. This evaluation should include sufficiency of information obtained to afford a reasonable basis for the conclusions reached and the resolution of significant exceptions or other unusual matters.

11. When the chief audit executive issues engagement communications, and an outside service provider was used, the chief audit executive may, as appropriate, refer to such services provided. The outside service provider should be informed and, if appropriate, concurrence should be obtained prior to such reference being made in engagement communications.

1210.A2 - The internal auditor should have sufficient knowledge to identify the indicators of fraud but is not expected to have the expertise of a person whose primary responsibility is detecting and investigating fraud.*

* Internal auditing's responsibilities with regard to fraud, including two Practice Advisories, are discussed in Study Unit 10.

1210.C1 - The chief audit executive should decline the consulting engagement or obtain competent advice and assistance if the internal audit staff lacks the knowledge, skills, or other competencies needed to perform all or part of the engagement.

Practice Advisory 1000.C1-2: Additional Considerations for Formal Consulting Engagements

The following is the portion of this omnibus Practice Advisory relevant to Standards 1210.C1 and 1220.C1.

1. The internal auditor should exercise due professional care in conducting a formal consulting engagement by understanding the following:

    *   *Needs of management officials, including the nature, timing, and communication of engagement results.*
    *   *Possible motivations and reasons of those requesting the service.*
    *   *Extent of work needed to achieve the engagement's objectives.*
    *   *Skills and resources needed to conduct the engagement.*
    *   *Effect on the scope of the audit plan previously approved by the audit committee.*
    *   *Potential impact on future audit assignments and engagements.*
    *   *Potential organizational benefits to be derived from the engagement.*

2. In addition to the independence and objectivity evaluation and due professional care considerations, the internal auditor should:

    *   *Conduct appropriate meetings and gather necessary information to assess the nature and extent of the service to be provided.*
    *   *Confirm that those receiving the service understand and agree with the relevant guidance contained in the internal audit charter, internal audit activity's policies and procedures, and other related guidance governing the conduct of consulting engagements. The internal auditor should decline to perform consulting engagements that are prohibited by the terms of the internal audit charter, conflict with the policies and procedures of the internal audit activity, or do not add value and promote the best interests of the organization.*
    *   *Evaluate the consulting engagement for compatibility with the internal audit activity's overall plan of engagements. The internal audit activity's risk-based plan of engagements may incorporate and rely on consulting engagements, to the extent deemed appropriate, to provide necessary audit coverage to the organization.*
    *   *Document general terms, understandings, deliverables, and other key factors of the formal consulting engagement in a written agreement or plan. It is essential that both the internal auditor and those receiving the consulting engagement understand and agree with the reporting and communication requirements.*

1220   **_Due Professional Care_** – *Internal auditors should apply the care and skill expected of a reasonably prudent and competent internal auditor. Due professional care does not imply infallibility.*

Practice Advisory 1220-1: Due Professional Care

1.   *Due professional care calls for the application of the care and skill expected of a reasonably prudent and competent internal auditor in the same or similar circumstances. Professional care should, therefore, be appropriate to the complexities of the engagement being performed. In exercising due professional care, internal auditors should be alert to the possibility of intentional wrongdoing, errors and omissions, inefficiency, waste, ineffectiveness, and conflicts of interest. They should also be alert to those conditions and activities where irregularities are most likely to occur. In addition, they should identify inadequate controls and recommend improvements to promote compliance with acceptable procedures and practices.*

2.   *Due care implies reasonable care and competence, not infallibility or extraordinary performance. Due care requires the auditor to conduct examinations and verifications to a reasonable extent, but does not require detailed reviews of all transactions. Accordingly, internal auditors cannot give absolute assurance that noncompliance or irregularities do not exist. Nevertheless, the possibility of material irregularities or noncompliance should be considered whenever an internal auditor undertakes an internal auditing assignment.*

1220.A1 - *The internal auditor should exercise due professional care by considering the:*

- *Extent of work needed to achieve the engagement's objectives.*
- *Relative complexity, materiality, or significance of matters to which assurance procedures are applied.*
- *Adequacy and effectiveness of risk management, control, and governance processes.*
- *Probability of significant errors, irregularities, or noncompliance.*
- *Cost of assurance in relation to potential benefits.*

1220.A2 - *The internal auditor should be alert to the significant risks that might affect objectives, operations, or resources. However, assurance procedures alone, even when performed with due professional care, do not guarantee that all significant risks will be identified.*

1220.C1 - *The internal auditor should exercise due professional care during a consulting engagement by considering the:*

- *Needs and expectations of clients including the nature, timing, and communication of engagement results.*
- *Relative complexity and extent of work needed to achieve the engagement's objectives.*
- *Cost of the consulting engagement in relation to potential benefits.*

Also see the portion of Practice Advisory 1000.C1-2 reproduced after Standard 1210.C1.

1230   ***Continuing Professional Development*** – *Internal auditors should enhance their knowledge, skills, and other competencies through continuing professional education.*

Practice Advisory 1230-1: Continuing Professional Development

1. *Internal auditors are responsible for continuing their education in order to maintain their proficiency. They should keep informed about improvements and current developments in internal auditing standards, procedures, and techniques. Continuing education may be obtained through membership and participation in professional societies; attendance at conferences, seminars, college courses, and in-house training programs; and participation in research projects.*

2. *Internal auditors are encouraged to demonstrate their proficiency by obtaining appropriate professional certification, such as the Certified Internal Auditor designation and other designations offered by The Institute of Internal Auditors.*

3. *Internal auditors with professional certifications should obtain sufficient continuing professional education to satisfy requirements related to the professional certification held.*

4. *Internal auditors not presently holding appropriate certifications are encouraged to pursue an educational program that supports efforts to obtain professional certification.*

2. Stop and review! You have completed the outline for this subunit. Study multiple-choice questions 5 through 30 beginning on page 85.

QUESTIONS

3.1 Professional Practices Framework

1. The purposes of the Standards include all of the following except

A. Establishing the basis for the measurement of internal audit performance.

B. Guiding the ethical conduct of internal auditors.

C. Delineating basic principles that represent the practice of internal auditing as it should be.

D. Fostering improved organizational processes and operations.

Answer (B) is correct. *(CIA, adapted)*
   REQUIRED: The item not a purpose of the Standards.
   DISCUSSION: The IIA Code of Ethics describes Rules of Conduct that constitute "behavior norms expected of internal auditors. These rules are intended as an aid to interpreting the Principles into practical applications and are intended to guide the ethical conduct of internal auditors." The purposes of the Standards are to

1. Delineate basic principles that represent the practice of internal auditing as it should be.

2. Provide a framework for performing and promoting a broad range of value-added internal audit activities.

3. Establish the basis for the measurement of internal audit performance.

4. Foster improved organizational processes and operations.

(Introduction to the Standards)

2. Administrative Directives are submitted to which group for approval?

    A. Board of Regents

    B. Executive Committee

    C. Internal Auditing Standards Board

    D. International Ethics Committee

Answer (B) is correct. *(Publisher)*
    REQUIRED: The group that Administrative Directives are submitted to for approval.
    DISCUSSION: Administrative Directives are submitted by the appropriate committee to the Executive Committee for approval.
    Answer (A) is incorrect because the Board of Regents establishes requirements for the CIA designation and continuing professional education (CPE) for the CIAs. Answer (C) is incorrect because the Internal Auditing Standards Board (IASB) is the official body charged by The IIA with developing professional standards for internal auditing. Its primary responsibility is to provide guidance to practitioners. Answer (D) is incorrect because the International Ethics Committee considers needed changes in the Code of Ethics and investigates complaints against members of The IIA and CIAs.

3. According to the Professional Practices Framework of The IIA, which pronouncements represent nonmandatory guidance for implementing the Standards?

    A. Attribute Standards.

    B. Implementation Standards.

    C. Performance Standards.

    D. Practice Advisories.

Answer (D) is correct. *(Publisher)*
    REQUIRED: The pronouncements that represent nonmandatory guidance for implementing the SPPIA.
    DISCUSSION: Practice Advisories are nonmandatory interpretations of the Standards or their application in specific situations. They represent best practices endorsed by The IIA as a means of implementing the Standards. The Code of Ethics, Attribute Standards, Implementation Standards, and Performance Standards constitute mandatory guidance.

4. Which type of standards applies to organizations and individuals performing the specific internal auditing services delineated by these Standards?

    A. Standards for the Professional Practice of Internal Auditing - Performance Standards.

    B. Standards for the Professional Practice of Internal Auditing - Attribute Standards.

    C. Standards for the Professional Practice of Internal Auditing - Implementation Standards.

    D. All of these types of standards.

Answer (C) is correct. *(Publisher)*
    REQUIRED: The type of standards that apply to organizations and individuals performing the specific internal auditing services delineated by these Standards.
    DISCUSSION: According to the Professional Practices Framework, Standards for the Professional Practice of Internal Auditing - Implementation Standards apply to organizations and individuals performing the specific internal auditing services delineated by these Standards. Board categories are assurance services and consulting services Implementation Standards.
    Answer (A) is incorrect because they apply to Standards for Performance of organizations and individuals performing internal auditing services. Answer (B) is incorrect because they apply to Standards for Attributes of organizations and individuals performing internal auditing services. Answer (D) is incorrect because only Implementation standards apply to organizations and individuals performing the specific internal auditing services delineated by these Standards.

3.2 Professional Proficiency

5. Use of outside service providers with expertise in health care benefits is appropriate when the internal audit activity is

- A. Evaluating the organization's estimate of its liability for postretirement benefits, which include health care benefits.
- B. Comparing the cost of the organization's health care program with other programs offered in the industry.
- C. Training its staff to conduct an audit of health care costs in a major division of the organization.
- D. All of the answers are correct.

Answer (D) is correct.   *(CIA, adapted)*
REQUIRED: The reason(s) for using specialists in health care benefits.
DISCUSSION: The IAA should collectively possess or obtain the knowledge, skills, and other competencies needed to perform its responsibilities (Standard 1210). In regard to an assurance engagement, the CAE should obtain competent advice and assistance if the internal audit staff lacks the knowledge, skills, and other competencies needed to perform all or part of the engagement (Standard 1210.A1). In regard to a consulting engagement, the CAE should decline the engagement or obtain competence advice and assistance if the internal audit staff lacks the knowledge, skills, and other competencies needed to perform all or part of the engagement (Standard 1210.C1). Accordingly, if the internal audit staff lacks expertise with regard to health care costs, outside service providers should be employed who can provide the requisite knowledge, skills, and other competencies. These outside service providers can provide assistance in estimating the company's liability for postretirement benefits, in developing a comparative analysis of health care costs, and in training the staff to audit health care costs.

6. A chief audit executive has reviewed credentials, checked references, and interviewed a candidate for a staff position. The CAE concludes that the candidate has a thorough understanding of internal auditing techniques, accounting, and finance. However, the candidate has limited knowledge of economics and information technology. Which action is most appropriate?

- A. Reject the candidate because of the lack of knowledge required by the Standards.
- B. Offer the candidate a position despite lack of knowledge in certain essential areas.
- C. Encourage the candidate to obtain additional training in economics and information technology and then reapply.
- D. Offer the candidate a position if other staff members possess sufficient knowledge in economics and information technology.

Answer (D) is correct.   *(CIA, adapted)*
REQUIRED: The proper hiring decision for an internal audit activity.
DISCUSSION: The internal audit activity should collectively possess or obtain the knowledge, skills, and other competencies needed to perform its responsibilities (Standard 1210). These attributes include proficiency in applying internal auditing standards, procedures, and techniques. The IAA should have employees or use outside service providers who are qualified in such disciplines as accounting, auditing, economics, finance, statistics, information technology, engineering, taxation, law, environmental affairs, and such other areas as needed to meet the IAA's responsibilities. Each member of the IAA, however, need not be qualified in all of these disciplines (PA 1210.A1-1).
Answer (A) is incorrect because the Standards do not require each internal auditor to possess a knowledge of all relevant subjects. Answer (B) is incorrect because the IAA's needs may be for additional expertise in economics or information technology. Answer (C) is incorrect because encouraging the candidate to obtain additional training does not adequately address the IAA's current needs.

7. An internal audit activity has scheduled an engagement relating to a construction contract. One portion of this engagement will include comparing materials purchased with those specified in the engineering drawings. The IAA does not have anyone on staff with sufficient expertise to complete this procedure. The chief audit executive should

- A. Delete the engagement from the schedule.
- B. Perform the entire engagement using current staff.
- C. Engage an engineering consultant to perform the comparison.
- D. Accept the contractor's written representations.

Answer (C) is correct.   *(CIA, adapted)*
REQUIRED: The appropriate action when internal auditors lack the expertise to make a crucial determination.
DISCUSSION: The IAA should have employees or use outside service providers who are qualified in such disciplines as accounting, auditing, economics, finance, statistics, information technology, engineering, taxation, law, environmental affairs, and such other areas as needed to meet the IAA's responsibilities. Each member of the IAA, however, need not be qualified in all of these disciplines (PA 1210.A1-1). Thus, hiring an outside service provider is also necessary as an exercise of due professional care.
Answer (A) is incorrect because the engagement is within the scope of the IAA. Answer (B) is incorrect because performing the engagement using the current (unqualified) staff is inappropriate. Answer (D) is incorrect because accepting the contractor's representations without adequate testing is inappropriate.

8. A chief audit executive for a large manufacturer is considering revising the internal audit activity's charter with respect to the minimum educational and experience qualifications required. The CAE wants to require all staff auditors to possess specialized training in accounting and a professional auditing certification such as the Certified Internal Auditor or the Chartered Accountant (CA). One of the disadvantages of imposing this requirement would be

    A. The policy might negatively affect the internal audit activity's ability to perform quality engagements relating to the organization's financial and accounting systems.

    B. The policy would not promote the professionalism of the internal audit activity.

    C. The policy would prevent the internal audit activity from using outside service providers when it did not have the knowledge, skills, and other competencies required in certain engagements.

    D. The policy could limit the range of services that could be performed due to the internal audit activity's narrow expertise and backgrounds.

Answer (D) is correct. *(CIA, adapted)*
    REQUIRED: The disadvantage of requiring all staff auditors to possess specialized training in accounting and a professional auditing certification.
    DISCUSSION: The IAA should have employees or use outside service providers who are qualified in such disciplines as accounting, auditing, economics, finance, statistics, information technology, engineering, taxation, law, environmental affairs, and such other areas as needed to meet the IAA's responsibilities. Each member of the IAA, however, need not be qualified in all of these disciplines (PA 1210.A1-1). Thus, the IAA should have an appropriate balance of experience, training, and skills to permit the performance of a wide range of services.
    Answer (A) is incorrect because the policy might result in better engagements relating to financial and accounting systems. Answer (B) is incorrect because setting minimum professional standards promotes professionalism. Answer (C) is incorrect because this requirement would not affect whether outside service providers were used.

9. If the internal audit activity does not have the skills to perform a particular task, an outside service provider could be brought in from

I.   The organization's external audit firm
II. An outside consulting firm
III. The engagement client
IV. A college or university

    A. I, II.

    B. II, IV.

    C. I, II, III.

    D. I, II, IV.

Answer (D) is correct. *(CIA, adapted)*
    REQUIRED: The appropriate sources of outside service providers.
    DISCUSSION: The IAA should have employees or use outside service providers who are qualified in such disciplines as accounting, auditing, economics, finance, statistics, information technology, engineering, taxation, law, environmental affairs, and such other areas as needed to meet the IAA's responsibilities. Each member of the IAA, however, need not be qualified in all of these disciplines (PA 1210.A1-1). Qualified outside service providers may be recruited from a variety of sources. However, an outside service provider from the engagement client is unacceptable because the person would not be independent or objective.
    Answer (A) is incorrect because an outside service provider from a college or university is acceptable. Answer (B) is incorrect because an outside service provider from the organization's external audit firm is acceptable. Answer (C) is incorrect because an outside service provider from the engagement client is unacceptable.

10. A professional engineer applied for a position in the internal audit activity of a high technology firm. The engineer became interested in the position after observing several internal auditors while they were performing an engagement in the engineering department. The chief audit executive

    A. Should not hire the engineer because of the lack of knowledge of internal auditing standards.

    B. May hire the engineer despite the lack of knowledge of internal auditing standards.

    C. Should not hire the engineer because of the lack of knowledge of accounting and taxes.

    D. May hire the engineer because of the knowledge of internal auditing gained in the previous position.

Answer (B) is correct. *(CIA, adapted)*
    REQUIRED: The appropriate decision whether to hire a specialist.
    DISCUSSION: The IAA should have employees or use outside service providers who are qualified in such disciplines as accounting, auditing, economics, finance, statistics, information technology, engineering, taxation, law, environmental affairs, and such other areas as needed to meet the IAA's responsibilities. Each member of the IAA, however, need not be qualified in all of these disciplines (PA 1210.A1-1).
    Answer (A) is incorrect because each new employee of an IAA is not required to have knowledge of internal auditing standards. However, the IAA collectively must have this knowledge. Answer (C) is incorrect because each individual internal auditor is not required to have knowledge of accounting or taxes. Answer (D) is incorrect because the knowledge acquired by observation is irrelevant to the skills necessary for internal auditing.

11. Your organization has selected you to develop an internal audit activity. Your approach will most likely be to hire

A. Internal auditors each of whom possesses all the skills required to handle all engagements.

B. Inexperienced personnel and train them the way the organization wants them trained.

C. Degreed accountants because most internal audit work is accounting related.

D. Internal auditors who collectively have the knowledge and skills needed to perform the responsibilities of the internal audit activity.

Answer (D) is correct. *(CIA, adapted)*
REQUIRED: The personnel required by an IAA.
DISCUSSION: The internal audit activity should collectively possess or obtain the knowledge, skills, and other competencies needed to perform its responsibilities (Standard 1210). The IAA should have employees or use outside service providers who are qualified in such disciplines as accounting, auditing, economics, finance, statistics, information technology, engineering, taxation, law, environmental affairs, and such other areas as needed to meet the IAA's responsibilities. Each member of the IAA, however, need not be qualified in all of these disciplines (PA 1210.A1-1).
Answer (A) is incorrect because the scope of internal auditing is so broad that one individual cannot have the requisite expertise in all areas. Answer (B) is incorrect because the IAA should have personnel with various skill levels to permit appropriate matching of internal auditors with varying engagement complexities. Furthermore, experienced internal auditors should be available to train and supervise less experienced staff members. Answer (C) is incorrect because many skills are needed in internal auditing. For example, computer skills are needed in engagements involving information technology.

12. Reasonable assurance should be obtained as to each prospective internal auditor's qualifications and proficiency. Which of the following is the least useful application of this principle?

A. Determining that all applicants have an accounting degree.

B. Obtaining college transcripts.

C. Checking an applicant's references.

D. Determining previous job experience.

Answer (A) is correct. *(CIA, adapted)*
REQUIRED: The least useful application of the principle concerning internal auditor qualifications and proficiency.
DISCUSSION: "Internal auditors should possess the knowledge, skills, and other competencies needed to perform their individual responsibilities. The internal audit activity collectively should possess or obtain the knowledge, skills, and other competencies needed to perform its responsibilities" (Standard 1210). Each member of the IAA, however, need not be qualified in all disciplines (PA 1210.A1-1).
Answer (B) is incorrect because obtaining college transcripts is an appropriate procedure to determine a prospective auditor's qualifications. Answer (C) is incorrect because checking an applicant's references is an appropriate procedure to determine a prospective auditor's qualifications. Answer (D) is incorrect because determining previous job experience is appropriate during the hiring process.

13. Internal auditing is unique in that its scope often encompasses all areas of an organization. Thus, it is not possible for each internal auditor to possess detailed competence in all areas that might be the subject of engagements. Which of the following competencies is required of every internal auditor?

A. Understanding of taxation and law as it applies to operation of the organization.

B. Proficiency in accounting principles.

C. Understanding of management principles.

D. Proficiency in information technology.

Answer (C) is correct. *(CIA, adapted)*
REQUIRED: The competencies required of an internal auditor.
DISCUSSION: An understanding of management principles is required of all internal auditors. An understanding is "the ability to apply broad knowledge to situations likely to be encountered, to recognize significant deviations, and to be able to carry out the research necessary to arrive at reasonable solutions" (PA 1210-1).
Answer (A) is incorrect because an internal auditor must have only an appreciation of taxation and law. Answer (B) is incorrect because proficiency in accounting principles is required only of those auditors who work extensively with financial records and reports. Answer (D) is incorrect because an auditor need only have an appreciation of information technology.

14. Proficiency is required of internal auditors with respect to which discipline?

    A. Internal auditing procedures and techniques.

    B. Accounting principles and techniques.

    C. Management principles.

    D. Marketing techniques.

Answer (A) is correct. *(CIA, adapted)*
REQUIRED: The organizational discipline that matches the skill level described.
DISCUSSION: Proficiency in applying internal auditing standards, procedures, and techniques is required in performing engagements. Proficiency means the ability to apply knowledge to situations likely to be encountered and to deal with them without extensive recourse to technical research and assistance (PA 1210-1).
Answer (B) is incorrect because proficiency in accounting principles and techniques is required only of auditors who work extensively with financial records and reports. Answer (C) is incorrect because an internal auditor is required to have an understanding of, not a proficiency in, management principles. Answer (D) is incorrect because internal auditors ordinarily need not be proficient in marketing techniques.

15. An understanding is required of internal auditors with respect to which discipline?

    A. Internal auditing procedures and techniques.

    B. Accounting principles and techniques.

    C. Management principles.

    D. Marketing techniques.

Answer (C) is correct. *(CIA, adapted)*
REQUIRED: The organizational discipline that matches the skill level described.
DISCUSSION: An understanding of management principles is required to recognize and evaluate the materiality and significance of deviations from good business practice. An understanding means the ability to apply broad knowledge to situations likely to be encountered, to recognize significant deviations, and to be able to carry out the research necessary to arrive at reasonable solutions (PA 1210-1).
Answer (A) is incorrect because internal auditors must have proficiency in, not an understanding of, internal auditing standards, procedures, and techniques. Answer (B) is incorrect because proficiency in accounting principles and techniques is required only of auditors who work extensively with financial records and reports. Answer (D) is incorrect because internal auditors ordinarily need not be proficient in, or have an understanding or appreciation of, marketing techniques.

16. The internal auditor should exercise due professional care in conducting a formal consulting engagement by understanding all of the following except

    A. Possible motivations and reasons of those requesting the service.

    B. Potential benefits in the form of compensation to be derived from the engagement.

    C. Skills and resources needed to conduct the engagement.

    D. Potential impact on future audit assignments and engagements.

Answer (B) is correct. *(Publisher)*
REQUIRED: The item that the internal auditor of a formal consulting engagement should not consider when exercising due professional care.
DISCUSSION: (PA 1000.C1-2) The internal auditor should exercise due professional care in conducting a formal consulting engagement by understanding the following:

- Needs of management officials, including the nature, timing, and communication of engagement results.
- Possible motivations and reasons of those requesting the service.
- Extent of work needed to achieve the engagement's objectives.
- Skills and resources needed to conduct the engagement.
- Effect on the scope of the audit plan previously approved by the audit committee.
- Potential impact on future audit assignments and engagements.
- Potential organizational benefits to be derived from the engagement.

Any benefit related to compensation for the engagement is not one of the considerations for an internal auditor who is exercising due professional care.

17. Jack is conducting a formal consulting engagement for XYZ Corp. In addition to the independence and objectivity evaluation and due professional care considerations, Jack should do which of the following?

I. Document general terms, understandings, deliverables, and other key factors of the formal consulting engagement in a written agreement or plan.

II. Evaluate the consulting engagement for comparability with the internal audit activity's overall plan of engagements.

III. Conduct appropriate meetings and gather necessary information to assess the nature and extent of the services to be provided.

    A. I and II.

    B. II and III.

    C. I and III.

    D. I, II, and III.

Answer (D) is correct. *(Publisher)*
REQUIRED: The procedures the internal auditor should perform when conducting a formal consulting engagement.
DISCUSSION: In addition to the independence and objectivity evaluation and due professional care considerations, the internal auditor should:

- Conduct appropriate meetings and gather necessary information to assess the nature and extent of the service to be provided.
- Confirm that those receiving the service understand and agree with the relevant guidance contained in the internal audit charter, internal audit activity's policies and procedures, and other related guidance governing the conduct of consulting engagements. The internal auditor should decline to perform consulting engagements that are prohibited by the terms of the internal audit charter, conflict with the policies and procedures of the internal audit activity, or do not add value and promote the best interests of the organization.
- Evaluate the consulting engagement for compatibility with the internal audit activity's overall plan of engagements. The internal audit activity's risk-based plan of engagements may incorporate and rely on consulting engagements, to the extent deemed appropriate, to provide necessary audit coverage to the organization.
- Document general terms, understandings, deliverables, and other key factors of the formal consulting engagement in a written agreement or plan. It is essential that both the internal auditor and those receiving the consulting engagement understand and agree with the reporting and communication requirements.

(PA 1000.C1-2)

18. An appreciation is required of internal auditors with respect to which discipline?

    A. Internal auditing procedures and techniques.

    B. Accounting principles and techniques.

    C. Management principles.

    D. Marketing techniques.

Answer (B) is correct. *(CIA, adapted)*
REQUIRED: The organizational discipline that matches the skill level described.
DISCUSSION: An appreciation is required of the fundamentals of such subjects as accounting, economics, commercial law, taxation, finance, quantitative methods, and information technology. An appreciation means the ability to recognize the existence of problems or potential problems and to determine the further research to be undertaken or the assistance to be obtained. However, proficiency in accounting principles and techniques is required of auditors who work extensively with financial records and reports (PA 1210-1).

Answer (A) is incorrect because proficiency, not an appreciation, is required of internal auditors in applying internal auditing standards, procedures, and techniques. Answer (C) is incorrect because an internal auditor must have an understanding, not an appreciation, of management principles. Answer (D) is incorrect because internal auditors ordinarily need not be proficient in, or have an understanding or appreciation of, marketing techniques.

19. Internal auditors should possess all of the following except

    A. Proficiency in applying internal auditing standards.

    B. An understanding of management principles.

    C. The ability to maintain good interpersonal relations.

    D. The ability to conduct training sessions in quantitative methods.

Answer (D) is correct. *(CIA, adapted)*
REQUIRED: The item that is not one of the qualifications of internal auditors.
DISCUSSION: Internal auditors require an appreciation of the fundamentals of such subjects as accounting, economics, commercial law, taxation, finance, quantitative methods, and information technology. An appreciation means the ability to recognize the existence of problems or potential problems and to determine the further research to be undertaken or the assistance to be obtained (PA 1210-1).
Answer (A) is incorrect because an internal auditor should be proficient in applying internal auditing standards, procedures, and techniques. Answer (B) is incorrect because an understanding of management principles is required to recognize and evaluate the materiality and significance of deviations from good business practice. Answer (C) is incorrect because internal auditors should understand human relations and maintain satisfactory relationships with engagement clients.

20. Communication skills are important to internal auditors. They should be able to convey effectively all of the following to engagement clients except

    A. The objectives designed for a specific engagement.

    B. The engagement evaluations based on a preliminary survey.

    C. The risk assessment used in selecting the area for investigation.

    D. Recommendations that are generated in relationship to a specific engagement client.

Answer (C) is correct. *(CIA, adapted)*
REQUIRED: The matter that internal auditors need not communicate to engagement clients.
DISCUSSION: Internal auditors should be skilled in oral and written communications so that they can clearly and effectively convey such matters as engagement objectives, evaluations, conclusions, and recommendations (PA 1210-1). However, the risk assessment is not necessarily a matter that must be communicated.

21. What is the most appropriate solution to resolve staff communication problems with engagement clients?

    A. Provide staff with sufficient training to enhance communication skills.

    B. Avoid unnecessary communication with engagement clients.

    C. Discuss communication problems with staff auditors.

    D. Meet with engagement clients to resolve communication problems.

Answer (A) is correct. *(CIA, adapted)*
REQUIRED: The most appropriate solution to resolve staff communication problems with engagement clients.
DISCUSSION: Internal auditors should be skilled in oral and written communications so that they can clearly and effectively convey such matters as engagement objectives, evaluations, conclusions, and recommendations (PA 1210-1).
Answer (B) is incorrect because the issue is the quality rather than the quantity of communication. Answer (C) is incorrect because communication problems should be resolved through effective training. Answer (D) is incorrect because meeting with engagement clients will not resolve problems caused by poor staff communication skills.

22. Internal auditors are responsible for continuing their education in order to maintain their proficiency. Which of the following is true regarding the continuing education requirements of the practicing internal auditor?

A. Internal auditors are required to obtain 40 hours of continuing professional education each year and a minimum of 120 hours over a 3-year period.

B. CIAs have formal requirements that must be met in order to continue as CIAs.

C. Attendance, as an officer or committee member, at formal Institute of Internal Auditors meetings does not meet the criteria of continuing professional development.

D. In-house programs meet continuing professional education requirements only if they have been preapproved by The Institute of Internal Auditors.

Answer (B) is correct. *(CIA, adapted)*
REQUIRED: The true statement about continuing professional education (CPE) requirements.
DISCUSSION: Internal auditors should enhance their knowledge, skills, and other competencies through CPE (Standard 1230). To maintain the CIA designation, the CIA must commit to a formal program of CPE and report to the Certification Department of The IIA.
Answer (A) is incorrect because the Standards do not state formal hour requirements for internal auditors. The intent of the Standards is to provide flexibility in meeting the requirements. Answer (C) is incorrect because continuing education may be obtained by participation in professional societies. Answer (D) is incorrect because prior approval by The IIA is not necessary for CPE courses.

23. Which of the following statements is true with respect to due professional care?

A. An internal auditor should perform detailed tests of all transactions before communicating results.

B. An item should not be mentioned in an engagement communication unless the internal auditor is absolutely certain of the item.

C. An engagement communication should never be viewed as providing an infallible truth about a subject.

D. An internal auditor has no responsibility to recommend improvements.

Answer (C) is correct. *(CIA, adapted)*
REQUIRED: The true statement about due professional care.
DISCUSSION: Due professional care implies reasonable care and competence, not infallibility or extraordinary performance. Due professional care requires the internal auditor to conduct examinations and verifications to a reasonable extent, but it does not require detailed reviews of all transactions. Accordingly, internal auditors cannot give absolute assurance that noncompliance or irregularities do not exist. Nevertheless, the possibility of material irregularities or noncompliance should be considered whenever an internal auditor undertakes an internal auditing assignment (PA 1220-1).
Answer (A) is incorrect because an internal auditor should conduct reasonable examinations and verifications, but detailed tests of all transactions are not required. Answer (B) is incorrect because absolute assurance need not, and cannot, be given. Answer (D) is incorrect because an internal auditor should recommend improvements to promote compliance with acceptable procedures and practices.

24. An internal auditor has some suspicion of, but no information about, potential misstatement of financial statements. The internal auditor has failed to exercise due professional care if (s)he

A. Identified potential ways in which a misstatement could occur and ranked the items for investigation.

B. Informed the engagement manager of the suspicions and asked for advice on how to proceed.

C. Did not test for possible misstatement because the engagement work program had already been approved by engagement management.

D. Expanded the engagement work program, without the engagement client's approval, to address the highest ranked ways in which a misstatement may have occurred.

Answer (C) is correct. *(CIA, adapted)*
REQUIRED: The act in violation of the due professional care standard.
DISCUSSION: Due professional care requires the exercise of the care and skill expected of a reasonably prudent and competent internal auditor in the same or similar circumstances (PA 1220-1). Because engagement work programs are expected to be modified to reflect changing circumstances, the internal auditor would fail to exercise due professional care if (s)he did not investigate a suspected misstatement solely because the engagement work program had already been approved.
Answer (A) is incorrect because ranking the ways in which a misstatement could occur is consistent with the due professional care standard. Answer (B) is incorrect because seeking advice is consistent with the due professional care standard. Answer (D) is incorrect because the internal auditor does not need the engagement client's approval to expand the engagement work program.

25. An internal auditor observes that a receivables clerk has physical access to and control of cash receipts. The auditor worked with the clerk several years before and has a high level of trust in the individual. Accordingly, the auditor notes in the engagement working papers that controls over receipts are adequate. Has the auditor exercised due professional care?

A. Yes, reasonable care has been taken.

B. No, irregularities were not noted.

C. No, alertness to conditions most likely indicative of irregularities was not shown.

D. Yes, the engagement working papers were annotated.

Answer (C) is correct. *(CIA, adapted)*
REQUIRED: The true statement as to whether the internal auditor has exercised due professional care.
DISCUSSION: These facts indicate that the internal auditor has failed to exercise due professional care. Internal auditors must be alert to those conditions and activities where irregularities are most likely to occur (PA 1220-1). Cash has a high degree of inherent risk and should therefore be subject to stringent controls. Access to cash and the record-keeping functions should be separated regardless of the personal qualities of the individuals involved. That the clerk is a friend of the internal auditor is irrelevant. Management still needs to be aware that internal control over receivables is inadequate.
Answer (A) is incorrect because the auditor's engagement observation is inappropriate given the lack of segregation of functions. Answer (B) is incorrect because no indication is given that irregularities have occurred. Answer (D) is incorrect because following instructions by rote is unacceptable. Professional judgment and alertness are necessary.

26. Due professional care implies reasonable care and competence, not infallibility or extraordinary performance. Thus, which of the following is unnecessary?

A. The conduct of examinations and verifications to a reasonable extent.

B. The conduct of extensive examinations.

C. The reasonable assurance that compliance does exist.

D. The consideration of the possibility of material irregularities.

Answer (B) is correct. *(CIA, adapted)*
REQUIRED: The obligation not imposed by the due professional care standard.
DISCUSSION: Due professional care implies reasonable care and competence, not infallibility or extraordinary performance. It requires the internal auditor to conduct examinations and verifications to a reasonable extent, but it does not require detailed reviews of all transactions. Accordingly, the internal auditor cannot give absolute assurance that noncompliance or irregularities do not exist. Nevertheless, the possibility of material irregularities or noncompliance should be considered whenever an internal auditor undertakes an internal auditing assignment (PA 1220-1).
Answer (A) is incorrect because examination and verification need only be undertaken to a reasonable extent. Answer (C) is incorrect because an internal auditor cannot give absolute assurance. Answer (D) is incorrect because the possibility of material irregularities should be considered.

27. An internal auditor judged an item to be immaterial when planning an assurance engagement. However, the assurance engagement may still include the item if it is subsequently determined that

A. Sufficient staff is available.

B. Adverse effects related to the item are likely to occur.

C. Related information is reliable.

D. Miscellaneous income is affected.

Answer (B) is correct. *(CIA, adapted)*
REQUIRED: The basis for including an item in the engagement although it is immaterial.
DISCUSSION: Internal auditors should exercise due professional care by considering the relative complexity, materiality, or significance of matters to which assurance procedures are applied (Standard 1220.A1). Materiality judgments are made in the light of all the circumstances and involve qualitative as well as quantitative considerations. Moreover, internal auditors must also consider the interplay of risk with materiality. Consequently, engagement effort may be required for a quantitatively immaterial item if adverse effects are likely to occur, for example, a material contingent liability arising from an illegal payment that is otherwise immaterial.
Answer (A) is incorrect because, in the absence of other considerations, devoting additional engagement effort to an immaterial item is inefficient. Answer (C) is incorrect because additional engagement procedures might not be needed if related information is reliable. Answer (D) is incorrect because the item is more likely to be included if it affects recurring income items rather than miscellaneous income.

28. The internal audit activity can perform an important role in preventing and detecting significant fraud by being assigned all but which one of the following tasks?

    A. Review large, abnormal, or unexplained expenditures.

    B. Review sensitive expenses such as legal fees, consultant fees, and foreign sales commissions.

    C. Review every control feature pertaining to petty cash receipts.

    D. Review contributions by the organization that appear to be unusual.

Answer (C) is correct. *(CIA, adapted)*
    REQUIRED: The task not appropriate to the prevention and detection of significant fraud.
    DISCUSSION: The internal auditor should exercise due professional care by considering the relative complexity, materiality, or significance of matters to which assurance procedures are applied. The cost of assurance in relation to potential benefits also should be considered (Standard 1220.A1). Hence, an exhaustive review of petty cash is not an efficient and effective use of limited IAA resources because it will not prevent or detect significant fraud. The amount of any theft of petty cash will not be substantial.

29. An internal auditor fails to discover an employee fraud during an assurance engagement. The nondiscovery is most likely to suggest a violation of the Standards if it was the result of a

    A. Failure to perform a detailed review of all transactions in the area.

    B. Determination that any possible fraud in the area would not involve a material amount.

    C. Determination that the cost of extending procedures in the area would exceed the potential benefits.

    D. Presumption that the internal controls in the area were adequate and effective.

Answer (D) is correct. *(CIA, adapted)*
    REQUIRED: The most likely reason failure to detect fraud is a violation of the Standards.
    DISCUSSION: Exercising due professional care entails considering the adequacy and effectiveness of risk management, control, and governance processes (Standard 1220.A1).
    Answer (A) is incorrect because due professional care does not require detailed reviews of all transactions (PA 1220-1). Answer (B) is incorrect because the relative complexity, materiality, or significance of matters to which assurance procedures are applied should be considered. Answer (C) is incorrect because the internal auditor should consider the cost of assurance in relation to potential benefits.

30. Assurance engagements should be performed with proficiency and due professional care. Accordingly, the Standards require internal auditors to

I. Consider the probability of significant noncompliance

II. Perform assurance procedures with due professional care so that all significant risks are identified

III. Weigh the cost of assurance against the benefits

    A. I and II only.

    B. I and III only.

    C. II and III only.

    D. I, II, and III.

Answer (B) is correct. *(Publisher)*
    REQUIRED: The responsibility(ies) of internal auditors regarding proficiency and due professional care.
    DISCUSSION: Standard 1220.A1 states that the exercise of due professional care involves considering the extent of work needed to achieve management's objectives; the relative complexity, materiality, or significance of matters to which assurance procedures are applied; the adequacy and effectiveness of risk management, control, and governance processes; the probability of significant errors, irregularities, or noncompliance; and the cost of assurance in relation to the benefits. Moreover, Standard 1220.A2 states that the internal auditor should be alert to the significant risks that might affect objectives, operations, or resources. However, assurance procedures alone, even when performed with due professional care, do not guarantee that all significant risks will be identified.

Use Gleim's ***CIA Test Prep*** for interactive testing with over 2,000 additional multiple-choice questions!

STUDY UNIT FOUR
INTERNAL AUDIT ROLES AND RESPONSIBILITIES

(22 pages of outline)

4.1 Nature of Work - Pronouncements ....

This study unit concerns the scope of the internal audit activity's work as defined in pronouncements of The IIA. One General Performance Standard, two Specific Performance Standards, three Consulting Implementation Standards, and three Assurance Implementation Standards are presented here. In addition, eleven Practice Advisories, which constitute endorsed but nonmandatory guidance, are included. These pronouncements elaborate on the description of the services performed by the internal audit activity provided in the definition of internal auditing, which stresses the improvement of risk management, control, and governance processes. The internal auditors' work regarding **control** is such a vital part of their responsibilities that it is treated separately in Study Units 5 and 6.

4.1 NATURE OF WORK - PRONOUNCEMENTS

2100 **Nature of Work** — *The internal audit activity evaluates and contributes to the improvement of risk management, control, and governance systems.*

Practice Advisory 2100-1: Nature of Work

1. *The scope of internal auditing work encompasses a systematic, disciplined approach to evaluating and improving the adequacy and effectiveness of risk management, control, and governance processes and the quality of performance in carrying out assigned responsibilities. The purpose of evaluating the adequacy of the organization's existing risk management, control, and governance processes is to provide reasonable assurance that these processes are functioning as intended and will enable the organization's objectives and goals to be met, and to provide recommendations for improving the organization's operations, in terms of both efficient and effective performance. Senior management and the board might also provide general direction as to the scope of work and the activities to be audited.*

2. *Adequacy of risk management, control, and governance processes is present if management has planned and designed them in a manner which provides reasonable assurance that the organization's objectives and goals will be achieved efficiently and economically. Efficient performance accomplishes objectives and goals in an accurate, timely, and economical fashion. Economical performance accomplishes objectives and goals with minimal use of resources (i.e., cost) commensurate with the risk exposure. Reasonable assurance is provided if the most cost-effective measures are taken in the design and implementation stages to reduce risks and restrict expected deviations to a tolerable level. Thus, the design process begins with the establishment of objectives and goals. This is followed by connecting or interrelating concepts, parts, activities, and people in such a manner as to operate together to achieve the established objectives and goals.*

3. *Effectiveness of risk management, control, and governance processes is present if management directs processes in such a manner as to provide reasonable assurance that the organization's objectives and goals will be achieved. In addition to accomplishing the objectives and planned activities, management directs by authorizing activities and transactions, monitoring resulting performance, and verifying that the organization's processes are operating as designed.*

4.   Broadly, management is responsible for the sustainability of the whole organization and accountability for the organization's actions, conduct, and performance to the owners, other stakeholders, regulators, and general public. Specifically, the primary objectives of the overall management process are to achieve:

- Relevant, reliable, and credible financial and operating information.
- Effective and efficient use of the organization's resources.
- Safeguarding of the organization's assets.
- Compliance with laws, regulations, ethical and business norms, and contracts.
- Identification of risk exposures and use of effective strategies to control them.
- Established objectives and goals for operations or programs.

5.   Management plans, organizes, and directs the performance of sufficient actions to provide reasonable assurance that objectives and goals will be achieved. Management periodically reviews its objectives and goals and modifies its processes to accommodate changes in internal and external conditions. Management also establishes and maintains an organizational culture, including an ethical climate that fosters control.

6.   Control is any action taken by management to enhance the likelihood that established objectives and goals will be achieved. Controls may be preventive (to deter undesirable events from occurring), detective (to detect and correct undesirable events which have occurred), or directive (to cause or encourage a desirable event to occur). The concept of a system of control is the integrated collection of control components and activities that are used by an organization to achieve its objectives and goals.

7.   Internal auditors evaluate the whole management process of planning, organizing, and directing to determine whether reasonable assurance exists that objectives and goals will be achieved. Internal auditors should be alert to actual or potential changes in internal or external conditions that affect the ability to provide assurance from a forward-looking perspective. In those cases, internal auditors should address the risk that performance may deteriorate.

8.   These internal auditing evaluations, in the aggregate, provide information to appraise the overall management process. All business systems, processes, operations, functions, and activities within the organization are subject to the internal auditors' evaluations. The comprehensive scope of work of internal auditing should provide reasonable assurance that management's:

- Risk management system is effective.
- System of internal control is effective and efficient.
- Governance process is effective by establishing and preserving values, setting goals, monitoring activities and performance, and defining the measures of accountability.

Practice Advisory 2100-2: Information Security

1.   Internal auditors should determine that management and the board, audit committee, or other governing body have a clear understanding that information security is a management responsibility. This responsibility includes all critical information of the organization regardless of media in which the information is stored.

2.   The chief audit executive should determine that the internal audit activity possesses, or has access to, competent auditing resources to evaluate information security and associated risk exposures. This includes both internal and external risk exposures, including exposures relating to the organization's relationships with outside entities.

3. *Internal auditors should determine that the board, audit committee, or other governing body, has sought assurance from management that information security breaches and conditions that might represent a threat to the organization will promptly be made known to those performing the internal auditing activity.*

4. *Internal auditors should assess the effectiveness of preventive, detective, and mitigative measures against past attacks, as deemed appropriate, and future attempts or incidents deemed likely to occur. Internal auditors should confirm that the board, audit committee, or other governing body has been appropriately informed of threats, incidents, vulnerabilities exploited, and corrective measures.*

5. *Internal auditors should periodically assess the organization's information security practices and recommend, as appropriate, enhancements to, or implementation of, new controls and safeguards. Following an assessment, an assurance report should be provided to the board, audit committee, or other appropriate governing body. Such assessments can either be conducted as separate stand-alone engagements or as multiple engagements integrated into other audits or engagements conducted as part of the approved audit plan.*

NOTE: **Physical security**, such as safeguards against environmental risks and unauthorized access to computer terminals, remains an internal auditing concern even though software controls now provide most protection for information.

Another aspect of internal auditing's role regarding information security is to evaluate compliance with laws and regulations concerning **privacy**. Thus, internal auditors determine the existence and content of requirements relating to privacy (after consulting with legal counsel). Systems are designed accordingly, compliance is achieved, and compliance is documented.

Practice Advisory 2100-3: Internal Audit's Role in the Risk Management Process

1. *Risk management is a key responsibility of management. To achieve its business objectives, management should ensure that sound risk management processes are in place and functioning. Boards and audit committees have an oversight role to determine that appropriate risk management processes are in place and that these processes are adequate and effective. Internal auditors should assist both management and the audit committee by examining, evaluating, reporting, and recommending improvements on the adequacy and effectiveness of management's risk processes. Management and the board are responsible for their organization's risk management and control processes. However, internal auditors acting in a consulting role can assist the organization in identifying, evaluating, and implementing risk management methodologies and controls to address those risks.*

2. *Developing assessments and reports on the organization's risk management processes is normally a high audit priority. Evaluating management's risk processes is different from the requirement that auditors use risk analysis to plan audits. However, information from a comprehensive risk management process, including the identification of management and board concerns, can assist the internal auditor in planning audit activities.*

3. *The chief audit executive should obtain an understanding of management's and the board's expectations of the internal audit activity in the organization's risk management process. This understanding should be codified in the charters of the internal audit activity and audit committee.*

4. *Responsibilities and activities should be coordinated among all groups and individuals with a role in the organization's risk management process. These responsibilities and activities should be appropriately documented in the organization's strategic plans, board policies, management directives, operating procedures, and other governance type instruments. Examples of some of the activities and responsibilities that should be documented include:*

    - *Setting strategic direction may reside with the board or a committee;*
    - *Ownership of risks may be assigned at the senior management level;*

- *Acceptance of residual risk may reside at the executive management level;*
- *Identifying, assessing, mitigating, and monitoring activities on a continuous basis may be assigned at the operating level; and*
- *Periodic assessment and assurance to others should reside with the internal audit activity.*

5. *Internal auditors are expected to identify and evaluate significant risk exposures in the normal course of their duties.*

6. *The internal audit activity's role in the risk management process of an organization can change over time and may be found at some point along a continuum that ranges from:*

- *no role, to*
- *auditing the risk management process as part of the internal audit plan, to*
- *active, continuous support and involvement in the risk management process such as participation on oversight committees, monitoring activities, and status reporting, to*
- *managing and coordinating the risk management process.*

7. *Ultimately, it is the role of executive management and the audit committee to determine the role of internal audit in the risk management process. Management's view on internal audit's role is likely to be determined by factors such as the culture of the organization, ability of the internal auditing staff, and local conditions and customs of the country.*

8. *Additional guidance can be found in the following Practice Advisories:*

- *PA 2100-4 Internal Audit's Role in Organizations without a Risk Management Process*
- *PA 1130.A1-2 Internal Audit Responsibility for Other (Non-Audit) Functions*
- *PA 2110-1 Assessing the Adequacy of Risk Management Processes*
- *PA 2010-2 Linking the Audit Plan to Risk and Exposures*

Practice Advisory 2100-4: Internal Audit's Role in Organizations Without a Risk Management Process

1.-3. *Same as PA 2100-3, paragraphs 1. through 3.*

4. *If an organization has not established a risk management process, the internal auditor should bring this to management's attention along with suggestions for establishing such a process. The internal auditor should seek direction from management and the board as to the internal audit activity's role in the risk management process. The charters for the internal audit activity and audit committee should document the role of each in the risk management process.*

5. *If requested, internal auditors can play a proactive role in assisting with the initial establishment of a risk management process for the organization. A more proactive role supplements traditional assurance activities with a consultative approach to improving fundamental processes. If such assistance exceeds normal assurance and consulting activities conducted by internal auditors, independence could be impaired. In these situations, internal auditors should comply with the disclosure requirements of the Standards. Additional guidance can also be found in Practice Advisory 1130.A1-2: Internal Audit Responsibility for Other (Non-Audit) Functions.*

6. *A proactive role in developing and managing a risk management process is not the same as an "ownership of risks" role. In order to avoid an "ownership of risk" role, internal auditors should seek confirmation from management as to its responsibility for identification, mitigation, monitoring, and "ownership" of risks.*

7. *In summary, internal auditors can facilitate or enable risk management processes, but they should not "own" or be responsible for the management of the risks identified.*

Practice Advisory 2100-5: Legal Considerations in Evaluating Regulatory Compliance Programs

Caution – Internal auditors are encouraged to consult legal counsel in all matters involving legal issues as requirements may vary significantly in different jurisdictions. The guidance contained in this Practice Advisory is based primarily on the United States' legal system.

1. Compliance programs assist organizations in preventing inadvertent employee violations, detecting illegal activities, and discouraging intentional employee violations. They can also help prove insurance claims, determine director and officer liability, create or enhance corporate identity, and decide the appropriateness of punitive damages. Internal auditors should evaluate an organization's regulatory compliance programs in light of the following suggested steps for effective compliance programs.

2. The organization should establish compliance standards and procedures to be followed by its employees and other agents that are reasonably capable of reducing the prospect of criminal conduct.

    - The organization should develop a written business code of conduct that clearly identifies prohibited activities. This code should be written in language that all employees can understand, avoiding legalese.

    - A good code provides guidance to employees on relevant issues. Checklists, a question and answer section and reference to additional sources for further information all help make the code user friendly.

    - The organization should create an organizational chart identifying board members, senior officers, senior compliance officer, and department personnel who are responsible for implementing compliance programs.

    - Codes of conduct that are viewed as legalistic and "one-sided" by employees may increase the risk that employees will engage in unethical or illegal behavior, whereas codes that are viewed as straightforward and fair tend to decrease the risk that employees will engage in such activity.

    - Companies using reward systems that attach financial incentives to apparently unethical or illegal behavior can expect a poor compliance environment.

    - Companies with international operations should institute a compliance program on a global basis, not just for selective geographic locations. Such programs should reflect appropriate local conditions, laws, and regulations.

3. Specific individual(s) within high-level personnel of the organization should be assigned overall responsibility to oversee regulatory compliance with standards and procedures.

    - High-level personnel of the organization means individuals who have substantial control of the organization or who have a substantial role in the making of policy within the organization.

    - High-level personnel of the organization includes: a director; an executive officer; an individual in charge of a major business or functional unit of the organization, such as sales, administration or finance; and an individual with a substantial ownership interest.

    - To be fully effective, the CEO and other senior management must have significant involvement in the program.

    - In some organizations assigning chief compliance responsibilities to the company's general counsel may convince employees that management is not committed to the program, that the program is important to the legal department only, not the firm as a whole. In other organizations the opposite may be true.

- *In a large company with several business units, compliance responsibilities should be assigned to high-level personnel in each unit.*

- *It is not enough for the company to create the position of chief compliance officer and to select the rest of the compliance unit. The company should also ensure that those personnel are appropriately empowered and supplied with the resources necessary for carrying out their mission. Compliance personnel should have adequate access to senior management. The chief compliance officer should report directly to the CEO.*

4. *The organization should use due care not to delegate substantial discretionary authority to individuals the organization knows, or should know through the exercise of due diligence, have a propensity to engage in illegal activities.*

- *Companies should screen applicants for employment at all levels for evidence of past wrongdoing, especially wrongdoing within the company's industry.*

- *Employment applications should inquire as to past criminal convictions. Professionals should be asked about any history of discipline in front of licensing boards.*

- *Care should be taken to ensure that the company does not infringe upon employees' and applicants' privacy rights under applicable laws. Many jurisdictions have laws limiting the amount of information a company can obtain in performing background checks on employees.*

5. *The organization should take steps to communicate effectively its standards and procedures to all employees and other agents, e.g., by requiring participation in training programs or by disseminating publications that explain in a practical manner what is required.*

- *The effectiveness of a compliance program will depend upon the ways in which it is communicated to employees. Generally, an interactive format works better than a lecture. Programs communicated in person tend to work better than programs communicated entirely through video or game formats. Programs that are periodically repeated work better than one-time presentations.*

- *The best programs include employee training that allows employees to practice new techniques and use new information. Such activities are particularly appropriate with regard to management training but are effective with regard to employees at all levels.*

- *The language used by an organization's code of conduct and employee manual should be easy to understand. Alternative methods of communicating the code and the employee manual to employees lacking more formal education must be found and implemented.*

- *Compliance tips, statements, and warnings should be disseminated to employees through a variety of available media: newsletters, posters, e-mail, questionnaires and presentations.*

- *Organizations should present the program on multiple occasions to different sets of employees, targeting the information presented to the areas important to each functional group of employees. The information should be tailored to that group's job requirements. For example, environmental compliance information should be directed to those departments, such as manufacturing or real property management, that have an increased likelihood of violating or detecting violations of such laws and regulations. On the other hand, providing such training to a department with no such responsibilities could be detrimental, inspiring employee apathy or a belief that the program was not well constructed.*

- *New employees should receive basic compliance training as part of their orientation. Later, they can be incorporated into ongoing compliance efforts in their departments.*

- *Agents of the organization should be asked to attend a presentation specifically geared toward them. It is important that an organization inform its agents of the organization's core values, and that the actions of its agents that are attributable to the company will be monitored in connection with the compliance program. The organization should be prepared to cease doing business with agents who fail to adhere to the organization's compliance standards.*

- *Organizations should require employees to periodically certify that they have read, understood and complied with the company's code of conduct. This information should be related annually to senior management and the board of directors.*

- *All ethics related documents - codes of conduct, human resources policies/manuals, etc. - should be readily available to all employees. Continuous access availability, such as through the organization's intranet, is strongly encouraged.*

6. *The organization should take reasonable steps to achieve compliance with its standards, e.g., by utilizing monitoring and auditing systems reasonably designed to detect criminal conduct by its employees and other agents and by having in place and publicizing a reporting system whereby employees and other agents could report criminal conduct by others within the organization without fear of retribution.*

    - *The organization should devote an amount of resources to the internal audit plan that is appropriate given the size of the company and the difficulty of the audit task. The audit plan should concentrate on the organization's activities in each of its businesses.*

    - *The audit plan should also include a review of the organization's compliance program and its procedures, including reviews to determine whether: written materials are effective, communications have been received by employees, detected violations have been appropriately handled, discipline has been even-handed, whistle blowers have not been retaliated against, and the compliance unit has fulfilled its responsibilities. The auditors should review the compliance program to determine whether it can be improved, and should solicit employee input in that regard.*

    - *Each program should have a "hotline" or other reporting system under which employees can report activity that they believe to be unethical, illegal or against the company's code of conduct. Employees must be free to report such behavior without fear of reprisal.*

    - *Although an attorney monitoring the hotline is better able to protect attorney-client and work-product privileges, one study observed that employees have little confidence in hotlines answered by the legal department or by an outside service. The same study showed that employees have even less confidence in write-in reports or an off-site ombudsperson, but have the most confidence in hotlines answered by an in-house representative and backed by a nonretaliation policy.*

    - *Use of an on-site ombudsperson is more effective if the ombudsperson reports directly to the chief compliance officer or the board of directors, if the ombudsperson can keep the names of whistle blowers secret, if the ombudsperson provides guidance to whistle blowers, and if the ombudsperson undertakes follow-up review to ensure that retaliation has not occurred. Additionally, some jurisdictions now recognize a limited ombudsperson privilege, under which the ombudsperson is protected from disclosing confidential communications made by whistle blowers to the ombudsperson.*

- *An effective tool for uncovering unethical or illegal activity is the ethics questionnaire. Each employee of the organization should receive a questionnaire, which asks whether the employee is aware of kickbacks, bribes or other wrongdoing. To protect privilege, the questionnaire should: be sent by organization counsel; contain a statement that the questionnaire is protected by privilege; require the employee to complete, sign and return the questionnaire without making a copy; and contain a statement that the organization retains the right to disclose information provided to the company to government agencies or in litigation. Note that privilege will be lost if the questionnaire is disclosed to outside parties.*

7.   *The standards should be consistently enforced through appropriate disciplinary mechanisms, including, as appropriate, discipline of individuals responsible for the failure to detect an offense. Adequate discipline of individuals responsible for an offense is a necessary component of enforcement; however, the form of discipline that will be appropriate will be case specific.*

- *The compliance program should contain a disciplinary system under which those who violate the organization's code of conduct receive punishment appropriate to the offense, such as warning, loss of pay, suspension, transfer or termination. But if an employee is found to have committed some illegal act, the organization might have to terminate that employee, in keeping with the organization's obligation to use "due care not to delegate substantial discretionary authority to individuals whom the organization knew, or should have known through the exercise of due diligence, had a propensity to engage in illegal activities."*

- *Discipline under the program must be fair. The program has slight chance of succeeding if unethical or illegal activity goes unpunished, especially if tied to the activities of senior management or big producers. Ignored wrongdoing by such persons will encourage such behavior in the rest of the workforce.*

- *Termination or other discipline of employees may be limited by whistle-blower laws, exceptions to the employee-at-will doctrine, employee or union contracts, and employer responsibilities with regard to discrimination, wrongful discharge and employer bad faith laws/doctrines.*

- *The program should provide for the discipline of managers and other responsible persons who knew or should have known of misconduct and did not report it. Failure of the program to do so may cause a court to find that the program is not effective; the program will then have no beneficial effect on sentencing.*

8.   *Organizations should be scrupulous and thorough in documenting employee discipline. The organization should be able to prove that it made its best efforts to collect information with regard to any incident and took appropriate action based upon the information available.*

9.   *After an offense has been detected, the organization should take all reasonable steps to respond appropriately to the offense and to prevent further similar offenses - including any necessary modifications to its program to prevent and detect violations of law.*

- *The organization should respond appropriately to each offense detected by the compliance program. Appropriate responses include disciplinary action taken with regard to those who engaged in misconduct.*

- *In some circumstances, an appropriate response could require self-reporting the violation to the government, cooperation with governmental investigations and the acceptance of responsibility for the violation. Note that similar to the existence of an effective compliance program, making these responses could result in a court lowering the amount of the organization's fine.*

- Failure to detect or prevent a serious violation could indicate that the compliance program needs a major overhaul. At a minimum, after any violation is detected compliance personnel should examine the program to determine whether changes need to be made.
- One change that may be required in light of a violation could be the replacement or shuffling of compliance personnel. In fact, the organization may need to discipline or replace any manager who fails to detect or prevent misconduct in the areas under the manager's supervision, especially if the violation is one that the manager should have detected.

Practice Advisory 2100-6: Control and Audit Implications of E-commerce Activities

1. Electronic commerce (e-commerce) is generally defined as "conducting commercial activities over the Internet." These commercial activities can be business-to-business (B2B), business-to-consumer (B2C), and business-to-employee (B2E). The growth of e-commerce has been dramatic and is anticipated to grow even more rapidly in the years ahead. The recent publication by the IIA Research Foundation, **Systems Assurance and Control (SAC)**, and the success of the web-based **www.ITAudit.org** and various email IIA newsletters confirms that technology not only supports e-commerce strategies, but is an integral part. Web-based and other technology changes have a dramatic impact on society, governance, economics, competition, markets, organizational structure, and national defense. Clearly, these changes and the dramatic growth of e-commerce create significant control and management challenges that should be considered by internal auditors in developing and implementing their audit plans.

Understanding and Planning an E-commerce Engagement

2. Continuous changes in technology offer the internal auditing profession both great opportunity and risk. Before attempting to provide assurance on the systems and processes, an internal auditor should understand the changes in business and information systems, the related risks, and the alignment of strategies with the enterprise's design and market requirements. The internal auditor should review management's strategic planning and risk assessment processes and its decisions about:

   - Which risks are serious?
   - Which risks can be insured?
   - What current controls will mitigate the risks?
   - Which additional compensating controls are necessary?
   - What type of monitoring is required?

3. The major components of auditing e-commerce activities are:

   - Assess the internal control structure, including the tone set by senior management,
   - Provide reasonable assurance that goals and objectives can be achieved,
   - Determine if the risks are acceptable,
   - Understand the information flow,
   - Review the interface issues (such as hardware to hardware, software to software, and hardware to software), and
   - Evaluate the business continuity and disaster recovery plans.

4. The Chief Audit Executive's (CAE's) concerns in performing an e-commerce engagement relate to the competency and capacity of the internal audit activity. Among the possible factors that may constrain the internal audit activity are:

   - Does the internal audit activity have sufficient skills? If not, can the skills be acquired?
   - Are training or other resources necessary?
   - Is the staffing level sufficient for the near-term and long-term?
   - Can the expected audit plan be delivered?

5.   ***Internal auditor's questions during risk assessment.*** *The IIA's SAC publication can assist the internal auditor in audit planning and risk assessment. It includes a list of e-commerce areas that should be of interest to an internal auditor who is undertaking an engagement and assessing risks. The questions for internal auditors to consider are:*

- *Is there a business plan for the e-commerce project or program?*
- *Does the plan cover the integration of the planning, design, and implementation of the e-commerce system with the strategies of the organization?*
- *What will be the impact on the performance, security, reliability, and availability of the system?*
- *Will the functionality meet the end user's needs (e.g., employees, customers, business partners) as well as management's objectives?*
- *Have governmental and regulatory requirements been analyzed and considered?*
- *How secure is the hardware and software, and will they prevent or detect unauthorized access, inappropriate use, and other harmful effects and losses?*
- *Will transaction processing be current, accurate, complete, and indisputable?*
- *Does the control environment allow the organization to achieve its e-commerce objectives as it moves from concepts to results?*
- *Does the risk assessment include internal and external forces?*
- *Have the inherent risks associated with the Internet and Internet provider (such as reliability of basic communications, authentication of users, and who has access) been addressed?*
- *Have other issues been addressed (for example, disclosures of confidential business information, misuse of intellectual property, violations of copyrights, trademark infringement, libelous statements on Web sites, fraud, misuse of electronic signatures, privacy violations, and reputation damage)?*
- *If outside vendors are used, has a "going concern" evaluation been conducted by a trusted third party who is qualified to certify the vendor?*
- *If vendors provide hosting services, do they have a tested business contingency plan? Have they provided a recent SAS-70 report? (SAS-70 reports can offer valuable information about internal controls to user organizations.) Also, have privacy issues been resolved?*
- *Does the contract include audit rights?*

E-commerce Risks and Control Issues

6.   *The e-commerce risk and control environment is complex and evolving. Risk can be defined as the uncertainty of an event occurring that could have a negative impact on the achievement of objectives. Risk is inherent to every business or government entity. Opportunity risks assumed by management are often drivers of organizational activities. Beyond these opportunities may be threats and other dangers that are not clearly understood and fully evaluated and too easily accepted as part of doing business. In striving to manage risk, it is essential to have an understanding of risk elements. It is also important to be aware of new threats and changes in technology that open new vulnerabilities in information security. For management purposes, the seven key questions below can serve to identify organizational risk and target potential ways to control or mitigate the exposures. (Risk practitioners use a variety of different risk management approaches; these questions illustrate one approach.) Risk elements associated with the questions are displayed in brackets.*

    (a)   **Risk Identification and Quantification:**

- *What could happen that would adversely affect the organization's ability to achieve its objectives and execute its strategies? [Threat Events]*
- *If it happens, what is the potential financial impact? [Single Loss Exposure Value]*
- *How often might it happen? [Frequency]*
- *How probable are the answers to the first three questions? [Uncertainty]*

    (b)   ***Risk Management and Mitigation:***

- *What can be done to prevent and avoid, mitigate, and detect risks and provide notification? [Safeguards and Controls]*
- *How much will it cost? [Safeguard and Control Costs]*
- *How efficient would that be? [Cost/Benefit or ROI Analysis]*

7.   *Some of the more critical risk and control issues to be addressed by the internal auditor are:*

- *General project management risks.*
- *Specific security threats, such as denial of service, physical attacks, viruses, identity theft, and unauthorized access or disclosure of data.*
- *Maintenance of transaction integrity under a complex network of links to legacy systems and data warehouses.*
- *Website content review and approval when there are frequent changes and sophisticated customer features and capabilities that offer around-the-clock service.*
- *Rapid technology changes.*
- *Legal issues, such as increasing regulations throughout the world to protect individual privacy; enforceability of contracts outside of the organization's country; and tax and accounting issues.*
- *Changes to surrounding business processes and organizational structures.*

Auditing E-commerce Activities

8.   *The overall audit objective should be to ensure that all e-commerce processes have effective internal controls. Management of e-commerce initiatives should be documented in a strategic plan that is well developed and approved. If there is a decision not to participate in e-commerce, that decision should be carefully analyzed, documented, and approved by the governing board.*

9.   *Audit objectives for an e-commerce engagement may include:*

- *Evidence of e-commerce transactions*
- *Availability and reliability of security system*
- *Effective interface between e-commerce and financial systems*
- *Security of monetary transactions*
- *Effectiveness of customer authentication process*
- *Adequacy of business continuity processes, including the resumption of operations*
- *Compliance with common security standards*
- *Effective use and control of digital signatures*
- *Adequacy of systems, policies, and procedures to control Public Key Certificates (using public key cryptographic techniques)*
- *Adequacy and timeliness of operating data and information*
- *Documented evidence of an effective system of internal control*

10. The details of the audit program used to audit e-commerce activities in specific organizations will vary depending on industry, country, and legal and business models. The following is an outline of a possible e-commerce audit protocol for key areas.

(a) **e-commerce organization** – The internal auditor should do the following:

- Determine the value of transactions.
- Identify the stakeholders (external and internal).
- Review the change management process.
- Examine the approval process.
- Review the business plan for e-commerce activities.
- Evaluate the policies over Public Key Certificates.
- Review the digital signature procedures.
- Examine service level agreements between buyer, supplier, and certification authority.
- Ascertain the quality assurance policy.
- Assess the privacy policy and compliance in e-commerce activities.
- Assess the incident response capability.

(b) **Fraud** – The internal auditor should be alert for the following conditions.

- Unauthorized movement of money (e.g., transfers to jurisdictions where the recovery of funds would be difficult).
- Duplication of payments.
- Denial of orders placed or received, goods received, or payments made.
- Exception reports and procedures: and effectiveness of the follow up.
- Digital signatures: Are they used for all transactions? Who authorizes them? Who has access to them?
- Protections against viruses and hacking activities (history file, use of tools).
- Access rights: Are they reviewed regularly? Are they promptly revised when staff members are changed?
- History of interception of transactions by unauthorized persons.

(c) **Authentication** – The internal auditor should review the policies for authenticating transactions and evaluating controls.

- Evidence of regular reviews.
- Control self-assessment (CSA) tools used by management.
- Regular independent checks.
- Segregation of duties.
- Tools that management should have in place: firewalls (multi-level to partition e-commerce and other activities), password management, independent reconciliation, and audit trails.

(d) **Corruption of data** – The internal auditor should evaluate controls over data integrity.

- Who can amend catalogues and prices or rates? What is the approval mechanism?
- Can someone destroy audit trails?
- Who can approve bulletin board amendments?
- What are the procedures for ordering and recording?
- Is the process of on-line tendering providing adequate documentation?
- Tools that should be in-place include: intrusion management (monitoring software, automatic timeout, and trend analysis), physical security for e-commerce servers, change controls, and reconciliation.

(e) **Business Interruptions** – *The internal auditor should review the business continuity plan and determine if it has been tested. Management should have devised an alternative means to process the transactions in the event of an interruption. Management should have a process in place to address the following potential conditions:*

- *Volume attacks*
- *Denial of service attacks*
- *Inadequacies in interfacing between e-commerce and financial management systems*
- *Backup facilities*
- *Strategies to counter: hacking, intrusion, cracking, viruses, worms, Trojan horses, and back doors.*

(f) **Management Issues** – *The internal auditor should evaluate how well business units are managing the e-commerce process. The following are some relevant topics:*

- *Project management reviews of individual initiatives and development projects*
- *System Development Life Cycle reviews*
- *Vendor selection, vendor capabilities, employee confidentiality, and bonding.*
- *Post-implementation economic reviews: Are anticipated benefits being achieved? What metrics are being used to measure success?*
- *Post-implementation process reviews: Are new processes in place and working effectively?*

Practice Advisory 2100-7: Internal Audit's Role in Identifying and Reporting Environmental Risks

Potential Risks

1. *Chief Audit Executive (CAE) should include the environmental, health, and safety (EH&S) risks in any entity-wide risk management assessment and assess the activities in a balanced manner relative to other types of risk associated with an entity's operations. Among the risk exposures that should be evaluated are: organizational reporting structures; likelihood of causing environmental harm, fines, and penalties; expenditures mandated by Environmental Protection Agency (EPA) or other governmental agencies; history of injuries and deaths; record of losses of customers, and episodes of negative publicity and loss of public image and reputation.*

2. *If the CAE finds that the management of the EH&S risks largely depends on an environmental audit function, the CAE needs to consider the implications of that organizational structure and its effects on operations and the reporting mechanisms. If the CAE finds that the exposures are not adequately managed and residual risks exist, that conclusion would normally result in changes to the internal audit activity's plan of engagements and further investigations.*

3. *The majority of environmental audit functions report to their organization's environmental component or general counsel, not to the CAE. The typical organizational models for environmental auditing fall into one of the following scenarios:*

- *The CAE and environmental audit chief are in separate functional units with little contact with each other.*
- *The CAE and environmental audit chief are in separate functional units and coordinate their activities.*
- *The CAE has responsibility for auditing environmental issues.*

4.   *According to an IIA flash report on environmental auditing issues:*

- *About one-half of the environmental auditors seldom meet with a committee of the governing board and only 40 percent have some contact with the CAE.*

- *Seventy percent of the organizations reported that environmental issues are not regularly included on the agenda of the governing board.*

- *About 40 percent of the organizations reported that they had paid fines or penalties for environmental violations in the past three years. Two-thirds of the respondents described their environmental risks as material.*

5.   *The Environmental, Health, and Safety Auditing Roundtable (new name is The Auditing Roundtable) commissioned Richard L. Ratliff of Utah State University and a group of researchers to perform a study of environmental, health, and safety auditing. The researchers' findings related to the risk and independence issues are as follows.*

- *The EH&S audit function is somewhat isolated from other organizational auditing activities. It is organized separately from internal auditing, only tangentially related to external audits of financial statements, and reports to an EH&S executive, rather than to the governing board or to senior management. This structure suggests that management believes EH&S auditing to be a technical field which is best placed within the EH&S function of the organization.*

- *With that organizational placement, EH&S auditors could be unable to maintain their independence, which is considered one of the principal requirements of an effective audit function. EH&S audit managers typically report administratively to the executives who are responsible for the physical facilities being audited. Thus, poor EH&S performance would reflect badly on the facilities management team, who would therefore try to exercise their authority and influence over what is reported in audit findings, how audits are conducted, or what is included in the audit plan. This potential subordination of the auditors' professional judgment, even when only apparent, violates auditor independence and objectivity.*

- *It is also common for written audit reports to be distributed no higher in the organization than to senior environmental executives. Those executives may have a potential conflict of interest, and they may curtail further distribution of EH&S audit findings to senior management and the governing board.*

- *Audit information is often classified as either (a) attorney-client privilege or attorney work product, (b) secret and confidential, or (c) if not confidential, then closely held. This results in severely restricted access to EH&S audit information.*

Suggestions for the Chief Audit Executive

6.   *CAE should foster a close working relationship with the chief environmental officer and coordinate activities with the plan for environmental auditing. In those instances where the environmental audit function reports to someone other than the CAE, the CAE should offer to review the audit plan and the performance of engagements. Periodically, the CAE should schedule a quality assurance review of the environmental audit function if it is organizationally independent of the internal audit activity. That review should determine if the environmental risks are being adequately addressed. An EH&S audit program could be either (a) compliance-focused (i.e., verifying compliance with laws, regulations and the entity's own EH&S policies, procedures and performance objectives) or (b) management systems-focused (i.e., providing assessments of management systems intended to ensure compliance with legal and internal requirements and the mitigation of risks), or (c) a combination of both approaches.*

7. *CAE should evaluate whether the environmental auditors, who are not part of the CAE's organization, are in compliance with recognized professional auditing standards and a recognized code of ethics. The Board of Environmental, Health, & Safety Auditor Certifications (BEAC) as well as the IIA publish practice standards and ethical codes.*

8. *CAE should evaluate the organizational placement and independence of the environmental audit function to ensure that significant matters resulting from serious risks to the enterprise are reported up the chain of command to the audit or other committee of the governing board. CAE should also facilitate the reporting of significant EH&S risk and control issues to the audit (or other board) committee.*

2110 **Risk Management** — *The internal audit activity should assist the organization by identifying and evaluating significant exposures to risk and contributing to the improvement of risk management and control systems.*

Practice Advisory 2110-1: Assessing the Adequacy of Risk Management Processes

1.-2. *Same as PA 2100-3, paragraphs 1. and 2.*

3. *Each organization may choose a particular methodology to implement its risk management process. The internal auditor should determine the methodology is understood by key groups or individuals involved in corporate governance, including the board and audit committee. Internal auditors must satisfy themselves that the organization's risk management processes address five key objectives to formulate an opinion on the overall adequacy of the risk management processes. The five key objectives of a risk management process are:*

   - *Risks arising from business strategies and activities are identified and prioritized.*
   - *Management and the board have determined the level of risks acceptable to the organization, including the acceptance of risks designed to accomplish the organization's strategic plans.*
   - *Risk mitigation activities are designed and implemented to reduce, or otherwise manage, risk at levels that were determined to be acceptable to management and the board.*
   - *Ongoing monitoring activities are conducted to periodically reassess risk and the effectiveness of controls to manage risk.*
   - *The board and management receive periodic reports of the results of the risk management processes. The corporate governance processes of the organization should provide periodic communication of risks, risk strategies, and controls to stakeholders.*

4. *Internal auditors should recognize that there could be significant variations in the techniques used by various organizations for their risk management practices. Risk management processes should be designed for the nature of an organization's activities. Depending on the size and complexity of the organization's business activities, risk management processes can be;*

   - *formal or informal*
   - *quantitative or subjective*
   - *embedded in the business units or centralized at a corporate level.*

The specific process used by an organization must fit that organization's culture, management style, and business objectives. For example, the use of derivatives or other sophisticated capital markets products by the organization would require the use of quantitative risk management tools. Smaller, less complex organizations may use an informal risk committee to discuss the organization's risk profile and to initiate periodic actions. The auditor should determine that the methodology chosen is both comprehensive and appropriate for the nature of the organization's activities.

5.   *Internal auditors should obtain sufficient information to satisfy themselves that the five key objectives of the risk management processes are being met in order to form an opinion on the adequacy of risk management processes. In gathering such information, the internal auditor should consider the following types of engagement procedures:*

- *Research and review reference materials and background information on risk management methodologies as a basis to assess whether or not the process used by the organization is appropriate and represents best practices for the industry.*

- *Research and review current developments, trends, industry information related to the business conducted by the organization, and other appropriate sources of information to determine risks and exposures that may affect the organization and related control procedures used to address, monitor, and reassess those risks.*

- *Review corporate policies, board, and audit committee minutes to determine the organization's business strategies, risk management philosophy and methodology, appetite for risk, and acceptance of risks.*

- *Review previous risk evaluation reports by management, internal auditors, external auditors, and any other sources that may have issued such reports.*

- *Conduct interviews with line and executive management to determine business unit objectives, related risks, and management's risk mitigation and control monitoring activities.*

- *Assimilate information to independently evaluate the effectiveness of risk mitigation, monitoring, and communication of risks and associated control activities.*

- *Assess the appropriateness of reporting lines for risk monitoring activities.*

- *Review the adequacy and timeliness of reporting on risk management results.*

- *Review the completeness of management's risk analysis, actions taken to remedy issues raised by risk management processes, and suggest improvements.*

- *Determine the effectiveness of management's self-assessment processes through observations, direct tests of control and monitoring procedures, testing the accuracy of information used in monitoring activities, and other appropriate techniques.*

- *Review risk related issues that may indicate weakness in risk management practices and, as appropriate, discuss with management, the audit committee, and the board of directors. If the auditor believes that management has accepted a level of risk that is inconsistent with the organization's risk management strategy and policies, or that is deemed unacceptable to the organization, the auditor should refer to Standard 2600, Management's Acceptance of Risks, and any related guidance for additional direction.*

Practice Advisory 2110-2: Internal Audit's Role in the Business Continuity Process

1.   *Business interruption can result from natural occurrences and accidental or deliberate criminal acts. Those interruptions can have significant financial and operational ramifications. Auditors should evaluate the organization's readiness to deal with business interruptions. A comprehensive plan would provide for emergency response procedures, alternative communication systems and site facilities, information systems backup, disaster recovery, business impact assessments and resumption plans, procedures for restoring utility services, and maintenance procedures for ensuring the readiness of the organization in the event of an emergency or disaster.*

2.   *Internal auditing activity should assess the organization's business continuity planning process on a regular basis to ensure that senior management is aware of the state of disaster preparedness.*

3. Many organizations do not expect to experience an interruption or lengthy delay of normal business processes and operations due to a disaster or other unforeseen event. Many business experts say that it is not **if** a disaster will occur, but **when** it will occur. Over time, an organization will experience an event that will result in the loss of information, access to properties (tangible or intangible), or the services of personnel. Exposure to those types of risks and the planning for business continuity is an integral part of an organization's risk management process. Advance planning is necessary to minimize the loss and ensure continuity of an organization's critical business functions. It may enable the organization to maintain an acceptable level of service to its stakeholders.

4. A crucial element of business recovery is the existence of a comprehensive and current disaster recovery plan. Internal auditors can play a role in the organization's planning for disaster recovery. Internal audit activity can (a) assist with the risk analysis, (b) evaluate the design and comprehensiveness of the plan after it has been drawn up, and (c) perform periodic assurance engagements to verify that the plan is kept up to date.

Planning

5. Organizations rely upon internal auditors for analysis of operations and assessment of risk management and control processes. Internal auditors acquire an understanding of the overall business operations and the individual functions and how they interrelate with one another. This positions the internal audit activity as a valuable resource in evaluating the disaster recovery plan during its formulation process.

6. Internal audit activity can help with an assessment of an organization's internal and external environment. Internal factors that may be considered include the turnover of management and changes in information systems, controls, and major projects and programs. External factors may include changes in outside regulatory and business environment and changes in markets and competitive conditions, international financial and economic conditions, and technologies. Internal auditors can help identify risks involving critical business activities and prioritize functions for recovery purposes.

Evaluation

7. Internal auditors can make a contribution as objective participants when they review the proposed business continuity and disaster recovery plans for design, completeness, and overall adequacy. The auditor can examine the plan to determine that it reflects the operations that have been included and evaluated in the risk assessment process and contains sufficient internal control concerns and prescriptions. The internal auditor's comprehensive knowledge of the organization's business operations and applications enables it to assist during the development phase of the business continuity plan by evaluating its organization, comprehensiveness, and recommended actions to manage risks and maintain effective controls during a recovery period.

Periodic Assurance Engagements

8. Internal auditors should periodically audit the organization's business continuity and disaster recovery plans. The audit objective is to verify that the plans are adequate to ensure the timely resumption of operations and processes after adverse circumstances, and that it reflects the current business operating environment.

9. Business continuity and disaster recovery plans can become outdated very quickly. Coping with and responding to changes is an inevitable part of the task of management. Turnover of managers and executives and changes in system configurations, interfaces, and software can have a major impact on these plans. Internal audit activity should examine the recovery plan to determine whether (a) it is structured to incorporate important changes that could take place over time and (b) the revised plan will be communicated to the appropriate people, inside and outside the organization.

10.   During the audit, internal auditors should consider:

- Are all plans up to date? Do procedures exist for updating the plans?
- Are all critical business functions and systems covered by the plans? If not, are the reasons for omissions documented?
- Are the plans based on the risks and potential consequences of business interruptions?
- Are the plans fully documented and in accordance with organizational policies and procedures? Have functional responsibilities been assigned?
- Is the organization capable of and prepared to implement the plans?
- Are the plans tested and revised based on the results?
- Are the plans stored properly and safely? Is the location of and access to the plans known to management?
- Are the locations of alternate facilities (backup sites) known to employees?
- Do the plans call for coordination with local emergency services?

Internal Audit's Role After a Disaster

11.   There is an important role for the internal auditors to play immediately after a disaster occurs. An organization is more vulnerable after a disaster has occurred, and it is trying to recover. During that recovery period, internal auditors should monitor the effectiveness of the recovery and control of operations. Internal audit activity should identify areas where internal controls and mitigating actions should be improved, and recommend improvements to the entity's business continuity plan. Internal audit can also provide support during the recovery activities.

12.   After the disaster, usually within several months, internal auditors can assist in identifying the lessons learned from the disaster and the recovery operations. Those observations and recommendations may enhance activities to recover resources and update the next version of the business continuity plan.

13.   In the final analysis, it is senior management that will determine the degree of the internal auditor's involvement in the business continuity and disaster recovery processes, considering their knowledge, skills, independence, and objectivity.

2110.A1 - The internal audit activity should monitor and evaluate the effectiveness of the organization's risk management system.

2110.A2 - The internal audit activity should evaluate risk exposures relating to the organization's governance, operations, and information systems regarding the

- Reliability and integrity of financial and operational information.
- Effectiveness and efficiency of operations.
- Safeguarding of assets.
- Compliance with laws, regulations, and contracts.

2110.C1 - During consulting engagements, internal auditors should address risk consistent with the engagement's objectives and should be alert to the existence of other significant risks.

2110.C2 - Internal auditors should incorporate knowledge of risks gained from consulting engagements into the process of identifying and evaluating significant risk exposures of the organization.

Practice Advisory 1000.C 1-2: Additional Considerations for Formal Consulting Engagements

The following is the portion of this omnibus Practice Advisory relevant to Standards 2110.C1 and 2110.C2:

11. *Internal auditors should should reach an understanding about the objectives and scope of the consulting engagement with those receiving the service. Any reservations about the value, benefit, or possible negative implications of the consulting engagement should be communicated to those receiving the service. Internal auditors should design the scope of work to ensure that professionalism, integrity, credibility, and reputation of the internal audit activity will be maintained.*

12. *In planning formal consulting engagements, internal auditors should design objectives to meet the appropriate needs of management officials receiving these services. In the case of special requests by management, internal auditors may consider the following actions if they believe that the objectives that should be pursued go beyond those requested by management:*

- *Persuade management to include the additional objectives in the consulting engagement; or*
- *Document the fact that the objectives were not pursued and disclose that observation in the final communication of consulting engagement results; and*
- *Include the objectives in a separate and subsequent assurance engagement.*

13. *Work programs for formal consulting engagements should document the objectives and scope of the engagement as well as the methodology to be used in satisfying the objectives. The form and content of the program may vary depending on the nature of the engagement. In establishing the scope of the engagement, internal auditors may expand or limit the scope to satisfy management's request. However, the internal auditor should be satisfied that the projected scope of work will be adequate to meet the objectives of the engagement. The objectives, scope, and terms of the engagement should be periodically reassessed and adjusted during the course of the work.*

14. *Internal auditors should be observant of the effectiveness of risk management and control processes during formal consulting engagements. Substantial risk exposures or material control weaknesses should be brought to the attention of management. In some situations the auditor's concerns should also be communicated to executive management, the audit committee, and/or the board of directors. Auditors should use professional judgment (a) to determine the significance of exposures or weaknesses and the actions taken or contemplated to mitigate or correct these exposures or weaknesses and (b) to ascertain the expectations of executive management, the audit committee, and board in having these matters reported.*

2130 *Governance* — *The internal audit activity should contribute to the organization's governance process by evaluating and improving the process through which (1) values and goals are established and communicated, (2) the accomplishment of goals is monitored, (3) accountability is ensured, and (4) values are preserved.*

Practice Advisory 2130-1: Role of the Internal Audit Activity and Internal Auditor in the Ethical Culture of an Organization

1.   *This Practice Advisory underscores the importance of organizational culture in establishing the ethical climate of an enterprise and suggests the role that internal auditors could play in improving that ethical climate. Specifically, the Practice Advisory:*

     •   *Describes the nature of the governance process.*
     •   *Links it to the ethical culture of the organization.*
     •   *States that all people associated with the organization, and specifically internal auditors, should assume the role of ethics advocates.*
     •   *Lists the characteristics of an enhanced ethical culture.*

2.   *An organization uses various legal forms, structures, strategies, and procedures to ensure that it:*

     •   *Complies with society's legal and regulatory rules.*
     •   *Satisfies the generally accepted business norms, ethical precepts, and social expectations of society.*
     •   *Provides overall benefit to society and enhances the interests of the specific stakeholders in both the long- and short-term.*
     •   *Reports fully and truthfully to its owners, regulators, other stakeholders, and general public to ensure accountability for its decisions, actions, conduct, and performance.*

     The way in which an organization chooses to conduct its affairs to meet those four responsibilities is commonly referred to as its governance process. The organization's governing body (such as a board of directors or trustees or a managing board) and its senior management are accountable for the effectiveness of the governance process.

3.   *An organization's governance practices reflect a unique and ever-changing culture that affects roles, specifies behavior, sets goals and strategies, measures performance, and defines the terms of accountability. That culture affects the values, roles, and behavior that will be articulated and tolerated by the organization and determines how sensitive - thoughtful or indifferent - the enterprise is in meeting its responsibilities to society. Thus, how effective the overall governance process is in performing its expected function largely depends on the organization's culture.*

4.   *All people associated with the organization share some responsibility for the state of its ethical culture. Because of the complexity and dispersion of decision-making processes in most enterprises, each individual should be encouraged to be an ethics advocate, whether the role is delegated officially or merely conveyed informally. Codes of conduct and statements of vision and policy are important declarations of the organization's values and goals, the behavior expected of its people, and the strategies for maintaining a culture that aligns with its legal, ethical, and societal responsibilities. A growing number of organizations have designated a chief ethics officer as counselor of executives, managers, and others and as champion within the organization for "doing the right thing."*

5.   *Internal auditors and the internal audit activity should take an active role in support of the organization's ethical culture. They possess a high level of trust and integrity within the organization and the skills to be effective advocates of ethical conduct. They have the competence and capacity to appeal to the enterprise's leaders, managers, and other employees to comply with the legal, ethical, and societal responsibilities of the organization.*

6.   *The internal audit activity may assume one of several different roles as an ethics advocate. Those roles include chief ethics officer (ombudsperson, compliance officer, management ethics counselor, or ethics expert), member of an internal ethics council, or assessor of the organization's ethical climate. In some circumstances, the role of chief ethics officer may conflict with the independence attribute of the internal audit activity.*

7.   At a minimum, the internal audit activity should periodically assess the state of the ethical climate of the organization and the effectiveness of its strategies, tactics, communications, and other processes in achieving the desired level of legal and ethical compliance. Internal auditors should evaluate the effectiveness of the following features of an enhanced, highly effective ethical culture:

- Formal Code of Conduct, which is clear and understandable, and related statements, policies (including procedures covering fraud and corruption), and other expressions of aspiration.
- Frequent communications and demonstrations of expected ethical attitudes and behavior by the influential leaders of the organization.
- Explicit strategies to support and enhance the ethical culture with regular programs to update and renew the organization's commitment to an ethical culture.
- Several, easily accessible ways for people to confidentially report alleged violations of the Code, policies, and other acts of misconduct.
- Regular declarations by employees, suppliers, and customers that they are aware of the requirements for ethical behavior in transacting the organization's affairs.
- Clear delegation of responsibilities to ensure that ethical consequences are evaluated, confidential counseling is provided, allegations of misconduct are investigated, and case findings are properly reported.
- Easy access to learning opportunities to enable all employees to be ethics advocates.
- Positive personnel practices that encourage every employee to contribute to the ethical climate of the organization.
- Regular surveys of employees, suppliers, and customers to determine the state of the ethical climate in the organization.
- Regular reviews of the formal and informal processes within the organization that could potentially create pressures and biases that would undermine the ethical culture.
- Regular reference and background checks as part of hiring procedures, including integrity tests, drug screening, and similar measures.

2130.A1 - Internal auditors should review operations and programs to ensure consistency with organizational values.

2130.C1 - Consulting engagement objectives should be consistent with the overall values and goals of the organization.

Practice Advisory 1000.C1-2: Additional Considerations for Formal Consulting Engagements

The following is the portion of this omnibus Practice Advisory relevant to Standards 2130.C1:

9.   The internal auditor should exercise due professional care in conducting a formal consulting engagement by understanding the following:

- Needs of management officials, including the nature, timing, and communication of engagement results.
- Possible motivations and reasons of those requesting the service.
- Extent of work needed to achieve the engagement's objectives.
- Skills and resources needed to conduct the engagement.
- Effect on the scope of the audit plan previously approved by the audit committee.
- Potential impact on future audit assignments and engagements.
- Potential organizational benefits to be derived from the engagement.

10.   In addition to the independence and objectivity evaluation and due professional care considerations, the internal auditor should:

- Conduct appropriate meetings and gather necessary information to assess the nature and extent of the service to be provided.

- Confirm that those receiving the service understand and agree with the relevant guidance contained in the internal audit charter, internal audit activity's policies and procedures, and other related guidance governing the conduct of consulting engagements. The internal auditor should decline to perform consulting engagements that are prohibited by the terms of the internal audit charter, conflict with the policies and procedures of the internal audit activity, or do not add value and promote the best interests of the organization.

- Evaluate the consulting engagement for compatibility with the internal audit activity's overall plan of engagements. The internal audit activity's risk-based plan of engagements may incorporate and rely on consulting engagements, to the extent deemed appropriate, to provide necessary audit coverage to the organization.

- Document general terms, understandings, deliverables, and other key factors of the formal consulting engagement in a written agreement or plan. It is essential that both the internal auditor and those receiving the consulting engagement understand and agree with the reporting and communication requirements.

1.   Stop and review! You have completed the outline for this subunit. Study multiple-choice questions 1 through 40 beginning on page 116.

QUESTIONS

4.1 Nature of Work - Pronouncements

1. The scope of internal auditing work encompasses a systematic, disciplined approach to evaluating and improving the adequacy and effectiveness of all of the following factors except:

A. Risk management.

B. Control.

C. Financial statements.

D. Corporate governance.

Answer (C) is correct. *(Publisher)*
REQUIRED: The scope of internal auditing.
DISCUSSION: Financial statements are the responsibility of management and evaluating the adequacy of the statements is a role of the external auditor. The internal auditor evaluates and contributes to the improvement of risk management, control, and governance systems (Standard 2100). The comprehensive scope of work of internal auditing should provide reasonable assurance that:

- The risk management system is effective.
- The system of internal control is effective and efficient.
- The governance process is effective by establishing and preserving values, setting goals, monitoring activities and performance, and defining the measures of accountability.

2. Adequacy of risk management, control, and governance processes is present if management has planned and designed these processes in a manner that provides reasonable assurance that the organization's objectives and goals will be achieved efficiently and economically. Which of the following statements is not true regarding the efficient and economical achievement of the organization's objectives and goals?

A. Economical performance accomplishes objectives and goals with minimal use of resources with no regard to risk exposure.

B. Efficient performance accomplishes objectives and goals in a timely manner.

C. Economical performance accomplishes objectives and goals with minimal use of resources commensurate with the risk exposure.

D. Efficient performance accomplishes objectives and goals in an accurate and economical manner.

Answer (A) is correct. *(Publisher)*
REQUIRED: The meaning of efficient and economic performance of an organization's objectives and goals.
DISCUSSION: Efficient performance accomplishes objectives and goals in an accurate, timely, and economical fashion. Economical performance accomplishes objectives and goals with minimal use of resources (i.e., cost) commensurate with risk exposure (Practice Advisory 2100-1). Thus, in order to achieve economical performance when accomplishing objectives and goals, the minimal cost should correspond to the degree of risk exposure.

3. All of the following are primary objectives of the overall management process except:

A. Improving the effectiveness of risk management, control, and governance processes.

B. Compliance with laws, regulations, ethical and business norms, and contracts.

C. Identification of risk exposures and use of effective strategies to control them.

D. Safeguarding of the organization's assets.

Answer (A) is correct. *(Publisher)*
REQUIRED: The primary objectives of the overall management process.
DISCUSSION: Improving the effectiveness of risk management, control, and governance processes is the scope of internal auditing work. Broadly, management is responsible for the sustainability of the whole organization and accountability for the organization's actions, conduct, and performance to the owners, other stakeholders, regulators, and general public. Specifically, the primary objectives of the overall management process are to achieve (Practice Advisory 2100-1):

- Relevant, reliable, and credible financial and operating information.
- Effective and efficient use of the organization's resources.
- Safeguarding of the organization's assets.
- Compliance with laws, regulations, ethical and business norms, and contracts.
- Identification of risk exposures and use of effective strategies to control them.
- Established objectives and goals for operations or programs.

4. Which of the following is not a type of control?

A. Preventive.

B. Reactive.

C. Detective.

D. Directive.

Answer (B) is correct. *(Publisher)*
REQUIRED: The types of controls.
DISCUSSION: Control is any action taken by management to enhance the likelihood that established objectives and goals will be achieved (Practice Advisory 2100-1). Controls may be preventive (to deter undesirable events from occurring), detective (to detect and correct undesirable events which have occurred), or directive (to cause or encourage a desirable event to occur). "Reactive" is not a specified type of control. However, controls may be reactive in the sense that they detect an undesirable event and react to it or correct it.

5. Which of the following is subject to the internal auditors' evaluations?

I.   The human resources function.

II. The purchasing process.

III. The manufacturing and production database system.

    A. I only.

    B. II only.

    C. I, II, and III.

    D. None of the answers are correct.

Answer (C) is correct. *(Publisher)*
    REQUIRED: The organizational systems, processes, operations, functions, and activities that are subject to internal auditor evaluations.
    DISCUSSION: The internal auditing evaluations, in the aggregate, provide information to appraise the overall management process. Thus, all business systems, processes, operations, functions, and activities within the organization are subject to the internal auditors' evaluations (Practice Advisory 2100-1).

6. Management's view of the internal audit activity's role is likely to be determined by all of the following factors except:

    A. Organizational culture.

    B. Preferences of the independent auditor.

    C. Ability of the internal auditing staff.

    D. Local conditions and customs of the country.

Answer (B) is correct. *(Publisher)*
    REQUIRED: The factors influencing management's view on the role of internal audit.
    DISCUSSION: It is the role of executive management and the audit committee to determine the role of internal audit in the risk management process. Management's view on internal audit's role is likely to be determined by factors such as the culture of the organization, ability of the internal auditing staff, and local conditions and customs of the country (Practice Advisory 2100-3).

7. Internal auditors can play a more proactive role in assisting with the initial establishment of a risk management process for the organization. However, if such assistance exceeds normal assurance and consulting activities conducted by internal auditors, independence may be impaired. Which of the following would impair the independence of an internal auditor who had participated in the initial establishment of a risk management process?

    A. Developing assessments and reports on the risk management process.

    B. Managing the identified risks.

    C. Evaluating the adequacy and effectiveness of management's risk processes.

    D. Implementing controls to address the risks identified.

Answer (B) is correct. *(Publisher)*
    REQUIRED: The activity that an internal auditor may not do in the establishment and evaluation of a risk management process that the auditor helped create.
    DISCUSSION: A more proactive role in the initial establishment of a risk management process supplements traditional assurance activities with a consultative approach to improving fundamental processes. However, a proactive role in developing a risk management process is not the same as an "ownership of risks" role, which is a role of management (Practice Advisory 2100-4). The internal auditor cannot assume this role, or any other management, board, or audit committee role in the risk management process, without impairing independence. Boards and audit committees have an oversight role to determine that adequate and effective processes are in place, and managers have the responsibility for the management of the risks identified, and for ensuring that sound risk management processes are in place and functioning (Practice Advisory 2100-3). By managing the identified risks, the internal auditor impairs his/her independence by assuming management's role.
    Answer (A) is incorrect because developing assessments and reports on the organization's risk management processes is not only an internal auditing role, but it is normally also a high audit priority. Answer (C) is incorrect because internal auditors should assist both management and the audit committee by examining, evaluating, reporting, and recommending improvements on the adequacy and effectiveness of management's risk processes. Answer (D) is incorrect because internal auditors acting in a consulting role may assist the organization in identifying, evaluating, and implementing risk management methodologies and controls to address those risks (Practice Advisory 2100-3).

8. Compliance programs assist organizations by doing which of the following?

I. Evaluating business continuity.
II. Determining director and officer liability.
III. Evaluating disaster recovery plans.

   A. I only.

   B. II only.

   C. I and II only.

   D. I, II, and III.

Answer (B) is correct. *(Publisher)*
REQUIRED: The way(s) in which compliance programs help organizations.
DISCUSSION: Compliance programs assist organizations in preventing inadvertent employee violations, detecting illegal activities, and discouraging intentional employee violations. They can also help prove insurance claims, determine director and officer liability, create or enhance corporate identity, and decide the appropriateness of punitive damages. Evaluating the business continuity and evaluating the disaster recovery plans are both major components of auditing e-commerce activities.

9. An organization should establish compliance standards and procedures, and should develop a written business code of conduct to be followed by its employees. Which of the following is true concerning business codes of conduct and the compliance standards?

   A. Compliance standards should be straightforward and reasonably capable of reducing the prospect of criminal conduct.

   B. The compliance standards should be codified in the charters of the audit committee.

   C. Companies with international operations should institute various compliance programs based on selective geographic locations, that reflect appropriate local regulations.

   D. In order to prevent future legal liability, the code should consist of legal terms and definitions.

Answer (A) is correct. *(Publisher)*
REQUIRED: The true statement regarding the code of conduct and compliance standards.
DISCUSSION: The code of conduct should clearly identify prohibited activities, making compliance standards reasonably capable of reducing the prospect of criminal conduct (i.e., discouraging intentional employee violations). In addition, codes that are straightforward and fair tend to decrease the risk that employees will engage in unethical or illegal behavior (Practice Advisory 2100-5).
Answer (B) is incorrect because the compliance standards need only be codified in the code of conduct. The item that should be codified in the charters of the audit committee is the chief audit executive's understanding of the expectations of management and the board for the internal audit activity in the organization's risk management process (Practice Advisory 2100-3). Answer (C) is incorrect because companies with international operations should institute a compliance program on a global basis, not just for selective geographic locations. Such programs should reflect appropriate local conditions, laws, and regulations (Practice Advisory 2100-5). Answer (D) is incorrect because the code should be written in a language that all employees can understand, avoiding legalese (Practice Advisory 2100-5).

10. Which of the following is least likely to exemplify a good compliance environment?

   A. An international company that institutes a global compliance program that reflects local conditions, laws, and regulations.

   B. A company that creates an organizational chart, identifying personnel who are responsible for implementing compliance programs.

   C. A company whose code of conduct provides guidance to employees on relevant issues.

   D. A company that rewards employees for charging travel hours, in order to take advantage of the tax benefits.

Answer (D) is correct. *(Publisher)*
REQUIRED: The entity with the poorest compliance environment.
DISCUSSION: Companies using reward systems that attach financial incentives to apparently unethical or illegal behavior can expect a poor compliance environment. For instance, a company rewarding its employees for charging travel hours makes itself vulnerable to fraud. Employees may start charging false travel hours to receive additional rewards. Thus, the tax benefit that the company is trying to take advantage of by offering such an incentive may be negated by fraudulent employee practices. A good compliance environment is created when an organization does the following:

- Develops a written, straightforward business code of conduct that clearly identifies prohibited activities, provides guidance to employees on relevant issues, and decreases the risk that employees will engage in unethical or illegal behavior (Practice Advisory 2100-5).

- Creates an organizational chart identifying board members, senior officers, senior compliance officer, and department personnel who are responsible for implementing compliance programs (Practice Advisory 2100-5).

- Institutes a compliance program on a global basis, not just for selective geographic locations, which reflects appropriate local conditions, laws, and regulations (Practice Advisory 2100-5).

11. The chief compliance officer of an organization should report to

A. The chief executive officer.

B. The chief general counsel.

C. The chief operating officer.

D. The chief audit executive.

Answer (A) is correct. *(Publisher)*
REQUIRED: The supervisor to whom the chief compliance officer reports.
DISCUSSION: It is not enough for a company to create the position of chief compliance officer and to select the rest of the compliance unit. The company should also ensure that these personnel are appropriately empowered and supplied with the resources necessary for carrying out their mission. Furthermore, compliance personnel should have adequate access to senior management. A reporting structure in which the chief compliance officer reports directly to the chief executive officer (CEO) is indicative of this access (Practice Advisory 2100-5).
Answer (B) is incorrect because the chief general counsel, in many organizations, is assigned chief compliance responsibilities. In many companies, however, such a structure may convince employees that management is not committed to the program, and that the program is important only to the legal department. Anyone assigned chief compliance responsibilities should report to the CEO. Answer (C) is incorrect because the chief compliance officer should report to the CEO, not the COO. Answer (D) is incorrect because the chief compliance officer should report to the CEO, not the chief audit executive.

12. An organization should use due care not to delegate substantial discretionary authority to individuals the organization knows have a propensity to engage in illegal activities. Which of the following are steps an organization can take to ensure that such individuals are detected?

I. Screening of applicants for employment at all levels for evidence of past wrongdoing, especially past criminal convictions within the company's industry.

II. Asking professionals about any history of discipline in front of licensing boards.

III. Performing background checks on employees' or applicants' credit reports to ensure that they are financially sound and are unlikely to commit theft or fraud.

A. I only.

B. III only.

C. I and II only.

D. I, II, and III.

Answer (C) is correct. *(Publisher)*
REQUIRED: The due diligence steps an organization can take when hiring individuals.
DISCUSSION: As part of the exercise of due diligence, an organization can take a number of steps to protect itself against individuals who have a propensity to engage in illegal activities. For instance, a company can screen applicants for employment at all levels for evidence of past wrongdoing, especially wrongdoing within the company's industry. Furthermore, it may inquire as to past criminal convictions, and professionals may be asked about any history of discipline in front of licensing boards. Care should be taken, however, to ensure that the company does not infringe upon employees' and applicants' privacy rights under applicable laws, since many jurisdictions have laws limiting the amount of information a company may obtain in performing background checks on employees (Practice Advisory 2100-5).

13. Environmental compliance information and training is most applicable, and should be provided, to which of the following departments?

A. Sales.

B. Human resources.

C. Manufacturing.

D. Information technology.

Answer (C) is correct. *(Publisher)*
REQUIRED: The department to which environmental compliance information and training most applies.
DISCUSSION: When presenting compliance information and training, different sets of employees should be targeted based on areas important to each functional group, and the information should be tailored to that group's job requirements (Practice Advisory 2100-5). Environmental compliance, in this case, is not in reference to the market or information technology environment, but the physical environment. Thus, information regarding environmental compliance is most applicable to the manufacturing department, since this department has an increased likelihood of violating or detecting violations of such laws and regulations.

14. An ombudsperson is most effective when (s)he:

I. Is located on-site.

II. Reports to the chief compliance officer or the board of directors.

III. Is located off-site.

IV. Reports to no one, thus ensuring a whistle blower's secrecy.

    A. II only.

    B. I and II only.

    C. I and IV only.

    D. III and IV only.

Answer (B) is correct. *(Publisher)*
    REQUIRED: The characteristic(s) of an effective ombudsperson.
    DISCUSSION: Use of an ombudsperson is more effective if the ombudsperson is located on-site, reports directory to the chief compliance officer or the board of directors, keeps the names of whistle blowers secret, provides guidance to whistle blowers, and undertakes follow-up review to ensure that retaliation has not occurred. An ombudsperson must report to someone at a high level in the organization that is empowered to initiate a change in organization policies based on the ombudsperson's findings; thus, reporting to no one is not an option. In addition, an ombudsperson's location on-site promotes employee confidence in the ombudsperson.

15. Employees have the most confidence in a hotline monitored by which of the following?

    A. An expert from the legal department, backed by a non-retaliation policy.

    B. An in-house representative, backed by a retaliation policy.

    C. An on-site ombudsperson, backed by a non-retaliation policy.

    D. An off-site attorney who can better protect attorney-client privilege.

Answer (C) is correct. *(Publisher)*
    REQUIRED: The hotline monitor that employees have the most confidence in.
    DISCUSSION: Although an attorney monitoring the hotline is better able to protect attorney-client and work-product privileges, one study observed that employees have little confidence in hotlines answered by the legal department or by an outside service. The same study showed that employees have even less confidence in write-in reports or an off-site ombudsperson, but have the most confidence in hotlines answered by an in-house representative (or an on-site ombudsperson) and backed by a non-retaliation policy.
    Answer (A) is incorrect because employees have little confidence in hotlines answered by the legal department. Answer (B) is incorrect because a retaliation policy would dissuade whistle blowers from coming forth due to concern of possible backlash. Answer (D) is incorrect because employees have little confidence in hotlines monitored by the legal department or by an outside service. Thus, they would have even less confidence in an outside attorney.

16. An internal audit plan should include a review of the organization's compliance program and its procedures, including reviews to determine all but which of the following?

    A. The effectiveness of written materials.

    B. The receipt of communications by employees.

    C. The appropriate handling of detected violations.

    D. The performance of full background checks on employees and new hires.

Answer (D) is correct. *(Publisher)*
    REQUIRED: The review that is not included in an internal audit plan, with regard to the organization's compliance program.
    DISCUSSION: The audit plan should include a review of the organization's compliance program and its procedures, including reviews to determine whether: written materials are effective, communications have been received by employees, detected violations have been appropriately handled, discipline has been even-handed, whistle blowers have not been retaliated against, and the compliance unit has fulfilled its responsibilities. The auditors should review the compliance program to determine whether it can be improved, and should solicit employee input. Moreover, companies should screen applicants for employment at all levels and should inquire as to past criminal convictions, taking care not to infringe upon employees' and applicants' privacy rights. However, a review of the performance of full background checks is not included in an audit plan as part of the review of an organization's compliance program.

17. Which of the following is an effective tool for uncovering unethical or illegal activity in an organization?

    A. The screening of applicants.

    B. The ethics interview.

    C. The background check.

    D. The ethics questionnaire.

Answer (D) is correct. *(Publisher)*
    REQUIRED: The tool used to uncover unethical or illegal activity.
    DISCUSSION: An effective tool for uncovering unethical or illegal activity is the ethics questionnaire. Each employee of the organization should receive a questionnaire that asks whether the employee is aware of kickbacks, bribes or other wrongdoing. To protect privilege, the questionnaire should: be sent by organization counsel; contain a statement that the questionnaire is protected by privilege; require the employee to complete, sign and return the questionnaire without making a copy; and contain a statement that the organization retains the right to disclose information provided to the company to government agencies or in litigation. The questionnaire's instructions should also note that privilege will be lost if the questionnaire is disclosed to outside parties.
    Answer (A) is incorrect because screening applicants for employment is a way to detect past criminal activity and wrongdoing. Thus, it is of no use in uncovering unethical or illegal activity currently ongoing in an organization. Answer (B) is incorrect because an ethics interview may cause discomfort to an employee, and an employee may not believe that the interview is protected by privilege or as confidential as an ethics questionnaire. Answer (C) is incorrect because the background check is a way to detect past wrongdoing, not ongoing or current unethical or illegal activities.

18. Which of the following are forms of punishment for those who violate an organization's code of conduct?

    I. A warning.
    II. Loss of pay.
    III. Suspension.
    IV. Termination.

    A. I and II only.

    B. I, III, and IV only.

    C. I, II, and III only.

    D. I, II, III, and IV.

Answer (D) is correct. *(Publisher)*
    REQUIRED: The forms of punishment for a violation of an organization's code of conduct
    DISCUSSION: Those who violate the organization's code of conduct should receive punishment appropriate to the offense, such as warning, loss of pay, suspension, transfer, or termination. Nevertheless, if an employee is found to have committed some illegal act, the organization might have to terminate that employee, in keeping with the organization's obligation to use "due care not to delegate substantial discretionary authority to individuals whom the organization knew, or should have known through the exercise of due diligence, had a propensity to engage in illegal activities."

19. Termination or other discipline of employees may be limited by all of the following except:

    A. Whistle-blowers laws.

    B. Employer responsibilities with regard to employer good faith doctrines.

    C. Union contracts.

    D. Exceptions to the employee-at-will doctrine.

Answer (B) is correct. *(Publisher)*
    REQUIRED: The item that does not limit the termination or other discipline of employees.
    DISCUSSION: Termination or other discipline of employees may be limited by whistle-blower laws, exceptions to the employee-at-will doctrine, employee or union contracts, and employer responsibilities with regard to discrimination, wrongful discharge, and employer bad faith laws/doctrines.

20. An organization with an effective regulatory compliance program displays which of the following characteristics?

- A. It punishes unethical or illegal activity based on seniority.

- B. It disciplines those who knew of the misconduct and did not report it, and holds harmless those who should have known, but did not know.

- C. After an offense is detected, the organization takes the necessary steps – short of modifying its entire program – to prevent further similar offenses.

- D. It is scrupulous in documenting employee discipline.

Answer (D) is correct. *(Publisher)*
REQUIRED: The characteristics of an organization with an effective regulatory compliance program.
DISCUSSION: Organizations should be scrupulous and thorough in documenting employee discipline. The organization should be able to prove that it made its best efforts to collect information with regard to any incident and took appropriate action based upon the information available.
Answer (A) is incorrect because discipline under the program must be fair. The program has slight chance of succeeding if unethical or illegal activity goes unpunished, especially if tied to the activities of senior management or big producers. Ignored wrongdoing by such persons will encourage wrongful behavior in the rest of the workforce. Answer (B) is incorrect because the program should provide for the discipline of managers and other responsible persons who knew or should have known of misconduct and did not report it. Answer (C) is incorrect because after an offense has been detected, the organization should take all reasonable steps to respond appropriately to the offense and to prevent further similar offenses, including any necessary modifications to its program to prevent and detect violations of law.

21. Which of the following is true regarding appropriate responses to an offense detected by an organization's compliance program?

I. Disciplinary action taken against those engaged in misconduct is an appropriate response.

II. Self-reporting the violation to the government is an appropriate response.

III. Acceptance of responsibility for the violation is an appropriate response.

IV. An appropriate response can lower the amount of an organization's court fines.

- A. I and II only.

- B. I and III only.

- C. I, II, and III only.

- D. I, II, III, and IV.

Answer (D) is correct. *(Publisher)*
REQUIRED: The true statement(s) regarding appropriate responses to an offense detected by an organization's compliance program.
DISCUSSION: An organization should respond appropriately to each offense detected by the compliance program. Appropriate responses include disciplinary action taken with regard to those who engaged in misconduct. In some circumstances, an appropriate response could require self-reporting the violation to the government, cooperation with governmental investigations and the acceptance of responsibility for the violation. Similar to the existence of an effective compliance program, making these responses could result in a court lowering the amount of the organization's fine.

22. Electronic commerce (e-commerce) is generally defined as "conducting commercial activities over the Internet." These commercial activities can be all but which of the following?

- A. Business-to-business.

- B. Business-to-consumer.

- C. Business-to-employee.

- D. Consumer-to-business.

Answer (D) is correct. *(Publisher)*
REQUIRED: The activity that is not considered part of e-commerce.
DISCUSSION: These commercial activities can be business-to-business (B2B), business-to-consumer (B2C), and business-to-employee (B2E). Consumer-to-business is not a commercial activity because it does not originate from a business; therefore, it is not considered part of e-commerce.

23. Which of the following is not a major component of auditing e-commerce activities?

   A. Make certain that goals and objectives can be achieved.

   B. Assess the internal control structure.

   C. Review the interface issues.

   D. Evaluate the business continuity and disaster recovery plans.

Answer (A) is correct. *(Publisher)*
REQUIRED: The item that is not a major component of auditing e-commerce activities.
DISCUSSION: Auditing e-commerce activities should provide reasonable assurance – not ensure or make certain – that goals and objectives can be achieved. This is because there is no way to be absolutely certain that goals and objectives will be achieved. Other major components of auditing e-commerce activities are:

- Assess the internal control structure, including the tone set by senior management,
- Determine if the risks are acceptable,
- Understand the information flow,
- Review the interface issues (such as hardware to hardware, software to software, and hardware to software), and
- Evaluate the business continuity and disaster recovery plans.

24. With regard to an e-commerce project, which of the following will an auditor assess as having the lowest risk?

   A. A project with a business plan that covers the integration of the planning, design, and implementation of the e-commerce system with the strategies of the organization.

   B. A project with a business plan that considers governmental and regulatory requirements, and other external factors in its risk assessment.

   C. A project with a business plan that calls for using outside vendors to provide hosting services.

   D. A project with a business plan that addresses the security of the software and the accuracy of transaction processing.

Answer (A) is correct. *(Publisher)*
REQUIRED: The item, with regard to an e-commerce project, that an auditor is likely to assess as having the lowest risk.
DISCUSSION: The following are a few issues that an internal auditor should consider when undertaking an e-commerce engagement and assessing risks:

- Is there a business plan for the e-commerce project or program?
- Does the plan cover the integration of the planning, design, and implementation of the e-commerce system with the strategies of the organization?
- Have governmental and regulatory requirements been analyzed and considered?
- How secure is the hardware and software, and will they prevent or detect unauthorized access, inappropriate use, and other harmful effects and losses?
- Will transaction processing be current, accurate, complete, and indisputable?
- Does the risk assessment include internal and external forces?
- If outside vendors are used, has a "going concern" evaluation been conducted by a trusted third party who is qualified to certify the vendor?
- If vendors provide hosting services, do they have a tested business contingency plan? Have they provided a recent SAS-70 report? Also, have privacy issues been resolved?

Based on how well the e-commerce project addresses these questions, the project likely to receive the lowest risk assessment is one that has a business plan that covers the integration of the planning, design, and implementation of the e-commerce system with the strategies of the organization.
Answer (B) is incorrect because the project's business plan should include internal forces in its risk assessment, in addition to external forces, for it to be considered low risk. Answer (C) is incorrect because the use of outside vendors will increase the risk of an e-commerce project, unless assessments such as a "going concern" evaluation have been conducted by a trusted third party who is qualified to certify the vendor, the vendor has a tested business contingency plan, the vendor has provided a recent SAS-70 report, etc. Answer (D) is incorrect because a project's business plan should address hardware security in addition to software security. Moreover, the plan should not only ensure that transaction processing is accurate, but it should also make certain that a processed transaction is current, complete, and indisputable.

25. With regard to e-commerce, risk is best defined as

    A. The uncertainty of an event occurring that could have a negative impact on the achievement of objectives.

    B. The uncertainty of an event occurring that could positively impact management's ability to safeguard organizational assets.

    C. The uncertainty of an event occurring that could have a positive impact on the achievement of objectives.

    D. The uncertainty of an event occurring that could have an impact on the effective and efficient use of an organization's resources.

Answer (A) is correct. *(Publisher)*
    REQUIRED: The best definition of risk, with regard to e-commerce.
    DISCUSSION: The e-commerce risk and control environment is complex and evolving. Risk can be defined as the uncertainty of an event occurring that could have a negative impact on the achievement of objectives.
    Answer (B) is incorrect because management's objective to safeguard organizational assets is just one of the many management objectives. Answer (C) is incorrect because the impact on the achievement of objectives should be negative, not positive. Answer (D) is incorrect because, although the effective and efficient use of organizational resources is a valid objective, the impact of the uncertain event upon this objective is not strictly negative.

26. Which of the following is not one of the seven elements of risk?

    A. Frequency.

    B. Timing.

    C. ROI analysis.

    D. Uncertainty.

Answer (B) is correct. *(Publisher)*
    REQUIRED: The item that is not one of the seven risk elements.
    DISCUSSION: The seven elements of risk include threat events, single loss exposure value, frequency, uncertainty, safeguards and controls, safeguard and control costs, and cost/benefit or ROI analysis. Timing, which is not a risk element, is when a risk may occur. It is different from frequency, which is how often an uncertain event might occur.

27. Which of the following are elements of risk management and mitigation?

    I. Threat events and cost/benefit analysis.
    II. Safeguards, controls, and ROI analysis.
    III. Frequency and uncertainty.
    IV. Safeguard and control costs.

    A. I only.

    B. II only.

    C. I and III only.

    D. II and IV only.

Answer (D) is correct. *(Publisher)*
    REQUIRED: The risk elements that are part of risk management and mitigation.
    DISCUSSION: The elements relating to risk management and mitigation include safeguards and controls, safeguard and control costs, and cost/benefit or ROI analysis. The other elements of risk–threat events, single loss exposure value, frequency, and uncertainty–comprise risk identification and quantification.

28. Which of the following questions is best associated with the safeguards and controls risk element?

A. What could happen that would adversely affect the organization's ability to achieve its objectives and execute its strategies?

B. What can be done to prevent and avoid, mitigate, and detect risks and provide notification?

C. What is the potential financial impact of the occurrence of an uncertain event?

D. How often might an uncertain event occur?

Answer (B) is correct. *(Publisher)*
REQUIRED: The question that best incorporates the safeguards and controls risk element.
DISCUSSION: For the purposes of management, there are seven key questions that can serve to identify organizational risk and target potential ways to control or mitigate the exposures. These questions, along with the risk elements associated with them (in brackets), include the following:

● What could happen that would adversely affect the organization's ability to achieve its objectives and execute its strategies? [Threat Events]
● If it happens, what is the potential financial impact? [Single Loss Exposure Value]
● How often might it happen? [Frequency]
● How probable are the answers to the first three questions? [Uncertainty]
● What can be done to prevent and avoid, mitigate, and detect risks and provide notification? [Safeguards and Controls]
● How much will it cost? [Safeguard and Control Costs]
● How efficient would that be? [Cost/Benefit or ROI Analysis]

Answer (A) is incorrect because it is a key question associated with the threat events element of risk. Answer (C) is incorrect because it is a key question associated with the single loss exposure value element of risk. Answer (D) is incorrect because it is a key question associated with the frequency element of risk.

29. Which of the following are critical risk and control issues that an internal auditor must address?

I. Rapid technology changes.
II. Maintenance of transaction integrity.
III. Website content review and approval.
IV. Changes to organizational structures.

A. I and II only.
B. I and III only.
C. II and III only.
D. I, II, III, and IV.

Answer (D) is correct. *(Publisher)*
REQUIRED: The critical risk and control issues that an internal auditor must address.
DISCUSSION: Some of the more critical risk and control issues to be addressed by the internal auditor are:

● General project management risks.
● Specific security threats, such as denial of service, physical attacks, viruses, identity theft, and unauthorized access or disclosure of data.
● Maintenance of transaction integrity under a complex network of links to legacy systems and data warehouses.
● Website content review and approval when there are frequent changes and sophisticated customer features and capabilities that offer around-the-clock service.
● Rapid technology changes.
● Legal issues, such as increasing regulations throughout the world to protect individual privacy; enforceability of contracts outside of the organization's country; and tax and accounting issues.
● Changes to surrounding business processes and organizational structures.

30. A decision not to participate in e-commerce should be carefully analyzed, documented, and approved by whom?

A. The chief audit executive.
B. The chief executive officer.
C. The governing board.
D. The audit committee.

Answer (C) is correct. *(Publisher)*
REQUIRED: The entity responsible for analyzing, documenting, and approving e-commerce initiatives.
DISCUSSION: The overall audit objective should be to ensure that all e-commerce processes have effective internal controls. Management of e-commerce initiatives should be documented in a strategic plan that is well developed and approved. If there is a decision not to participate in e-commerce, that decision should be carefully analyzed, documented, and approved by the governing board.

31. Security of monetary transactions is one example of an audit objective for an e-commerce engagement. Which of the following is not an audit objective for an e-commerce engagement?

    A. Effective use and control of digital signatures.

    B. Adequacy and timeliness of operating data and information.

    C. Effectiveness of customer authentication process.

    D. Appropriateness of reporting lines.

Answer (D) is correct. *(Publisher)*
    REQUIRED: The item that is not an audit objective for an e-commerce engagement.
    DISCUSSION: Audit objectives for an e-commerce engagement may include:

- Evidence of e-commerce transactions
- Availability and reliability of security system
- Effective interface between e-commerce and financial systems
- Security of monetary transactions
- Effectiveness of customer authentication process
- Adequacy of business continuity processes, including the resumption of operations
- Compliance with common security standards
- Effective use and control of digital signatures
- Adequacy of systems, policies, and procedures to control Public Key Certificates (using public key cryptographic techniques)
- Adequacy and timeliness of operating data and information
- Documented evidence of an effective system of internal control

32. The details of the audit program used to audit e-commerce activities in specific organizations will vary depending on all but which of the following factors?

    A. Industry.

    B. Organizational culture.

    C. Country.

    D. Legal and business models.

Answer (B) is correct. *(Publisher)*
    REQUIRED: The factor upon which the details of the audit program used to audit e-commerce activities are not dependent.
    DISCUSSION: The details of the audit program used to audit e-commerce activities in specific organizations will vary depending on industry, country, and legal and business models.

33. Tools that should be in place to prevent corruption of data include.

I. Monitoring software
II. Change controls
III. Trend analysis
IV. Automatic timeout

    A. I and III only.

    B. II, III, and IV only.

    C. I, III, and IV only.

    D. I, II, III, and IV.

Answer (D) is correct. *(Publisher)*
    REQUIRED: The tools that should be in place to prevent the corruption of data.
    DISCUSSION: The internal auditor should evaluate controls over data integrity in order to prevent the corruption of data. Tools that should be in place in order to ensure data integrity include intrusion management (monitoring software, automatic timeout, and trend analysis), physical security for e-commerce servers, change controls, and reconciliation.

34. Which of the following e-commerce audit protocol items relates to the area of fraud?

    A. Segregation of duties.

    B. Inadequacies in interfacing between e-commerce and financial management systems.

    C. Examination of service level agreements between buyer, supplier, and certification authority.

    D. Denial of orders placed or received, goods received, or payments made.

Answer (D) is correct.   *(Publisher)*
REQUIRED: The e-commerce audit protocol item that relates to the area of fraud.
DISCUSSION: With regard to the e-commerce audit protocol in the area of fraud, the internal auditor should be alert for the following conditions:

- Unauthorized movement of money (e.g., transfers to jurisdictions where the recovery of funds would be difficult).
- Duplication of payments.
- Denial of orders placed or received, goods received, or payments made.
- Exception reports and procedures, and effectiveness of the follow up.
- Digital signatures: Are they used for all transactions? Who authorizes them? Who has access to them?
- Protections against viruses and hacking activities (history file, use of tools).
- Access rights: Are they reviewed regularly? Are they promptly revised when staff members are changed?
- History of interception of transactions by unauthorized persons.

Answer (A) is incorrect because segregation of duties is an e-commerce audit protocol in the area of authentication, which includes reviewing the policies for authenticating transactions and evaluating controls. Answer (B) is incorrect because inadequacies in interfacing between e-commerce and financial management systems is an e-commerce audit protocol in the area of business interruptions, which includes reviewing the business continuity plan and determining if it has been tested. Answer (C) is incorrect because examination of service level agreements between buyer, supplier, and certification authority has to do with the area of e-commerce organization.

35. Based on the facts given, which of the following carries the least environmental, health, and safety risk?

    A. A malfunction at a nuclear plant that causes a blackout and results in a loss of public confidence.

    B. A chemical plant that disposes of waste in a nearby river.

    C. A hydroelectric power plant that is located several miles from a small town.

    D. A skyscraper construction site that has had several mishaps, including injuries and death.

Answer (C) is correct.   *(Publisher)*
REQUIRED: The item that poses the least environmental, health, and safety risk.
DISCUSSION: The Chief Audit Executive (CAE) should include the environmental, health, and safety (EH&S) risks in any entity-wide risk management assessment and assess the activities in a balanced manner relative to other types of risk associated with an entity's operations. Among the risk exposures that should be evaluated are: organizational reporting structures; likelihood of causing environmental harm, fines and penalties; expenditures mandated by the Environmental Protection Agency (EPA) or other governmental agencies; history of injuries and deaths; record of losses of customers, and episodes of negative publicity and loss of public image and reputation. As such, based on the risk exposures mentioned, a hydroelectric plant that is located several miles from a small town poses the least EH&S risk.

Answer (A) is incorrect because the blackout risks exposing the plant to negative publicity and a loss of public image and reputation. Answer (B) is incorrect because the disposal of chemical waste into a river increases the likelihood of causing environmental harm, fines, and penalties. Answer (D) is incorrect because the construction site is exposed to risk due to its history of injuries and death.

36. Access to EH&S audit information is severely restricted by all but which of the following classifications?

- A. Attorney-client privilege.
- B. Accountant-client privilege.
- C. Attorney work product.
- D. Closely held.

Answer (B) is correct. *(Publisher)*
REQUIRED: The item that limits access to EH&S audit information.
DISCUSSION: Audit information is often classified as either (a) attorney-client privilege or attorney work product, (b) secret and confidential, or (c) if not confidential, then closely held. This results in severely restricted access to EH&S audit information. The accountant-client privilege, which is not one of the aforementioned classifications, does not limit access to EH&S audit information.

37. Which of the following are key objectives of a risk management process?

I. Risks arising from business strategies and activities are identified and prioritized.

II. Ongoing monitoring activities are conducted to periodically reassess risk and the effectiveness of controls to manage risk.

III. Review of previous risk evaluation reports by management, internal auditors, external auditors, and any other sources that may have issued such reports.

- A. I and II only.
- B. I and III only.
- C. II and III only.
- D. I, II, and III.

Answer (A) is correct. *(Publisher)*
REQUIRED: The items that are key objectives of a risk management process.
DISCUSSION: Internal auditors must determine that the organization's risk management processes address five key objectives to formulate an opinion on the overall adequacy of the risk management processes. The five key objectives of a risk management process are:

- Risks arising from business strategies and activities are identified and prioritized.
- Management and the board have determined the level of risks acceptable to the organization, including the acceptance of risks designed to accomplish the organization's strategic plans.
- Risk mitigation activities are designed and implemented to reduce, or otherwise manage, risk at levels that were determined to be acceptable to management and the board.
- Ongoing monitoring activities are conducted to periodically reassess risk and the effectiveness of controls to manage risk.
- The board and management receive periodic reports of the results of the risk management processes. The corporate governance processes of the organization should provide periodic communication of risks, risk strategies, and controls to stakeholders.

38. A comprehensive plan to deal with business interruptions will provide for all but which of the following?

- A. Segregation of duties.
- B. Alternative site facilities.
- C. Business impact assessments.
- D. Procedures for restoring utility services.

Answer (A) is correct. *(Publisher)*
REQUIRED: The item that is not included in a comprehensive plan to deal with business interruptions.
DISCUSSION: Auditors should evaluate the organization's readiness to deal with business interruptions. A comprehensive plan would provide for emergency response procedures, alternative communication systems and site facilities, information systems backup, disaster recovery, business impact assessments and resumption plans, procedures for restoring utility services, and maintenance procedures for ensuring the readiness of the organization in the event of an emergency or disaster. Segregation of duties, however, is an audit protocol item in the authentication key area of an audit program.

39. Internal auditors can play a role in an organization's planning for business continuity and disaster recovery. Which of the following is a way in which the internal audit activity helps with the planning phase of a business continuity or disaster recovery plan?

A. Assessing an organization's internal and external environment during the plan formulation process, including the turnover of management, changes in market conditions, and changes in controls.

B. Examining the plan to determine that it reflects the operations that have been included and evaluated in the risk assessment process and contains sufficient internal control concerns and prescriptions.

C. Verifying the adequacy of the plan to ensure the timely resumption of operations and processes after adverse circumstances.

D. Examining the plan to determine whether it is structured to incorporate important changes that could take place over time.

Answer (A) is correct. *(Publisher)*
REQUIRED: The item that is an internal audit activity in the planning phase of a business continuity or disaster recovery plan.
DISCUSSION: Organizations rely upon internal auditors for analysis of operations and assessment of risk management and control processes. Internal auditors acquire an understanding of the overall business operations, the individual functions, and how they interrelate with one another. This positions the internal audit activity as a valuable resource in evaluating the disaster recovery plan during its formulation process. Internal audit activity can help with an assessment of an organization's internal and external environment. Internal factors that may be considered include the turnover of management and changes in information systems, controls, and major projects and programs. External factors may include changes in outside regulatory and business environment and changes in markets and competitive conditions, international financial and economic conditions, and technologies.
Answer (B) is incorrect because it is an internal audit activity in the evaluation phase of a business continuity or disaster recovery plan. Answers (C) and (D) are incorrect because they are part of the internal audit activity's periodic assurance engagements phase of a business continuity or disaster recovery plan.

40. The governance process is also referred to as the way in which an organization chooses to conduct its affairs to meet four key responsibilities. Which of the following is a part of those responsibilities?

I.   Complying with society's legal and regulatory rules.

II. Satisfying the generally accepted business norms of society.

III. Providing overall benefit to society and enhancing the interests of the specific stakeholders.

IV. Reporting fully and truthfully to its owners, regulators, other stakeholders, and the general public.

A. I and II only.

B. II and IV only.

C. I, III, and IV only.

D. I, II, III, and IV.

Answer (D) is correct. *(Publisher)*
REQUIRED: The four key responsibilities of an organization that make up its governance process.
DISCUSSION: An organization uses various legal forms, structures, strategies, and procedures to ensure that it:

● Complies with society's legal and regulatory rules.
● Satisfies the generally accepted business norms, ethical precepts, and social expectations of society.
● Provides overall benefit to society and enhances the interests of the specific stakeholders in both the long- and short-term.
● Reports fully and truthfully to its owners, regulators, other stakeholders, and general public to ensure accountability for its decisions, actions, conduct, and performance.

The way in which an organization chooses to conduct its affairs to meet those four responsibilities is commonly referred to as its governance process.

Use Gleim's *CIA Test Prep* for interactive testing with over 2,000 additional multiple-choice questions!

STUDY UNIT FIVE
CONTROL I

(20 pages of outline)

Governance, risk, and control are interrelated concepts that are fundamental to the field of internal auditing and the work of internal auditors. Study Unit 4 primarily addressed risk management and governance. Study Units 5 and 6 relate to control.

The definition of internal auditing includes helping an organization accomplish its objectives by bringing a systematic, disciplined approach to evaluating and improving the effectiveness of risk management, control, and governance processes. The **Glossary** appended to the Standards defines **control** as follows:

> Any action taken by management, the board, and other parties to enhance risk management and increase the likelihood that established objectives and goals will be achieved. Management plans, organizes, and directs the performance of sufficient actions to provide reasonable assurance that objectives and goals will be achieved.

Practice Advisory 2100-1 provides another definition of control:

> Control is any action taken by management to enhance the likelihood that established objectives and goals will be achieved. Controls may be preventive (to deter undesirable events from occurring), detective (to detect and correct undesirable events that have occurred), or directive (to cause or encourage a desirable event to occur). The concept of a system of control is the integrated collection of control components and activities that are used by an organization to achieve its objectives and goals.

The definition in Practice Advisory 2100-1 describes three categories of controls. When such controls are absent or are too costly relative to their benefits, mitigating (compensating) controls should be in place. Examples are supervisory review when segregation of duties (a preventive control) is not feasible or monitoring of budget variances in the absence of transaction processing controls.

The first subunit of Study Unit 5 concerns The IIA's approach to control. Study Unit 5 then continues with a description of a systems approach to control and an outline from the internal auditing perspective of the means of achieving control. Study Unit 6 will address approaches to control by entities other than The IIA.

5.1 CONTROL PRONOUNCEMENTS

1. Pronouncements specifically pertaining to control include one General Performance Standard, one Specific Performance Standard, four Assurance Implementation Standards, two Consulting Implementation Standards, and three Practice Advisories. Furthermore, the Practice Advisories related to Standard 2100 and the Standards and Practice Advisories related to risk management and governance processes presented in Study Unit 4 are especially relevant.

2100   *Nature of Work — The internal audit activity evaluates and contributes to the improvement of risk management, control, and governance systems.*

> **2120**   *Control — The internal audit activity should assist the organization in maintaining effective controls by evaluating their effectiveness and efficiency and by promoting continuous improvement.*
>
> **2120.A1** – *Based on the results of the risk assessment, the internal audit activity should evaluate the adequacy and effectiveness of controls encompassing the organization's governance, operations, and information systems. This should include:*
>
> - *Reliability and integrity of financial and operational information.*
> - *Effectiveness and efficiency of operations.*
> - *Safeguarding of assets.*
> - *Compliance with laws, regulations, and contracts.*

Practice Advisory 2120.A1-1: Assessing and Reporting on Control Processes

1. *One of the tasks of a board of directors is to establish and maintain the organization's governance processes and obtain assurances concerning the effectiveness of the risk management and control processes. Senior management's role is to oversee the establishment, administration, and assessment of that system of risk management and control processes. The purpose of that multifaceted system of control processes is to support people of the organization in the management of risks and the achievement of the established and communicated objectives of the enterprise. More specifically, those control processes are expected to ensure, among other things, that the following conditions exist:*

    - *Financial and operational information is reliable and possesses integrity.*
    - *Operations are performed efficiently and achieve effective results.*
    - *Assets are safeguarded.*
    - *Actions and decisions of the organization are in compliance with laws, regulations, and contracts.*

2. *Among the responsibilities of the organization's managers is the assessment of the control processes in their respective areas. Internal and external auditors provide varying degrees of assurance about the state of effectiveness of the risk management and control processes in select activities and functions of the organization.*

3. *Senior management and the audit committee normally expect that the chief audit executive will perform sufficient engagement work and gather other available information during the year so as to form a judgment about the adequacy and effectiveness of the control processes. The chief audit executive should communicate that overall judgment about the organization's system of controls to senior management and the audit committee. A growing number of organizations have included a management's report on the system of internal controls in their annual or periodic reports to external stakeholders.*

4. The chief audit executive should develop a proposed engagement plan for the coming year that ensures that sufficient information will be obtained to evaluate the effectiveness of the control processes. The plan should call for engagements or other procedures to gather relevant information about all major operating units and business functions. The engagement plan should also give special consideration to those operations most affected by recent or expected changes. Those changes in circumstances may result from marketplace or investment conditions, acquisitions and divestitures, or restructures and new ventures. The proposed plan should be flexible so that adjustments may be made during the year as a result of changes in management strategies, external conditions, or revised expectations about achieving the organization's objectives.

5. In determining the proposed engagement plan, the chief audit executive should consider relevant work that will be performed by others. To minimize duplication and inefficiencies, the work planned or recently completed by management in its assessments of controls and quality improvement processes as well as the work planned by the external auditors should be considered in determining the expected coverage of the audit plan for the coming year.

6. Finally, the chief audit executive should evaluate the coverage of the proposed plan from two viewpoints: adequacy across organizational entities and inclusion of a variety of transaction and business-process types. If the scope of the proposed engagement plan is insufficient to enable the expression of assurance about the organization's control processes, the chief audit executive should inform senior management and the audit committee of the expected deficiency, its causes, and the probable consequences.

7. The challenge for the internal audit activity is to evaluate the effectiveness of the organization's system of controls based on the aggregation of many individual assessments. Those assessments are largely gained from internal auditing engagements, management's self assessments, and external auditor's work. As the engagements progress, internal auditors should communicate, on a timely basis, the observations to the appropriate levels of management so that prompt action can be taken to correct or mitigate the consequences of discovered control discrepancies or weaknesses.

8. Three key considerations in reaching an evaluation of the overall effectiveness of the organization's control processes are:

    • Were significant discrepancies or weaknesses discovered from the audit work performed and other assessment information gathered?
    • If so, were corrections or improvements made after the discoveries?
    • Do the discoveries and their consequences lead to the conclusion that a pervasive condition exists resulting in an unacceptable level of business risk?

    The temporary existence of a significant control discrepancy or weakness does not necessarily lead to the judgment that it is pervasive and poses an unacceptable residual risk. The pattern of discoveries, degree of intrusion, and level of consequences and exposures are factors to be considered in determining whether the effectiveness of the whole system of controls is jeopardized and unacceptable risks exist. The report of the chief audit executive on the state of the organization's control processes should be presented, usually once a year, to senior management and the audit committee.

9.   The report should emphasize the critical role played by the control processes in the quest to achieve the organization's objectives, and it should refer to major work performed by internal audit and to other important sources of information that were used to formulate the overall assurance judgment. The opinion section of the report is normally expressed in terms of negative assurance; that is, the engagement work performed for the period and other information gathered did not disclose any significant weaknesses in the control processes that have a pervasive effect. If the control deficiencies or weaknesses are significant and pervasive, the assurance section of the report may be a qualified or adverse opinion, depending on the projected increase in the level of residual risk and its impact on the organization's objectives.

10.   The target audiences for the annual report are senior executives and audit committee members. Because these readers have divergent understandings of auditing and business, the chief audit executive's annual report should be clear, concise, and informative. It should be composed and edited to be understandable by them and targeted to meet their informational needs. Its value to these readers can be enhanced by including major recommendations for improvement and information about current control issues and trends, such as technology and information security exposures, patterns of control discrepancies or weaknesses across business units, and potential difficulties in complying with laws or regulations.

11.   Ample evidence exists of an "expectation gap" surrounding the internal audit activity's work in evaluating and providing assurance about the state of control processes. One such gap exists between management and the audit committee's normally high expectations about the value of internal auditing services and the internal auditor's more modest expectations that derive from knowledge of practical limitations on audit coverage and from self-doubt about generating sufficient evidence to support an informed and objective judgment. The chief audit executive should be mindful of the possible gap between what is presumed by the report reader and what actually happened during the year. He or she should use the report as another way to address different mental models and to suggest improving the capacity of the function or reducing the constraints to access and audit effectiveness.

Practice Advisory 2120.A1-2: Using Control Self-Assessment for Assessing the Adequacy of Control Processes

1.   Senior management is charged with overseeing the establishment, administration, and evaluation of the processes of risk management and control. Operating managers' responsibilities include assessment of the risks and controls in their units. Internal and external auditors provide varying degrees of assurance about the state of effectiveness of the risk management and control processes of the organization. Both managers and auditors have an interest in using techniques and tools that sharpen the focus and expand the efforts to assess risk management and control processes that are in place and to identify ways to improve their effectiveness.

2.   *A methodology encompassing self-assessment surveys and facilitated-workshops called CSA is a useful and efficient approach for managers and internal auditors to collaborate in assessing and evaluating control procedures. In its purest form, CSA integrates business objectives and risks with control processes. Control self-assessment is also referred to as "control/risk self-assessment" or "CRSA." Although CSA practitioners use a number of differing techniques and formats, most implemented programs share some key features and goals. An organization that uses self-assessment will have a formal, documented process that allows management and work teams, who are directly involved in a business unit, function, or process to participate in a structured manner for the purpose of:*

- *Identifying risks and exposures.*
- *Assessing the control processes that mitigate or manage those risks.*
- *Developing action plans to reduce risks to acceptable levels.*
- *Determining the likelihood of achieving the business objectives.*

3.   *The outcomes that may be derived from self-assessment methodologies are:*

- *People in the business units become trained and experienced in assessing risks and associating control processes with managing those risks and improving the chances of achieving business objectives.*
- *Informal, "soft" controls are more easily identified and evaluated.*
- *People are motivated to take "ownership" of the control processes in their units and corrective actions taken by the work teams are often more effective and timely.*
- *The entire objectives-risks-controls infrastructure of an organization is subject to greater monitoring and continuous improvement.*
- *Internal auditors become involved in and knowledgeable about the self-assessment process by serving as facilitators, scribes, and reporters for the work teams and as trainers of risk and control concepts supporting the CSA program.*
- *Internal audit activity acquires more information about the control processes within the organization and can leverage that additional information in allocating their scarce resources so as to spend a greater effort in investigating and performing tests of business units or functions that have significant control weaknesses or high residual risks.*
- *Management's responsibility for the risk management and control processes of the organization is reinforced, and managers will be less tempted to abdicate those activities to specialists, such as auditors.*
- *The primary role of the internal audit activity will continue to include the validation of the evaluation process by performing tests and the expression of its professional judgment on the adequacy and effectiveness of the whole risk management and control systems.*

4.   *The wide variety of approaches used for CSA processes in organizations reflects the differences in industry, geography, structure, organizational culture, degree of employee empowerment, dominant management style, and the manner of formulating strategies and policies. That observation suggests that the success of a particular type of CSA program in one enterprise may not be replicated in another organization. The CSA process should be customized to fit the unique characteristics of each organization. Also, it suggests that a CSA approach needs to be dynamic and change with the continual development of the organization.*

5.   The three primary forms of CSA programs are facilitated team workshops, surveys, and management-produced analysis. Organizations often combine more than one approach.

6.   Facilitated team workshops gather information from work teams representing different levels in the business unit or function. The format of the workshop may be based on objectives, risks, controls, or processes.

- Objective-based format focuses on the best way to accomplish a business objective. The workshop begins by identifying the controls presently in place to support the objective and, then, determining the residual risks remaining. The aim of the workshop is to decide whether the control procedures are working effectively and are resulting in residual risks within an acceptable level.

- Risk-based format focuses on listing the risks to achieving an objective. The workshop begins by listing all possible barriers, obstacles, threats, and exposures that might prevent achieving an objective and, then, examining the control procedures to determine if they are sufficient to manage the key risks. The aim of the workshop is to determine significant residual risks. This format takes the work team through the entire objective-risks-controls formula.

- Control-based format focuses on how well the controls in place are working. This format is different than the two above because the facilitator identifies the key risks and controls before the beginning of the workshop. During the workshop, the work team assesses how well the controls mitigate risks and promote the achievement of objectives. The aim of the workshop is to produce an analysis of the gap between how controls are working and how well management expects those controls to work.

- Process-based format focuses on selected activities that are elements of a chain of processes. The processes are usually a series of related activities that go from some beginning point to an end, such as, the various steps in purchasing, product development, or revenue generation. This type of workshop usually covers the identification of the objectives of the whole process and the various intermediate steps. The aim of the workshop is to evaluate, update, validate, improve, and even streamline the whole process and its component activities. This workshop format may have a greater breadth of analysis than a control-based approach by covering multiple objectives within the process and by supporting concurrent management efforts, such as, reengineering, quality improvement, and continuous improvement initiatives.

7.   The survey form of CSA utilizes a questionnaire that tends to ask mostly simple "Yes-No" or "Have-Have Not" questions that are carefully written to be understood by the target recipients. Surveys are often used if the desired respondents are too numerous or widely dispersed to participate in a workshop. They are also preferred if the culture in the organization may hinder open, candid discussions in workshop settings or if management desires to minimize the time spent and costs incurred in gathering the information.

8. The form of self-assessment called "management-produced analyses" covers most other approaches by management groups to produce information about selected business processes, risk management activities, and control procedures. The analysis is often intended to reach an informed and timely judgment about specific characteristics of control procedures and is commonly prepared by a team in staff or support role. The internal auditor may synthesize this analysis with other information to enhance the understanding about controls and to share the knowledge with managers in business or functional units as part of the organization's CSA program.

9. All self-assessment programs assume that managers and members of the work teams possess an understanding of risks and controls concepts and using those concepts in communications. For training sessions, to facilitate the orderly flow of workshop discussions and as a check on the completeness of the overall process, organizations often use a control framework, such as the COSO (Committee of Sponsoring Organizations) and CoCo (Canadian Criteria of Control Board) models.

10. In the typical CSA facilitated workshop, a report will be largely created during the deliberations. A group consensus will be recorded for the various segments of the discussions, and the group will review the proposed final report before the end of the final session. Some programs will use anonymous voting techniques to ensure the free flow of information and viewpoints during the workshops and to aid in negotiating differences between viewpoints and interest groups.

11. Internal audit's investment in some CSA programs is fairly significant. It may sponsor, design, implement and, in effect, own the process; conduct the training; supply the facilitators, scribes, and reporters; and orchestrate the participation of management and work teams. In other CSA programs, internal audit's involvement is minimal, serving as interested party and consultant of the whole process and as ultimate verifier of the evaluations produced by the teams. In most programs, internal audit's investment in the organization's CSA efforts is somewhere between the two extremes described above. As the level of internal audit's involvement in the CSA program and individual workshop deliberations increases, the chief audit executive should monitor the objectivity of the internal audit staff, take steps to manage that objectivity (if necessary), and augment internal audit testing to ensure that bias or partiality do not affect the final judgments of the staff. Standard 1120 states: "Internal auditors should have an impartial, unbiased attitude and avoid conflicts of interest."

12. A CSA program augments the traditional role of internal audit activity by assisting management in fulfilling its responsibilities to establish and maintain risk management and control processes and to evaluate the adequacy of that system. Through a CSA program, the internal audit activity and the business units and functions collaborate to produce better information about how well the control processes are working and how significant the residual risks are.

13. Although providing staff support for the CSA program as facilitator and specialist, the internal audit activity often finds that it may reduce the effort spent in gathering information about control procedures and eliminate some testing. A CSA program should increase the coverage of assessing control processes across the organization, improve the quality of corrective actions made by the process owners, and focus internal audit's work on reviewing high-risk processes and unusual situations. It can focus on validating the evaluation conclusions produced by the CSA process, synthesizing the information gathered from the components of the organization, and expressing its overall judgment about the effectiveness of controls to senior management and the audit committee.

Practice Advisory 2120.A1-3: Internal Audit's Role in Quarterly Financial Reporting, Disclosures, and Management Certifications

1.   The strength of all financial markets depends on investor confidence. Events involving allegations of misdeeds by corporate executives, independent auditors and other market participants have undermined that confidence. In response to this threat, the U.S. Congress and a growing number of legislative bodies and regulatory agencies in other countries passed legislation and regulations affecting corporate disclosures and financial reporting. Specifically, in the U.S., the Sarbanes-Oxley Act of 2002 (the "Sarbanes-Oxley Act") enacted sweeping reform requiring additional disclosures and certifications of financial statements by principal executive and financial officers.

2.   The new law challenges companies to devise processes that will permit senior officers to acquire the necessary assurances on which to base their personal certification. A key component of the certification process is the management of risk and internal controls over the recording and summarizing of financial information.

New Statutory Requirements

3.   Section 302 of the Sarbanes-Oxley Act outlines the corporate responsibility for financial reports and the SEC has issued guidance to implement the act. As adopted, SEC Rules 13a-14 and 15d-14 require an issuer's principal executive officer or officers and the principal financial officer or officers, or persons performing similar functions, to certify in each quarterly and annual report, including transition reports, filed or submitted by the issuer under Section 13(a) or 15(d) of the Exchange Act that:

   - He or she has reviewed the report;
   - Based on his or her knowledge, the report does not contain any untrue statement of a material fact or omit a material fact necessary to make a statement, in light of the circumstances under which such statements are made, not misleading with respect to the period covered by the report;
   - Based on his or her knowledge, the financial statements, and other financial information included in the report, fairly present in all material respects the financial condition, results of operations and cash flows of the issuer as of, and for, the periods presented in the report;
   - He or she and the other certifying officers:
      - Are responsible for establishing and maintaining "disclosure controls and procedures" (a newly-defined term reflecting the concept of controls and procedures related to disclosure embodied in Section 302(a)(4) of the Act) for the issuer;
      - Have designed such disclosure controls and procedures to ensure that material information is made known to them, particularly during the period in which the periodic report is being prepared;
      - Have evaluated the effectiveness of the issuer's disclosure controls and procedures as of a date within 90 days prior to the filing date of the report; and
      - Have presented in the report their conclusions about the effectiveness of the disclosure controls and procedures based on the required evaluation as of that date;

- • *He or she and the other certifying officers have disclosed to the issuer's auditors and to the audit committee of the board of directors (or persons fulfilling the equivalent function):*

  - ■ *All significant deficiencies in the design or operation of internal controls (a pre-existing term relating to internal controls regarding financial reporting) which could adversely affect the issuer's ability to record, process, summarize and report financial data and have identified for the issuer's auditors any material weaknesses in internal controls; and*

  - ■ *Any fraud, whether or not material, that involves management or other employees who have a significant role in the issuer's internal controls; and*

  - ■ *Whether or not there were significant changes in internal controls or in other factors that could significantly affect internal controls subsequent to the date of their evaluation, including any corrective actions with regard to significant deficiencies and material weaknesses.*

Recommended Actions for Internal Auditors

4. *The following actions and considerations are offered to internal auditors as value-added services that can be provided regarding quarterly financial reports, disclosures, and management certifications related to requirements of the SEC and the Sarbanes-Oxley Act. These recommended actions are also offered as best practices to non-publicly held companies and other organizations seeking to adopt similar processes over quarterly financial reporting.*

   a. *The internal auditor's role in such processes may range from initial designer of the process, participant on a disclosure committee, coordinator or liaison between management and its auditors, to independent assessor of the process.*

   b. *All internal auditors involved in quarterly reporting and disclosure processes should have a clearly defined role and evaluate responsibilities with appropriate IIA Consulting and Assurance Standards, and with guidance contained in related Practice Advisories.*

   c. *Internal auditors should ensure that organizations have a formal policy and documented procedures to govern processes for quarterly financial reports, related disclosures and regulatory reporting requirements. Appropriate review of any policies and procedures by attorneys, external auditors, and other experts can offer additional comfort that policies and procedures are comprehensive and accurately reflect applicable requirements.*

   d. *Internal auditors should encourage organizations to establish a "disclosure committee" to coordinate the process and provide oversight to participants. Representatives from key areas of the organization should be represented on the committee, including key financial managers, legal counsel, risk management, internal audit, and any area providing input or data for the regulatory filings and disclosures. Normally the chief audit executive (CAE) should be a member of the disclosure committee. Consideration should be given to CAEs status on the committee. CAEs who serve as committee chairs or regular or "voting" members need to be aware of independence considerations and are advised to review IIA Standards and related Practice Advisories for guidance and required disclosures. Status as an "ex-officio" member normally would not create independence problems.*

e. *Internal auditors should periodically review and evaluate quarterly reporting and disclosure processes, disclosure committee activities, and related documentation, and provide management and the audit committee with an assessment of the process and assurance concerning overall operations and compliance with policies and procedures. Internal auditors whose independence may be impaired due to their assigned role in the process should ensure that management and the audit committee are able to obtain appropriate assurance about the process from other sources. Other sources can include internal self-assessments as well as third parties such as external auditors and consultants.*

f. *Internal auditors should recommend appropriate improvements to the policies, procedures, and process for quarterly reporting and related disclosures based on the results of an assessment of related activities. Recommended best practices for such activities may include all, or components of, the following tools and procedures, depending on the specific process used by each organization:*

- *Properly documented policies, procedures, controls, and monitoring reports*
- *Quarterly checklist of procedures and key control elements*
- *Standardized control reports on key disclosure controls*
- *Management self-assessments (such as CSA)*
- *Sign-offs or representation statements from key managers*
- *Review of draft regulatory filings prior to submission*
- *Process maps to document the source of data elements for regulatory filings, key controls, and responsible parties for each element*
- *Follow-up on previously reported outstanding items*
- *Consideration of internal audit reports issued during the period*
- *Special or specifically targeted reviews of high-risk, complex, and problem areas; including material accounting estimates, reserve valuations, off-balance sheet activities, major subsidiaries, joint ventures, and special purpose entities*
- *Observation of the "closing process" for the financial statements and related adjusting entries, including waived adjustments*
- *Conference calls with key management from remote locations to ensure appropriate consideration of and participation by all major components of the organization*
- *Review of potential and pending litigation, and contingent liabilities*
- *CAE report on internal control, issued at least annually, and possibly quarterly*
- *Regularly scheduled disclosure and audit committee meetings*

g.   *Internal auditors should compare processes for complying with Section 302 of the Sarbanes-Oxley Act (quarterly financial reporting and disclosures) to procedures developed to comply with Section 404 concerning management's annual assessment and public report on internal controls. Processes designed to be similar or compatible will contribute to operational efficiencies and reduce the likelihood or risk for problems and errors to occur or go undetected. While processes and procedures may be similar, it is possible that the internal auditor's role may vary. In some organizations the work of internal auditors may form the basis for management's assertions about internal control, while in other organizations internal auditors may be called upon to evaluate management's assessment.*

- *The nature of internal audit's work, and use thereof, can potentially affect the treatment or degree of reliance placed upon the internal auditor's work by the external auditor. Internal auditors should ensure that each participant's role is clarified and activities are coordinated and agreed upon with management and the external auditors.*
- *In organizations where management conducts its own assessment of controls as the basis for an opinion, internal auditors should evaluate management's assessment and supporting documentation.*
- *Internal auditors should evaluate how internal audit report comments are classified and ensure that comments that may be subject to disclosure in quarterly certifications or the annual report on internal controls are appropriately communicated to management and the audit committee. Extra care should be taken to ensure such comments are adequately resolved in a timely manner.*

2120.A2 *– Internal auditors should ascertain the extent to which operating and program goals and objectives have been established and conform to those of the organization.*

2120.A3 *– Internal auditors should review operations and programs to ascertain the extent to which results are consistent with established goals and objectives to determine whether operations and programs are being implemented or performed as intended.*

2120.A4 *– Adequate criteria are needed to evaluate controls. Internal auditors should ascertain the extent to which management has established adequate criteria to determine whether objectives and goals have been accomplished. If adequate, internal auditors should use such criteria in their evaluation. If inadequate, internal auditors should work with management to develop appropriate evaluation criteria.*

Practice Advisory 2120.A4-1: Control Criteria

1.   *Internal auditors should evaluate the established operating targets and expectations and should determine whether those operating standards are acceptable and are being met. When such management targets and criteria are vague, authoritative interpretations should be sought. If internal auditors are required to interpret or select operating standards, they should seek agreement with engagement clients as to the criteria needed to measure operating performance.*

2120.C1 *– During consulting engagements, internal auditors should address controls consistent with the engagement's objectives and should be alert to the existence of any significant control weaknesses.*

2120.C2 – *Internal auditors should incorporate knowledge of controls gained from consulting engagements into the process of identifying and evaluating significant risk exposures of the organization.*

Practice Advisory 1000.C1-2: Additional Considerations for Formal Consulting Engagements

The following is the portion of this omnibus Practice Advisory relevant to Standards 2120.C1 and 2120.C2:

14.   *Internal auditors should be observant of the effectiveness of risk management and control processes during formal consulting engagements. Substantial risk exposures or material control weaknesses should be brought to the attention of management. In some situations the auditor's concerns should also be communicated to executive management, the audit committee, and/or the board of directors. Auditors should use professional judgment (a) to determine the significance of exposures or weaknesses and the actions taken or contemplated to mitigate or correct these exposures or weaknesses and (b) to ascertain the expectations of executive management, the audit committee, and board in having these matters reported.*

2.   **Organizational Control** (from The IIA's Research Committee Report #18)

    a.   **Organization** is the way individual work efforts within an entity are assigned and integrated for achievement of the organization's objectives and goals.

        1)   Assignments are defined in terms of **job descriptions** to avoid confusion and conflict of work efforts.

        2)   **Integration** is accomplished through specific organizational arrangements in a structure of roles, including

            a)   Coordinating committees
            b)   Requirements for review and approval
            c)   Specific assignment of authority and responsibility

    b.   **Organizational control** is the means of achieving the most effective possible use of organizational arrangements. Organizational control

        1)   Is part of the larger control process
        2)   Relates to the special control aspects of the organizing activity
        3)   Consists of

            a)   Design of arrangements to meet a particular entity's objectives
            b)   Continuous reappraisal and modification of the design

    c.   The general **elements of systems of control**, applicable to procedural efforts, are

        1)   Establishing standards for the operation to be controlled
        2)   Measuring performance against the standards
        3)   Examining and analyzing deviations
        4)   Taking corrective action
        5)   Reappraising the standards based on experience

    d.   Examples of the major **types of organizational problems** and conflicting issues may be useful in understanding the organizational process and its controls.

        1)   Objectives are accomplished through people; therefore, the organizational relationships must be among people.

            a)   The activity-authority relationships among individuals are emphasized.

        2)   An **activity** is divided into job assignments. The job assignments are then integrated to achieve the organization's objectives.

3) The design of organizational activity and its implementation are separate phases even though they are interrelated.

   a) In the **design phase**, the rationale (including objectives) is more important.

   b) In the **implementation phase**, the human dimension is more important.

4) Organizational arrangements are based on judgmental decisions.

5) Many organizational arrangements are based on trade-offs among alternatives.

6) Assignment of organizational responsibilities sometimes results in conflict between different responsibilities, personalities, etc.

7) Organizational arrangements must be based upon management objectives.

e. In implementing organizational structures, numerous application problems are encountered.

   1) **Grouping activities** effectively involves the following questions:

      a) How much specialization?
      b) How much control for protection and efficiency?
      c) Is departmentation functional or nonfunctional?
      d) How much decentralization?
      e) Can profit responsibility be fixed?
      f) How much staff?
      g) How many service departments?
      h) How is balance of emphasis achieved?
      i) What should be the span of control?
      j) How much formal coordination?

   2) Achieving effective **operational relationships** concerns

      a) Effectiveness of delegating
      b) Quality of supervision
      c) Adequacy of the information provided
      d) Adequacy of participation
      e) Effectiveness of staff usage
      f) Proper recognition of common objectives
      g) Fair definition of rewards and punishments
      h) Quality of leadership

   3) The following are additional considerations:

      a) Formal organizational charts are necessary, but the **informal organization** must be

         i) Monitored and understood
         ii) Modified as needed to encourage conformity with the organization's goals

      b) **Human resources** and their interrelationships must be administered effectively.

      c) Organizational arrangements should be

         i) Adapted to managerial style
         ii) Tied to the total management process
         iii) Responsive to changing conditions

f. **Maintaining organizational control**

1) Organizational control should be reappraised continually.

    a) Reappraisal of organizational arrangements is the basic element of the organizational control process.

2) **Managers should be responsible** for organizational control.

    a) A manager should initiate actions deemed appropriate, putting them into effect to the extent of his/her authority.

    b) A manager should channel information and **proposals for change** to the appropriate people who are responsible for the particular organizational arrangement.

    c) A considerable amount of a manager's time must be devoted to administering the department being supervised. This process constitutes **coordination** with other departments.

        i)   New employees must be added to the payroll.

        ii) Verified time sheets must be sent to the proper department.

        iii) In short, the manager is a funnel for transactions up and down the organizational chart.

3) The function of **special staff** regarding organizational control is to provide personnel who

    a) Have the overall responsibility of coordinating current organizational changes and studying ongoing organizational needs

    b) Assist managers with organizational arrangements

    c) Establish organization-wide control over and coordination of all organizational arrangements

4) **Role of the internal audit activity** in organizational control

    a) The internal audit activity is part of management's concern for the total control process. Internal auditors

        i)   Assist in providing organizational control
        ii) Monitor organizational changes

    b) Internal auditors must be familiar with organizational arrangements.

        i)   They should understand the nature of the relations among particular operations to be reviewed and the related organizational arrangements.

            • The understanding establishes a reference point for later determining how the organizational arrangements actually operate.

    c) Internal auditors must relate operational arrangements to operational deficiencies. They should

        i)   Understand the basic concepts for appraising the soundness of organizational arrangements

        ii) Probe for factors leading to the deficiency

        iii) Consider the extent to which existing organizational arrangements are the cause of operational deficiencies

d) The internal audit activity should implement the same degree of organizational control within its own function as it expects to find throughout the organization.

3. Stop and review! You have completed the outline for this subunit. Study multiple-choice questions 1 through 29 beginning on page 151.

5.2 SYSTEMS APPROACH TO CONTROL

1. A **system** is a set of related elements with a purpose.

   a. A process transforms an input to an output:

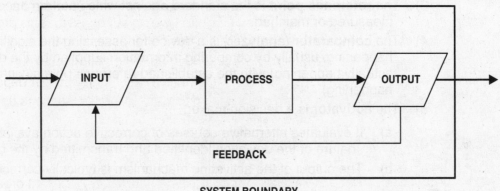

   b. **Feedback** provides information as to whether the desired state has been attained or maintained. This function is control.

   c. The **system boundary** determines what variables are internal or external to the system; they are internal if they are part of the system.

   d. **Subsystems** may extend the system's boundaries.

   e. Systems are open or closed.

      1) **Open** systems accept uncontrolled inputs that may affect the system.
      2) **Closed** systems do not accept uncontrolled inputs.

         a) Closed systems may be ineffective in rapidly changing environments.

   f. **Adaptive systems** alter their processes to produce outputs required in a changing environment.

      1) They have learning capacity and can react to nonroutine situations.
      2) They are open systems.

   g. **Corrective systems** can be open systems and can adapt to environmental change, but

      1) They have no learning ability.
      2) They operate only according to prescribed rules.

2. **Control systems** should attain and maintain a desired state or condition.

    a. There are five basic elements of control systems.

        1) The **control object** is the variable of the system's behavior chosen for monitoring.

            a) Some of the control objects must be chosen from the controlled system's outputs.

            b) Additional controls may apply to the input variables and conversion processes of the system under control.

        2) The **detector** measures what is happening in the control object (variable being controlled).

        3) The **reference point** is the standard against which performance may be measured or matched.

        4) The **comparator (analyzer)** is a device for assessing the significance of what is happening, usually by comparing information supplied by the detector (what is actually happening) with the established reference points (what should be happening).

        5) The **activator** is a decision maker.

            a) It evaluates alternative courses of corrective action available given the nature of the deviation identified and transmitted by the comparator.

            b) The output of the activating mechanism is typically corrective action.

    b. Types of controls

        1) **Yes/no** controls are preemptive.

            a) System activities may not proceed to the next step until a screening test has been passed.

            b) Approval to continue is required.

        2) **Steering** controls are preventive.

            a) They predict results and take corrective action before the system's processes are completed.

        3) **Post-action** controls are detective.

            a) System activities are completed before they apply.

            b) Results are then measured and compared with a standard before control action is taken.

            c) Control action is directed toward eliminating the deviation in future cycles of the process under control.

    c. Complexity of controls

        1) **First-order control systems** (corrective) monitor the object of control against a predetermined goal.

            a) The control system is given particular commands to be carried out regardless of changes in the environment.

            b) Nothing unpredictable about the system's response; the control is programmed to perform according to specifications.

2) **Second-order control systems** (adaptive) can perform all first-order functions and, in addition, can initiate alternative courses of action in response to changed external conditions.

   a) The control has the ability to change standards or decision rules that dictate lower-order control system behavior.

   b) In extreme cases, the control system has the capacity to trigger the redesign of the operating system, the control subsystem, or both.

d. Direction of the flow of information

   1) In a **feedback** situation, control information arises from judgments concerning the performance of conversion activities that have already occurred. This information is transmitted to the activator governing the behavior of the conversion processes under review.

   2) In a **feedforward** situation, control information is derived before the implementation of conversion activities to which it relates. This information is transmitted to an activator that adjusts conversion activities yet to be performed.

e. An **open, adaptive control system** is illustrated below.

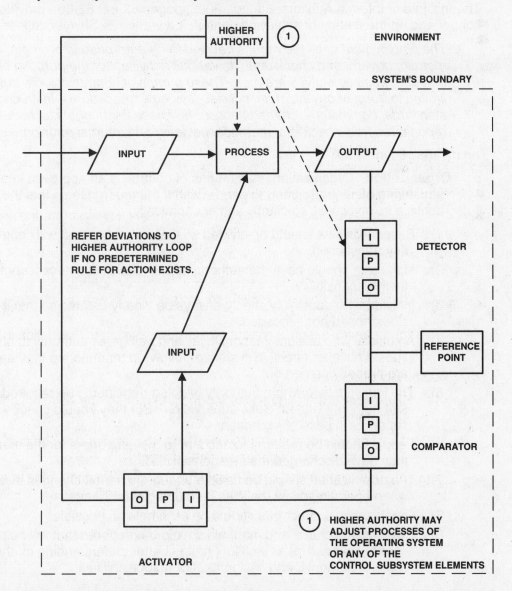

3.   **Studying organizational and control models** assists internal auditors in

    a.   Communicating within a multidisciplinary group of internal auditors and between the internal auditors and the engagement clients (The model provides a common basis for understanding the organization.)

    b.   Focusing on the organizational elements to be evaluated (scope of the engagement)

    c.   Determining and displaying the key operations of the organization under review (reasons for the existence of the organization)

    d.   Determining and displaying the management complement and the instruments through which it works (its mandate, etc.)

    e.   Focusing on organizational dynamics and cause-effect relationships

    f.   Understanding the interaction between the organization and its environment

4.   Stop and review! You have completed the outline for this subunit. Study multiple-choice questions 30 through 32 beginning on page 161.

5.3 MEANS OF ACHIEVING CONTROL

1.   Sawyer, Dittenhofer, and Scheiner in *Sawyer's Internal Auditing* (Altamonte Springs, FL: The Institute of Internal Auditors, 5th ed., 2003, pages 63-64; 82-86), provide definitions of control and list the means of achieving control. Lawrence B. Sawyer defines control as

> *The employment of all the means devised in an enterprise to promote, direct, restrain, govern, and check upon its various activities for the purpose of seeing that enterprise objectives are met. These means of control include, but are not limited to, form of organization, policies, systems, procedures, instructions, standards, committees, charts of accounts, forecasts, budgets, schedules, reports, records, checklists, methods, devices, and internal auditing.*

2.   The means of control are

    a.   **Organization**. Organization, as a means of control, is an approved intentional structuring of roles assigned to people within the enterprise so that the enterprise can achieve its objectives efficiently and economically.

       1) Responsibilities should be divided so that no one person will control all phases of any transaction.

       2) Managers should have the authority to take the action necessary to discharge their responsibility.

       3) Individual responsibility should always be clearly defined so that it can be neither sidestepped nor exceeded.

       4) An official who assigns responsibility and delegates authority to subordinates should have an effective system of follow-up for ensuring that tasks assigned are properly carried out.

       5) The individuals to whom authority is delegated should be required to exercise that authority without close supervision. But they should check with their superiors in case of exception.

       6) People should be required to account to their superiors for the manner in which they have discharged their responsibilities.

       7) The organization should be flexible enough to permit changes in its structure when operating plans, policies, and objectives change.

       8) Organizational structures should be as simple as possible.

       9) Organization charts and manuals should be prepared that will help plan and control changes in, as well as provide better understanding of, the organization, chain of authority, and assignment of responsibilities.

b. **Policies**. A policy is any stated principle that requires, guides, or restricts action. Policies should follow certain principles.

1) Policies should be clearly stated in writing in systematically organized handbooks, manuals, or other publications, and properly approved.

2) Policies should be systematically communicated to all officials and appropriate employees of the organization.

3) Policies must conform with applicable laws and regulations, and they should be consistent with objectives and general policies prescribed at higher levels.

4) Policies should be designed to promote the conduct of authorized activities in an effective, efficient, and economical manner and to provide a satisfactory degree of assurance that the resources of the enterprise are suitably safeguarded.

5) Policies should be periodically reviewed, and they should be revised when circumstances change.

c. **Procedures**. Procedures are methods employed to carry out activities in conformity with prescribed policies. The same principles applicable to policies are also applicable to procedures. In addition,

1) To reduce the possibility of fraud and error, procedures should be so coordinated that one employee's work is automatically checked by another who is independently performing separate prescribed duties. In determining the extent to which automatic internal checks should be built into the system of control, such factors as degree of risk, cost of preventive procedures, availability of personnel, operational impact, and feasibility should be considered.

2) For nonmechanical operations, prescribed procedures should not be so detailed as to stifle the use of judgment.

3) To promote maximum efficiency and economy, prescribed procedures should be as simple and as inexpensive as possible.

4) Procedures should not be overlapping, conflicting, or duplicative.

5) Procedures should be periodically reviewed and improved as necessary.

d. **Personnel**. People hired or assigned should have the qualifications to do the jobs assigned to them. The best form of control over the performance of individuals is supervision. Hence, high standards of supervision should be established. The following practices help improve control.

1) New employees should be investigated as to honesty and reliability.

2) Employees should be given training and refresher courses that provide the opportunity for improvement and keep them informed of new policies and procedures.

3) Employees should be given information on the duties and responsibilities of other segments of the organization so they may better understand how and where their jobs fit into the organization as a whole.

4) The performance of all employees should be periodically reviewed to see whether all essential requirements of their jobs are being met. Superior performance should be given appropriate recognition. Shortcomings should be discussed with employees so that they are given an opportunity to improve their performance or upgrade their skills.

e. **Accounting**. Accounting is the indispensable means of financial control over activities and resources. It furnishes a framework that can be fitted to assignments of responsibility. Moreover, it is the financial scorekeeper of the organization. The problem lies in what scores to keep. Some basic principles for accounting systems follow:

1) Accounting should fit the needs of managers for rational decision making rather than the dictates of some textbook or canned check list.
2) Accounting should be based on lines of responsibility.
3) Financial reports of operating results should parallel the organizational units responsible for carrying out operations.
4) Accounting should be such that controllable costs can be identified.

f. **Budgeting**. A budget is a statement of expected results expressed in numerical terms. As a control, it sets a standard for input of resources and what should be achieved as output and outcomes.

1) Those who are responsible for meeting a budget should participate in its preparation.
2) Those responsible for meeting a budget should be provided with adequate information that compares budgets with actual events and shows reasons for any significant variances.
3) All subsidiary budgets should tie into the overall budget for the enterprise.
4) Budgets should set measurable objectives; they are meaningless unless managers know what they are budgeting for.
5) Budgets should help sharpen the organizational structure because objective budgeting standards are difficult to set in a confused combination of subsystems. Budgeting is therefore a form of discipline and coordination.

g. **Reporting**. In most organizations, management functions and makes decisions on the basis of reports it receives. Thus, reports should be timely, accurate, meaningful, and economical. The following are some principles for establishing a satisfactory internal reporting system:

1) Reports should be made in accordance with assigned responsibilities.
2) Individuals or units should be required to report only on those matters for which they are responsible.
3) The cost of accumulating data and preparing reports should be weighed against the benefits to be obtained from them.
4) Reports should be as simple as possible, and consistent with the nature of the subject matter. They should include only information that serves the needs of the readers. Common classifications and terminology should be used as much as possible to avoid confusion.
5) When appropriate, performance reports should show comparisons with predetermined standards of cost, quality, and quantity. Controllable costs should be segregated.
6) When performance cannot be reported in quantitative terms, the reports should be designed to emphasize exceptions or other matters requiring management attention.
7) For maximum value, reports should be timely. Timely reports based partly on estimates may be more useful than delayed reports that are more precise.
8) Report recipients should be polled periodically to see whether they still need the reports they are receiving or whether the report could be improved.

3. Stop and review! You have completed the outline for this subunit. Study multiple-choice questions 33 through 48 beginning on page 162.

QUESTIONS

5.1 Control Pronouncements

1. Which of the following best defines control?

A. Control is the result of proper planning, organizing, and directing by management.

B. Controls are statements of what the organization chooses to accomplish.

C. Control is provided when cost-effective measures are taken to restrict deviations to a tolerable level.

D. Control accomplishes objectives and goals in an accurate, timely, and economical fashion.

Answer (A) is correct. *(CIA, adapted)*
REQUIRED: The best definition of control.
DISCUSSION: According to the Glossary appended to the Standards, a control is "any action taken by management, the board, and other parties to enhance risk management and increase the likelihood that established objectives and goals will be achieved. Management plans, organizes, and directs the performance of sufficient actions to provide reasonable assurance that objectives and goals will be achieved." Thus, control is the result of proper planning, organizing, and directing by management.
Answer (B) is incorrect because established objectives and goals are what the organization chooses to accomplish. Answer (C) is incorrect because, during the development of risk management, control, and governance processes, reasonable assurance of achieving objectives and goals efficiently and economically is provided when the most cost-effective measures are taken in the design and implementation stages to reduce risks and restrict deviations to a tolerable level (PA 2100-1). Answer (D) is incorrect because efficient performance accomplishes objectives and goals in an accurate, timely, and economical fashion (PA 2100-1).

2. Controls that are designed to provide management with assurance of the realization of specified minimum gross margins on sales are

A. Directive controls.

B. Preventive controls.

C. Detective controls.

D. Output controls.

Answer (A) is correct. *(CIA, adapted)*
REQUIRED: The control that provides management with assurance of the realization of specified minimum gross margins on sales.
DISCUSSION: A control is any action taken by management, the board, and other parties to enhance the likelihood that established objectives and goals will be achieved (Glossary). The objective of directive controls is to cause or encourage desirable events to occur (PA 2100-1), e.g., providing management with assurance of the realization of specified minimum gross margins on sales.
Answer (B) is incorrect because preventive controls deter undesirable events from occurring. Answer (C) is incorrect because detective controls detect and correct undesirable events that have occurred. Answer (D) is incorrect because output controls relate to the accuracy and reasonableness of information processed by a system, not to operating controls.

3. Controls should be designed to provide reasonable assurance that

A. Organizational objectives and goals will be achieved economically and efficiently.

B. Management's plans have not been circumvented by worker collusion.

C. The internal audit activity's guidance and oversight of management's performance is accomplished economically and efficiently.

D. Management's planning, organizing, and directing processes are properly evaluated.

Answer (A) is correct. *(CIA, adapted)*
REQUIRED: The purpose of controls.
DISCUSSION: Risk management, control, and governance processes are adequate if management has planned and designed them in a manner providing reasonable assurance that the organization's objectives and goals will be achieved economically and efficiently. Reasonable assurance is provided when the most cost-effective actions are taken in the design and implementation stages to reduce risks and restrict deviations to a tolerable level (PA 2100-1).
Answer (B) is incorrect because collusion is an inherent limitation of internal control. Answer (C) is incorrect because representatives of the organization's stakeholders (e.g., the board) provide oversight of risk and control processes administered by management (Glossary). Answer (D) is incorrect because internal auditors evaluate management processes to determine whether reasonable assurance exists that objectives and goals will be achieved (PA 2100-1).

4. Management has a role in the maintenance of control. In fact, management sometimes is a control. Which of the following involves managerial functions as a control?

- A. Monitoring performance.
- B. Use of an organizational policies manual.
- C. Maintenance of a quality assurance program.
- D. Establishment of an internal audit activity.

Answer (A) is correct.   *(CIA, adapted)*
REQUIRED: The item that involves managerial functions as a control.
DISCUSSION: Risk management, control, and governance processes are effective when management directs processes in such a manner as to provide reasonable assurance that the organization's objectives and goals will be achieved. In addition to accomplishing the objectives and planned activities, management directs by authorizing activities and transactions, monitoring resulting performance, and verifying that the organization's processes are operating as designed (PA 2100-1).
Answer (B) is incorrect because the manual advises but does not control. Answer (C) is incorrect because a quality assurance program is a form of internal assessment. The manager of the program should be independent of the operations assessed. Answer (D) is incorrect because an internal audit activity should be independent of the operations reviewed and is not a managerial function.

5. The procedure requiring preparation of a prelisting of incoming cash receipts, with copies of the pre-list going to the cashier and to accounting, is an example of which type of control?

- A. Preventive.
- B. Corrective.
- C. Detective.
- D. Directive.

Answer (A) is correct.   *(CIA, adapted)*
REQUIRED: The kind of control exemplified by a pre-list of cash receipts.
DISCUSSION: A prelisting of cash receipts in the form of checks is a preventive control. It is intended to deter undesirable events from occurring (PA 2100-1). Because irregularities involving cash are most likely before receipts are recorded, either remittance advices or a prelisting of checks should be prepared in the mailroom so as to establish recorded accountability for cash as soon as possible. A cash register tape is a form of prelisting for cash received over the counter. One copy of a prelisting will go to accounting for posting to the cash receipts journal, and another is sent to the cashier for reconciliation with checks and currency received.
Answer (B) is incorrect because a corrective control rectifies an error or irregularity. Answer (C) is incorrect because a detective control uncovers an error or irregularity that has already occurred. Answer (D) is incorrect because a directive control causes or encourages a desirable event.

6. Controls may be classified according to the function they are intended to perform, for example, as detective, preventive, or directive. Which of the following is a directive control?

- A. Monthly bank statement reconciliations.
- B. Dual signatures on all disbursements over a specific amount.
- C. Recording every transaction on the day it occurs.
- D. Requiring all members of the internal audit activity to be CIAs.

Answer (D) is correct.   *(CIA, adapted)*
REQUIRED: The directive control.
DISCUSSION: Requiring all members of the internal audit activity to be CIAs is a directive control. The control is designed to cause or encourage a desirable event to occur (PA 2100-1). The requirement enhances the professionalism and level of expertise of the internal audit activity.
Answer (A) is incorrect because monthly bank statement reconciliation is a detective control. The events under scrutiny have already occurred. Answer (B) is incorrect because dual signatures on all disbursements over a specific amount is a preventive control. The control is designed to deter an undesirable event. Answer (C) is incorrect because recording every transaction on the day it occurs is a preventive control. The control is designed to deter an undesirable event.

7. Directors, management, external auditors, and internal auditors all play important roles in creating proper control processes. Senior management is primarily responsible for

    A. Establishing and maintaining an organizational culture.

    B. Reviewing the reliability and integrity of financial and operational information.

    C. Ensuring that external and internal auditors oversee the administration of the system of risk management and control processes.

    D. Implementing and monitoring controls designed by the board of directors.

Answer (A) is correct. *(CIA, adapted)*

    REQUIRED: The best description of senior management's responsibility.

    DISCUSSION: Management plans, organizes, and directs the performance of sufficient actions to provide reasonable assurance that goals and objectives will be achieved. Management periodically reviews its objectives and goals and modifies its processes to accommodate changes in internal and external conditions. Management also establishes and maintains an organizational culture, including an ethical climate that fosters control (PA 2100-1).

    Answer (B) is incorrect because internal auditors are responsible for evaluating the adequacy and effectiveness of controls, including those relating to the reliability and integrity of financial and operational information (Standard 2120.A1). Answer (C) is incorrect because senior management's role is to oversee the establishment, administration, and assessment of the system of risk management and control processes (PA 2120.A1-1). Answer (D) is incorrect because the board has oversight responsibilities but ordinarily does not become involved in the details of operations.

8. Internal auditors regularly evaluate controls. Which of the following best describes the concept of control as recognized by internal auditors?

    A. Management regularly discharges personnel who do not perform up to expectations.

    B. Management takes action to enhance the likelihood that established goals and objectives will be achieved.

    C. Control represents specific procedures that accountants and internal auditors design to ensure the correctness of processing.

    D. Control procedures should be designed from the "bottom up" to ensure attention to detail.

Answer (B) is correct. *(CIA, adapted)*

    REQUIRED: The best description of the concept of control as recognized by internal auditors.

    DISCUSSION: A control is any action taken by management to enhance the likelihood that established goals and objectives will be achieved. Management plans, organizes, and directs the performance of sufficient actions to provide reasonable assurance that objectives and goals will be achieved (PA 2100-1). Thus, control is the result of proper planning, organizing, and directing by management.

    Answer (A) is incorrect because termination of employees who perform unsatisfactorily is not a comprehensive definition of control. Answer (C) is incorrect because control is not limited to processing. Moreover, it is instituted by management, not internal auditors. Answer (D) is incorrect because some control procedures may be designed from the bottom up, but the concept of control flows from management down through the organization.

9. Which of the following are elements included in the control environment?

    A. Organizational structure, management philosophy, and planning.

    B. Integrity and ethical values, assignment of authority, and human resource policies.

    C. Competence of personnel, backup facilities, laws, and regulations.

    D. Risk assessment, assignment of responsibility, and human resource practices.

Answer (B) is correct. *(Publisher)*

    REQUIRED: The elements of the control environment.

    DISCUSSION: According to the Glossary appended to the Standards, the control environment includes the attitude and actions of the board and management regarding the significance of control within the organization. The control environment provides the discipline and structure for the achievement of the primary objectives of the system of internal control. The control environment includes the following elements:

- Integrity and ethical values
- Management's philosophy and operating style
- Organizational structure
- Assignment of authority and responsibility
- Human resource policies and practices
- Competence of personnel

    Answer (A) is incorrect because planning is not an element of the control environment. Answer (C) is incorrect because backup facilities, laws, and regulations are not elements of the control environment. Answer (D) is incorrect because risk assessment is part of planning the internal audit activity and specific engagements.

10. Internal control can provide only reasonable assurance that the organization's objectives and goals will be met efficiently and effectively. One factor limiting the likelihood of achieving those objectives is that

   A. The internal auditor's primary responsibility is the detection of fraud.

   B. The audit committee is active and independent.

   C. The cost of internal control should not exceed its benefits.

   D. Management monitors performance.

Answer (C) is correct. *(Publisher)*
REQUIRED: The true statement about the limitation of internal control.
DISCUSSION: A limiting factor is that the cost of internal control should not exceed the benefits that are expected to be derived. Thus, the potential loss associated with any exposure or risk is weighed against the cost to control it. Although the cost-benefit relationship is a primary criterion that should be considered in designing and implementing internal control, the precise measurement of costs and benefits usually is not possible.
Answer (A) is incorrect because the internal auditor's responsibility regarding internal control is to examine and evaluate the adequacy and effectiveness of the system of internal control. Answer (B) is incorrect because an active audit committee strengthens the control environment. Answer (D) is incorrect because management's directing function includes authorizing activities and transactions, monitoring resulting performance, and verifying that processes are operating as designed (PA 2100-1).

11. Which of the following is not an interrelated concept that is fundamental to the field of internal auditing and the work of internal auditors?

   A. Governance.

   B. Materiality.

   C. Risk.

   D. Control.

Answer (B) is correct. *(Publisher)*
REQUIRED: The answer choice that is not an interrelated concept that is fundamental to the field of internal auditing and the work of internal auditors.
DISCUSSION: Governance, risk, and control are interrelated concepts that are fundamental to the field of internal auditing and the work of internal auditors. Materiality is a concept related to external auditing.

12. The primary responsibility for overseeing the establishment and administration of internal control rests with

   A. The external auditor.

   B. Senior management.

   C. The controller.

   D. The treasurer.

Answer (B) is correct. *(CMA, adapted)*
REQUIRED: The person(s) primarily responsible for establishing and administering internal control.
DISCUSSION: The board establishes and maintains governance processes and obtains assurances about the effectiveness of the risk management and control processes. Senior management's role is to oversee the establishment, administration, and assessment of that system of processes (PA 2120.A1-1).
Answer (A) is incorrect because external auditors must consider internal control, but they do not establish and maintain it. Answer (C) is incorrect because the controller is responsible only to the extent that (s)he is a part of the management team. Answer (D) is incorrect because the treasurer is responsible only to the extent that (s)he is a part of the management team.

13. SEC Rules 13a-14 and 15d-14 require an issuer's principal executive officer or officers and the principal financial officer or officers, or persons performing similar functions, to certify that he or she and other certifying officers have performed which of the following?

I.   Are responsible for establishing and maintaining "disclosure controls and procedures" for the issuer.

II. Have designed such disclosure controls and procedures to ensure that material information is made known to them, particularly during the period in which the periodic report is being prepared.

III. Have evaluated the effectiveness of the issuer's disclosure controls and procedures as of a date within 180 days prior to the filing date of the report.

    A. I and II.

    B. II and III.

    C. I and III.

    D. I, II, and III.

Answer (A) is correct. *(Publisher)*
REQUIRED: The items that SEC Rules 13a-14 and 15d-14 require an issuer's principal executive officer or officers and the principal financial officer or officers, or persons performing similar functions, to certify that he or she and other certifying officers have performed.
DISCUSSION: PA 2120.A 1-3 lists a number of new statutory requirements. Section 302 of the Sarbanes-Oxley Act outlines the corporate responsibility for financial reports and the SEC has issued guidance to implement the act. As adopted, SEC Rules 13a-14 and 15d-14 require an issuer's principal executive officer or officers and the principal financial officer or officers, or persons performing similar functions, to certify in each quarterly and annual report, including transition reports, filed or submitted by the issuer under Section 13(a) or 15(d) of the Exchange Act that, among other things, (s)he and the other certifying officers:

- Are responsible for establishing and maintaining "disclosure controls and procedures" (a newly-defined term reflecting the concept of controls and procedures related to disclosure embodied in Section 302(a)(4) of the act) for the issuer;

- Have designed such disclosure controls and procedures to ensure that material information is made known to them, particularly during the period in which the periodic report is being prepared;

- Have evaluated the effectiveness of the issuer's disclosure controls and procedures as of a date within 90 days prior to the filing date of the report; and

- Have presented in the report their conclusions about the effectiveness of the disclosure controls and procedures based on the required evaluation as of that date.

14. The chief audit executive's responsibility for assessing and reporting on control processes includes

    A. Communicating to senior management and the audit committee an annual judgment about internal control.

    B. Overseeing the establishment of internal control processes.

    C. Maintaining the organization's governance processes.

    D. Arriving at a single assessment based solely on the work of the internal audit activity.

Answer (A) is correct. *(Publisher)*
REQUIRED: The chief audit executive's responsibility for assessing and reporting on control processes.
DISCUSSION: Senior management and the audit committee normally expect that the chief audit executive will perform sufficient engagement work and gather other available information during the year so as to form a judgment about the adequacy and effectiveness of the control processes. The chief audit executive should communicate that overall judgment about the organization's system of controls to senior management and the audit committee. A growing number of organizations have included a management's report on the system of internal controls in their annual or periodic reports to external stakeholders. The report of the chief audit executive should therefore be presented, usually once a year, to senior management and the audit committee (PA 2120.A1-1).
Answer (B) is incorrect because senior management is responsible for overseeing the establishment of internal control processes. Answer (C) is incorrect because the board is responsible for establishing and maintaining the organization's governance processes. Answer (D) is incorrect because the challenge for the internal audit activity is to evaluate the effectiveness of the organization's system of controls based on the aggregation of many individual assessments. Those assessments are largely gained from internal auditing engagements, management's self assessments, and external auditor's work (PA 2120.A1-1).

15. Which of the following is not a role that the internal auditor can accept with respect to processes over quarterly financial reporting as stated in the new requirements of the SEC and the Sarbanes-Oxley Act?

    A. Initial designer of the required process.

    B. Independent assessor of the process.

    C. Fulfiller of SEC Rules 13a-14 and 15d-14.

    D. Coordinator or liaison between management and its auditors.

Answer (C) is correct. *(Publisher)*
    REQUIRED: The role that the internal auditor cannot accept with respect to processes over quarterly financial reporting as stated in the new requirements of the SEC and the Sarbanes-Oxley Act.
    DISCUSSION: PA 2120.A1-3 includes recommended actions for internal auditors. The actions and considerations are offered to internal auditors as value-added services that can be provided regarding quarterly financial reports, disclosures, and management certifications related to requirements of the SEC and the Sarbanes-Oxley Act. The internal auditors' role in such processes may range from initial designer of the process, participant on a disclosure committee, coordinator or liaison between management and its auditors, to independent assessor of the process. The internal auditor cannot fulfill SEC Rules 13a-14 and 15d-14. These rules must be fulfilled by an issuer's principal executive officer or officers and the principal financial officer or officers, or persons performing similar functions.

16. Which of the following is most likely to be regarded as a strength in internal control in a traditional external audit?

    A. The performance of financial audits by the internal audit activity.

    B. The performance of operational engagements by internal auditors.

    C. The routine supervisory review of production planning.

    D. The existence of a preventive maintenance program.

Answer (A) is correct. *(CMA, adapted)*
    REQUIRED: The activity most likely regarded as a strong internal control in a traditional external audit.
    DISCUSSION: The external auditor's traditional role is to perform an audit to determine whether the externally reported financial statements are fairly presented. Thus, a financial audit by the IAA is relevant to the traditional external audit because it is an engagement in which the reliability and integrity of financial information is evaluated. Such an engagement is consistent with the Standards. According to Standard 2120.A1, based on the results of the risk assessment, the internal audit activity should evaluate the adequacy and effectiveness of controls encompassing the organization's governance, operations, and information systems. This evaluation should extend to the reliability and integrity of financial and operational information; effectiveness and efficiency of operations; safeguarding of assets; and compliance with laws, regulations, and contracts.
    Answer (B) is incorrect because operational engagements are concerned with operational efficiency and effectiveness, matters that are not the primary focus of an external audit of financial statements. Answer (C) is incorrect because routine supervisory review of production planning is a concern of management but does not directly affect the fair presentation of the financial statements. Answer (D) is incorrect because the existence of a preventive maintenance program is not directly relevant to a financial statement audit.

17. An adequate system of internal controls is most likely to detect a fraud perpetrated by a

    A. Group of employees in collusion.

    B. Single employee.

    C. Group of managers in collusion.

    D. Single manager.

Answer (B) is correct. *(CIA, adapted)*
    REQUIRED: The fraud most likely to be detected by an adequate system of internal controls.
    DISCUSSION: Segregation of duties and other control processes serve to prevent or detect a fraud committed by an employee acting alone. One employee may not have the ability to engage in wrongdoing or may be subject to detection by other employees in the course of performing their assigned duties. However, collusion may circumvent controls. For example, comparison of recorded accountability for assets with the assets known to be held may fail to detect fraud if persons having custody of assets collude with record keepers.
    Answer (A) is incorrect because a group has a better chance of successfully perpetrating a fraud than does an individual employee. Answer (C) is incorrect because management can override controls. Answer (D) is incorrect because even a single manager may be able to override controls.

18. Factors that should be considered when assessing risk in a functional area include

1. Volume of transactions
2. Degree of system integration
3. Years since last engagement
4. Significant management turnover
5. Value of assets at risk
6. Average value per transaction
7. Results of last engagement

Factors that best define the significance of risk are

A. 1 through 7.

B. 2, 4, and 7.

C. 1, 5, and 6.

D. 3, 4, and 6.

Answer (C) is correct. *(CIA, adapted)*
REQUIRED: The factors that best define the significance of risk.
DISCUSSION: Risk is the uncertainty of an event's occurrence that could have an effect on the achievement of objectives. It is measured in terms of consequences and likelihood (Glossary appended to the Standards). Significance is a function of quantitative and qualitative factors, of which the former are obviously more readily defined. Factors 1, 5, and 6 can all be quantified in a way that contributes to meaningful measurement of the monetary amount of a risk exposure.
Answer (A) is incorrect because factors 2, 3, 4, and 7 do not contribute to the measurement of risk. These factors do not, for example, help to quantify the monetary amount (the consequences) of a risk exposure. Answer (B) is incorrect because factors 2, 4, and 7 are not quantifiable. Answer (D) is incorrect because factors 3 and 4 do not help in measuring risk in a meaningful way.

19. Internal auditors document the engagement in their working papers, which may include control questionnaires, flowcharts, checklists, and narrative descriptions. A questionnaire consists of a series of questions concerning controls that internal auditors consider necessary to prevent or detect errors and fraud. The most appropriate question designed to contribute to the internal auditors' understanding of the completeness of the expenditure cycle concerns the

A. Internal verification of quantities, prices, and mathematical accuracy of sales invoices.

B. Use and accountability of prenumbered checks.

C. Disposition of cash receipts.

D. Qualifications of accounting personnel.

Answer (B) is correct. *(CMA, adapted)*
REQUIRED: The most appropriate question designed to contribute to the internal auditors' understanding of the completeness of the expenditure cycle.
DISCUSSION: A completeness assertion concerns whether all transactions and accounts that should be presented are so presented. The exclusive use of sequentially numbered documents facilitates control over expenditures. An unexplained gap in the sequence alerts the internal auditor to the possibility that not all transactions have been recorded. A failure to use prenumbered checks therefore suggests a control discrepancy or weakness. If an organization uses prenumbered checks, determining exactly which checks were used during a period is easy.
Answer (A) is incorrect because determination of proper amounts of sales invoices concerns the valuation assertion. Also, sales invoices are part of the sales-receivables (revenue) cycle. Answer (C) is incorrect because cash receipts are part of the revenue cycle. Answer (D) is incorrect because consideration of the qualifications of accounting personnel is not a test of controls over the completeness of any cycle. This procedure is appropriate during the consideration of the control environment.

20. Status as an "ex-officio" or unofficial member of the "disclosure committee" normally avoids which kind of problems for the CAE?

A. Disclosure problems.

B. Internal control problems.

C. Independence problems.

D. Audit committee problems.

Answer (C) is correct. *(Publisher)*
REQUIRED: The problem that is avoided by the CAE when (s)he has a status as an "ex-officio" member of the "disclosure committee."
DISCUSSION: Normally, the chief audit executive (CAE) should be a member of the disclosure committee. Consideration should be given to the CAE's status on the committee. CAEs who serve as committee chairs or regular or "voting" members need to be aware of independence considerations and are advised to review IIA Standards and related Practice Advisories for guidance and required disclosures. Status as an "ex-officio" member normally would not create independence problems (PA 2120.A1-3).
Answer (A) is incorrect because allowing the CAE to have a status as an "ex-officio" member of the disclosure committee does not have any effect on disclosure. Answer (B) is incorrect because allowing the CAE to have a status as an "ex-officio" member of the disclosure committee does not affect internal controls of an organization. Answer (D) is incorrect because allowing the CAE to have a status as an "ex-officio" member of the disclosure committee does not have any effect on the audit committee.

21. Two organizations have recently merged. The audit committee has asked the internal auditors from both organizations to assess risks that should be addressed after the merger. One manager has suggested that the engagement teams jointly examine the organizational culture and the "tone at the top" to identify control risks associated with the proposed merger. Which of the following statements is true?

A. The organizational culture is not a part of the control environment and therefore should not be considered for a proposed engagement.

B. Although the organizational culture could be considered part of the control environment, the assessment of such an environment would be highly subjective and therefore not useful.

C. Differences in the organizational culture should be systematically identified because the differences may present major risks to the success of the merger. However, identifying differences is not an appropriate activity because it is political and subjective.

D. None of the answers are correct.

Answer (D) is correct. *(CIA, adapted)*
REQUIRED: The true statement about the corporate culture.
DISCUSSION: According to the Glossary appended to the Standards, the control environment includes the attitude and actions of the board and management regarding the significance of control within the organization. The control environment provides the discipline and structure for the achievement of the primary objectives of the system of internal control. The control environment includes the following elements:

- Integrity and ethical values
- Management's philosophy and operating style
- Organizational structure
- Assignment of authority and responsibility
- Human resource policies and practices
- Competence of personnel

Answer (A) is incorrect because the organizational culture is an integral part of the control environment. Answer (B) is incorrect because subjectivity is a significant factor in engagements. Answer (C) is incorrect because identifying differences in organizational cultures is an appropriate activity. The differences may affect internal control.

22. In evaluating the effectiveness and efficiency with which resources are employed, an internal auditor is responsible for

A. Determining the extent to which adequate operating criteria have been established.

B. Verifying the existence of assets.

C. Reviewing the reliability of operating information.

D. Verifying the accuracy of asset valuation.

Answer (A) is correct. *(CIA, adapted)*
REQUIRED: The internal auditor's responsibility for evaluating economic and efficient use of resources.
DISCUSSION: The internal audit activity evaluates the controls encompassing governance, operations, and information systems. This evaluation includes the effectiveness and efficiency of operations (Standard 2120.A1). Moreover, the internal auditors should "ascertain the extent to which management has established adequate criteria to determine whether objectives and goals have been accomplished" (Standard 2120.A4). They should also "evaluate the established operating targets and expectations and should determine whether those operating standards are acceptable and are being met" (PA 2120.A4-1). Verifying existence relates to the safeguarding of assets. The reliability of operating information and the accuracy of asset valuation concern the reliability and integrity of information.

23. In organizations where management conducts its own assessment of controls as the basis for an opinion, what is the internal auditor's role with respect to internal controls?

    A. Internal auditors have no responsibility over internal control assessment.

    B. Internal auditors should form their opinion based on their assessment of controls.

    C. Internal auditors should evaluate management's assessment and supporting documentation.

    D. Internal auditors should evaluate management's assessment and supporting documentation against their own assessment and discuss any differences with management.

Answer (C) is correct. *(Publisher)*
    REQUIRED: The role of an internal auditor with respect to internal controls in organizations where management conducts its own assessment of controls as the basis for an opinion.
    DISCUSSION: According to PA 2120.A1-3, Internal auditors should compare processes for complying with Section 302 of the Sarbanes-Oxley Act (quarterly financial reporting and disclosures) to procedures developed to comply with Section 404 concerning management's annual assessment and public report on internal controls. Processes designed to be similar or compatible will contribute to operational efficiencies and reduce the likelihood or risk for problems and errors to occur or go undetected. While processes and procedures may be similar, it is possible that the internal auditor's role may vary. In some organizations the work of internal auditors may form the basis for management's assertions about internal control, while in other organizations internal auditors may be called upon to evaluate management's assessment.
    Answer (A) is incorrect because internal auditors do have a responsibility with respect to internal controls in organizations where management conducts its own assessment of controls as the basis for an opinion. Answer (B) is incorrect because internal auditors should not do their own assessment, rather they should evaluate management's assessment and supporting documentation to ensure that management has formed a good opinion. Answer (D) is incorrect because to have management and the internal auditors do separate assessments would be time consuming, costly, and unnecessary.

24. An internal auditor's role with respect to operating objectives and goals includes

    A. Approving the operating objectives or goals to be met.

    B. Seeking authoritative interpretations when management's targets and criteria are vague.

    C. Developing and implementing control procedures.

    D. Accomplishing desired operating program results.

Answer (B) is correct. *(CIA, adapted)*
    REQUIRED: The internal auditor's role regarding operating objectives and goals.
    DISCUSSION: "Internal auditors should evaluate the established operating targets and expectations and should determine whether those operating standards are acceptable and are being met. When such management targets and criteria are vague, authoritative interpretations should be sought. If internal auditors are required to interpret or select operating standards, they should seek agreement with engagement clients as to the criteria needed to measure operating performance" (PA 2120.A4-1). Operational matters are the responsibility of management. "Internal auditors should not assume operating responsibilities" (PA 1130.A1-1).

25. Internal auditors need to ascertain the extent to which management has established adequate criteria to determine whether goals and objectives have been accomplished. Which of the following actions may be appropriate?

    I. Determining whether operating and program goals and objectives conform with those of the organization.

    II. Reviewing operations to ascertain the extent to which results are consistent with established goals and objectives.

    III. Working with management to develop appropriate control evaluation criteria.

    A. I only.

    B. I and II only.

    C. I, II, and III.

    D. II only.

Answer (C) is correct. *(Publisher)*
    REQUIRED: The action(s) that may be taken if management has not established criteria for achievement of goals and objectives.
    DISCUSSION: "Internal auditors should ascertain the extent to which operating and program goals and objectives have been established and conform to those of the organization" (Standard 2120.A2). Internal auditors also "should review operations and programs to ascertain the extent to which results are consistent with established goals and objectives to determine whether operations and programs are being implemented or performed as intended" (Standard 2120.A3). Furthermore, "Adequate criteria are needed to evaluate controls. Internal auditors should ascertain the extent to which management has established adequate criteria to determine whether objectives and goals have been accomplished. If adequate, internal auditors should use such criteria in their evaluation. If inadequate, internal auditors should work with management to develop appropriate evaluation criteria" (Standard 2120.A4).

26. What is the role of the principal executive officer and other certifying officers in disclosing fraud to the issuer's auditors and to the audit committee, according to SEC Rules 13a-14 and 15d-14?

- A. They have no responsibility to disclose fraud to the issuer's auditors or the audit committee.
- B. They have a responsibility to disclose material fraud that involves management or other employees who have a significant role in the issuer's internal controls.
- C. They have a responsibility to disclose any fraud that involves management or other employees regardless of whether they play a significant role in the issuer's internal controls.
- D. They have a responsibility to disclose any fraud that involves management or other employees who have a significant role in the issuer's internal controls.

Answer (D) is correct. *(Publisher)*
REQUIRED: The role of the principal executive officer and other certifying officers in disclosing fraud to the issuer's auditors and to the audit committee.
DISCUSSION: The principal executive officer and other certifying officers have a responsibility to disclose any fraud, whether or not material, that involves management or other employees who have a significant role in the issuer's internal controls. This is now required as part of SEC Rules 13a-14 and 15d-14 which is covered in PA 2120.A1-3.
Answer (A) is incorrect because the principal executive officer and other certifying officers do have a responsibility to disclose fraud to the issuer's auditors and the audit committee. Answer (B) is incorrect because all fraud, whether material or not, that involves management or other employees who have a significant role in the issuer's internal controls should be disclosed. Answer (C) is incorrect because all fraud, whether material or not, that involves management or other employees who have a significant role in the issuer's internal controls should be disclosed.

27. If an engagement client's operating standards are vague and thus subject to interpretation, the internal auditor should

- A. Seek agreement with the engagement client as to the criteria to be used to measure operating performance.
- B. Determine best practices in this area and use them as the standard.
- C. Interpret the standards in their strictest sense because standards are otherwise only minimum measures of acceptance.
- D. Omit any comments on standards and the engagement client's performance in relationship to those standards because such an analysis would be meaningless.

Answer (A) is correct. *(CIA, adapted)*
REQUIRED: The internal auditor's action if an engagement client's operating standards are vague.
DISCUSSION: Management is responsible for establishing adequate criteria for determining whether objectives and goals have been accomplished (Standard 2120.A4). However, established internal auditors should evaluate the operating targets and expectations and should determine whether those operating standards are acceptable and are being met. When such management targets and criteria are vague, authoritative interpretations should be sought. If internal auditors are required to interpret or select operating standards, they should seek agreement with engagement clients as to the criteria needed to measure operating performance (PA 2120.A4-1).
Answer (B) is incorrect because the internal auditor need not apply the principles of competitive benchmarking. Answer (C) is incorrect because circumstances will dictate the interpretation of vague operating standards. Answer (D) is incorrect because the internal auditor must interpret or select standards if an engagement client's operating standards are vague.

28. During a formal consulting engagement, the internal auditor should always bring substantial risk exposures or material control weaknesses to the attention of whom?

- A. Executive management.
- B. Management.
- C. Audit committee.
- D. Board of directors.

Answer (B) is correct. *(Publisher)*
REQUIRED: The group that the internal auditor should always communicate substantial risk exposure or material control weaknesses to during a formal consulting engagement.
DISCUSSION: Internal auditors should be observant of the effectiveness of risk management and control processes during formal consulting engagements. Substantial risk exposures or material control weaknesses should be brought to the attention of management. In some situations the auditor's concerns should also be communicated to executive management, the audit committee, or the board of directors.

29. An internal auditor should exercise due professional care in performing engagements. Due professional care includes

   A. Establishing direct communication between the chief audit executive and the board of directors.

   B. Evaluating established operating standards and determining whether those standards are acceptable and are being met.

   C. Accumulating sufficient information so that the internal auditor can give absolute assurance that irregularities do not exist.

   D. Establishing suitable criteria of education and experience for filling internal auditing positions.

Answer (B) is correct. *(CIA, adapted)*
   REQUIRED: The internal auditor's action consistent with due professional care.
   DISCUSSION: In the exercise of due professional care, an internal auditor should, among other things, consider the adequacy and effectiveness of risk management, control, and governance processes (Standard 1220.A1). Furthermore, adequate criteria are needed to evaluate controls. Thus, internal auditors should ascertain the extent to which management has established adequate criteria to determine whether objectives and goals have been accomplished (Standard 2120.A4). Internal auditors should evaluate the established operating targets and expectations and should determine whether those operating standards are acceptable and are being met (PA 2120.A4-1).
   Answer (A) is incorrect because such communication promotes the independence of the internal audit activity rather than the performance of engagements with due professional care. Answer (C) is incorrect because assurance procedures alone, even when performed with due professional care, cannot guarantee that all significant risks will be identified (Standard 1220.A2). Answer (D) is incorrect because establishing suitable criteria of education and experience for filling internal auditing positions pertains to proficiency, not due professional care.

5.2 Systems Approach to Control

30. Which of the following are elements of a feedback control system?

   A. Detectors, comparators, and activators.

   B. Sender, medium, and receiver.

   C. Achievement, recognition, and aptitude.

   D. Planning, organizing, and directing.

Answer (A) is correct. *(CIA, adapted)*
   REQUIRED: The elements of a feedback control system.
   DISCUSSION: A feedback control system ensures that a desired state is attained or maintained. The control object is the variable of the system's behavior chosen for monitoring. A detector measures what is happening in the variable being controlled. A reference point represents the standards against which performance may be measured or matched. A comparator (analyzer) is a device for assessing the significance of what is happening, usually by comparing information supplied by the detector (what is actually happening) with the established reference points (what should be happening). An activator is a decision maker. It evaluates alternative courses of corrective action available given the nature of the deviation identified and transmitted by the comparator. The output of the activating mechanism is typically corrective action.
   Answer (B) is incorrect because sender, medium, and receiver are elements in a communication network. Answer (C) is incorrect because achievement, recognition, and aptitude are behavior motivators. Answer (D) is incorrect because planning, organizing, and directing are management functions other than controlling.

31. Control may be described as a closed system consisting of six elements. One of the six elements is

   A. Setting performance standards.

   B. Adequately securing data files.

   C. Approval of the internal audit activity's charter.

   D. Establishment of an independent internal audit activity.

Answer (A) is correct. *(CIA, adapted)*
   REQUIRED: The element of control.
   DISCUSSION: Sawyer's Internal Auditing (IIA 1988, p. 979), on which this question is based, describes a six-element control system: (1) setting standards, (2) measuring performance, (3) analyzing performance and comparing it with the standards, (4) evaluating deviations and bringing them to the attention of appropriate persons, (5) correcting deviations, and (6) following up on corrective action.
   Answer (B) is incorrect because adequately securing data files is not an element of a closed control system. Answer (C) is incorrect because approval of the IAA's charter is not an element of a closed control system. Answer (D) is incorrect because establishment of an independent IAA is not an element of a closed control system.

32. Specific airline ticket information, including fare, class, purchase date, and lowest available fare options, as prescribed in the organization's travel policy, is obtained and reported to department management when employees purchase airline tickets from the organization's authorized travel agency. Such a report provides information for

- A. Quality of performance in relation to the organization's travel policy.
- B. Identifying costs necessary to process employee business expense report data.
- C. Departmental budget-to-actual comparisons.
- D. Supporting employer's business expense deductions.

Answer (A) is correct. *(CIA, adapted)*
REQUIRED: The information provided by reporting employee airline ticket information.
DISCUSSION: Feedback is a part of the internal control cycle. It provides a basis for comparing actual performance (purchases of tickets given the available options) with standards (organizational policy).
Answer (B) is incorrect because this ticket information is preliminary; employees may change tickets and routings prior to their trip. Answer (C) is incorrect because departmental budget-to-actual comparisons do not necessarily reflect the actual costs ultimately incurred. Answer (D) is incorrect because supporting expense deductions may not necessarily reflect actual costs.

5.3 Means of Achieving Control

33. Internal control should follow certain basic principles to achieve its objectives. One of these principles is the segregation of functions. Which one of the following examples does not violate the principle of segregation of functions?

- A. The treasurer has the authority to sign checks but gives the signature block to the assistant treasurer to run the check-signing machine.
- B. The warehouse clerk, who has the custodial responsibility over inventory in the warehouse, may authorize disposal of damaged goods.
- C. The sales manager has the responsibility to approve credit and the authority to write off accounts.
- D. The department time clerk is given the undistributed payroll checks to mail to absent employees.

Answer (A) is correct. *(CMA, adapted)*
REQUIRED: The situation that does not violate the principle of segregation of functions.
DISCUSSION: Controls include segregation of duties to reduce the risk that any person may be able to perpetrate and conceal errors or fraud in the normal course of his/her duties. Different persons should authorize transactions, record transactions, and maintain custody of assets. The treasurer's department should have custody of assets but should not authorize or record transactions. Because the assistant treasurer reports to the treasurer, the treasurer is merely delegating an assigned duty related to asset custody. The use of the check-signing machine does not conflict with any other duty of the assistant treasurer and does not involve authorization or recording of transactions.
Answer (B) is incorrect because authorization to dispose of damaged goods could be used to cover thefts of inventory for which the warehouse clerk has custodial responsibility. Transaction authorization is inconsistent with asset custody. Answer (C) is incorrect because the sales manager could approve credit to a controlled entity and then write off the account as a bad debt. The sales manager's authorization of credit is inconsistent with his/her indirect access to assets. Answer (D) is incorrect because the time clerk could conceal the termination of an employee and retain that employee's paycheck. Record keeping is inconsistent with asset custody.

34. If internal control is well designed, two tasks that should be performed by different persons are

A. Approval of bad debt write-offs, and reconciliation of the accounts payable subsidiary ledger and controlling account.

B. Distribution of payroll checks and approval of sales returns for credit.

C. Posting of amounts from both the cash receipts journal and cash payments journal to the general ledger.

D. Recording of cash receipts and preparation of bank reconciliations.

Answer (D) is correct. *(CMA, adapted)*
REQUIRED: The tasks that should be performed by different persons if internal control is well designed.
DISCUSSION: Recording of cash establishes accountability for assets. The bank reconciliation compares that recorded accountability with actual assets. The recording of cash receipts and preparation of bank reconciliations should therefore be performed by different individuals because the preparer of a reconciliation could conceal a cash shortage. For example, if a cashier both prepares the bank deposit and performs the reconciliation, (s)he could embezzle cash and conceal the theft by falsifying the reconciliation.
Answer (A) is incorrect because there is no conflict between writing off bad debts (accounts receivable) and reconciling accounts payable, which are liabilities. Answer (B) is incorrect because distribution of payroll checks and approval of sales returns are independent functions. People who perform such disparate tasks are unlikely to be able to perpetrate and conceal a fraud. In fact, some organizations use personnel from an independent function to distribute payroll checks. Answer (C) is incorrect because posting both ledgers would cause no conflict as long as the individual involved did not have access to the actual cash. If a person has access to records but not the assets, no danger exists of embezzlement without collusion.

35. Which one of the following situations represents an internal control weakness in the payroll department?

A. Payroll department personnel are rotated in their duties.

B. Paychecks are distributed by the employees' immediate supervisor.

C. Payroll records are reconciled with quarterly tax reports.

D. The timekeeping function is independent of the payroll department.

Answer (B) is correct. *(CMA, adapted)*
REQUIRED: The internal control weakness in the payroll department.
DISCUSSION: Paychecks should not be distributed by supervisors because an unscrupulous person could terminate an employee and fail to report the termination. The supervisor could then clock in and out for the employee and keep the paycheck. A person unrelated to either payroll record keeping or the operating department should distribute checks.
Answer (A) is incorrect because periodic rotation of payroll personnel inhibits the perpetration and concealment of fraud. Answer (C) is incorrect because this analytical procedure may detect a discrepancy. Answer (D) is incorrect because timekeeping should be independent of asset custody and employee records.

36. Which of the following activities represents both an appropriate personnel department function and a deterrent to payroll fraud?

A. Distribution of paychecks.

B. Authorization of overtime.

C. Authorization of additions and deletions from the payroll.

D. Collection and retention of unclaimed paychecks.

Answer (C) is correct. *(CIA, adapted)*
REQUIRED: The activity that is both a personnel department function and a fraud deterrent.
DISCUSSION: The payroll department is responsible for assembling payroll information (record keeping). The personnel department is responsible for authorizing employee transactions such as hiring, firing, and changes in pay rates and deductions. Segregating the recording and authorization functions helps prevent fraud.
Answer (A) is incorrect because the treasurer should perform the asset custody function regarding payroll. Answer (B) is incorrect because authorizing overtime is a responsibility of operating management. Answer (D) is incorrect because unclaimed checks should be in the custody of the treasurer until they can be deposited in a special bank account.

37. Which of the following describes a control weakness?

A. Purchasing procedures are well designed and are followed unless otherwise directed by the purchasing supervisor.

B. Prenumbered blank purchase orders are secured within the purchasing department.

C. Normal operational purchases fall in the range from $500 to $1,000 with two signatures required for purchases over $1,000.

D. The purchasing agent invests in a publicly traded mutual fund that lists the stock of one of the organization's suppliers in its portfolio.

Answer (A) is correct. *(CIA, adapted)*
REQUIRED: The control weakness.
DISCUSSION: Well-designed procedures that are set aside at management's discretion are not adequate controls. Control procedures must be followed consistently to be effective. However, the possibility of management override is an inherent limitation of internal control.
Answer (B) is incorrect because use of prenumbered blank purchase orders secured within the purchasing department is a common control. Answer (C) is incorrect because requiring a more stringent authorization procedure for larger purchases is an appropriate control as long as documentation supports the purchases. Answer (D) is incorrect because the purchasing agent's mutual fund investment should not be a conflict of interest. The relationship between the return on the investment and any possible action by the agent to favor the supplier is very weak.

38. The most appropriate method to control the frequent movement of trailers loaded with valuable metal scrap from the manufacturing plant to the organization's scrap yard about 10 miles away would be to

A. Perform complete physical inventory of the scrap trailers before leaving the plant and upon arrival at the scrap yard.

B. Require existing security guards to log the time of plant departure and scrap yard arrival. The elapsed time should be reviewed by a supervisor for fraud.

C. Use armed guards to escort the movement of the trailers from the plant to the scrap yard.

D. Contract with an independent hauler for the removal of scrap.

Answer (B) is correct. *(CIA, adapted)*
REQUIRED: The most appropriate method to control the frequent movement of trailers loaded with valuable metal scrap.
DISCUSSION: Having the security guards record the times of departure and arrival is a cost-effective control because it entails no additional expenditures. Comparing the time elapsed with the standard time allowed and investigating material variances may detect a diversion of part of the scrap.
Answer (A) is incorrect because performing a complete physical inventory of the scrap at both locations would not be economically feasible. Answer (C) is incorrect because hiring armed guards to escort the scrap trailers is unlikely to be necessary unless the scrap is extremely valuable. Logging departures and arrivals will be sufficient in most cases. Answer (D) is incorrect because using an independent hauler would provide no additional assurance of prevention or detection of wrongdoing.

39. A utility with a large investment in repair vehicles would most likely implement which internal control to reduce the risk of vehicle theft or loss?

A. Review insurance coverage for adequacy.

B. Systematically account for all repair work orders.

C. Physically inventory vehicles and reconcile the results with the accounting records.

D. Maintain vehicles in a secured location with release and return subject to approval by a custodian.

Answer (D) is correct. *(CIA, adapted)*
REQUIRED: The internal control to reduce the risk of vehicle theft or loss.
DISCUSSION: Physical control of assets is a preventive control that reduces the likelihood of theft or other loss. Keeping the vehicles at a secure location and restricting access establishes accountability by the custodian and allows for proper authorization of their use.
Answer (A) is incorrect because insurance provides for indemnification if loss or theft occurs. It reduces financial exposure but does not prevent the actual loss or theft. Answer (B) is incorrect because an internal control designed to ensure control over repair work performed has no bearing on the risk of loss. Answer (C) is incorrect because taking an inventory is a detective, not a preventive, control.

40. To minimize the risk that agents in the purchasing department will use their positions for personal gain, the organization should

A. Rotate purchasing agent assignments periodically.

B. Request internal auditors to confirm selected purchases and accounts payable.

C. Specify that all items purchased must pass value-per-unit-of-cost reviews.

D. Direct the purchasing department to maintain records on purchase prices paid, with review of such being required each 6 months.

Answer (A) is correct. *(CIA, adapted)*
REQUIRED: The control to minimize the risk that agents in the purchasing department will use their positions for personal gain.
DISCUSSION: The risk of favoritism is increased when buyers have long-term relationships with specific vendors. Periodic rotation of buyer assignments will limit the opportunity to show favoritism. This risk is also reduced if buyers are required to take vacations.
Answer (B) is incorrect because confirmation does not enable internal auditors to detect inappropriate benefits received by purchasing agents or deter long-term relationships. Answer (C) is incorrect because value-per-unit-of-cost reviews could be helpful in assuring value received for price paid but do not directly focus on receipt of inappropriate benefits by purchasing agents. Answer (D) is incorrect because review of records every 6 months does not enable the organization to detect receipt of inappropriate benefits by an agent or deter relationships that could lead to such activity.

41. A system of internal control includes physical controls over access to and use of assets and records. A departure from the purpose of such procedures is that

A. Access to the safe-deposit box requires two officers.

B. Only storeroom personnel and line supervisors have access to the raw materials storeroom.

C. The mailroom compiles a list of the checks received in the incoming mail.

D. Only salespersons and sales supervisors use sales department vehicles.

Answer (B) is correct. *(Publisher)*
REQUIRED: The departure from the purpose of control activities that limit access to assets.
DISCUSSION: Storeroom personnel have custody of assets, and supervisors are in charge of execution functions. To give supervisors access to the raw materials storeroom is a violation of the essential internal control principle of segregation of functions.
Answer (A) is incorrect because it is appropriate for two officers to be required to open the safe-deposit box. One supervises the other. Answer (C) is incorrect because the mailroom typically compiles a prelisting of cash. The list is sent to the accountant as a control for actual cash sent to the cashier. Answer (D) is incorrect because use of sales department vehicles should be limited to sales personnel unless proper authorization is obtained.

42. Which of the following controls could be used to detect bank deposits that are recorded but never made?

A. Establishing accountability for receipts at the earliest possible time.

B. Linking receipts to other internal accountabilities, for example, collections to either accounts receivable or sales.

C. Consolidating cash receiving points.

D. Having bank reconciliations performed by a third party.

Answer (D) is correct. *(CIA, adapted)*
REQUIRED: The control to detect failure to make recorded bank deposits.
DISCUSSION: Having an independent third party prepare the bank reconciliations would reveal any discrepancies between recorded deposits and the bank statements. A bank reconciliation compares the bank statement with company records and resolves differences caused by deposits in transit, outstanding checks, NSF checks, bank charges, errors, etc.

43. Upon receipt of purchased goods, receiving department personnel match the quantity received with the packing slip quantity and mark the retail price on the goods based on a master price list. The annotated packing slip is then forwarded to inventory control and goods are automatically moved to the retail sales area. The most significant control strength of this activity is

- A. Immediately pricing goods for retail sale.
- B. Matching quantity received with the packing slip.
- C. Using a master price list for marking the sale price.
- D. Automatically moving goods to the retail sales area.

Answer (C) is correct.   *(CIA, adapted)*
REQUIRED: The most significant control strength of the procedure described.
DISCUSSION: Use of the master price list assures that the correct retail price is marked.
Answer (A) is incorrect because timing is not as important as the accuracy of prices. Answer (B) is incorrect because matching quantity received with the packing slip does not ensure receipt of the quantity ordered. Answer (D) is incorrect because goods may or may not be needed in retail sales.

44. Management can best strengthen internal control over the custody of inventory stored in an off-site warehouse by implementing

- A. Reconciliations of transfer slips to/from the warehouse with inventory records.
- B. Increases in insurance coverage.
- C. Regular reconciliation of physical inventories to accounting records.
- D. Regular confirmation of the amount on hand with the custodian of the warehouse.

Answer (C) is correct.   *(CIA, adapted)*
REQUIRED: The best method to strengthen control over off-site inventory.
DISCUSSION: The most effective control over off-site inventory is the periodic comparison of the recorded accountability for inventory with the actual physical inventory.
Answer (A) is incorrect because examination of documents is a less effective procedure than actual observation of the inventory. Answer (B) is incorrect because increasing insurance coverage helps protect the business against losses but does not strengthen internal control over the custody of inventory. Answer (D) is incorrect because confirming with the custodian the amount of inventory on hand does not verify that the inventory is actually at the warehouse.

45. A manufacturer uses large quantities of small inexpensive items such as nuts, bolts, washers, and gloves in the production process. As these goods are purchased, they are recorded in inventory in bulk amounts. Bins are located on the shop floor to provide timely access to these items. When necessary the bins are refilled from inventory, and the cost of the items is charged to a consumable supplies account, which is part of shop overhead. Which of the following would be an appropriate improvement of controls in this environment?

- A. Relocate bins to the inventory warehouse.
- B. Require management review of reports on the cost of consumable items used in relation to budget.
- C. Lock the bins during normal working hours.
- D. None of the above controls are needed for items of minor cost and size.

Answer (B) is correct.   *(CIA, adapted)*
REQUIRED: The control over small inexpensive items used in manufacturing.
DISCUSSION: In accordance with the cost-benefit criterion, control expenditures for manufacturing supplies (nuts, bolts, etc.) should be minimal. Nevertheless, some controls should be implemented. For example, usage should be estimated and compared with stock balances and also with the number of using personnel. Moreover, variances should be calculated for the difference between costs incurred and budgeted amounts.
Answer (A) is incorrect because the bins should be on the shop floor where the nuts, bolts, etc., are needed. Answer (C) is incorrect because locking the bins would limit the efficiency and effectiveness of shop personnel. Answer (D) is incorrect because controls are needed even for items of minor cost and size.

46. When a supplier of office products is unable to fill an order completely, it marks the out-of-stock items as back ordered on the customer's order and enters these items in a back order file that management can view or print. Customers are becoming disgruntled with the supplier because it seems unable to keep track of and ship out-of-stock items as soon as they are available. The best approach for ensuring prompt delivery of out-of-stock items is to

A. Match the back order file to goods received daily.

B. Increase inventory levels to minimize the number of times that out-of-stock conditions occur.

C. Implement electronic data interchange with supply vendors to decrease the time to replenish inventory.

D. Reconcile the sum of filled and back orders with the total of all orders placed daily.

Answer (A) is correct. *(CIA, adapted)*
REQUIRED: The best approach for ensuring prompt delivery of out-of-stock items.
DISCUSSION: The system should be designed automatically to reconcile the back-order file with shipments on a daily basis. The system could therefore identify unfilled orders for appropriate and prompt action.
Answer (B) is incorrect because an increase in inventory minimizes out-of-stock conditions but has no effect on tracking and shipping goods as soon as they are available. Answer (C) is incorrect because the use of EDI has no effect on tracking and shipping goods as soon as they are available. Answer (D) is incorrect because reconciling the sum of filled and back orders with the total of all orders placed daily ensures that orders were either filled or back ordered but will not affect delivery of the items that are out of stock.

47. A restaurant chain has over 680 restaurants. All food orders for each restaurant are required to be entered into an electronic device that records all food orders by food servers and transmits the order to the kitchen for preparation. All food servers are responsible for collecting cash for all their orders and must turn in cash at the end of their shift equal to the sales value of food ordered for their I.D. number. The manager then reconciles the cash received for the day with the computerized record of food orders generated. All differences are investigated immediately by the restaurant. Organizational headquarters has established monitoring controls to determine when an individual restaurant might not be recording all its revenue and transmitting the applicable cash to the corporate headquarters. Which one of the following is the best example of a monitoring control?

A. The restaurant manager reconciles the cash received with the food orders recorded on the computer.

B. All food orders must be entered on the computer, and segregation of duties is maintained between the food servers and the cooks.

C. Management prepares a detailed analysis of gross margin per store and investigates any store that shows a significantly lower gross margin.

D. Cash is transmitted to corporate headquarters on a daily basis.

Answer (C) is correct. *(CIA, adapted)*
REQUIRED: The best example of a monitoring control.
DISCUSSION: Monitoring is a process that assesses the quality of internal control over time. It involves assessment by appropriate personnel of the design and operation of controls and the taking of corrective action. Monitoring can be done through ongoing activities or separate evaluations. Ongoing monitoring procedures are built into the normal recurring activities of an entity and include regular management and supervisory activities. Thus, analysis of gross margin data and investigation of significant deviations is a monitoring process.
Answer (A) is incorrect because the manager's activity is an example of a reconciliation control applied at the store level. Monitoring is an overall control that determines whether other controls are operating effectively. Answer (B) is incorrect because the division of duties is an operational control. Answer (D) is incorrect because daily transmission of cash is an operational control.

48. Insurers may receive hospitalization claims directly from hospitals by computer media; no paper is transmitted from the hospital to the insurer. Which of the following controls is most effective in detecting fraud in such an environment?

A. Use integrated test facilities to test the correctness of processing in a manner that is transparent to data processing.

B. Develop monitoring programs to identify unusual types of claims or an unusual number of claims by demographic classes for investigation by the claims department.

C. Use generalized audit software to match the claimant identification number with a master list of valid policyholders.

D. Develop batch controls over all items received from a particular hospital and process those claims in batches.

Answer (B) is correct. *(CIA, adapted)*
REQUIRED: The most effective preventive control over transmission of insurance claims by computer.
DISCUSSION: Monitoring assesses the quality of internal control over time. Management considers whether internal control is properly designed and operating as intended and modifies it to reflect changing conditions. Monitoring may be in the form of separate, periodic evaluations or of ongoing monitoring. Ongoing monitoring occurs as part of routine operations. It includes management and supervisory review, comparisons, reconciliations, and other actions by personnel as part of their regular activities. Thus, monitoring of the number and nature of claims may serve to detect failures of internal control.

Answer (A) is incorrect because an ITF is useful in determining the correctness of processing of validly entered transactions. The issue in this case is the validity of the entered transactions. Answer (C) is incorrect because an edit control should be built into the application to test for valid policy numbers. Answer (D) is incorrect because batch controls are designed to ensure that all items submitted are processed, i.e., that they are not lost or added to. Batch controls serve a control purpose, but the major concern in this situation is the validity of the input.

Use Gleim's *CIA Test Prep* for interactive testing with over 2,000 additional multiple-choice questions!

STUDY UNIT SIX
CONTROL II

(30 pages of outline)

This study unit is the second of two devoted to internal control. Study Unit 5 emphasized authoritative pronouncements and certain theoretical considerations. Study Unit 6 enlarges upon those considerations, especially with regard to control frameworks. It also extends to related subjects such as management of change, organizational structures, leadership styles, and conflict management.

6.1 THE NATURE OF CONTROL

1. Control is the process of assuring that plans achieve the desired objectives and goals.

    a. The essence of control is feedback information on the results of actions taken by the enterprise for the purposes of measurement and regulation.

    b. Control can be precise, imprecise, formal, informal, good, or bad.

    c. Control has two aspects.

        1) Performance is measured against a standard.

        2) Performance is regulated or corrected (if necessary) in light of that measurement (thus, timeliness of feedback is important).

2. Controls are often classified as follows:

    a. **Feedback controls** obtain information about completed activities. They permit improvement in future performance by learning from past mistakes. Thus, corrective action occurs after the fact. Inspection of completed goods is an example.

    b. **Concurrent control** adjust ongoing processes. These real-time controls monitor activities in the present to prevent them from deviating too far from standards. An example is close supervision of production-line workers.

    c. **Feedforward controls** anticipate and prevent problems. These controls require a long-term perspective. Organizational policies and procedures are examples.

3. A typical sequence of control functions includes

    a. Selecting strategic control points at which to gather information about the activities being performed

    b. Observing the work, or collecting samples or other significant data

    c. Accumulating, classifying, and recording this information

    d. Comparing it with predetermined quality, schedule, and cost standards

e.   Determining whether performance is satisfactory

f.   Reporting significant deviations to managers concerned

g.   Determining, by repeating the steps, whether action taken is effective in correcting reported deviations (follow-up)

h.   Reviewing and revising standards

4.   A successful control process is one that institutes corrections before the deviations become serious.

5.   **Planning and control** overlap, and some common managerial tools apply to both.

a.   Comprehensive planning includes creation of control mechanisms, i.e., measurement and follow-up.

b.   Budgets, breakeven charts, and Program Evaluation and Review Technique (PERT) are examples of systematically combining planning with control.

6.   Control devices may be either **quantitative or qualitative**.

a.   Budgets, schedules, quotas, charts, etc., are quantitative.

b.   Job instructions, quality-control standards, and employment criteria are qualitative.

7.   The total control process is a **closed system** consisting of a series of control elements.

a.   As the final managerial function, control also closes the total managerial system by leading back to revised plans and corrective action when necessary to accomplish objectives.

8.   Effective control systems should display the following **characteristics**:

a.   Economical: Excessive controls are costly in time as well as money.

b.   Meaningful: They must measure performance in important areas.

c.   Appropriate: They must fairly reflect the events they are designed to measure.

d.   Congruent: They must be consistent with the need for and ability to obtain precision in measurement. For example, employee morale may be described as good or bad but is not precisely quantifiable.

e.   Timely: Outdated information is inappropriate.

f.   Simple: Control should be understandable to people using it.

g.   Operational: Controls should be relevant to a planned result and not just interesting.

9.   Control has been facilitated by improvements in information technology and reductions in its cost, which have made real-time information common, e.g., airline reservation systems, retail point-of-sale systems, and production-line status systems.

a.   Technological advances have increased the popularity of **total quality management (TQM)** techniques and reengineering.

1)   **Reengineering** (also called **business process reengineering**) entails process innovation and core process redesign. Instead of improving existing procedures, it finds new ways of doing things. Its emphasis is on simplification and elimination of nonvalue-adding activities. Thus, it is not continuous improvement, it is not simply downsizing or modifying an existing system, and it should be reserved for the most important processes.

a)   In the modern highly competitive business environment, a company may need to adapt quickly and radically to change. Thus, reengineering is usually a cross-departmental process of innovation requiring substantial investment in information technology and retraining. Successful reengineering may bring dramatic improvements in customer service and the speed with which new products are introduced.

b) Reengineering may be contrasted with **automation**, or the computerization of existing manual methods; **rationalization**, or the streamlining of procedures to make automation more efficient; and a paradigm shift, or a complete change in the very nature of the business.

2) One well-known tool useful in reengineering is **work measurement**, a process that involves analysis of activities. The nature and extent of a task, the procedures needed for its execution, and the efficiency with which it is carried out are determined by work measurement.

a) This technique is appropriate when management takes an engineered-cost approach to control. Such an approach is indicated when the workload is divisible into control-factor units, for example, accounting entries made, lines of text word processed, or number of packages shipped. In work measurement, the cost of a control-factor unit is treated as a variable cost for budgeting purposes.

b) One method used for work measurement is micromotion study, which entails videotaping performance of a job, e.g., assembly-line activities.

c) Another method is work sampling, a technique that involves making numerous random observations of an activity to determine what steps it normally requires.

b. Accordingly, reengineering and TQM techniques eliminate many traditional controls. They exploit modern technology to improve productivity and decrease the number of clerical workers. Thus, the emphasis is on developing controls that are automated and self-correcting and require minimal human intervention.

c. The emphasis therefore shifts to monitoring internal control so management can determine when an operation may be out of control and corrective action is needed.

1) Most reengineering and TQM techniques also assume that humans will be motivated to work actively in improving operations when they are full participants in the process.

d. **Monitoring** assesses the quality of internal control over time. Management considers whether internal control is properly designed and operating as intended and modifies it to reflect changing conditions. Monitoring may be in the form of separate, periodic evaluations or of ongoing monitoring.

1) Ongoing monitoring occurs as part of routine operations. It includes management and supervisory review, comparisons, reconciliations, and other actions by personnel as part of their regular activities.

10. Stop and review! You have completed the outline for this subunit. Study multiple-choice questions 1 through 12 beginning on page 198.

6.2 THE CONTROL SEQUENCE

1. **Setting Standards**. Standards are specific goals or objectives with which performance is compared.

a. Standards are commonly classified in terms of

1) **Quantity** – the number of units to be produced
2) **Quality** – rejects, rework costs
3) **Time** – schedules, promised deliveries
4) **Cost** – the number of dollars needed to produce the required number of units

   b.   **Control points.** Selection of points at which performance will be measured is critical.

   1)   It is not possible to oversee or measure the performance of every aspect of a business organization's activity.

   a)   The cost would be prohibitive.

   b)   The information system generating such data would overload the manager's capacity for review.

   c)   Too much control is demoralizing.

   d)   Measuring the wrong performance is unproductive.

   e)   Developing surrogate quantitative measures for many qualitative issues may focus attention on the wrong issues (an example is teaching students how to maximize test scores instead of teaching concepts).

   f)   The choices of control points and standards will affect behavior. Standards and control points must be selected so they are congruent with organizational goals.

   i)   EXAMPLE: One study of the management of a police force revealed a dysfunctional result of a poor choice of a control point. An administrator, who had noticed that those units with the most miles logged on their patrol car odometers also had the most arrests, began rewarding those units with the most miles driven. This choice of control point did not increase the number of arrests, but it did increase mileage greatly.

   2)   Key questions in the selection of control points

   a)   What will best reflect the goals of the department?

   b)   What will best indicate when these goals are not being met?

   c)   What will best measure critical deviations, i.e., those with the greatest impact on departmental goals?

   d)   Which standards will cost the least?

   3)   Examples of good control points are

   a)   Inspecting a motor **before** its cover is attached
   b)   Balancing columns of figures **before** entering the answers into a ledger
   c)   Inspecting components **before** assembly
   d)   Reviewing progress reports **at** intermediate points
   e)   Inspecting materials **before** approving payment

2.   **Additional Guides for Standards**

   a.   Standards should assist in implementing plans.

   b.   Standards should be applied at those points that significantly influence subsequent progress.

   c.   Standards must be **accepted** by those who will carry them out if they are to have maximum effectiveness.

   1)   Subordinates should believe that standards are both fair and achievable, or they will tend to sabotage, ignore, or circumvent them.

   2)   Participation in the standard-setting process will encourage acceptance of standards and increase understanding of their meanings, measures, and purposes by those affected.

   d.   Standards should be **reviewed** periodically for adjustment or elimination because of changed circumstances.

e.   Standards may need to be **flexible** in the same way budgets are flexible. The appropriate standard might be a ratio between cost and service produced rather than an absolute dollar amount of cost. For example,

1)   Labor hours per unit rather than total labor hours
2)   Pounds of material consumed per customer, not total pounds consumed

f.   Standards take different forms, depending on organizational function and level.

1)   Production standards
2)   Sales standards, such as percentage margin on sales
3)   Finance standards

a)   Return on investment at various levels
b)   Return on investment for decentralized divisions
c)   Budgets

4)   Personnel standards

a)   Turnover rates
b)   New hire rates
c)   Voluntary termination rates
d)   Absentee rates
e)   Sales per employee
f)   Return on investment per employee
g)   Affirmative action programs
h)   Human asset accounting
i)   Training needs and costs

5)   Management standards

a)   Management audits (operational audits of all activities of a particular function or department)
b)   Audits based on performance standards in social areas (social responsibility audits)

3.   **Setting Tight Standards**

a.   The degree of difficulty in meeting a standard is known as tightness. The more difficult a standard is to achieve, the tighter it is said to be.

b.   Tight standards can have positive behavioral implications if they motivate employees to strive for excellence.

c.   They can have negative effects if they are difficult or impossible to attain.

4.   **Measuring Performance**. Every product, output, or action can be measured in some way.

a.   The difficulty is in selecting appropriate measures for the performance activity being monitored. For example,

1)   A decentralized structure in which the manager is evaluated on a return on investment (ROI) basis forces the manager to seek short-run, profit-maximizing solutions to the detriment of long-run survival factors such as

a)   Social responsibility and ethics
b)   Research and development
c)   Capital purchase decisions

2)   The budgeting process may send unintended messages to managers who play the budget game instead of accomplishing objectives.

b.   The measurement must be carefully chosen because it is a message to the controlled activity's personnel and directs their behavior.

c. Complete measurement is often not possible (e.g., because of destructive tests) or not desirable (possibly because it is too costly) or inappropriate (the measure may be irrelevant to actual performance).

   1) Statistical sampling is useful for some quantitative measures (e.g., quality control).

   2) Sampling of the work process may be better than observing work output (e.g., behavior control).

d. The people doing the measuring may or may not be involved in the performance.

e. Behavioral considerations are important factors in selecting who does the measuring, as well as what is measured and what standards are used.

   1) Self-measurement may create confidence and trust. Moreover, feedback, correction, and learning may occur more quickly.

      a) It may also lead to distortion, concealment, and delay in reporting when goals and measurement criteria are unclear.

      b) It forces clear definition and open communication of organizational goals because employees must know the standards and measures.

   2) Second-party measurement may create hostility, concern, rebellion, and other negative reactions.

      a) It may also minimize bias, influence, and suspicion.

5. **Evaluation and Correction**. Care must be taken to compare like items. Thus, any alteration in the production process may make previously used or company-wide standards inapplicable to the case at hand.

a. Detection of a variation from standards is followed by the critical phases of evaluation and correction. A thorough understanding of applicable standards is required if appropriate corrective action is to result.

b. Some control situations require little evaluation and lead to immediate corrective action.

   1) In situations for which the number of possible future states is limited, a precise (usually quantitative) decision rule may be adopted. For example, a cash budget may call for a certain minimum balance in a given account. The automatic correction for this deviation calls for transferring into the account an amount of cash equal to the deficiency.

c. If subjective factors are important (e.g., employee evaluation), correction may need to be more gradual. Because the decision maker must rely on a number of less precise measures, the formulation of appropriate corrective action is more complex.

   1) One of the major disadvantages of trait-type performance appraisals is their inability to measure performance accurately, which makes corrective action difficult.

   2) One of the major advantages of management by objectives is that it closely ties job performance to a standard that can be used as a guide to corrective action.

    3) Participation by affected employees in all control systems (especially the judgmental areas) permits all concerned to understand both the performance levels desired and the measurement criteria being applied. Some benefits of participation are that it

       a) Develops a perception by those being evaluated that the process is fair

       b) Communicates to everyone the need for control

       c) Enhances acceptance of the need for control standards

       d) Indicates the direction of the desired behavior, which permits self-control and self-correction

6. Stop and review! You have completed the outline for this subunit. Study multiple-choice questions 13 through 20 beginning on page 201.

6.3 CONTROL FRAMEWORKS

1. The Committee of Sponsoring Organizations **(COSO)**, a consortium of organizations that includes The IIA and the AICPA among others, has developed the **Internal Control-Integrated Framework** model. The COSO model has served as the basis for control frameworks developed by other organizations, most notably the internal control pronouncements of the AICPA. That body's relevant Statements on Auditing Standards closely follow the COSO model.

    a. **Definition of control.** The COSO treats internal control as a **process** – effected by an entity's board of directors, management, and other **personnel** – designed to provide **reasonable assurance** regarding the achievement of **objectives** related to

       1) Reliability of financial reporting, e.g., published financial information;

       2) Effectiveness and efficiency of operations, e.g., achievement of performance and profit goals and the safeguarding of resources; and

       3) Compliance with applicable laws and regulations.

    b. Internal control is composed of five interrelated **components**.

       1) The **control environment** reflects the attitude and actions of the board and management regarding the significance of control within the organization. It sets the organization's tone and influences the central consciousness of its personnel. Moreover, the control environment provides discipline and structure for the achievement of the primary objectives of internal control. The control environment includes the following elements:

         a) **Integrity and ethical values.** Standards should be effectively communicated, e.g., by management example. Management should also remove incentives and temptations for dishonest or unethical acts.

         b) **Commitment to competence.** Management must consider the competence levels for particular jobs.

         c) **Board of directors or audit committee participation.** The independence, experience, and stature of their members are among the factors that affect the entity's control consciousness.

         d) **Management's philosophy and operating style**

           i) Relate to management's approach to taking and monitoring business risks

           ii) Include management's attitudes and actions towards financial reporting

           iii) Encompass management's attitudes towards information processing and accounting functions and personnel

e) **Organizational structure.** Key areas of authority and responsibility and appropriate lines of reporting should be considered.

f) **Assignment of authority and responsibility.** This factor concerns how authority over and responsibility for operating activities are assigned and how reporting relationships and authorization hierarchies are established.

g) **Human resource policies and practices** relate to hiring, orientation, training, evaluation, counseling, promoting, compensating, and remedial actions. Training policies should communicate roles and responsibilities and expected levels of performance and behavior.

2) **Risk assessment** is based on a set of complementary operational, financial reporting, and compliance **objectives** linked across all levels of the organization. Risk assessment identifies and analyzes external or internal risks to achievement of the objectives at the activity level as well as the entity level. The assessment provides a foundation for **managing change** in the economy, the industry and regulatory environments, and other operating conditions. The following factors affecting risk should be given special attention:

a) **Changes in operating environment.** A shift in the regulatory or operating environment may require reconsideration of risks.

b) **New personnel.** New employees may have a different focus on control issues.

c) **New or revamped information systems.** Significant and rapid changes in information systems can affect control risk, but IT is important to the risk assessment process because it provides timely information for identifying and managing risks.

d) **Rapid growth.** Expansion can strain controls and increase risk.

e) **New technology.** Integrating new technology into production or information processes may change risk.

f) **New business lines, products, or activities.** New business areas may change risk.

g) **Corporate restructurings.** Staffing changes can cause changes in risk.

h) **Expanded foreign operations.** Expansion to foreign markets may result in changes in risk.

3) **Control activities** are the policies and procedures helping to ensure that management directives are executed and actions are taken to address risks to achievement of objectives. Whether automated or manual, they have various objectives and are applied at all levels and in all functions of the organization.

a) **Performance reviews** by top managers include reviews of actual performance versus budgets, forecasts, prior performance, and competitors' results.

b) **Performance reviews at the functional or activity level** involve reviews of performance reports.

c) Analysis of **performance indicators**, that is, comparison of different sets of operating or financial data, may reveal unexpected results or trends that should be investigated.

d) **Information processing** requires checks of accuracy, completeness, and authorization of transactions. These controls include application controls and general controls. The latter include controls over data center operations, system software, access security, and applications development and maintenance.

e) **Physical controls** involve the security of assets and records and periodic counts and reconciliations.

f) **Segregation of duties** involves the separation of the functions of authorization, record keeping, and asset custody so as to minimize the opportunities for a person to be able to perpetrate and conceal errors or fraud in the normal course of his/her duties.

4) **Information and communication.** Relevant internal and external information should be identified, captured, and communicated in a timely manner and in appropriate forms.

 a) An **information system** may be formal or informal. It uses internal and external information to generate reports on financial, operational, and compliance matters.

   i) These reports facilitate the operation and control of the enterprise, decision-making, and external communications.

   ii) An information system may perform a routine **monitoring function** or be used for special tasks.

   iii) Information systems should be **integrated** not only with operations and the financial reporting process but also with the **strategic objectives** of the enterprise.

   iv) Information should be appropriate, timely, current, accurate, and accessible.

 b) **Communication** of information with the business may take many forms and should be two-way, both vertically and horizontally.

   i) Communication of information allows people in the organization to perform their duties regarding financial reporting, operations, and compliance.

   ii) However, communication also functions in a more general way. Thus, individuals in the organization should understand their obligations regarding **control** and how their work relates to the efforts of others.

   iii) Communications channels should be clear, and all parties should have good **listening** skills.

   iv) Effective communication between managers and directors is vital.

   v) Communication with such **external parties** as customers, suppliers, regulators, and shareholders should be open and effective.

5) **Monitoring** is "a process that assesses the quality of the system's performance over time."

 a) It consists of **ongoing activities** built into normal operations to ensure that they continue to be performed effectively. Supervision and other ordinary management functions, consideration of communications with external parties, and the actions of internal and external auditors are examples.

 b) Monitoring also involves **separate evaluations**. The extent of this form of monitoring depends on the effectiveness of the ongoing monitoring activities and the risk assessment.

   i) Separate evaluation may consist of control self-assessment or formal evaluations by internal or external auditors. Laws and regulations may require that an external assessment of internal control be performed periodically.

   ii) Deficiencies in internal control should be reported, with the most serious matters being communicated to senior management and the board.

c.   **Limitations of internal control.** Because of its inherent limitations, internal control can be designed and operated to provide only **reasonable assurance** that control objectives are met.

  1)   **Inherent limitations**

    a)   Human judgment is faulty, and controls may fail because of simple errors or mistakes.

    b)   Manual or automated controls can be circumvented by **collusion**.

    c)   Management may inappropriately **override** internal control.

    d)   Custom, culture, the corporate governance system, and an effective control environment are not absolute deterrents to fraud. For example, if the nature of management incentives increases the risk of material misstatements, the effectiveness of controls may be diminished.

    e)   **Costs should not exceed the benefits of control**. Although this relationship is a primary design criterion for internal control, the precise measurement of costs and benefits is not feasible.

d.   **Responsibility** for internal control resides with (is "owned" by) the chief executive, but all people in the organization share this responsibility.

  1)   Parties with significant roles are the financial and accounting officers, other managers, the internal auditors (who nevertheless do not have primary responsibility for establishing or maintaining internal control), the board and the audit committee, and external parties (e.g., the external auditors).

2.   The **CoCo model** is an adaptation of the COSO model by the Criteria of Control Board of the Canadian Institute of Chartered Accountants. It is thought to be better designed for internal auditing purposes.

  a.   The CoCo model consists of **20 criteria** grouped into **four components**. The following listing is from **Sawyer's Internal Auditing**, 5th Ed., L.B. Sawyer, et al., 2003, The Institute of Internal Auditors (pages 68-69):

    1)   *Purpose*

      a)   **Objectives** should be established and communicated.

      b)   The significant internal and external **risks** faced by an organization in the achievement of its objectives should be identified and assessed.

      c)   **Policies** designed to support the achievement of an organization's objectives and the management of its risks should be established, communicated, and practiced so that people understand what is expected of them and the scope of their freedom to act.

      d)   **Plans** to guide efforts in achieving the organization's objectives should be established and communicated.

      e)   Objectives and related plans should include measurable **performance targets and indicators**.

    2)   *Commitment*

      a)   Shared **ethical values**, including integrity, should be established, communicated, and practiced through the organization.

      b)   **Human resource** policies and practices should be consistent with an organization's ethical values and with achievement of its objectives.

      c)   **Authority, responsibility, and accountability** should be clearly defined and consistent with an organization's objectives so that decisions and actions are taken by the appropriate people.

      d)   An atmosphere of **mutual trust** should be fostered to support the flow of information between people and their effective performance toward achieving the organization's objectives.

   3) *Capability*

      a)   People should have the necessary **knowledge, skills, and tools** to support the achievement of the organization's objectives.

      b)   **Communication** processes should support the organization's values and the achievement of its objectives.

      c)   **Sufficient and relevant information** should be identified and communicated in a timely manner to enable people to perform their assigned responsibilities.

      d)   The decisions and actions of different parts of the organization should be **coordinated**.

      e)   **Control activities** should be designed as an integral part of the organization, taking into consideration its objectives, the risks to their achievement, and the interrelatedness of control elements.

   4) *Monitoring and Learning*

      a)   **External and internal environments** should be monitored to obtain information that may signal a need to reevaluate the organization's objectives or controls.

      b)   **Performance** should be monitored against the targets and indicators identified in the organization's objectives and plans.

      c)   The **assumptions** behind an organization's objectives and systems should be periodically challenged.

      d)   **Information** needs and related information systems should be reassessed as objectives change or as reporting deficiencies are identified.

      e)   **Follow-up** procedures should be established and performed to ensure appropriate change or action occurs.

      f)   Management should periodically **assess the effectiveness of control** in its organization and communicate the results to those whom it is accountable.

  b.   The COSO and CoCo models emphasize **soft controls** (see Roth, "Taking a Hard Look at Soft Controls," Internal Auditor, February 1998). For example, the communication of ethical values and the fostering of mutual trust are soft controls in the CoCo model. In the COSO model, soft controls are embodied in the control environment.

    1) Soft controls should be distinguished from the **hard controls** represented by compliance with specific policies and procedures imposed upon employees from above.

    2) Soft controls have become more necessary as **technology advances** have empowered employees. Technology has given them access to large amounts of critical information and enabled them to make decisions formerly made by those higher in the organizational structure.

      a)   In addition to making many hard controls obsolete, technology advances also have permitted the **automation** of hard controls, for example, the embedding of audit modules in computer programs.

3) One approach to auditing soft controls is **control self-assessment**, which is the involvement of management and staff in the assessment of internal controls within their workgroup.

4) Hard and soft controls can be associated with particular risks and measured. The vulnerability (V) addressed can be stated as the product of the probability of occurrence (P) and the significance of the occurrence (S). Accordingly, the formula is

$$PS = V$$

3. The IIA's own **Systems Auditability and Control study** (1991) defined the system of internal controls as the
    "means established to provide reasonable assurance that the overall objectives and goals of the organization are achieved in an efficient, effective, and economical manner. For the purpose of this report, a system of internal control is defined as a set of processes, functions, activities, subsystems, and people who are grouped together or consciously segregated to ensure the effective achievement of objectives."

    a. **Key concepts** are

        1) Reasonable assurance
        2) Objectives as desired accomplishments of the organization
        3) Goals as specific targets that are identifiable, measurable, attainable, and consistent with the objectives.

    b. **Components**

        1) **Control environment**

            a) Organization structure
            b) Control framework

                i)   Segregation of incompatible duties
                ii)   Competence and integrity of people
                iii) Appropriate levels of authority and responsibility
                iv)   Tracing transactions or events to responsible persons
                v)   Adequate resources, time, and knowledgable personnel
                vi)   Supervision of staff and review of work

            c) Organization policies and procedures
            d) External influence

        2) **Manual and automated systems**

            a) Systems software
            b) Application systems

                i)   Core business and financial systems
                ii) Specific operational systems

            c) End-user and departmental systems

        3) **Control procedures**

            a) General controls
            b) Application controls
            c) Compensating controls

4. Stop and review! You have completed the outline for this subunit. Study multiple-choice questions 21 through 25 beginning on page 203.

6.4 CONTROL TECHNIQUES

1. Control includes such planning devices as PERT, Gantt charts, and budgets. All these tools are considered here for their contribution to the control process.

   a. A **budget** is the traditional control device. The word has developed some negative connotations, and more positive phrases (**profit plan** or **business plan**) are sometimes used.

      1) A budget is a formal statement, usually in financial terms, of the goals and plans of an organization.

      2) A budget may also be stated in terms other than financial (e.g., budgets of direct labor hours, materials, or unit sales).

      3) The budget of an organization has the same structure as the organization itself; i.e., the total organizational budget is made up of a hierarchy of smaller budgets, each representing the plan of a division, department, or other unit in the organizational structure.

      4) Successful budgeting requires completion of a plan that states organizational goals before the budgeting process.

      5) Prevention and detection of deviations from budget are the control purposes of budgets. Such deviations have obvious implications for the success of planning.

         a) The amount of deviation and the portion of the budget affected are the starting points for corrective action.

         b) **Management by exception** is often used to foster cost control. Deviations from budget are the exceptions that attract the attention of management and consume the majority of management time and effort. However, management by exception has the disadvantages of not spotting trends at an early stage and not reinforcing employees for work well done.

         c) If deviations from the budget become more common than conformity to the budget, management by exception degenerates into putting out fires, and a serious reappraisal of either the budget or the managers is necessary.

   b. **PERT** is a control technique that breaks down a project into a set of events, arranges the events into a strict priority network, and establishes a completion time for each event.

      1) With PERT, it is possible to find a **critical path**, i.e., the order of events that determines the time required for completion of the project.

      2) The critical path is important for control purposes because

         a) Management can concentrate its efforts on the most important activities and not waste time controlling noncritical activities.

         b) As the plan is executed and variations change the critical path, PERT provides a means of identifying the new critical path and applying the appropriate management effort.

   c. **Gantt charts** compare scheduled production with actual production. Their control use comes from the ability to identify variations and thus stimulate corrective action. Gantt charts are not as effective as PERT because interactions between various steps in a project are not identified.

   d. **Flowcharting** is a useful tool for conducting a preliminary survey and understanding internal control as well as for systems development. A flowchart is a pictorial diagram of the definition, analysis, or solution of a problem in which symbols are used to represent operations, data flow, equipment, etc.

e. **Cause-effect analysis** uses fishbone diagrams to determine the causes of problems. Construction begins with a problem statement (the head of the fish), and the potential causes are grouped by categories, with each category assigned a main branch off the backbone of the skeleton. Each cause within a category is listed on a line attached to the branch. The most recent causes are nearest to the problem statement.

f. **Pareto analysis** (named for an Italian economist) is based on the 80-20 principle; that is, only about 20% of the people or events cause about 80% of the effects under investigation. The analysis entails developing a bar chart that depicts frequencies of events in absolute terms. The tallest bar requires the most attention.

g. **Statistical quality control techniques** are used when measurement of 100% of the output is impossible because the cost of measurement would exceed the benefit gained by physically identifying all errors, or testing destroys the product. Thus, a fuse factory would have to ruin all of its products to measure their quality.

1) Statistical control charts are graphic aids for monitoring the status of any process subject to random variations.

a) A statistical control chart consists of three horizontal lines plotted on a horizontal time scale. The center line represents the average or mean value for the process being controlled. The other two lines are the upper control limit (UCL) and the lower control limit (LCL). The processes are measured periodically, and the values are plotted on the chart (X). If the value falls within the control limits, no action is taken. If the value falls outside the limits, the process is considered out of control, and an investigation is made for possible corrective action. Another advantage of the chart is that it makes trends visible.

h. A **histogram** represents a frequency distribution by means of contiguous rectangles. Their widths are the class intervals, and their areas correspond to the frequencies plotted. Thus, the variable that is subject to repeated measurement is plotted on the horizontal axis, and the frequency for each class interval is plotted on the vertical axis. The result may be compared with the bell-shaped curve of the normal distribution. Significant deviations may need corrective action. For example, examination scores might be depicted using a histogram.

i. **Correlation analysis** is used to measure the strength of the linear relationship between two or more variables. Correlation between two variables can be seen by plotting their values on a single graph to form a **scatter diagram**. If the points tend to form a straight line, correlation is high. If they form a random pattern, there is little correlation. Correlation measures only linear relationships.

j. Time series (trend or run) charts analyze the change in a dependent variable over a period of time (the independent variable).

2. Special control programs have been effective in educating employees about control requirements. In these programs, the problem (the deviation from the plan) is defined, and the employees are given feedback about the effect of their actions on the problem.

   a. A program of **zero defects** sets a goal for employees that may seem unreasonable but is surprisingly approachable. Employees' awareness of the results of their actions is heightened by

      1) Education about the program
      2) Periodic notification of the results
      3) An emphasis on the desirability of high quality
      4) An emphasis on the minimization of defects through individual and group efforts **before** errors occur

         a) EXAMPLE: Ongoing safety programs emphasizing zero defects help to reduce accidents.

   b. A short-run effect is often observed, however. Zero-defect programs require continuous implementation to be effective.

3. Management control processes can take two approaches.

   a. **Imposed control** is the traditional, mechanical approach, consisting of measuring performance against standards and then taking corrective action through the individual responsible for the function or area being evaluated.

      1) Though common in organizations, it has one striking drawback: Corrective action tends to come **after** the performance has taken place (often resulting in negative disciplinary action).

   b. **Self-control** is an emerging and increasingly important approach. It evaluates the entire process of management and the functions performed, as well as attempts to improve the managerial process (in contrast to correcting specific output performance of the manager). Management by objectives (MBO) is a good example of this approach.

4. Stop and review! You have completed the outline for this subunit. Study multiple-choice questions 26 through 28 beginning on page 204.

6.5 SURVEILLANCE OF CONTROL SYSTEMS

1. The control process must itself be controlled. No control system is so perfect that it can function without outside review of its effectiveness or ability to provide adequate results.

   a. The control system should evolve continuously because of changes in

      1) The nature of the firm's business
      2) The managers who are available to implement the plans
      3) The nature of the plans themselves

   b. Overreliance on a control system merely because it seemed adequate in the past can be disastrous to a business.

      1) No control system can anticipate all possible events.
      2) Employees, in providing feedback, may deliberately or unintentionally omit or distort information.
      3) Resistance to a control system that employees do not believe in or understand may lead to attempts to subvert the system.

2.   Unreliable feedback is a significant problem for any control system. Managers must observe the control process critically and imaginatively to uncover difficulties in the generation of feedback that could lead to erroneous information. Sources of problems include

    a.   Technical difficulties in measurement because of

        1)   Mechanical problems
        2)   Poor statistical design
        3)   Delays in transmission of data

    b.   Behavioral problems because of

        1)   Failure to observe employee morale
        2)   Training inadequacies
        3)   Fraud
        4)   Malicious behavior

    c.   Failure to use appropriate internal audits periodically to measure the effectiveness of control systems

    d.   Inappropriate measurement criteria leading to unintended or undesired behavior

    e.   Inappropriate standards

3.   Exogenous or input variables are outside the control of the decision maker. However, managerial decisions and their outcomes are related to and dependent on many outside (exogenous) variables:

    a.   Technological developments

    b.   Weather

    c.   National fiscal or monetary policies

    d.   Competitors (However, competitors may not be exogenous if affected by the company's own decisions.)

4.   Stop and review! You have completed the outline for this subunit. Study multiple-choice questions 29 through 31 on page 205.

6.6 CHANGE MANAGEMENT

1.   Change management is important to all organizations whether or not TQM techniques are adopted. Organizational change anticipates expected changes in circumstances or may be a reaction to the unexpected. The nature of the change may be incremental, or it may entail a strategic alteration of the structure or purpose of the organization.

    a.   Organizational and procedural changes often are resisted by the individuals and groups affected. **Resistance** may be caused by simple surprise or by inertia, but it also may arise from fear of

        1)   **Personal adjustments** that may be required

            a)   Concern about usefulness
            b)   Apparent disregard for workers' feelings
            c)   Deviations from past procedures for implementing change (especially if procedures used are less participative than before)
            d)   Downgrading of job status

        2)   **Social adjustments** that may be required

            a)   Potential violation of the behavior norms of informal groups
            b)   Disruption of the social situation within groups

3) **Economic adjustments**, e.g., potential economic loss and insecurity based on perceived threats to jobs

4) In general, any perceived deterioration in the work situation that is seen as a threat to needs -- economic, social, or psychological

b. Resistance may be overcome by a **participative management** approach that

1) Communicates fully to reduce fear of adjustments

2) Avoids arbitrary, capricious, or prejudicial actions

3) Times the change so ample notice is given, including the reasons for the change, the precise nature of the change, and expected outcomes or results of the change

4) Allows participation in the implementation of changes by those affected

5) Includes informal and formal conferences and problem-solving groups

6) Provides express guarantees against economic loss

7) Anticipates and accommodates the perceived impact of a change on the needs – economic, social, or psychological – of those involved

c. Nadler and Tushman have developed a model for categorizing organizational changes.

1) Change is either **anticipatory or reactive**.

   a) Anticipatory changes are systematically planned changes intended to take advantage of expected situations.

   b) Reactive changes are necessitated by unexpected environmental events or pressures.

2) The scope of change is either **incremental or strategic**.

   a) Incremental changes involve subsystem adjustments needed to keep the organization on its chosen path.

   b) Strategic changes alter the overall shape or direction of the organization.

3) **Tuning** is an incremental anticipatory change. Preventive maintenance and continuous improvement (kaizen) are examples.

4) **Adaptation** is an incremental reactive change. An example is a change in the styling of an automobile to meet competition.

5) **Reorientation** is a strategic anticipatory change. It is "frame bending" because it is a redirection. For example, some fast-food companies are offering their products in dramatically different locations, such as department stores.

6) **Re-creation** is a strategic reactive change. It is risky because it is "frame breaking." Moving into an entirely new business is an example.

2. Stop and review! You have completed the outline for this subunit. Study multiple-choice questions 32 through 36 beginning on page 206.

6.7 CONTROL IMPLICATIONS OF ORGANIZATIONAL STRUCTURE

1. A number of relationships are present in the structure of an organization, including authority, responsibility, and accountability.

    a. Authority is the right to direct and exact performance from others, including the right to prescribe the means and methods by which the work will be done.

    b. Responsibility is the obligation to perform.

        1) In the classical view, this obligation is formally imposed by a superior and is inherent in any job.

        2) In the behavioral view, responsibility must and should be delegated; a successive dividing and passing down of responsibility is necessary.

            a) The appropriate amount of authority must be delegated with the responsibility, but a higher position can never rid itself of ultimate responsibility.

    c. Accountability is the duty to account for the fulfillment of the responsibility. In practice, accountability is

        1) The duty to report performance to one's superior

            a) The principle of single accountability or unity of command means that each subordinate should report to only one superior.

            b) Unity of command permits more than one person as superior only under conditions in which there is complete coordination of plans so that no conflicting instructions are given.

        2) The physical means for reporting or being able to substantiate performance, i.e., record keeping

2. **Unity of Objective.** An organizational structure is effective if it facilitates the contribution of individuals toward the attainment of enterprise objectives. Thus, organizational objectives must be clearly formulated in the planning process.

    a. In other words, the purpose of organizing is coordination, ensuring that all individuals in the organization are working toward the same organizational goals.

    b. Organizing also allows management to determine when goals are not achieved and where the problems exist within the organization (e.g., monitoring, feedback). Organizing is therefore the beginning of control.

3. **Efficiency.** An organizational structure is efficient if it facilitates the accomplishment of organizational objectives with minimum resources and fewest unsought consequences. An efficient organizational structure maximizes output for a given amount of input and provides inputs of all resources required, whether physical, financial, or human, with minimum waste.

4. **Effectiveness.** An organization that reaches its objectives is effective.

    a. Effectiveness can be assessed on a short-, medium-, or long-term basis.

5. **Elements of Organizational Structure.** Structure can be defined in terms of complexity, formalization, and centralization.

    a. The following are three kinds of differentiation that contribute to complexity:

        1) **Vertical differentiation** concerns the depth of the organizational hierarchy. The greater the number of levels, the more complex the organization, the greater the potential for information distortion, the more difficult the coordination of management activities, and the slower and less effective the response to changing conditions.

2) **Horizontal differentiation** concerns the extent to which tasks in the organization require special skills and knowledge. The greater the diversity of these orientations, the greater the organizational complexity, and the more difficult communication and coordination become.

3) **Spatial differentiation** concerns the extent of the geographical separation of the organization's operations.

b. **Formalization** concerns the extent to which job performance is standardized by job descriptions and clear procedures that define how tasks are to be accomplished. Low formalization enhances worker discretion.

c. **Centralization** concerns the concentration of authority in an organization and the degree and levels at which it occurs.

6. **Departmentation** is the grouping of organizational subsystems.

a. **Departmentation by function** is the most widely used method, found in almost every enterprise at some level. The most common departments are selling, production, and finance (though other terms may be used). These often extend upward in the organizational chart to the level below the CEO.

b. **Departmentation by territory** is favored by national or multinational firms and government agencies with scattered offices or plants.

c. **Departmentation by product** is growing in importance for multiline, large-scale enterprises. It is often an outgrowth of functional departmentation and permits extensive authority for a division executive over a given product or product line.

d. **Departmentation by customer** permits service to a particular customer to be managed by a department head. This form of departmentation seldom appears at the top level of an organizational structure, but it is often found at middle levels (e.g., the loan officer of a large bank who handles one account exclusively). Customer departmentation is often found within the sales department of a firm organized by function.

e. **Project departmentation** is for experimental or onetime activities, e.g., the construction of a ship, a large building, or a major design project (such as a military weapons system).

f. **Matrix organization** is usually seen as a combination of any of the previously mentioned approaches to departmentation, such as functional-product in manufacturing. It is a compromise between functional and product departmentation. A manager for each product is appointed and draws on personnel who are organized by function and who simultaneously report to a manager for each function. This form is used in research and development and in project management.

1) The emphasis of the arrangement is on the result or the product.

2) The functional organization remains, while parts of it are temporarily lent or assigned to a given project.

3) The project may be to make a product indefinitely or to accomplish a limited but lengthy task, such as construction of a submarine.

4) It is difficult for large organizations to use matrix organization because they typically have many levels (both vertically and horizontally), thus slowing communications.

g. The method of departmentation chosen is contingent upon

1) Organizational plans, programs, policies, and purpose
2) Environmental constraints
3) Training and preferences of available personnel

7. **Mechanistic versus Organic Structures**

   a. The extremes of the structural continuum are mechanistic and organic organizations.

      1) A **mechanistic structure** is appropriate for organizations focusing on a cost-minimization strategy through tight controls, extensive division of labor, high formalization, and centralization. The information network is limited, and employees rarely participate in decision making.

      2) An **organic structure** is characterized by low complexity, low formalization, and decentralization. It has an extensive information system, and employees participate in decision making. Organic organizations tend to be flexible and adaptive to change.

   b. Structure is a function of the organization's fundamental strategy.

      1) An **innovation strategy** focuses on developing important new products or services. An organic structure provides the flexibility for this strategy.

      2) A **cost-minimization strategy** imposes tight controls over expenditures and attempts to reduce prices of products. The mechanistic structure is appropriate.

      3) An **imitation strategy** is not adopted by true innovators but rather by companies that move into new markets only after smaller competitors have demonstrated the potential for success. Imitation strategies are best suited to a structure that combines mechanistic and organic components.

   c. Structure is also a function of

      1) **Organizational size**. Larger organizations tend to be mechanistic because greater formalization is needed. Strategies also change as organizations change size. Growing organizations often expand their activities within their industry.

      2) **Technology**. An organic structure may be best for coping with nonroutine technology since formalization is low.

      3) **Environment**. In general, the more stable the environment, the more mechanistic the organization. A mechanistic structure is also appropriate when the environment has little capacity for growth. Dynamic environments require an organic structure because of their unpredictability. Moreover, a complex environment (e.g., one with numerous and constantly changing competitors) also requires the flexibility and adaptability of an organic structure.

         a) Every organization's environment has three key dimensions: capacity, volatility, and complexity. Capacity is the degree of growth an environment can support. Volatility concerns the relative instability in the environment. Complexity refers to the amount of heterogeneity and concentration in the environment; e.g., an industry with a few very large firms is homogeneous and concentrated.

         b) Uncertainty is not a specific environmental factor. Rather, the foregoing factors determine the level of uncertainty present in the environment.

8. According to Henry Mintzberg, an organization has five components. Depending on which is in control, one of five different structures will evolve.

   a. The five organizational components include the

      1) **Operating core** – workers who perform the basic tasks related to production

      2) **Strategic apex** – top managers

      3) **Middle line** – managers who connect the core to the apex

        4)   **Technostructure** – analysts who achieve a certain standardization in the organization

        5)   **Support staff** – indirect support services

   b.   The five structures include the following:

        1)   A **simple structure**, such as that of a small retailer, has low complexity and formality, and authority is centralized. Its small size and simplicity usually precludes significant inefficiency in the use of resources. The strategic apex is the dominant component.

        2)   A **machine bureaucracy** is a complex, formal, and centralized organization that performs highly routine tasks, groups activities into functional departments, has a strict chain of command, and distinguishes between line and staff relationships. The technostructure dominates.

        3)   A **professional bureaucracy** (e.g., a university or library) is a complex and formal but decentralized organization in which highly trained specialists have great autonomy. Duplication of functions is minimized. For example, a university would have only one history department. Thus, the operating core is in control.

        4)   A **divisional structure** is essentially a self-contained organization. Hence, it must perform all or most of the functions of the overall organization of which it is a part. It is characterized by substantial duplication of functions compared with more centralized structures. The middle line dominates.

        5)   An **adhocracy** (an organic structure) has low complexity, formality, and centralization. Vertical differentiation is low and horizontal differentiation is high. The emphasis is on flexibility and response. Thus, the support staff dominates.

9.   **Centralization and Decentralization**

   a.   Centralization concerns the concentration of authority in an organization and the degree and levels at which it occurs.

   b.   Decentralization is a philosophy of organizing and managing. Careful selection of which decisions to push down the hierarchy and which to hold at the top is required. The degree of decentralization will be greater if

        1)   More decisions are made lower in the management hierarchy.
        2)   Some important decisions are made lower in the management hierarchy.
        3)   More functions are affected by decisions made at lower levels.
        4)   Fewer approvals are required before implementation of a decision.

   c.   Centralization and decentralization are relative terms. Absolute centralization or decentralization is impossible.

   d.   Neither centralization nor decentralization is good or bad in itself. The degree to which either is used depends upon the situation.

        1)   Information. Decisions cannot be decentralized to those who do not have necessary information, e.g., knowledge of job objectives or measures for evaluation of job performance.

        2)   Ability. Decisions cannot be decentralized to people who do not have training, experience, knowledge, or the ability to make decisions.

        3)   Timeliness. The organization should decentralize decisions requiring a quick response to those near the action.

        4)   Degree of coordination. The organization cannot decentralize below the level at which coordination must be maintained.

5)   Significance of decision. Decisions cannot be decentralized to lower levels if they are of critical importance to the organization.

6)   Morale. The organization should decentralize, when possible, for the positive influence on morale.

e.   Organizational restructuring has been successfully accomplished by setting up **strategic business units (SBUs)**. Establishment of SBUs is a means of decentralization.

1)   An SBU is an independent business that serves a specific market outside the parent, has outside competition, makes key decisions about such matters as strategic planning and product development even though it shares the parent's resources, and constitutes a profit center.

a)   An SBU must operate as a profit center to provide a measure of its effectiveness independent of the original organization.

2)   The purpose of an SBU is to allow for entrepreneurial risk taking, which might otherwise be limited by the parent's bureaucratic structure and concomitant reluctance to take risks.

a)   An SBU is a more appropriately sized unit for coping with competition. The larger parent may make decisions more slowly and hence less competitively.

10.   **Span of Control**

a.   The number of subordinates who can be effectively and efficiently supervised by one person is limited.

b.   Expansion of span of control may be advantageous if it improves morale of individual workers by reducing the extent of supervision and reduces communication and control problems by reducing the number of organizational levels.

c.   Flat organizational structures have relatively few levels from top to bottom. Tall organizational structures have many levels between top and bottom.

1)   Flat structures have the advantages of fast information flow from top to bottom of the organization and increased employee satisfaction.

2)   Tall structures are faster and more effective at problem resolution because of the increased frequency of interaction between superior and subordinate and the greater order imposed by the hierarchy of the tall organizational structure.

3)   Studies do not indicate great advantages for either flat or tall structures.

d.   As an organization grows, spans of control may become unworkable, necessitating the hiring of more managers. In addition, more formalized policies and procedures must be developed, and the structure of the organization tends to become more mechanistic.

1)   The relationship between growth and structure, however, is linear only within a certain range. For example, adding 100 employees to a company with 100 employees is likely to cause significant structural change, but adding the same number to a workforce of 10,000 is likely to have little structural impact.

11.   Stop and review! You have completed the outline for this subunit. Study multiple-choice questions 37 through 45 beginning on page 207.

6.8 LEADERSHIP

1. Leadership, also called the **directing process**, is the act or process of influencing people so they will strive willingly toward the achievement of group goals. Leadership is a key factor in the governance of an organization, particularly regarding attitude toward tolerance of risk and the nature and extent of (and commitment to) control.

   a. The classical position focused on the idea that authority, decision making, and responsibility may all be decentralized in the organization to some extent, but leadership is a characteristic of the individual's personality and cannot be subdivided.

   b. **The traitist approach** was characteristic of studies before 1949, in which attempts were made to identify traits possessed by leaders. Starting with the theory that leaders are born, not made, attempts were made to identify the physical, mental, and psychological traits of various leaders. The traitist approach has produced such a long list of leadership traits that, in effect, it identifies nothing. A few traits do seem to have significant correlation with a leader's effectiveness, however.

      1) Intelligence
      2) Maturity
      3) Social participation and interest
      4) Socioeconomic status (in comparison to nonleaders)

2. With so little useful guidance from the leader characteristics approach, behavior-oriented researchers examined **leader behavior** to see if leaders conducted themselves in certain ways.

   a. Styles of leadership are emphasized in behavioral approaches. The proper leadership style depends on the situation. The personal background of the manager is also a determining factor, as are the personalities and backgrounds of the employees being supervised.

      1) These styles have been characterized as

         a) **Autocratic.** The manager dictates all decisions to the employees. This is considered the classical approach to leadership. Employees are not allowed to give input. Autocratic leaders rely on threats and punishment and do not trust workers. However, autocratic leadership can sometimes be the most effective, such as when there is limited time to make a decision or when workers do not respond to any other leadership style.

         b) **Consultative.** The manager takes the employee's view into account but still makes the decisions.

         c) **Participative** (also known as **democratic**). The employee has a definite input into decision making and the manager must include subordinates' views in the decision. The employee is encouraged to grow on the job and be promoted.

            i) But not all employees are willing to participate.
            ii) Many employees like the trust they receive.

         d) **Free-rein** (also known as **laissez-faire**). The employees make their own decisions.

e) **Bureaucratic**. A manager manages "by the book." Everything must be done according to procedure or policy. If there is no policy to cover a situation, the manager refers to the next level above him/herself. Bureaucratic leaders are essentially policemen rather than leaders. Bureaucratic leaders are sometimes necessary when employees are working with dangerous or highly delicate equipment or chemicals. Cash handling functions are sometimes policed by a bureaucratic leader.

    i) Management theoretician Max Weber argued that bureaucracy is essential in structuring governments and administrations. He viewed it as functional, efficient, and necessary for capitalism to be successful. Within the bureaucratic type there are specific rules and regulations for every goal. These rules must be followed by employees. Officials are subject to a hierarchy, and fulfill their duties impersonally. Weber began by discussing how work is carried out within the bureaucratic organization. Activities for governing are official duties and are assigned by a set of rules that determine who will perform what specialized task. These are completed only by employees who have received the adequate education. In this manner, the functions become bureaucratic authority. Within the bureaucracy there exists labor hierarchy directed by more regulations. That is, there are levels of authority. Supervision by a higher official ensures that management remains orderly. Also, subordinate officials have the opportunity to appeal a decision to a higher authority.

2) The behaviorists believe that leadership traits are not hereditary, except for physical characteristics like stature or health.

b. **Employee vs. task orientation**. A greater concern for people than for task accomplishment (although a certain degree of task orientation is vital) is believed to be more productive. The leader must balance the personal needs of subordinates with task accomplishment.

c. **Initiating structure vs. initiating consideration** behavior. Two behavior patterns that are consistently found in the study of leadership are the initiation of structure and the initiation of consideration by the leader (production-centered versus employee-centered behavior).

1) Initiating structure behavior is directed towards accomplishing tasks. Structure includes

    a) Defining duties
    b) Establishing procedures
    c) Planning and organizing the work

2) Consideration behavior is the establishment of a personal relationship between the leader and the subordinate. High consideration by the leader includes

    a) Warmth toward the employee as a person
    b) Psychological support for the employee
    c) Helpfulness with problems in the work

3) Both structure initiation and consideration behavior are present in all job situations, and the relative amounts of each must be appropriate to the situation.

    a) EXAMPLES:

        i) A highly structured situation (like assembly-line work) may respond negatively to further structure initiated by the manager but positively to increased consideration.

ii) A manager of research and development may find the initiation of structure much more productive than increased consideration. Creative personnel working on a disorganized project may find a better-defined project plan much more satisfying than a demonstration of concern by the manager.

d. A **transformational leader** is an agent of change. The transformational leader is able to inspire the members of the organization to aspire to, and to achieve, more than they thought was possible.

1) Transformational leadership emphasizes vision, development of the individual, empowerment of the worker, and the challenging of traditional assumptions.

2) Transformational leaders articulate a vision, use nontraditional thinking, encourage individual development, provide workers with regular feedback, use participative decision-making, and promote a cooperative and trusting work environment.

3) The tranformational leader normally has charisma, is inspirational, motivational, provides intellectual stimulation to workers, and gives individualized consideration.

3. The modern view follows a **contingency approach** in looking for even better answers to the questions, "What is an effective leader?" and "How do we train and identify leaders?"

a. According to Fred E. Fiedler's contingency theory, people become leaders not only because of personality attributes but also because of various situational factors and the interaction between the leaders and the situation.

1) Thus, the right person at the right time may rise to a position of leadership if his/her personality and the needs of the situation complement each other. The same person might not become a leader in different circumstances because of failure to interact successfully with that situation.

2) There are three dimensions to the contingency theory model:

a) **Position power** is a function of the formal authority structure and is the degree to which the position held enables a leader to evaluate, reward, sanction, or promote the group members independent of other sources of power, such as personality or expertise.

b) **Task structure** is how clearly and carefully the worker's responsibilities for various tasks are defined. Quality of performance is more easily controlled when tasks are clearly defined.

c) **Leader-member relations** reflect the extent to which group members like and trust and are willing to follow a leader.

i) Relationship to group members is the most important dimension from the leader's point of view, since position power and task structure may be largely under the control of the enterprise.

ii) The "least preferred coworker" test is one way to assess the optimal arrangement of group members by asking the leader to rank possible subordinates from least to most preferred. Previously unrecognized biases may surface that the leader can evaluate and learn to deal with.

3) Fiedler's research showed two types of leaders:

a) Task-oriented style is most effective when the situation is very favorable or very unfavorable.

b) Relationship-oriented style is most effective in the middle, less extreme situations.

4)   The most effective leadership style is contingent upon the definition of the three dimensions.

5)   Leadership is therefore as much a responsibility of the organization's placement of leaders as it is of the leaders themselves. An organization should identify leadership situations and its managers' leadership styles and engineer the job to suit the manager if necessary.

b.   According to Hersey and Blanchard's **situational leadership theory**, the appropriate leadership style depends on followers' maturity, which is their degree of willingness to be responsible for directing their own behavior.

1)   Maturity includes both job and psychological maturity. For example, experienced and knowledgeable workers who are highly motivated need little external direction.

2)   The dimensions of leadership involve task and relationship behaviors.

a)   One leadership style is **participative**. Task emphasis should be low, but relationship emphasis should be high. The leader's primary activities are facilitating and communicating, and decisions should be shared.

b)   The **delegating** style does not emphasize tasks or relationships.

c)   The **selling** style emphasizes both tasks and relationships.

d)   A **directive (telling)** leadership style is characterized by a high task, low relationship emphasis.

c.   **Path-goal theory** combines the research on initiating structure and consideration with expectancy theory.

1)   According to path-goal theory, two groups of contingency factors affect the relationship between leadership behavior and outcomes (performance and satisfaction).

a)   Environmental factors are those beyond subordinates' control (task structure, the formal authority system, and the work group).

b)   Subordinate factors include the subordinate's locus of control, experience, and perceived ability.

2)   A leadership style should be chosen that complements but does not duplicate the factors in the environment and is consistent with subordinates' characteristics.

a)   The **directive** leader lets subordinates know what is expected of them, schedules work to be done, and gives specific guidance on how to accomplish tasks.

i)   A directive style is most effective when the subordinate's locus of control is external, tasks are ambiguous or stressful, and substantial conflict exists in the work group. Thus, a directive style is appropriate when subordinates do not have high perceived ability or experience.

b)   The **supportive** leader is friendly and shows concern for the needs of the subordinates.

i)   Supportive style is best when tasks are highly structured and the authority relationships are clear and bureaucratic.

ii)   This approach depends on subordinates who want to work, grow, and achieve.

        c) The **participative** leader consults with subordinates and uses their suggestions before making a decision.

           i) Participative style is most useful when subordinates believe they control their own destinies, that is, when they have an internal locus of control. Such individuals may be resentful if they are not consulted.

        d) The **achievement-oriented** leader sets challenging goals and expects subordinates to perform at their highest level.

           i) Achievement-oriented leadership is appropriate when tasks are nonrepetitive and ambiguous and employee competence is high.

4. The **Vroom/Yetton/Jago** model describes leadership as a decision making process. The model helps leaders to determine how to arrive at, communicate, and implement decisions for various situations in an organization.

    a. The model identifies five decision making styles and provides tools for reaching decisions under each style. Two of the decision making styles are autocratic, two are consultative, and the fifth is group-directed. The degree of subordinate participation ranges from none or low (the autocratic styles), to moderate (the consultative styles), to high (the group-directed style).

    b. Computer software programs or decision-trees are used to guide leaders in the decision making process, including the choice of the decision-making style that is appropriate to a given situation.

        1) The guidance consists of diagnostic questions concerning such issues as the significance of the technical quality of the decision, the need for subordinates' commitment to the decision, the sufficiency of information available to the leader and to subordinates, the degree to which the problem is structured, potential conflict among subordinates regarding solutions, the probability that subordinates will be committed to a decision made by the leader, and the degree to which subordinates' goals and those of the organization are congruent.

5. **Influence** is an attempt to change the behavior of others in the workplace, whether they are superiors, subordinates, or coworkers. The following categories of influence tactics have been identified:

    a. **Consultation** permits the other person(s) to participate in the decision or change.

    b. **Rational persuasion** tries to convince others by reliance on a detailed plan, supporting evidence, and reason.

    c. **Inspirational appeals** are calls to superordinate goals. They are appeals to emotions, values, or ideals.

    d. **Ingratiating tactics** attempt to raise the other person's self-esteem prior to a request.

    e. **Coalition tactics** seek the aid of others to persuade someone to agree.

    f. **Pressure tactics** involve intimidation, threats, and demands.

    g. **Upward appeals** are based on the formal or informal support of higher management.

    h. **Exchange tactics** entail an exchange of favors, a reminder of a past favor, or an offer of a personal sacrifice.

6. Stop and review! You have completed the outline for this subunit. Study multiple-choice questions 46 through 54 beginning on page 210.

6.9 NEGOTIATION AND CONFLICT MANAGEMENT

1.   Conflict inevitably arises within (and between) organizations. Thus, effective conflict management is vital to governance and control. It improves the likelihood that established objectives and goals will be achieved.

2.   One method of conflict resolution is **negotiation**, which strives for an exchange and an agreement as to the rate of exchange.

   a.   According to Walton and McKensie, *A Behavioral Theory of Labor Negotiations: An Analysis of a Social Interaction System*, the general approaches to negotiation are distributive bargaining and integrative bargaining.

      1)   **Distributive bargaining** is typical of negotiators who are in a zero-sum situation, such as labor-management negotiations about wages. What one side gains, the other loses. Thus, the interests of the parties diverge because they are competing for shares of a fixed amount of resources.

         a)   The negotiators in distributive bargaining operate with a maximum desired result and a minimum acceptable result in mind. If the ranges of feasible outcomes of the parties overlap, an agreement is possible.

      2)   **Integrative bargaining** occurs in a positive sum situation; that is, the parties believe that a solution exists that permits both sides to win. The parties have shared interests, the amount of resources to be allocated is not fixed, and the relationship tends to be long-term.

         a)   Integrative bargaining is the preferable mode within an organization because it fosters cooperation, minimizes conflict, and develops constructive long-term relationships. However, it works only when the negotiators are open, flexible, able to trust the other side, sympathetic to each other's concerns, and committed to finding creative solutions.

         b)   Effective negotiators are good listeners, ask frequent questions, avoid defensiveness and attacks on the opponents, do not use language calculated to be irritating, and phrase their arguments clearly and directly.

            i)   They also understand that reciprocity is often a characteristic of negotiation. A tough stance encourages a similar response, and concessions usually result in reciprocal concessions. In the latter case, however, the amount of concessions received will usually be less than those offered.

         c)   Third parties as negotiators

            i)   **Mediation** is an intervention between conflicting parties by a neutral and noncoercive agency to facilitate an agreement. A mediator offers solutions, facilitates communications, and presents arguments.

            ii) **Arbitration** is the hearing and determination of a case in controversy by a person chosen by the parties or appointed under statutory authority. The results of arbitration are binding although the process may be entered voluntarily or compulsorily (under law or contract).

            iii) **Conciliation** is similar to mediation. A conciliator is a trusted individual who provides an informal communication link, interprets messages, etc.

            iv) **Consultation** is performed by a neutral individual whose expertise is in conflict management. The consultant's function is less to arrive at a settlement than to improve interactions between the parties.

b. The benefits of negotiating include resolving an issue without litigation, recognizing that each party values the other party's needs and rights, and impartially treating tension while finding compromise solutions.

3. **Conflict Management**. Conflict may be constructive or destructive.

    a. Communication, structure, and personal variables are the broad categories of conditions that may result in conflict.

        1) **Communication variables** pertain to semantical issues, noise in communication channels, and other problems in communication that impair cooperation and cause misunderstanding.

        2) **Structural conditions** include the size of the work group, specialization of tasks, the clarity of lines of authority, leadership practices, compensation schemes, and the interdependence of groups.

        3) **Personal variables** include individual personality characteristics and value systems.

    b. **Conflict triggers** include ambiguous jurisdictions (unclear job boundaries); competition for scarce resources; status differentials; time pressures, personality clashes; unreasonable standards, rules, etc.; communication breakdowns; and unrealized expectations.

    c. **Interactionist theory** regards conflict as potentially beneficial. Functional conflict improves performance and helps the organization to achieve its objectives.

    d. Whether conflict is functional depends on the intentions of the parties.

        1) In **competition**, individuals display the maximum of assertiveness (behavior intended to achieve one's own objectives) and the minimum of cooperativeness (behavior intended to meet the concerns of others). Generally, this technique does not effectively resolve conflict.

        2) **Collaboration** is an attempt by all parties to the conflict to attain everyone's objectives.

        3) **Avoidance** is withdrawal from the conflict (the minimum of both cooperation and assertiveness).

        4) **Compromise** is a position in which each party to the conflict both gains and loses. It is characterized by moderate cooperation and moderate assertiveness.

        5) **Accommodation** is an intention that reflects a high degree of cooperation and a low degree of assertiveness.

    e. Conflict may result in better decision making, a reduction in complacency, more self-criticism, greater creativity, and solutions to problems. Functional conflict drives the change processes that all organizations need to survive and prosper.

        1) Thus, **intentional stimulation of conflict** may be desirable. For example, management may intentionally trigger conflict by issuing threatening communications; by making changes in the organizational structure; by hiring new employees with different values, managerial styles, attitudes, and backgrounds; or by designating individuals to oppose the majority views of the group.

    f. Conflicts may be resolved in a variety of ways.

        1) **Problem solving** is a means of confronting the conflict and removing its causes. The emphasis is on facts and solutions, not personalities and assignment of blame. The disadvantage is that problem solving takes time.

        2) **Smoothing** is a short-term avoidance approach. The parties in conflict are asked by management to submerge their differences temporarily.

3) **Forcing** occurs when a superior uses his/her formal authority to order a particular resolution of the conflict.

4) **Superordinate goals** are the overriding goals of the entity to which subunit and personal goals are subordinate. An appeal to these goals is another short-term solution.

5) **Compromise** entails negotiation by the parties in conflict. The conflict is avoided rather than solved through a process by which each side makes concessions. Thus, the parties both gain and lose.

6) **Expanding resources** resolves conflicts that result from scarcity.

7) **Avoidance** withdraws from and suppresses the conflict but does not solve the underlying problem.

8) **Changing the human element** involves use of behavioral techniques to change attitudes and behavior.

9) **Changing structure** alters formal organizational arrangements.

10) **Diffusion** is an approach to resolving conflict in which critical issues are temporarily set aside while an attempt is made to reach an agreement on less controversial issues first.

11) The **public media** hinders communication because issues are addressed to the public, not the other party. However, the media may help resolve the problem through public pressure.

4.   Stop and review! You have completed the outline for this subunit. Study multiple-choice questions 55 through 63 beginning on page 213.

QUESTIONS

6.1 The Nature of Control

1. Which of the following is an example of a feedback control?

A. Preventive maintenance.

B. Inspection of completed goods.

C. Close supervision of production-line workers.

D. Measuring performance against a standard.

Answer (B) is correct. *(Publisher)*
REQUIRED: The example of a feedback control.
DISCUSSION: Feedback controls obtain information about completed activities. They permit improvement in future performance by learning from past mistakes. Thus, corrective action occurs after the fact. Inspection of completed goods is an example of a feedback control.
Answer (A) is incorrect because preventive maintenance is a feedforward control. It attempts to anticipate and prevent problems. Answer (C) is incorrect because the close supervision of production-line workers is a concurrent control. It adjusts an ongoing process. Answer (D) is incorrect because measuring performance against a standard is a general aspect of control.

2. An organization's policies and procedures are part of its overall system of internal controls. The control function performed by policies and procedures is

A. Feedforward control.

B. Implementation control.

C. Feedback control.

D. Application control.

Answer (A) is correct. *(CIA, adapted)*
REQUIRED: The control function of policies and procedures.
DISCUSSION: Feedforward control anticipates and prevents problems. Policies and procedures serve as feedforward controls because they provide guidance on how an activity should be performed to best insure that an objective is achieved.
Answer (B) is incorrect because implementation controls are controls applied during systems development. Answer (C) is incorrect because policies and procedures provide primary guidance before and during the performance of some task rather than give feedback on its accomplishment. Answer (D) is incorrect because application controls apply to specific applications, e.g., payroll or accounts payable.

3. The steps in a typical control process include

1. Selecting strategic control points at which to gather information about activities being performed

2. Accumulating, classifying, and recording data samples

3. Observing the work or collecting samples of data

4. Determining whether performance is satisfactory

5. Reviewing and revising standards

6. Reporting significant deviations to managers concerned

What is the proper order of these steps?

A. 1, 3, 2, 4, 6, 5.

B. 1, 2, 3, 4, 5, 6.

C. 1, 3, 4, 2, 6, 5.

D. 1, 3, 4, 2, 5, 6.

Answer (A) is correct. *(Publisher)*
REQUIRED: The proper sequence of steps in a typical control process.
DISCUSSION: The proper sequence of steps in a typical control process is as follows:

1. Selecting strategic control points at which to gather information about activities being performed

2. Observing the work or collecting samples of data

3. Accumulating, classifying, and recording data samples

4. Comparing samples with predetermined quality, schedule, and cost standards

5. Determining whether performance is satisfactory

6. Reporting significant deviations to managers concerned

7. Determining, by repeating the above steps, whether action taken is effective in correcting reported deviations (follow-up)

8. Reviewing and revising standards

Answer (B) is incorrect because observation must occur before classifying and recording data samples. Answers (C) and (D) are incorrect because data must be recorded before comparisons can occur.

4. What is the name of the model that is an adaptation of the COSO model by the Criteria Board of the Canadian Institute of Chartered Accountants and consists of 20 criteria grouped into four components?

A. The COSO model.

B. The CoCo model.

C. The government model.

D. The 11A model.

Answer (B) is correct. *(Publisher)*
REQUIRED: The model adapted from COSO.
DISCUSSION: The CoCo Model is the name of the model that is an adaptation of the COSO model by the Criteria Board of the Canadian Institute of Chartered Accountants and consists of 20 criteria grouped into four components. The model is thought to be better designed for internal auditing purposes.
Answer (A) is incorrect because the CoCo model was adapted from the COSO model. Answer (C) is incorrect because the CoCo model was adapted from the COSO model by the Criteria Board of the Canadian Institute of Chartered Accountants and consists of 20 criteria grouped into four components. Answer (D) is incorrect because it is a nonsense answer.

5. Which of the following is not a component of the CoCo model?

A. Commitment.

B. Capability.

C. Control environment.

D. Monitoring and learning.

Answer (C) is correct. *(Publisher)*
REQUIRED: The item that is not a component of the CoCo model.
DISCUSSION: Control environment is not one of the four components of the CoCo model. The four components are commitment, capability, monitoring and learning, and purpose.
Answer (A) is incorrect because commitment is a component of the CoCo model. Answer (B) is incorrect because capability is a component of the CoCo model. Answer (D) is incorrect because monitoring and learning is a component of the CoCo model.

6. In regards to the IIA's own Systems Auditability and Control study, what are some activities that completed within the control framework?

A. Segregation of incompatible duties.

B. Appropriate levels of authority and responsibility.

C. Supervision of staff and review of work.

D. All of these.

Answer (D) is correct. *(Publisher)*
REQUIRED: Activities within the control framework of the IIA's Systems Auditability and Control study.
DISCUSSION: Answer (D) is correct because all of the activities are listen under the control framework of the IIA's own Systems Auditability and Control Study.
Answer (A) is incorrect because appropriate levels of authority and responsibility and supervision of staff and review of work are activities within the control framework. Answer (B) is incorrect because the segregation of incompatible duties and supervision of staff and review of work are also activities within the control framework. Answer (C) is incorrect because segregation of incompatible duties and appropriate levels of authority and responsibility are also within the control framework.

7. Which of the following management practices involves concentrating on areas that deserve attention and giving less attention to areas operating as expected?

- A. Management by objectives.
- B. Responsibility accounting.
- C. Benchmarking.
- D. Management by exception.

Answer (D) is correct. *(CIA, adapted)*
REQUIRED: The practice that gives less attention to areas operating as expected.
DISCUSSION: Controls should be configured so that they detect exceptions. This emphasis on exceptions to planned performance allows managers to devote more of their scarce time to significant matters. Thus, the exception principle includes an understanding that managers must concentrate their efforts on deviations from expectations that are critical.
Answer (A) is incorrect because under MBO, the subordinate and the manager jointly formulate the subordinate's objectives and the plans for attaining those objectives for a subsequent period. Answer (B) is incorrect because responsibility accounting assigns revenues, costs, and capital to responsibility centers. Answer (C) is incorrect because benchmarking involves building upon the best practices of organizational role models.

8. A bank has changed from a system in which lines are formed in front of each teller to a one-line, multiple-server system. When a teller is free, the person at the head of the line goes to that teller. Implementing the new system will

- A. Decrease the bank's wage expenses because the new system uses fewer tellers.
- B. Decrease time customers spend in the line.
- C. Increase accuracy in teller reconciliations at the end of the day because fewer customers are served by each teller.
- D. Improve on-the-job training for bank employees because each teller will perform different duties.

Answer (B) is correct. *(CIA, adapted)*
REQUIRED: The effect of implementing the new queuing system.
DISCUSSION: When all customers must wait in a single queue, it is possible to decrease waiting time given multiple servers. An added effect is to increase customer satisfaction.
Answer (A) is incorrect because it is unlikely that the number of employees will change due to the new system. Answer (C) is incorrect because assuming a Poisson process, the number of customers per teller will not change. Answer (D) is incorrect because tellers' duties will not change, so on-the-job training will not improve.

9. The Gantt chart shows that the project is

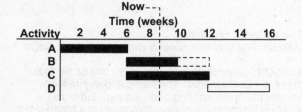

- A. Complete.
- B. Ahead of schedule.
- C. On schedule.
- D. Behind schedule.

Answer (B) is correct. *(CIA, adapted)*
REQUIRED: The status of a project according to the Gantt chart.
DISCUSSION: Assuming that each of the bars represents the expected time necessary to complete an activity and that the shaded regions represent the portions completed, it can be seen that activity A has been completed as scheduled and activities B and C are ahead of schedule. Therefore, the project is ahead of schedule but not yet complete.

10. Control devices may be

	Quantitative	Qualitative
A.	Yes	Yes
B.	Yes	No
C.	No	Yes
D.	No	No

Answer (A) is correct. *(Publisher)*
REQUIRED: The form of control devices.
DISCUSSION: Control devices may be either qualitative or quantitative. Budgets, schedules, quotas, and charts are examples of quantitative control devices. Job instructions, quality-control standards, and employment criteria are qualitative control devices.

11. Which of the following statements regarding effective control systems is false?

A. Excessive controls are costly in time and money.

B. Outdated information is inappropriate.

C. Controls should measure the performance of all areas.

D. Controls should be simple.

Answer (C) is correct. *(Publisher)*
REQUIRED: The false statement regarding effective control systems.
DISCUSSION: An effective control system should be meaningful. Thus, controls should be in place to measure performance only in important areas. Excessive controls in minor areas are not economical because the added benefits do not outweigh the loss of time and money.
Answer (A) is incorrect because effective controls should be economical because excessive controls are costly in time and money. Answer (B) is incorrect because effective controls need to be timely because outdated information may be unreliable. Answer (D) is incorrect because effective controls need to be simple enough that the people using the control can understand it.

12. Reengineering is the thorough analysis, fundamental rethinking, and complete redesign of essential business processes. The intended result is a dramatic improvement in service, quality, speed, and cost. An internal auditor's involvement in reengineering should include all of the following except

A. Determining whether the process has senior management's support.

B. Recommending areas for consideration.

C. Developing audit plans for the new system.

D. Directing the implementation of the redesigned process.

Answer (D) is correct. *(CIA, adapted)*
REQUIRED: The item not included in an internal auditor's involvement in reengineering.
DISCUSSION: Internal auditors should not become directly involved in the implementation of the redesign process. This involvement would impair their independence and objectivity. Staff assignments of internal auditors should be rotated periodically whenever it is practicable to do so. Internal auditors may perform the function of determining whether the process has senior management's support, recommending areas for consideration, and developing audit plans for the new system.

6.2 The Control Sequence

13. Which one of the following statements pertaining to performance measurement and behavior is false?

A. The use of residual income to measure divisional performance can cause goal congruence problems for corporations with divisions that have unequal operating asset bases.

B. The lack of commitment on the part of top management can turn budgets into ritualistic exercises without significance.

C. An organization using measures such as growth in market share, increases in productivity, and throughput time, in addition to various financial ratios, is relying on a more balanced approach to performance evaluation.

D. The development of information technology can permit organizations to do away with feedback in the design of management control systems.

Answer (D) is correct. *(CMA, adapted)*
REQUIRED: The false statement regarding performance measurement and behavior.
DISCUSSION: Control is the process of making certain that plans are achieving the desired objectives. The essence of control is feedback on the results of action. Thus, the development of information technology will in no way permit organizations to eliminate feedback in the design of management control systems.
Answer (A) is incorrect because the use of the residual income method can cause goal congruency problems. Residual income equals income after deduction of an imputed interest charge on the asset base. A division with a large asset base would normally have more residual income than a smaller division when the two divisions are equally profitable in percentage terms. Answer (B) is incorrect because lower-level managers will take a serious approach to budgeting if they know that their superiors are strongly committed to the process. Answer (C) is incorrect because a company using a balanced approach to performance evaluation will have a variety of measurement devices.

14. Benefits of employee participation in the design of control systems include all of the following except

    A. Development of a perception by those being evaluated that the process is fair.

    B. Communication to everyone involved of the need for control.

    C. Enhanced acceptance of the need for control standards.

    D. Easier implementation of the standards being used in other divisions.

Answer (D) is correct. *(Publisher)*
    REQUIRED: The item that is not a benefit of employee participation in the design of control systems.
    DISCUSSION: The ease of implementing company-wide standards is not a benefit of employee participation. Employees should be involved in the establishment of their own standards, based on the conditions in their own workplaces.

15. Standards are classified in terms of

    A. Quantity.

    B. Quality.

    C. Time.

    D. All of the answers are correct.

Answer (D) is correct. *(Publisher)*
    REQUIRED: The terms for which standards are classified.
    DISCUSSION: Standards are classified in terms of quantity, quality, and time. Quantity involves the number of units to be produced. Quality relates to rework costs and rejects. Time corresponds to schedules and promised deliveries. In addition, standards are classified in terms of cost or the number of dollars needed to produce the required number of units.
    Answer (A) is incorrect because quality is not the only term for which standards are classified. Answer (B) is incorrect because quantity and time are terms for which standards are classified. Answer (C) is incorrect because quantity and quality are also terms for which standards are classified.

16. Which of the following is not an example of good control points?

    A. Deciding not to inspect materials before approving payment.

    B. Inspecting a motor before its cover is attached.

    C. Balancing columns of figures before entering the answers into a ledger.

    D. Inspecting components before assembly.

Answer (A) is correct. *(Publisher)*
    REQUIRED: The statement that is not an example of good control points.
    DISCUSSION: Deciding not to inspect materials before approving payment is not an example of good control points. Inspecting materials before approving payment is an example of good control points.
    Answer (B) is incorrect because inspecting a motor before its cover is attached is an example of good control points. Answer (C) is incorrect because balancing columns of figures before entering the Answer (D) is incorrect because inspecting components before assembly is an example of good control points.

17. Standards must

    A. Fail to assist in implementing plans.

    B. Not be applied at those points that significantly influence subsequent progress.

    C. Be accepted by those who carry them out if they are to have maximum effectiveness.

    D. Not be reviewed periodically for adjustment or elimination because of changed circumstances.

Answer (C) is correct. *(Publisher)*
    REQUIRED: Additional guidelines for standards.
    DISCUSSION: Standards must be accepted by those who will carry them out if they are to have maximum effectiveness. Subordinates should believe that standards are both fair and achievable. Participation in the standard-setting process will encourage acceptance of standards.
    Answer (A) is incorrect because standards should assist in implementing plans. Answer (B) is incorrect because standards should be applied at those points that significantly influence subsequent progress. Answer (D) is incorrect because standards should be reviewed periodically for adjustment or elimination because of changed circumstances.

18. Which of the following is an example of a finance standard?

    A. Turnover rates.

    B. Audits based on performance standards in social areas.

    C. Return on investment at various levels.

    D. Percentage margin on sales.

Answer (C) is correct. *(Publisher)*
    REQUIRED: An example of a finance standard.
    DISCUSSION: Examples of finance standards include returns on investment at various levels, returns on investment for decentralized divisions, and and budgets.
    Answer (A) is incorrect because turnover rates are examples of personnel standards. Answer (B) is incorrect because audits based on performance standards in social areas are examples of management standards. Answer (D) is incorrect because percentage margin on sales are example of sales standards.

19. With regard to measuring performance, a decentralized structure in which the manager is evaluated on a return on investment basis forces the manager to seek short-run profit-maximizing solutions to the detriment of long-run survival factors such as

A. Social responsibility and ethics.

B. Research and development.

C. Capital purchase decisions.

D. All of the answers are correct.

Answer (D) is correct.   *(Publisher)*
    REQUIRED: The true statement about long-run survival factors.
    DISCUSSION: A decentralized structure in which the manager is evaluated on a return on investment basis forces the manager to seek short-run profit-maximizing solutions to the detriment of long-run survival factors such as social responsibility and ethics, research and development, and capital purchase decisions.
    Answer (A) is incorrect because research and development and capital purchase decisions are also correct. Answer (B) is incorrect because social responsibility and ethics and capital purchase decisions are also correct. Answer (C) is incorrect because social responsibility and ethics and research and development are also correct.

20. Participation by affected employees in all control systems permits employees to understand both the performance levels desired and the measurement criteria being applied. A benefit of participation is that it

A. Fails to develop a perception by those being evaluated that the process is fair.

B. Communicates to everyone the need for control.

C. Does not enhance acceptance of the need for control standards.

D. Fails to indicate the direction of the desired behavior.

Answer (B) is correct.   *(Publisher)*
    REQUIRED: A benefit of participation by affected employees in all control systems.
    DISCUSSION: The benefits associated with participation by affected employees in all control systems includes developing a perception by those being evaluated that the process is fair, communicating to everyone about the need for control, enhancing acceptance of the need for control standards, and indicating the direction of the desired behavior, which permits self-control and self-correction.
    Answer (A) is incorrect because developing a perception by those being evaluated that the process is fair is a benefit. Answer (C) is incorrect because enhancing acceptance of the need for control standards is a benefit. Answer (D) is incorrect because indicating the direction of the desired behavior, which permits self-control and self-correction is a benefit.

6.3 Control Frameworks

21. What is the name of the consortium of organizations that developed the Internal Control-Integrated Framework model?

A. The IRS

B. The Committee of Sponsoring Organizations (COSO).

C. The federal government.

D. The SEC.

Answer (B) is correct.   *(Publisher)*
    REQUIRED: The organization that developed the Control-Integrated Framework Model.
    DISCUSSION: The Committee of Sponsoring Organizations (COSO) is a consortium of organizations that includes The IIA and the AICPA, among others. It has developed the Internal Control-Integrated Framework.

22. COSO treats internal control as a process designed to provide reasonable assurance regarding the achievement of objectives related to

A. Reliability of financial reporting.

B. Effectiveness and efficiency of operations.

C. Compliance with applicable laws and regulations.

D. All of the answers are correct.

Answer (D) is correct.   *(Publisher)*
    REQUIRED: The true statement regarding COSO's objectives in relation to internal control.
    DISCUSSION: The COSO treats internal control as a process designed to provide a reasonable assurance regarding the achievement of objectives related to reliability of financial reporting, effectiveness and efficiency of operations, and compliance with applicable laws and regulations. The reliability of financial reporting concerns published financial information. The effectiveness and efficiency of operations relates to achievement of performance and profit goals and the safeguarding of resources. A final related objective is the compliance with applicable laws and regulations.

23. Which of the following are elements of the control environment?

    A. Integrity and ethical value.

    B. Organizational structure.

    C. Assignment of authority and responsibility.

    D. All of the answers are correct.

Answer (D) is correct.   *(Publisher)*
REQUIRED: The elements of the control environment.
DISCUSSION: The elements of the control environment include: integrity and ethical value, commitment to competence, board of directors or audit committee participation, management's philosophy and operating style, organizational structure, assignment of authority and responsibility, and human resource policies and practices.

24. Which of the following is a factor affecting risk?

    A. New personnel.

    B. New or revamped information systems.

    C. Rapid Growth.

    D. All of the answers are correct.

Answer (D) is correct.   *(Publisher)*
REQUIRED: The item that is a factor affecting risk.
DISCUSSION: New personnel, new or revamped information systems, and rapid growth are all factors that affect risk.

25. The policies and procedures helping to ensure that management directives are executed and actions are taken to address risks to achievement of objectives describes

    A. Risk assessments.

    B. Control environments.

    C. Control activities

    D. Monitoring.

Answer (C) is correct.   *(Publisher)*
REQUIRED: The definition of control activities.
DISCUSSION: Control activities are the policies and procedures helping to ensure that management directives are executed and actions are taken to address risks to achievement of objectives.
    Answer (A) is incorrect because risk assessment identifies and analyzes external or internal risks to achievement of the objectives at the activity level as well as the entity level. Answer (B) is incorrect because control environments reflect the attitude and actions of the board and management regarding the significance of control within the organization. Answer (D) is incorrect because monitoring is a process that assesses the quality of the system's performance over time.

6.4 Control Techniques

26. Is PERT analysis a control tool or a planning tool?

	Planning	Control
A.	Yes	No
B.	Yes	Yes
C.	No	Yes
D.	No	No

Answer (B) is correct.   *(Publisher)*
REQUIRED: The functions of PERT.
DISCUSSION: PERT (Program Evaluation Review Technique) is applied in the management of complex projects. It analyzes the project in terms of its component activities and determines their sequencing and timing. Thus, it systematically combines planning with control.

27. Budgets are a necessary component of financial decision making because they help provide a(n)

    A. Efficient allocation of resources.

    B. Means to use all the firm's resources.

    C. Automatic corrective mechanism for errors.

    D. Means to check managerial discretion.

Answer (A) is correct.   *(CIA, adapted)*
REQUIRED: The major benefit of budgets.
DISCUSSION: A budget is a quantitative model of a plan of action developed by management. A budget functions as an aid to planning, coordination, and control. Thus, a budget helps management to allocate resources efficiently.
    Answer (B) is incorrect because budgets are designed to use resources efficiently, not just use them. Answer (C) is incorrect because budgets per se provide for no automatic corrections. Answer (D) is incorrect because budgets are a management tool and are not designed to thwart managerial discretion.

28. Which of the following is the principal advantage of budgeting?

   A. Employee motivation.

   B. Performance evaluation.

   C. Forced planning.

   D. Communication.

Answer (C) is correct. *(CIA, adapted)*
   REQUIRED: The major contribution of budgeting to management.
   DISCUSSION: Managers in a formal budget setting are compelled to examine the future and be prepared to respond to future conditions. Without budgets, many operations would fail because of inadequate planning. Answer (A) is incorrect because employee motivation is a significant but secondary purpose of budgets. Answer (B) is incorrect because performance evaluation is a significant but secondary purpose of budgets. Answer (D) is incorrect because communication is a significant but secondary purpose of budgets. Planning is the foundation of other managerial functions, such as communication.

6.5 Surveillance of Control Systems

29. Variables that are important to the decision-making process but are out of the control of the decision maker, e.g., economic conditions, are considered to be

   A. Exogenous variables.

   B. Decision variables.

   C. Performance criteria.

   D. Constraints.

Answer (A) is correct. *(CMA, adapted)*
   REQUIRED: The term for variables that are outside the control of the decision maker.
   DISCUSSION: Exogenous or input variables are outside the control of the decision maker. Exogenous means "originating externally." These influence the decision model (system) but are not influenced by it.
   Answer (B) is incorrect because at least one of the decision variables in a model must be under the decision maker's control; that is, at least one variable cannot be exogenous. Answer (C) is incorrect because performance criteria are the means of measuring the results of a decision after the fact. Answer (D) is incorrect because constraints are limitations (constants, not variables) that must be considered as part of the decision process.

30. Unreliable feedback is a significant problem for any control system. Which of the following is not a source of unreliable feedback?

   A. Failure to use appropriate internal audits periodically.

   B. Inappropriate measurement criteria leading to unintended or undesired behavior.

   C. Behavior problems are not a source of problems.

   D. Inappropriate standards.

Answer (C) is correct. *(Publisher)*
   REQUIRED: The item that is not a source of unreliable feedback.
   DISCUSSION: Behavior problems like fraud or malicious behavior are sources of problems with unreliable feedback.
   Answer (A) is incorrect because failure to use appropriate internal audits periodically is a source of problems with unreliable feedback. Answer (B) is incorrect because inappropriate measurement criteria leading to unintended or undesired behavior is a source of problems with unreliable feedback. Answer (D) is incorrect because inappropriate standards is a source of problems with unreliable feedback.

31. Which of the following is not an example of an exogenous variable?

   A. Weather.

   B. Technological development.

   C. National fiscal or momentary policies.

   D. Labor negotiations.

Answer (D) is correct. *(Publisher)*
   REQUIRED: The item that is not an exogenous variable.
   DISCUSSION: Weather, technological developments, and national fiscal and monetary policies are examples of exogenous variables. Managerial decisions and their outcomes are related to and dependent on many of these outside variables. Labor negotiations are internal variables.
   Answer (A) is incorrect because weather is an example of exogenous variables. Answer (B) is incorrect because technological development is an example of an exogenous variable. Answer (C) is incorrect because national fiscal or monetary policies are examples of exogenous variables.

6.6 Change Management

32. A major corporation is considering significant organizational changes. Which of the following groups will not be responsible for implementing these changes?

- A. Employees.
- B. Top management.
- C. Common shareholders.
- D. Outside consultants.

Answer (C) is correct. *(CIA, adapted)*
REQUIRED: The group not responsible for implementing organizational changes.
DISCUSSION: Common shareholders are not responsible for implementing decisions within the organization. If members of the management team are also common shareholders, they must make decisions consistent with their stewardship function. Thus, they must separate their ownership interests from their managerial responsibilities. Organizational change is conducted through change agents, who may include employees, managers, or outside consultants.

33. Lack of skills, threats to job status and security, and fear of failure have all been identified as reasons that employees often

- A. Want to change the culture of their organization.
- B. Are dissatisfied with the structure of their organization.
- C. Are unable to perform their jobs.
- D. Resist organizational change.

Answer (D) is correct. *(CIA, adapted)*
REQUIRED: The result of lack of skills, threats to job security, and fear of failure.
DISCUSSION: Employees resist change for many reasons: surprise, inertia, misunderstanding, ignorance, lack of skills, emotional effects, lack of trust, fear of failure, personality conflicts, poor timing, lack of tact, threats to job status and security, and breakup of the work group. Resistance may be overcome by involving employees to gain feedback and allay fears.
Answer (A) is incorrect because these factors inhibit changes in the culture of the organization. Answer (B) is incorrect because the three factors are not symptoms of dissatisfaction with the structure of the organization. Answer (C) is incorrect because the three factors do not indicate an inability to perform.

34. Organizational development (OD) is one of the major approaches to proactive management of change in organizations. One of the major objectives of OD is to

- A. Increase the power of leaders.
- B. Align the organization's and the employees' goals.
- C. Attract better employees to the organization.
- D. Provide the organization and its managers with ways to increase efficiency.

Answer (B) is correct. *(CIA, adapted)*
REQUIRED: The major objective of organizational development.
DISCUSSION: The objectives of OD are to deepen the sense of organizational purpose and align individuals with it; to promote interpersonal trust, communication, cooperation, and support; to encourage a problem-solving approach; to develop a satisfying work experience; to supplement formal authority with authority based on expertise; to increase personal responsibility; and to encourage willingness to change.
Answer (A) is incorrect because OD focuses on participation and power sharing. Answer (C) is incorrect because attracting better applicants to an organization is not a major goal of OD. Answer (D) is incorrect because OD provides an organization and its managers with higher effectiveness.

35. An organization's management perceives the need to make significant changes. Which of the following factors is management least likely to be able to change?

- A. The organization's members.
- B. The organization's structure.
- C. The organization's environment.
- D. The organization's technology.

Answer (C) is correct. *(CIA, adapted)*
REQUIRED: The factor management is least likely to be able to change.
DISCUSSION: The environment of an organization consists of external forces outside its direct control that may affect its performance. These forces include competitors, suppliers, customers, regulators, climate, culture, politics, technological change, and many other factors. The organization's members are a factor that managers are clearly able to change.

36. An internal auditor is conducting an operational review that affects several different functional units. The auditor believes that the process under review can be improved, but the operating managers are resistant to suggestions for change. There are several methods the auditor could use to overcome the operating managers' resistance. Identify the technique that will produce the highest probability of success with the fewest negative side effects.

A. Negotiation with the operating managers.

B. Participation by the managers in the decision process.

C. Coercion of the managers through threats.

D. Cooperation by approaching each manager individually.

Answer (B) is correct. *(CIA, adapted)*
REQUIRED: The best method for overcoming resistance to change.
DISCUSSION: Participation by the operating managers in the decision process can improve the overall decision, reduce resistance, and secure their commitment to the change.
Answer (A) is incorrect because negotiation may result in sacrifice by one or both parties. Also, if significant concessions are made to one manager, the others will try to gain a similar advantage. Answer (C) is incorrect because coercion is a temporary solution. Resistance will only be subdued, not eliminated. In addition, future cooperation between the auditor and operating managers will be severely restricted. Answer (D) is incorrect because cooperation of individual managers is not optimal. A manager approached to obtain his/her endorsement may feel that (s)he is being used.

6.7 Control Implications of Organizational Structure

37. Organizations in which new product groups are often created, a structure that combines functional and product departmentation and creates dual lines of authority would be optimal. The best structure for this organization is

A. Professional bureaucracy.

B. Mechanistic.

C. Matrix.

D. Machine bureaucracy.

Answer (C) is correct. *(CIA, adapted)*
REQUIRED: The structure that combines functional and product departmentation and creates dual lines of authority.
DISCUSSION: A matrix organization is characterized by vertical and horizontal lines of authority because the product manager borrows specialists from various functions who continue to report to their functional managers. Thus, the resulting arrangement is a hybrid of functional and product departmentation. The advantage is flexibility and rapidity of response to new conditions. The disadvantage is violation of the unity-of-command concept.
Answer (A) is incorrect because a professional bureaucracy is a structure with high complexity and low formalization in which highly trained specialists have great autonomy. Answer (B) is incorrect because a mechanistic structure is complex, formal, and centralized. It adheres to the unity-of-command concept. Answer (D) is incorrect because a machine bureaucracy is formal and complex.

38. The following principles characterize certain organizational structures:

I. A superior can delegate the authority to make decisions but cannot delegate the ultimate responsibility for the results of those decisions.

II. A supervisor's span of control should not exceed seven subordinates.

III. Responsibility should be accompanied by adequate authority.

IV. Employees at all levels should be empowered to make decisions.

Which of these principles are shared by both hierarchical and open organizational structures?

A. I and III.

B. I and IV.

C. II and III.

D. III and IV.

Answer (A) is correct. *(CIA, adapted)*
REQUIRED: The principles shared by hierarchical and open organizational structures.
DISCUSSION: Certain basic concepts of authority and responsibility apply in all organizations. Authority is the right to direct the actions of others. Responsibility is the duty to perform. Responsibility and commensurate authority can and should be delegated, but the person in the higher position nevertheless retains ultimate responsibility. Employee empowerment is not a characteristic of a hierarchical organization. In accordance with the principles of contingency design, an open or organic organization adopts a span of control that reflects situational factors. Hence, a wide span of control may be indicated, for example, when subordinates perform similar duties in the same work area and little direction is required.

39. A new manager of a production department has been asked to assess the effectiveness of that department. The organization needs to satisfy both internal and external constituents and takes a broad approach to effectiveness. In order to complete the assignment successfully, the manager should

A. Measure the daily productivity of the department.

B. Do a survey of employee morale, as it is often a major underlying factor in productivity.

C. Compare the past year's production against annual goals.

D. Consider short-, medium-, and long-term effectiveness.

Answer (D) is correct. *(CIA, adapted)*
REQUIRED: The approach to assessing departmental effectiveness.
DISCUSSION: Kreitner (6th ed., pages 279-80) states, "Organizational effectiveness can be defined as meeting organizational objectives and prevailing societal expectations in the near future, adapting and developing in the intermediate future, and surviving in the distant future. In the near term (about one year), it should be effective in achieving its goals, efficient in its use of resources, and a source of satisfaction to its constituencies (owners, employees, customers, and society). In the intermediate term (2 to 4 years), it should adapt to new possibilities and obstacles and develop its abilities and those of its members. In the long term (5+ years), the organization should be able to survive in an uncertain world."
Answer (A) is incorrect because daily productivity relates to short-term effectiveness only. Answer (B) is incorrect because a survey of employee morale may contribute to assessing effectiveness, but it is not sufficient for assessing overall effectiveness. Answer (C) is incorrect because comparing production against goals is a measure of short-term effectiveness.

40. When an organization depends to a great extent on its environment, which of the following statements best characterizes the relationship among an organization's environment, the level of uncertainty it faces, and its structure? The more dynamic and complex the environment, the

A. More uncertainty the organization will face and the more organic the structure should be.

B. More uncertainty the organization will face and the more mechanistic the structure should be.

C. Less uncertainty the organization will face and the more autocratic the structure should be.

D. Less uncertainty the organization will face and the more organic the structure should be.

Answer (A) is correct. *(CIA, adapted)*
REQUIRED: The statement best characterizing the relationship among an organization's environment, the level of uncertainty it faces, and its structure.
DISCUSSION: A dynamic and complex organizational environment faces constant change, so the level of uncertainty increases. The more uncertainty an organization faces, the more organic the structure should be. Organic organizations tend to be flexible and adaptive to change.

41. In what form of organization does an employee report to multiple managers?

A. Bureaucracy.

B. Matrix.

C. Departmental.

D. Mechanistic.

Answer (B) is correct. *(CIA, adapted)*
REQUIRED: The organization in which an employee reports to multiple managers.
DISCUSSION: A matrix organization (project management) is characterized by vertical and horizontal lines of authority. The project manager borrows specialists from line functions as needed. This manager's authority is limited to the project, and the specialists will otherwise report to the line managers.
Answer (A) is incorrect because in a bureaucracy, each subordinate reports to a single manager. Answer (C) is incorrect because departmental organization structures represent the typical organization with unified and clear single lines of authority. Answer (D) is incorrect because mechanistic organization structure is another term for a bureaucracy.

42. The relationship between organizational structure and technology suggests that, in an organization using mass production technology (for example, automobile manufacturing), the best structure is

   A. Organic, emphasizing loose controls and flexibility.

   B. Matrix, in which individuals report to both product and functional area managers.

   C. Mechanistic, that is, highly formalized, with tight controls.

   D. Integrated, emphasizing cooperation among departments.

Answer (C) is correct. *(CIA, adapted)*
   REQUIRED: The best structure for an organization using mass production technology.
   DISCUSSION: According to Joan Woodward's work on the relationship of technology and structure in manufacturing, companies may be categorized as engaged in unit production (units or small batches), mass production (large batches), or process production (continuous processing). Mass production is most effective if the entity has a mechanistic structure characterized by moderate vertical differentiation, high horizontal differentiation, and high formalization. This structure is one in which tasks are well-defined, most communication is downward, and control is tight.
   Answer (A) is incorrect because an organic structure is flexible and therefore not suited to mass production. Answer (B) is incorrect because matrix is not a type of structure but rather a type of departmentation. Answer (D) is incorrect because an integrated structure is a nonsense term in this context.

43. As an organization increases the number of employees, its structure becomes more complex. Rules become more formalized and more supervisors are hired to direct the increased numbers of subordinates. What is the nature of the size-structure relationship?

   A. The size-structure relationship is linear.

   B. The structure becomes fixed once an organization attains a level of about 200 employees.

   C. The size-structure relationship is concave.

   D. None of the answers are correct.

Answer (D) is correct. *(CIA, adapted)*
   REQUIRED: The nature of the size-structure relationship in an increasingly complex organization.
   DISCUSSION: As an organization increases in size, its structure tends to become more formal and mechanistic. More policies and procedures are necessary to coordinate the increased number of employees, and more managers must be hired. However, the relationship between size and changes in structure is linear only within a certain range. For example, adding 100 employees to a company with 100 employees is likely to cause significant structural change, but adding the same number to a workforce of 10,000 is likely to have little impact. By the time a company reaches a certain size (1,500 to 2,000 or more), it usually has most of the qualities of a mechanistic structure.

44. Centralization and decentralization are defined according to the relative delegation of decision-making authority by top management. Many managers believe that decentralized organizations have significant advantages over centralized organizations. A major advantage of a decentralized organization is that

   A. Decentralized organizations are easier to control.

   B. Decentralized structures streamline organizations and eliminate duplication of resources.

   C. Decentralized organizations have fewer managers than centralized organizations.

   D. Decentralized organizations encourage increased initiative among employees.

Answer (D) is correct. *(CIA, adapted)*
   REQUIRED: The major advantage of a decentralized organization.
   DISCUSSION: A decentralized organization allows lower-level employees to participate in decision making. This increased involvement encourages initiative and creative thinking and is especially appropriate in complex and rapidly changing environments.
   Answer (A) is incorrect because decentralized organizations are more difficult to control. Answer (B) is incorrect because centralized structures streamline organizations and eliminate duplication of resources. Answer (C) is incorrect because the number of managers is not related to the degree of centralization or decentralization but is a function of the span of control.

45. The optimal span of control of a manager is contingent upon several situational variables. For instance, a manager supervising workers within the same work area who are performing identical tasks that are simple and repetitive would best be able to supervise

    A. An unlimited number of employees.

    B. Only a few workers (a narrow span of control).

    C. A relatively large number of employees (a wide span of control).

    D. Fewer workers than if the workers were geographically dispersed.

Answer (C) is correct. *(CIA, adapted)*
    REQUIRED: The optimal span of control of a manager supervising workers within the same work area who are performing identical tasks that are simple and repetitive.
    DISCUSSION: In any situation, there are underlying variables that influence the number of subordinates a manager can supervise. In general, if jobs are similar, procedures are standardized, and physical dispersion is minimized, a wide span of control is most effective.
    Answer (A) is incorrect because although a manager under these conditions would be able to supervise a large number of employees, an upper limit must exist. Answer (B) is incorrect because the conditions described support a wide rather than a narrow span. Answer (D) is incorrect because geographical dispersion would decrease rather than increase the span of control.

6.8 Leadership

46. According to the contingency theory of leadership, a manager will be most effective when (s)he

    A. Consistently initiates structure.

    B. Adapts his/her style to specific circumstances.

    C. Is task-oriented.

    D. Is relationship-oriented.

Answer (B) is correct. *(Publisher)*
    REQUIRED: The most effective management approach according to contingency theory.
    DISCUSSION: Fred E. Fiedler's contingency theory of management holds that no single style of directing is best for all occasions. A successful director (leader) must, for each situation, balance his/her formal authority, the task structure, and the leader's relationships with the pertinent group members. A relationship (employee)-oriented approach may be preferable when tasks are highly structured. When tasks are ill-defined, the more effective manager may be one who concentrates on defining and organizing the jobs to be done rather than on motivating employees.

47. Leadership situations vary with regard to the degree to which the leader can determine what subordinates will do, how they will do it, and what the results will be. According to Fiedler's contingency theory, a leader with a relationship-oriented management style will be most effective when (s)he exerts

    A. Great control.

    B. Moderate control.

    C. Little control.

    D. Great or little control.

Answer (B) is correct. *(Publisher)*
    REQUIRED: The situation in which a relationship-oriented management style will be most effective.
    DISCUSSION: A relationship-oriented manager is employee centered. His/her self-esteem is strongly affected by personal interactions with subordinates. Fiedler indicated that such a manager is most effective when not faced with the extremes of high or low control situations. High control follows from strong position power, a structured task, and good leader-member relations. A low control situation has just the opposite characteristics. In a high-control environment, a concern for personal relations may be unimportant. In a low-control situation, the relationship-oriented leader may be unable to provide the needed task structuring. Thus, the moderate control situation is best. An example is an assembly-line situation (a structured task) in which leader-member relations are poor.

48. If a supervisor uses a supportive management approach, evidenced by positive feelings and concern for subordinates, a problem might result because

    A. An approach based on pure power makes it difficult to motivate staff.

    B. This approach depends on material rewards for the worker.

    C. This approach depends on people who want to work, grow, and achieve.

    D. The manager must believe in the teamwork approach.

Answer (C) is correct. *(CIA, adapted)*
    REQUIRED: The problem that could result from using a supportive management approach.
    DISCUSSION: Supportive management techniques orient workers toward performance rather than obedience or happiness. The leader should have positive feelings for his/her employees and should attempt to encourage participation and involvement. This approach is effective when used with employees who are motivated to work, improve themselves and their abilities, and accomplish goals.
    Answer (A) is incorrect because an approach based on pure power is an autocratic style of leadership, not a supportive approach. Answer (B) is incorrect because the custodial model depends on material rewards for the worker. This model is predicated on the belief that a happy worker is a productive worker. Answer (D) is incorrect because the manager's beliefs are not sufficient. The workers must also believe in the system.

Questions 49 through 51 are based on the following information.

The following question presents a scenario in which a manager needs to decide what leadership style to use to obtain employee satisfaction and effective employee performance. For the purposes of this question, the manager has a choice of four styles.

- The <u>directive</u> leader lets subordinates know what is expected of them, schedules work to be done, and gives specific guidance on how to accomplish tasks.
- The <u>supportive</u> leader is friendly and shows concern for the needs of the subordinates.
- The <u>participative</u> leader consults with subordinates and uses their suggestions before making a decision.
- The <u>achievement-oriented</u> leader sets challenging goals and expects subordinates to perform at their highest level.

49. The workers in a factory have been told that their machines are obsolete and will be replaced by new, computer-assisted machines. The workers must be retrained and are eager to learn everything about the new machines. The manager was recently hired from a company where the new machines were extensively used and is very familiar with them. In this case, what is the best leadership style for the manager?

- A. Directive.
- B. Supportive.
- C. Participative.
- D. Achievement-oriented.

Answer (A) is correct. *(CIA, adapted)*
REQUIRED: The best leadership style for the manager when workers must be retrained and are eager to learn.
DISCUSSION: According to path-goal theory, two groups of contingency factors affect the relationship between leadership behavior and outcomes (performance and satisfaction): environmental factors beyond subordinates' control (task structure, the formal authority system, and the work group) and subordinate factors. The latter include the subordinate's locus of control, experience, and perceived ability. A leadership style should be chosen that complements but does not duplicate the factors in the environment and is consistent with subordinates' characteristics. A directive style is most effective when the subordinate's locus of control is external, tasks are ambiguous or stressful, and substantial conflict exists in the work group. Thus, a directive style is appropriate when subordinates do not have high perceived ability or experience.
Answer (B) is incorrect because subordinates who are neither competent nor confident are best led using the directive style. Answer (C) is incorrect because subordinates with an internal locus of control need a leader with a participative style. Answer (D) is incorrect because achievement-oriented leadership is appropriate when tasks are nonrepetitive and ambiguous and employee competence is high.

50. A production team has been together for several years and has worked well together. However, severe arguments have recently occurred between two members of the group, and other members have begun to take sides. This problem has had a negative effect on production performance. The best leadership style for the manager in this situation is

- A. Directive.
- B. Supportive.
- C. Participative.
- D. Achievement-oriented.

Answer (A) is correct. *(CIA, adapted)*
REQUIRED: The best leadership style for the manager given substantive internal conflict.
DISCUSSION: Directive leadership provides highest subordinate satisfaction when a team encounters substantive internal conflict. Thus, directive leadership is the appropriate complement to the environmental factors. The leader should intervene to compensate for the stress and strife in the workplace.
Answer (B) is incorrect because supportive style is best when tasks and authority relationships are highly structured. Answer (C) is incorrect because participative style is most useful when subordinates believe they control their own destinies. Answer (D) is incorrect because achievement-oriented leadership is appropriate when tasks are nonrepetitive and ambiguous and employee competence is high.

51. Refer to the information preceding question 49 on page 211. The manager of a team of actuaries has been asked to develop the basic pricing structure for a new health insurance product. The team has successfully designed other pricing structures in recent years. The manager was assigned to the team 6 months ago. What is the best leadership style for the manager of this team?

A. Directive.

B. Supportive.

C. Participative.

D. Achievement-oriented.

Answer (C) is correct.   *(CIA, adapted)*
REQUIRED: The best leadership style for a new manager of a team that has successfully completed similar projects.
DISCUSSION: Participative style is most useful when subordinates believe they control their own destinies, that is, when they have an internal locus of control. Such individuals may be resentful if they are not consulted.
Answer (A) is incorrect because directive leadership provides highest subordinate satisfaction when a team encounters substantive internal conflict, when tasks are ambiguous, and when subordinates' locus of control is external. Answer (B) is incorrect because supportive style is best when tasks are highly structured and the authority relationships are clear and bureaucratic. Answer (D) is incorrect because achievement-oriented style will increase subordinates' expectations that high performance will result from their best efforts.

52. A manager implementing the directive leader approach should

A. Closely supervise each employee.

B. Show concern for each employee.

C. Work with the employee when developing goals.

D. Clearly signal that the employee is expected to be successful.

Answer (A) is correct.   *(Publisher)*
REQUIRED: The action that should be taken by a manager using the directive leader approach.
DISCUSSION: The situational approach to leadership (called path-goal theory) allows a manager to choose one of four approaches for implementing his/her leadership style. One of these is the directive leader approach in which a manager provides close guidance to the employee through the use of specific rules, policies, and procedures.
Answer (B) is incorrect because it is an action taken by a supportive leader. Answer (C) is incorrect because it is an action taken by a participative leader. Answer (D) is incorrect because it is an action taken by an achievement-oriented leader.

53. Which of the following is a benefit of implementing the achievement-oriented leader approach rather than the directive leader approach?

A. Employee development is enhanced.

B. The structured environment allows employees to better achieve the organization's goals.

C. Closer supervision is provided for those who perform better in a structured work atmosphere.

D. Employees have more opportunities to develop creativity and meet challenges.

Answer (D) is correct.   *(Publisher)*
REQUIRED: The benefit of using the achievement-oriented leader approach.
DISCUSSION: The benefits to the company of the achievement-oriented leader approach include greater employee confidence and commitment, more employee decision making, increased employee creativity, more challenging objectives, and reduced supervision for employees who work best independently.
Answer (A) is incorrect because employee development is also enhanced under the directive leader approach. Answer (B) is incorrect because a structured environment and close supervision is not a characteristic of the achievement-oriented leader approach. Answer (C) is incorrect because close supervision is not a characteristic of the achievement-oriented leader approach.

54. Marianne is a manager who believes that positive employee attitudes are extremely important. She cooperates with employees in solving problems. A likely effect on employee behavior of this leadership style is

A. Mistrust of the manager.

B. A lack of extraordinary performance.

C. High employee turnover.

D. Increased employee creativity.

Answer (D) is correct.   *(Publisher)*
REQUIRED: The effect on employee behavior most likely to result from the described leadership style.
DISCUSSION: When a manager works to maintain a positive attitude among employees and cooperates with them in problem solving, employees are likely to be more motivated, confident, and creative. This leadership style should also improve communication and decrease absenteeism.

6.9 Negotiation and Conflict Management

55. A construction manager is using a distributive-bargaining approach in negotiating the price of lumber with a supplier. The construction manager will

   A. Concede to the supplier's asking price in order to maintain a positive working relationship.

   B. Hire a mediator to negotiate the deal on behalf of the manager.

   C. Attempt to get agreement on a price within the settlement range (that is, within both the manager's and supplier's aspiration ranges).

   D. State the resistance point (that is, the highest price acceptable) and ask the supplier to concede.

Answer (C) is correct. *(CIA, adapted)*
   REQUIRED: The action based on a distributive-bargaining approach.
   DISCUSSION: When using a distributive-bargaining approach, the negotiator operates with a maximum desired result (target point) and a minimum acceptable result (resistance point) in mind. If the ranges of feasible outcomes (aspiration ranges) overlap, an agreement is possible.
   Answer (A) is incorrect because when using a distributive-bargaining approach, the manager should negotiate a price that both the manager and the supplier can agree on. Answer (B) is incorrect because a mediator is not used when the distributive-bargaining approach is used to resolve a conflict. Answer (D) is incorrect because the manager should not reveal the resistance point (the minimum acceptable result). Instead, (s)he should negotiate to induce the supplier to agree to an amount closer to the target point.

56. As a conflict resolution strategy, optimizing (or a win-win strategy) is most appropriate when

   A. The benefits being contested cannot be changed.

   B. The relationship between the parties is likely to continue.

   C. People are deeply committed to established habits and patterns.

   D. Time is scarce and the manager's patience is wearing thin.

Answer (B) is correct. *(CIA, adapted)*
   REQUIRED: The circumstances in which optimizing is most appropriate.
   DISCUSSION: Optimizing or problem solving entails addressing the source of conflict and finding alternative strategies that benefit all parties. It promotes cooperative, positive attitudes that transfer to other organizational behaviors. Hence, optimizing may be worth the expenditure of more resources than other strategies because it improves the future relationship of the parties.
   Answer (A) is incorrect because optimizing can usually discover more benefits to divide. Answer (C) is incorrect because to optimize, people need to think outside of established habits to find new benefits to divide. Answer (D) is incorrect because optimizing takes more time and energy than other conflict resolution strategies.

57. Two managers have been arguing about the distribution of money for capital investment projects affecting their respective production units. All of the projects are worthwhile and significantly exceed the organization's required rate of return. The approach that would create a win-win solution for the managers under these circumstances would be to

   A. Smooth the differences of the two managers by emphasizing their common interests.

   B. Alter the attitudes and behaviors of the managers so that agreement can be reached.

   C. Force the managers to compromise by asking each of them to give up something.

   D. Expand the resources available so that both manager's projects can be funded.

Answer (D) is correct. *(CIA, adapted)*
   REQUIRED: The conflict resolution method creating a win-win situation.
   DISCUSSION: Expanding the pool of scarce resources, in this case, the money available for capital projects, permits both managers to achieve his/her objectives without having to give up anything of value. Thus, each side wins.
   Answer (A) is incorrect because emphasizing common ground may resolve the conflict but does not allow each party to get what (s)he wants. Answer (B) is incorrect because altering attitudes and behaviors that cause conflict does not create a win-win situation. Answer (C) is incorrect because compromise forces each side to give up something of value.

58. While conducting field work, a strong conflict arises between two of your subordinates regarding possible scope expansion. You draw their attention to their shared views, downplaying the issues of contention. This technique for resolving conflict is called

A. Superordinate goals.

B. Smoothing.

C. Problem solving.

D. Compromise.

Answer (B) is correct. *(CIA, adapted)*
REQUIRED: The technique for resolving conflict.
DISCUSSION: Smoothing is a conflict resolution technique in which differences are deemphasized and common interests of the parties are emphasized. It has the disadvantage of not solving the underlying problems that created the conflict.
Answer (A) is incorrect because superordinate goals are shared goals that can be achieved only through cooperation. Answer (C) is incorrect because problem solving involves identifying and correcting the source of the conflict. Answer (D) is incorrect because compromise requires each party to give up something.

59. Which of the following is a benefit of the communication link represented by negotiating employee-supervisor differences?

A. Each employee perceives that management values his/her accomplishments.

B. A written communication link between the employees and management is provided.

C. Each employee is shown that management values his/her rights and needs.

D. The need for an informal grapevine is reduced.

Answer (C) is correct. *(Publisher)*
REQUIRED: The benefit of negotiations between the employees and the supervisor.
DISCUSSION: The benefits of negotiating employee-supervisor differences include communicating both sides of an issue without litigation, recognizing employee concerns to indicate that management values each subordinate's needs and rights, and impartially treating tensions in the work environment while finding compromise solutions.
Answer (A) is incorrect because the perception that management values employee accomplishments is a benefit of recognition of employee achievements rather than negotiation. Answer (B) is incorrect because a written communication link is a benefit of a device such as a periodic (e.g., monthly or quarterly) newsletter. Answer (D) is incorrect because a reduced need for the informal grapevine is a benefit of a device such as a periodic newsletter.

60. In a situation involving a disagreement between two parties, when one party's interests are more important than the other's (for example, a customer believes one product is most suitable while the seller disagrees, yet the seller's primary goal is to keep the customer satisfied), the best conflict-resolution strategy is

A. Accommodating.

B. Compromising.

C. Competing.

D. Challenging.

Answer (A) is correct. *(CIA, adapted)*
REQUIRED: The best conflict-resolution strategy when one party's interest is more important than the other's.
DISCUSSION: Accommodating is a conflict handling intention. The dimensions of conflict handling intentions are assertiveness and cooperation. An intention is what mediates between one's actual behavior and one's emotions and perceptions. Accommodating entails placing another person's interests above one's own. It represents the minimum of assertiveness and the maximum of cooperation. For example, the seller should accommodate the customer by providing the product the customer wants.
Answer (B) is incorrect because in a compromise, both parties give up something to reach accord. It represents moderate assertiveness and cooperation. Answer (C) is incorrect because in a competitive situation, each party seeks to satisfy his/her own needs without regard to the other. It represents the maximum of assertiveness and the minimum of cooperation. Answer (D) is incorrect because challenging is not a conflict handling intention.

61. Which one of the following techniques is not generally recognized as an effective conflict resolution technique for management to use in a dispute between employees?

A. Accommodation - management encourages a high degree of cooperation and a low degree of assertiveness.

B. Competition - management encourages the parties to seek their own interests, regardless of the effect on each other.

C. Reorganization - management transfers one of the disputants to another department.

D. Compromise - management persuades each party to make concessions.

Answer (B) is correct. *(CIA, adapted)*
REQUIRED: The technique not ordinarily regarded as effective in conflict resolution.
DISCUSSION: Competition is a conflict-handling intention characterized by considerable assertiveness (the degree to which the party seeks to achieve his/her goals) and a low degree of cooperativeness (the degree to which the party attempts to satisfy the concerns of others). Encouraging competition stimulates conflict.

62. Which of the following would be the best approach for negotiating the purchase of a large number of microcomputers, assuming that both parties follow the same approach?

A. Review previous demands, concessions, and settlements (precedents).

B. Attempt to get personal information about the opposing negotiators.

C. Enter without preconceived ideas about what should be accomplished.

D. Ask as few questions as possible during negotiations.

Answer (A) is correct. *(CIA, adapted)*
REQUIRED: The best negotiating approach.
DISCUSSION: The best approach to negotiating a large purchase, assuming that both parties follow the same approach, is to review previous settlements, demands, and concessions to determine what can be achieved. The history of past practices and interactions tends to define current standards of fairness in negotiations.
Answer (B) is incorrect because research indicates that personality traits have no material direct effect on the outcome of negotiation. Answer (C) is incorrect because negotiators should be prepared. They should know what they wish to gain and what their resistance point is. Answer (D) is incorrect because a skilled negotiator asks many questions, is a good listener, is not defensive, focuses arguments well, and avoids irritating the opponent.

63. The behavioral science literature identifies diffusion as an effective approach to resolving conflict. An auditor effectively using diffusion in working with a confrontational auditee would

A. Set aside critical issues temporarily and try to reach agreement on less controversial issues first.

B. Emphasize differences between the parties.

C. Avoid the conflict situation.

D. Identify the sources of conflict and address them directly.

Answer (A) is correct. *(CIA, adapted)*
REQUIRED: The action taken by an auditor using diffusion in working with a confrontational auditee.
DISCUSSION: Diffusion temporarily leaves the conflict unresolved. Smoothing (downplaying differences and emphasizing common interests) and compromise (requiring each party to make concessions) are diffusion approaches to conflict management. The disadvantage is that the underlying problems remain unresolved while the less controversial issues are being addressed first.
Answer (B) is incorrect because differences are downplayed while using a diffusion approach. Answer (C) is incorrect because diffusion addresses issues of conflict. Answer (D) is incorrect because directly addressing the conflict is a confrontational approach.

Use Gleim's *CIA Test Prep* for interactive testing with over 2,000 additional multiple-choice questions!

STUDY UNIT SEVEN
PLANNING AND SUPERVISING THE ENGAGEMENT

(13 pages of outline)

An engagement consists of planning, performing the engagement, communicating results, and monitoring progress. The internal auditor's responsibility is to plan and perform the engagement, subject to review and approval by supervisors. This study unit concerns the first and second phases of the engagement. Because supervision begins with planning, it is included with planning. Identifying, analyzing and evaluating, and recording information are considered in Part II. In accordance with The IIA's content specification outline, communicating results and monitoring progress are covered in Part II.

Subunit 1 presents the pronouncements by The IIA that are relevant to the planning phase. Subunits 2 and 3 provide supplementary information about certain aspects of the engagement and the relevant pronouncements on supervision.

7.1 ENGAGEMENT PLANNING

1. This subunit describes the planning process and provides criteria for evaluating that process. Internal auditors consider the objectives, resources, and operations of, and risks to, the activities reviewed; the relevant risk management and control systems; and possible improvements in those systems. The internal auditors can then establish the engagement's objectives, determine its scope, allocate resources appropriate to the achievement of the objectives, and develop a work program. The engagement planning process is addressed by one General Performance Standard, five Specific Performance Standards, four Assurance Implementation Standards, four Consulting Implementation Standards, and six Practice Advisories.

2200 **Engagement Planning** — *Internal auditors should develop and record a plan for each engagement.*

Practice Advisory 2200-1: Engagement Planning

1. *The internal auditor is responsible for planning and conducting the engagement assignment, subject to supervisory review and approval. The engagement program should:*

   - *Document the internal auditor's procedures for collecting, analyzing, interpreting, and documenting information during the engagement.*
   - *State the objectives of the engagement.*
   - *Set forth the scope and degree of testing required to achieve the engagement objectives in each phase of the engagement.*
   - *Identify technical aspects, risks, processes, and transactions that should be examined.*
   - *State the nature and extent of testing required.*
   - *Be prepared prior to the commencement of engagement work and be modified, as appropriate, during the course of the engagement.*

2.   The chief audit executive is responsible for determining how, when, and to whom engagement results will be communicated. This determination should be documented and communicated to management, to the extent deemed practicable, during the planning phase of the engagement. Subsequent changes that affect the timing or reporting of engagement results should also be communicated to management, if appropriate.

3.   Other requirements of the engagement, such as the engagement period covered and estimated completion dates, should be determined. The final engagement communication format should be considered because proper planning at this stage facilitates preparing the final engagement communication.

4.   All those in management who need to know about the engagement should be informed. Meetings should be held with management responsible for the activity being examined. A summary of matters discussed at meetings and any conclusions reached should be prepared; distributed to individuals, as appropriate; and retained in the engagement working papers. Topics of discussion may include:

- Planned engagement objectives and scope of work.
- The timing of engagement work.
- Internal auditors assigned to the engagement.
- The process of communicating throughout the engagement, including the methods, time frames, and individuals who will be responsible.
- Business conditions and operations of the activity being reviewed, including recent changes in management or major systems.
- Concerns or any requests of management.
- Matters of particular interest or concern to the internal auditor.
- Description of the internal auditing activity's reporting procedures and follow-up process.

2201   _Planning Considerations_ — In planning the engagement, internal auditors should consider:

- The objectives of the activity being reviewed and the means by which the activity controls its performance.
- The significant risks to the activity, its objectives, resources, and operations and the means by which the potential impact of risk is kept to an acceptable level.
- The adequacy and effectiveness of the activity's risk management and control systems compared to a relevant control framework or model.
- The opportunities for making significant improvements to the activity's risk management and control systems.

_2201.C1_ – Internal auditors should establish an understanding with consulting engagement clients about objectives, scope, respective responsibilities, and other client expectations. For significant engagements, this understanding should be documented.

2210   **<u>Engagement Objectives</u>** — *The engagement's objectives should address the risks, controls, and governance processes associated with the activities under review.*

<u>Practice Advisory 2210-1: Engagement Objectives</u>

1.   *Planning should be documented. Engagement objectives and scope of work should be established. Engagement objectives are broad statements developed by internal auditors and define what the engagement is intended to accomplish. Engagement procedures are the means to attain engagement objectives. Engagement objectives and procedures, taken together, define the scope of the internal auditor's work.*

2.   *Engagement objectives and procedures should address the risks associated with the activity under review. The term risk is the uncertainty of an event's occurring that could have an impact on the achievement of objectives. Risk is measured in terms of consequences and likelihood. The purpose of the risk assessment during the planning phase of the engagement is to identify significant areas of activity that should be examined as potential engagement objectives.*

2210.A1 – *When planning the engagement, the internal auditor should identify and assess risks relevant to the activity under review. The engagement objectives should reflect the results of the risk assessment.*

<u>Practice Advisory 2210.A1-1: Risk Assessment in Engagement Planning</u>

1.   *Background information should be obtained about the activities to be reviewed. A review of background information should be performed to determine the impact on the engagement. Such items include:*

- *Objectives and goals.*
- *Policies, plans, procedures, laws, regulations, and contracts that could have a significant impact on operations and reports.*
- *Organizational information, e.g., number and names of employees, key employees, job descriptions, and details about recent changes in the organization, including major system changes.*
- *Budget information, operating results, and financial data of the activity to be reviewed.*
- *Prior engagement working papers.*
- *Results of other engagements, including the work of external auditors, completed or in process.*
- *Correspondence files to determine potential significant engagement issues.*
- *Authoritative and technical literature appropriate to the activity.*

2.   *If appropriate, a survey should be conducted to become familiar with the engagement client's activities, risks, and controls; to identify areas for engagement emphasis; and to invite comments and suggestions from engagement clients. A survey is a process for gathering information, without detailed verification, on the activity being examined. The main purposes are to:*

- *Understand the activity under review.*
- *Identify significant areas warranting special emphasis.*
- *Obtain information for use in performing the engagement.*
- *Determine whether further auditing is necessary.*

3. A survey permits an informed approach to planning and carrying out engagement work. It is an effective tool for applying the internal audit activity's resources where they can be used most effectively. The focus of a survey will vary depending upon the nature of the engagement. The scope of work and the time requirements of a survey will vary. Contributing factors include the internal auditor's training and experience, knowledge of the activity being examined, the type of engagement being performed, and whether the survey is part of a recurring or follow-up assignment. Time requirements will also be influenced by the size and complexity of the activity being examined, and by the geographical dispersion of the activity.

4. A survey may involve use of the following procedures:
    - Discussions with the engagement client.
    - Interviews with individuals affected by the activity, e.g., users of the activity's output.
    - On-site observations.
    - Review of management reports and studies.
    - Analytical auditing procedures.
    - Flowcharting.
    - Functional "walk-through" (tests of specific work activities from beginning to end).
    - Documenting key control activities.

5. A summary of results should be prepared at the conclusion of the survey. The summary should identify:
    - Significant engagement issues and reasons for pursuing them in more depth.
    - Pertinent information developed during the survey.
    - Engagement objectives, engagement procedures, and special approaches such as computer-assisted audit techniques.
    - Potential critical control points, control deficiencies, and/or excess controls.
    - Preliminary estimates of time and resource requirements.
    - Revised dates for reporting phases and completing the engagement.
    - When applicable, reasons for not continuing the engagement.

2210.A2 – The internal auditor should consider the probability of significant errors, irregularities, noncompliance, and other exposures when developing the engagement objectives.

2210.C1 – Consulting engagement objectives should address risks, controls, and governance processes to the extent agreed upon with the client.

2220   **Engagement Scope** — The established scope should be sufficient to satisfy the objectives of the engagement.

2220.A1 – The scope of the engagement should include consideration of relevant systems, records, personnel, and physical properties, including those under the control of third parties.

2220.C1 – In performing consulting engagements, internal auditors should ensure that the scope of the engagement is sufficient to address the agreed-upon objectives. If internal auditors develop reservations about the scope during the engagement, these reservations should be discussed with the client to determine whether to continue with the engagement.

2230   **_Engagement Resource Allocation_** — *Internal auditors should determine appropriate resources to achieve engagement objectives. Staffing should be based on an evaluation of the nature and complexity of each engagement, time constraints, and available resources.*

Practice Advisory 2230-1: Engagement Resource Allocation

1.   *In determining the resources necessary to perform the engagement, evaluation of the following is important:*

   ● *The number and experience level of the internal auditing staff required should be based on an evaluation of the nature and complexity of the engagement assignment, time constraints, and available resources.*

   ● *Knowledge, skills, and other competencies of the internal auditing staff should be considered in selecting internal auditors for the engagement.*

   ● *Training needs of internal auditors should be considered because each engagement assignment serves as a basis for meeting developmental needs of the internal audit activity.*

   ● *Consideration of the use of external resources when additional knowledge, skills, and other competencies are needed.*

2240   **_Engagement Work Program_** — *Internal auditors should develop work programs that achieve the engagement objectives. These work programs should be recorded.*

Practice Advisory 2240-1: Engagement Work Program

1.   *Engagement procedures, including the testing and sampling techniques employed, should be selected in advance, if practicable, and expanded or altered if circumstances warrant. More detailed guidance is described in Practice Advisory 2200-1.*

2.   *The process of collecting, analyzing, interpreting, and documenting information should be supervised to provide reasonable assurance that the auditor's objectivity is maintained and engagement goals are met.*

2240.A1 – *Work programs should establish the procedures for identifying, analyzing, evaluating, and recording information during the engagement. The work program should be approved prior to the commencement of work, and any adjustments approved promptly.*

Practice Advisory 2240.A1-1: Approval of Work Programs

1.   *In obtaining approval of the engagement work plan, such plans should be approved in writing by the chief audit executive or designee prior to the commencement of engagement work. Adjustments to engagement work plans should be approved in a timely manner. Initially, approval may be obtained orally, if factors preclude obtaining written approval prior to commencing engagement work.*

2240.C1 – *Work programs for consulting engagements may vary in form and content depending upon the nature of the engagement.*

2.   Stop and review! You have completed the outline for this subunit. Study multiple-choice questions 1 through 24 beginning on page 229.

7.2 THE PRELIMINARY SURVEY

1. The preliminary or on-site survey allows for the gathering of information, without detailed verification, about the activities to be reviewed. It is also an opportunity for the internal auditor and the client to begin a participative engagement.

2. **Objectives of the Preliminary Survey**

    a. The preliminary survey should

    1) Result in thorough internal auditor familiarity with the engagement client's

        a) Objectives
        b) Organizational structure
        c) Operations
        d) Physical facilities
        e) Risk management, control, and governance systems (including documentation and procedures)

            i) Internal auditors must consider all such policies and procedures, not merely those relevant to a financial statement audit.

        f) Personnel
        g) Information systems

    2) Become the basis for an efficient, effective engagement work program, which

        a) Concentrates on matters of significance
        b) Reduces the time allocated to areas in which risk appears to be minimal

    3) Set a cooperative tone for the field work that follows

    b. The more complex and extensive the activity, the greater the need for the overview provided by the preliminary survey.

    c. The preliminary survey requires certain abilities. The internal auditor must

    1) Ask intelligent questions
    2) Prepare suitable questionnaires
    3) Have a clear understanding of

        a) The information needed
        b) Sources of that information
        c) How to obtain the information

    4) Understand and be adept at flowcharting and other means of documenting the information obtained
    5) Understand management's objectives and be able to identify the objectives of each activity reviewed
    6) Understand the purposes of risk management, control, and governance policies and procedures
    7) Identify the risks implicit in the areas under review

     d.   Defects in risk management and control processes discovered during the preliminary survey should be immediately communicated to the person who can best take corrective action.

         1)   The initial communication should be oral. If corrective action is taken, no further steps are needed until the final engagement communication.

         2)   If corrective action is not taken, if the defect is significant, and if, in the internal auditor's opinion, correction cannot be safely delayed, management should be alerted in an interim or progress communication.

     e.   The overall results of the preliminary survey, if warranted, may be communicated to management in an oral presentation.

3.   **Preparation for the Preliminary Meeting**

     a.   The internal auditor should gain as much familiarity as possible with the engagement client before the first meeting. Sources of information include

         1)   Management's charter for the activities to be reviewed

         2)   Organization charts

         3)   The internal auditor's permanent file

         4)   Prior engagement communications

         5)   Prior engagement working papers

         6)   Internal audit staff and supervisors assigned to previous engagements for this client

     b.   A questionnaire should be constructed to elicit the needed information. Examples of questions are

         1)   How many sections and people are in the activity or department?

         2)   What activities are carried out, and which are the most important or the most troublesome?

         3)   How is control exercised, and what reports are received?

         4)   How are employees trained, and what standards must they meet?

         5)   How are priorities set for the work?

         6)   What are normal backlogs?

         7)   What other entities are affected, and what type of feedback is received from them?

         8)   What areas need the most managerial attention?

         9)   What is the status of deficient conditions observed in the last engagement, and what changes have occurred since then?

         10) What means are used for recording employee attendance?

         11) Are time clock hours balanced to labor hours that were charged to jobs?

         12) What is the basis for distributing overhead charges?

         13) What methods are used to ensure proper payments to suppliers?

         14) What methods are used to safeguard assets and facilities?

         15) How are the entrance and exit of materials controlled?

         16) How is the need for repetitive reports determined?

         17) How are insurable values determined?

         18) How is telephone expense controlled?

     c.   The questionnaire may be sent to the engagement client for completion prior to the internal auditor's arrival for discussion at the preliminary meeting.

         1)   The internal auditor may request that the questionnaire be returned prior to the preliminary meeting.

d.   The engagement client should be formally notified of the engagement, including

1)   Objective and scope
2)   Schedule
3)   Names of personnel involved
4)   Preliminary questionnaire (if any) and instructions for it
5)   The following example letter is adapted from Sawyer and Dittenhofer, *Sawyer's Internal Auditing*, p. 149.

To: *Manager, Plant X*
From: *Vice President, Off-Site Plants*
Subject: *Review of Plant X Activities*

The Internal Audit Activity is planning to perform its periodic engagement to review activities at Plant X in the very near future. The engagement will be performed by two internal auditors: Jane A. Smith is the auditor-in-charge, and William B. Jones will assist her.

The internal auditors will arrive at Plant X on or about November 9. Ms. Smith will call you a few days before her arrival to tell you the exact date.

To save the time of both the internal auditors and your staff, they have developed a set of questionnaires that should elicit a good deal of the information they will need. The answers to the questions should be prepared in advance of their visit. This will simplify the engagement and reduce the length of the internal auditors' stay at Plant X.

The questions are divided into the areas of Administration, Manufacturing Services, Production, and Quality Control – conforming to the Plant X organization – and so can be assigned to several people for response, thereby reducing the burden on any one individual. The internal auditors have asked that you attach any relevant reports and records to the answered questions to illustrate the documentation being used.

Please hold the answered questions pending the internal auditors' visit. After they have had an opportunity to review the replies and the supporting documentation, please assign someone to provide them with a "walk-through" of the Plant X facility, to answer any further questions they may have, and to assist them through the remainder of their engagement.

I appreciate your giving the internal auditors full cooperation and providing them with any assistance they may need.

Vice President, Off-Site Plants

cc: J.A. Smith

4.   **The Preliminary Meeting**

a.   The preliminary meeting with the engagement client should set a cooperative tone for the engagement and should attempt to calm client anxieties.

b.   The internal auditor should be candid about the engagement objectives and should discuss engagement methods.

1)   Cash or securities engagements and fraud investigations are exceptions.

c.   The internal auditor should stress that all engagement observations and recommendations will be promptly discussed with the engagement client and that an opportunity will be afforded for corrective action prior to communication of results.

d.   The preliminary meeting will proceed systematically and efficiently if the internal auditor has prepared a list of questions and requests about matters such as the following:

1)   The charter and organization of the activity and of all subactivities including objectives
2)   Financial information and statistical or quantitative data
3)   Operating and job instructions
4)   Performance standards

        5)   Flow of records and processes depicted by flowcharts, if available

        6)   Areas that are experiencing difficulties or where risks appear likely

        7)   Matters that may be of interest to senior management

  e.   The internal auditor should consider in advance the probable sources for such information.

     1)   EXAMPLES:

        a)   Discussions with supervisors and employees

        b)   Discussions with managers in related departments

        c)   Correspondence files

        d)   Reports submitted to and by the engagement client

        e)   Budgets

        f)   Short- and long-range objectives and reports on their accomplishment

        g)   Procedures manuals

        h)   Reports by and to governmental agencies

  f.   A physical inspection of the premises (a "walk through") is essential if the internal auditor is to obtain a frame of reference for policies, procedures, and organization charts. During these inspections, the internal auditor may ask these questions:

     1)   Is work being completed on schedule and at acceptable quality levels?

     2)   Are reports made on difficulties encountered, and are the reports acted upon?

     3)   What problems are being experienced?

     4)   Has corrective action proven successful?

  g.   Precise and specific information can also be obtained by "walking through" sample transactions.

     1)   Key types of documents being processed are selected.

     2)   The documents are "walked through" the entire process to give internal auditors visual assurance that the controls said to exist are actually in effect.

  h.   The internal auditor can help to ensure good relations with the engagement client by suggesting another meeting after the preliminary survey to

     1)   Give a brief report of initial impressions

     2)   Discuss the engagement client's views on the key objectives of the organization

     3)   Set forth the general thrust of the engagement work program

5. **Documentation of the Preliminary Survey**

  a.   The internal auditor should document the results of the preliminary survey.

     1)   Written statements of objectives and goals can be photocopied.

     2)   The organizational structure is described in client-prepared organizational charts.

     3)   Operations are summarized in financial statements and in narrative descriptions of products, processing services, etc.

     4)   Physical facilities can be described in photographs, plant layouts, etc.

     5)   Descriptions of accounting systems are normally recorded in

        a)   Questionnaires

        b)   Narrative memoranda

        c)   Flowcharts

       6)   Descriptions of nonfinancial control systems are found in procedures manuals, delegation guides, operating instructions, etc.

       7)   Employees are described in statements of personnel objectives, job descriptions, labor contracts, organizational phone directories, etc.

6.   Stop and review! You have completed the outline for this subunit. Study multiple-choice questions 25 through 33 beginning on page 236.

7.3 ENGAGEMENT SUPERVISION

1.   This subunit includes the pronouncements relevant to supervision of engagements as well as some supplementary guidance. Engagement supervision is the subject of one Specific Performance Standard and one Practice Advisory.

2340   ***Engagement Supervision*** — *Engagements should be properly supervised to ensure objectives are achieved, quality is assured, and staff is developed.*

Practice Advisory 2340-1: Engagement Supervision

1.   *The chief audit executive is responsible for assuring that appropriate engagement supervision is provided. Supervision is a process that begins with planning and continues throughout the examination, evaluation, communication, and follow-up phases of the engagement. Supervision includes:*

- *Ensuring that the auditors assigned possess the requisite knowledge, skills, and other competencies to perform the engagement.*
- *Providing appropriate instructions during the planning of the engagement and approving the engagement program.*
- *Seeing that the approved engagement program is carried out unless changes are both justified and authorized.*
- *Determining that engagement working papers adequately support the engagement observations, conclusions, and recommendations.*
- *Ensuring that engagement communications are accurate, objective, clear, concise, constructive, and timely.*
- *Ensuring that engagement objectives are met.*
- *Providing opportunities for developing internal auditors' knowledge, skills, and other competencies.*

2.   *Appropriate evidence of supervision should be documented and retained. The extent of supervision required will depend on the proficiency and experience of internal auditors and the complexity of the engagement. The chief audit executive has overall responsibility for review but may designate appropriately experienced members of the internal audit activity to perform the review. Appropriately experienced internal auditors may be used to review the work of other less experienced internal auditors.*

3.   *All internal auditing assignments, whether performed by or for the internal audit activity, remain the responsibility of the chief audit executive. The chief audit executive is responsible for all significant professional judgments made in the planning, examination, evaluation, communication, and follow-up phases of the engagement. The chief audit executive should adopt suitable means to ensure that this responsibility is met. Suitable means include policies and procedures designed to:*

- *Minimize the risk that professional judgments may be made by internal auditors or others performing work for the internal audit activity that are inconsistent with the professional judgment of the chief audit executive such that a significant adverse effect on the engagement could result.*

- *Resolve differences in professional judgment between the chief audit executive and internal auditing staff members over significant issues relating to the engagement. Such means may include: (a) discussion of pertinent facts, (b) further inquiry or research, and (c) documentation and disposition of the differing viewpoints in the engagement working papers. In instances of a difference in professional judgment over an ethical issue, suitable means may include referral of the issue to those individuals in the organization having responsibility over ethical matters.*

4. *Supervision extends to staff training and development, employee performance evaluation, time and expense control, and similar administrative areas.*

5. *All engagement working papers should be reviewed to ensure that they properly support the engagement communications and that all necessary procedures have been performed. Evidence of supervisory review should consist of the reviewer's initialing and dating each working paper after it is reviewed. Other review techniques that provide evidence of supervisory review include completing an engagement working paper review checklist or preparing a memorandum specifying the nature, extent, and results of the review.*

6. *Reviewers may make a written record (review notes) of questions arising from the review process. When clearing review notes, care should be taken to ensure that the working papers provide adequate evidence that questions raised during the review have been resolved. Acceptable alternatives with respect to disposition of review notes are as follows:*

   - *Retain the review notes as a record of the questions raised by the reviewer and the steps taken in their resolution.*
   - *Discard the review notes after the questions raised have been resolved and the appropriate engagement working papers have been amended to provide the additional information requested.*

2. The internal audit activity should maintain the same degree of control over its own activities as it expects from other subunits of the organization.

3. All projects should be formally assigned. Each should be provided

   a. An assignment sheet, i.e., a work order authorizing expenditure of engagement work hours

   b. A job title indicating the activity covered

   c. A job number identifying the job and indicating its nature, e.g., a regular or special internal audit, a consultancy, or a fraud investigation

4. The chief audit executive should review the progress of each engagement periodically in terms of budgeted employee-days, actual employee-days, and estimated completion date.

5. Schedules for job completion should be set early, usually before the midpoint of the assignment.

6. Requests for budget adjustment should also be made well before job completion, i.e., as soon as it becomes apparent that the actual project differs significantly from that described in the engagement work schedule.

7. Adjusted budgets will normally be carried forward to future budgets and work schedules, but temporary obstacles, e.g., those created by inexperienced assistants and unexpected problems, should not justify budget adjustments.

8. Projects should be formally closed upon the issuance of a final engagement communication if there are no unresolved matters when it is released. Otherwise, they should be closed by the submission of a closure communication to the CAE when action on all unresolved matters discussed in the final engagement communication is complete.

9. Activity reports should be prepared for senior management and the board at least annually. These activity reports

   a. Highlight significant engagement observations, conclusions, and recommendations.

   b. Explain major deviations from approved engagement work schedules, staffing plans, and financial budgets.

10. All engagements should be kept under budgetary control.

   a. Project budgets are usually stated in employee-hours or employee-days.

   b. Financial budgets should include items other than internal audit activity staff payroll, e.g.,

      1) Administrative and clerical support
      2) Engagement-related and training-related travel
      3) Outside service providers
      4) Telephone
      5) Supplies
      6) Library
      7) Staff professional society membership dues

   c. Budgets on regular jobs should be the same as those shown in the engagement work schedule.

   d. Budgets on engagements for which there is no prior experience should be set as soon as possible after the scope of the engagement becomes known.

   e. Because no projects are precisely the same (even those covering the same activity), budgets should be reevaluated after the preliminary survey.

      1) Excessive budgets should be reduced.
      2) Insufficient budgets should be expanded or the scope of the job reduced.
      3) Adjustments and the reasons for them should be documented for future engagement work schedules.

   f. Budget adjustments should be justified and should be approved at a level higher than the engagement supervisor. Requests for budget adjustment should show

      1) The operational activities to be reviewed according to the engagement work schedule
      2) The activities actually being carried on
      3) The employee-days attributable to the difference

11. Administrative records should provide the CAE with control over engagements in progress and with sufficient information for useful reports to management on engagement accomplishments.

   a. Staff auditors should submit time sheets periodically, showing the employee-days charged against their projects and accounting for all employee-days in the reporting period.

      1) Time should be accumulated in registers by project, including time off, vacations, holidays, etc.

   b. Staff auditors should report weekly to their supervisors on the time spent and the status of the job.

c.   The internal audit activity should maintain records to gather data for

1) Status reports on all ongoing engagements
2) Communication of results
3) Suggestions adopted
4) Savings accomplished as a result of recommendations
5) Time expended by type of engagement in comparison with amounts budgeted

12. Stop and review! You have completed the outline for this subunit. Study multiple-choice questions 34 through 43 beginning on page 240.

QUESTIONS

7.1 Engagement Planning

1. Internal auditors should develop and record a plan for each engagement. The planning process should include all the following except

A. Establishing engagement objectives and scope of work.

B. Obtaining background information about the activities to be reviewed.

C. Identifying sufficient information to achieve engagement objectives.

D. Determining how, when, and to whom the engagement results will be communicated.

Answer (C) is correct. *(CIA, adapted)*
REQUIRED: The item not part of the planning process.
DISCUSSION: Planning should include establishing engagement objectives and scope of work, obtaining background information about the activities to be reviewed, determining the resources necessary to perform the engagement, and informing those in management who need to know about the engagement. It also includes performing, as appropriate, a survey to become familiar with activities, risks, and controls; to identify areas for engagement emphasis; and to invite comments and suggestions from engagement clients. Furthermore, planning extends to developing work programs; determining how, when, and to whom engagement results will be communicated; and obtaining approval of the engagement work program. Identifying sufficient information to achieve engagement objectives is done during field work, not planning.

2. The scope of an internal auditing engagement is initially defined by the

A. Engagement objectives.

B. Scheduling and time estimates.

C. Preliminary survey.

D. Engagement work program.

Answer (A) is correct. *(CIA, adapted)*
REQUIRED: The factor initially defining the scope of an internal auditing engagement.
DISCUSSION: According to Standard 2220, "The established scope should be sufficient to satisfy the objectives of the engagement." Moreover, according to PA 2210-1, "Planning should be documented. Engagement objectives and scope of work should be established. Engagement objectives are broad statements developed by internal auditors and define what the engagement is intended to accomplish. Engagement procedures are the means to attain engagement objectives. Engagement objectives and procedures, taken together, define the scope of the internal auditor's work."
Answer (B) is incorrect because the scheduling and time estimates are based on the objectives and scope of the engagement. Answer (C) is incorrect because the preliminary survey is performed before the objectives are determined, but the objectives and procedures define the scope of the engagement. Answer (D) is incorrect because the work program is developed after the preliminary survey and is based on the objectives of the engagement.

3. The established scope of the engagement should be sufficient to satisfy the objectives of the engagement. When developing the objectives of the engagement, the internal auditor should consider the

A. Probability of significant noncompliance.

B. The information included in the engagement work program.

C. The results of engagement procedures.

D. Resources required.

Answer (A) is correct. *(Publisher)*
REQUIRED: The factor the internal auditor should consider when developing the objectives of the engagement.
DISCUSSION: According to Standard 2210.A2, the internal auditor should consider the probability of significant errors, irregularities, noncompliance, and other exposures when developing assurance engagement objectives. In a consulting engagement, the objectives should address risks, controls, and governance processes to the extent agreed upon with the client (Standard 2210.C1).
Answer (B) is incorrect because engagement objectives must be determined before the engagement work program is written. Answer (C) is incorrect because the objectives determine the procedures to be performed. Answer (D) is incorrect because internal auditors determine the resources required to achieve the engagement objectives.

4. The scope of an internal auditing assurance engagement should include consideration of

    A. Only those systems and records under the control of the engagement client.

    B. Relevant physical properties under third-party control.

    C. Engagement observations, conclusions, and recommendations.

    D. Final engagement communications.

Answer (B) is correct. *(Publisher)*
REQUIRED: The item within the scope of an internal auditing assurance engagement.
DISCUSSION: The scope of the engagement should include consideration of relevant systems, records, personnel, and physical properties, including those under the control of third parties (Standard 2220.A1). Engagement results reported in final engagement communications follow from performing the procedures and achieving the objectives that define the engagement scope.

5. Which of the following is the best explanation of the difference, if any, between engagement objectives and procedures?

    A. Procedures establish broad general goals; objectives specify the detailed work to be performed.

    B. Objectives are tailor-made for each engagement; procedures are generic in application.

    C. Objectives define specific desired accomplishments; procedures provide the means of achieving objectives.

    D. Procedures and objectives are essentially the same.

Answer (C) is correct. *(CIA, adapted)*
REQUIRED: The difference between objectives and procedures.
DISCUSSION: According to PA 2210-1, "Planning should be documented. Engagement objectives and scope of work should be established. Engagement objectives are broad statements developed by internal auditors and define what the engagement is intended to accomplish. Engagement procedures are the means to attain engagement objectives. Engagement objectives and procedures, taken together, define the scope of the internal auditor's work."
Answer (A) is incorrect because objectives are specific goals, and procedures specify the detailed work. Answer (B) is incorrect because both objectives and procedures must be defined specifically for each engagement. Answer (D) is incorrect because procedures are the means of collecting, analyzing, interpreting, and documenting information during the engagement to achieve the objectives.

6. An outside consultant is developing methods for the management of a city's capital facilities. An appropriate scope of an engagement to evaluate the consultant's product is to

    A. Review the consultant's contract to determine its propriety.

    B. Establish the parameters of the value of the items being managed and controlled.

    C. Determine the adequacy of the risk management and control systems for the management of capital facilities.

    D. Review the handling of idle equipment.

Answer (C) is correct. *(CIA, adapted)*
REQUIRED: The appropriate scope of an engagement to evaluate a consultant's product.
DISCUSSION: According to Standard 2201, "In planning the engagement, internal auditors should consider:

- The objectives of the activity being reviewed and the means by which the activity controls its performance.
- The significant risks to the activity, its objectives, resources, and operations and the means by which the potential impact of risk is kept to an acceptable level.
- The adequacy and effectiveness of the activity's risk management and control systems compared to a relevant control framework or model.
- The opportunities for making significant improvements to the activity's risk management and control systems."

Answer (A) is incorrect because the review of the consultant's contract to determine its propriety is related to the procurement decision. Answer (B) is incorrect because the establishment of parameters for values of items being managed and controlled is a management responsibility. Answer (D) is incorrect because management must determine policies regarding idle equipment. Some equipment may be retained for emergency use.

7. As a particular engagement is being planned in a high-risk area, the chief audit executive determines that the available staff does not have the requisite skills to perform the assignment. The best course of action consistent with engagement planning principles is to

A. Not perform the engagement because the requisite skills are not available.

B. Use the engagement as a training opportunity and let the internal auditors learn as the engagement is performed.

C. Consider using external resources to supplement the needed knowledge, skills, and other competencies and complete the assignment.

D. Perform the engagement but limit the scope in light of the skill deficiency.

Answer (C) is correct. *(CIA, adapted)*
REQUIRED: The course of action when the internal auditing staff does not have adequate skills to perform the engagement.
DISCUSSION: In determining the resources needed to perform the engagement, the CAE should consider the knowledge, skills, and other competencies of the internal auditing staff in selecting internal auditors for the engagement. The CAE should consider the use of external resources when additional knowledge, skills, and other competencies are needed (PA 2230-1).
Answer (A) is incorrect because not performing the engagement is unacceptable, especially for a high-risk area. Answer (B) is incorrect because engagements should be properly supervised. The IAA has no one to provide this supervision. Answer (D) is incorrect because limiting the scope of the engagement should be done only when the requisite skills are not available even from external resources. If the scope is limited, management should be informed of the constraint in an interim report.

8. The chief audit executive of a multinational organization must form an engagement team to examine a newly acquired subsidiary in another country. Consideration should be given to which of the following factors?

I. Local customs
II. Language skills of the internal auditor
III. Experience of the internal auditor
IV. Monetary exchange rate

A. I, II, and III.

B. II, III, and IV.

C. I and III.

D. I and II.

Answer (A) is correct. *(CIA, adapted)*
REQUIRED: The factors considered in forming a team to conduct an engagement in another country.
DISCUSSION: Internal auditors should determine appropriate resources to achieve engagement objectives. Staffing should be based on an evaluation of the nature and complexity of each engagement, time constraints, and available resources (Standard 2230). Thus, the knowledge, skills, and other competencies of the internal auditing staff should be considered in selecting internal auditors for the engagement (PA 2230-1). Thus, in an engagement to be performed in a foreign country, the language skills of the internal auditor and knowledge of local customs must be considered. For example, gender and ethnic issues may be important in some countries because of religious restrictions and incompatibilities. As always, experience levels are relevant in making staff assignments.
Answer (B) is incorrect because the exchange rate is irrelevant to determining the needed traits of the team members. Answer (C) is incorrect because the language skills of the internal auditor must be considered. Answer (D) is incorrect because experience must always be considered.

9. Documentation required to plan an internal auditing engagement should include information that

A. Resources needed to complete the engagement were considered.

B. Planned engagement work will be completed on a timely basis.

C. Intended engagement observations have been clearly identified.

D. Internal audit activity resources are efficiently and effectively employed.

Answer (A) is correct. *(CIA, adapted)*
REQUIRED: The information included in the documentation required to plan an engagement.
DISCUSSION: Planning should be documented. It includes establishing engagement objectives and scope of work, obtaining background information about activities to be reviewed, determining the resources required for the engagement, and informing those in management who need to know about the engagement. It also includes performing, as appropriate, a survey to become familiar with activities, risks, and controls; to identify areas for engagement emphasis; and to invite comments and suggestions from engagement clients. Furthermore, planning extends to developing work programs; determining how, when, and to whom engagement results will be communicated; and obtaining approval of the engagement work program.
Answer (B) is incorrect because whether the planned work will actually be completed on time cannot be known in the planning phase. Answer (C) is incorrect because intended engagement observations should be identified when determining the scope of work to be performed. Answer (D) is incorrect because documenting the economic and efficient use of resources can be done only on completion of the engagement.

10. Which of the following is least likely to be placed on the agenda for discussion at a pre-engagement meeting?

A. Purpose and scope of the engagement.

B. Records and client personnel needed.

C. Sampling plan and key criteria.

D. Expected starting and completion dates.

Answer (C) is correct. *(CIA, adapted)*
REQUIRED: The item least likely to be discussed at a pre-engagement meeting.
DISCUSSION: Meetings should be held with management responsible for the activity being examined (PA 2200-1). These pre-engagement meetings between the internal auditor and engagement client are opportunities to discuss planning and housekeeping matters regarding the forthcoming engagement. The sampling plan would probably not be discussed because it is not determined until the preliminary survey and evaluation of controls are completed.

11. In planning an engagement, the internal auditor should establish objectives and procedures to address the risk associated with the activity. Risk is defined as

A. The possibility that the balance or class of transactions and related assertions contains misstatements that could be material to the financial statements.

B. The uncertainty of the occurrence of an event that could affect the achievement of objectives.

C. The failure to adhere to organizational policies, plans, and procedures or to comply with relevant laws and regulations.

D. The failure to accomplish established objectives and goals for operations or programs.

Answer (B) is correct. *(CIA, adapted)*
REQUIRED: The definition of risk.
DISCUSSION: According to PA 2210-1, "Engagement objectives and procedures should address the risks associated with the activity under review. The term risk is the uncertainty of an event's occurring that could have an impact on the achievement of objectives. Risk is measured in terms of consequences and likelihood. The purpose of the risk assessment during the planning phase of the engagement is to identify significant areas of activity that should be examined as potential engagement objectives."
Answer (A) is incorrect because the risk of material misstatement in financial statement assertions consists of inherent risk, control risk, and detection risk as defined in the AICPA's auditing standards. Answer (C) is incorrect because the failure to adhere to organizational policies, plans, and procedures or to comply with relevant laws and regulations is just one type of adverse effect that can result from unmitigated risk. Answer (D) is incorrect because the failure to accomplish established objectives and goals for operations or programs is just one type of adverse effect that can result from unmitigated risk.

12. Which of the following activities represents the greatest risk to a post-merger manufacturing organization and is therefore most likely be the subject of an internal auditing engagement?

A. Combining imprest funds.

B. Combining purchasing functions.

C. Combining legal functions.

D. Combining marketing functions.

Answer (B) is correct. *(CIA, adapted)*
REQUIRED: The activity representing the greatest risk.
DISCUSSION: According to Standard 2210.A1, "When planning the engagement, the internal auditor should identify and assess risks relevant to the activity under review. The engagement objectives should reflect the results of the risk assessment." In a consulting engagement, the objectives should address risks, controls, and governance processes to the extent agreed upon with the client (Standard 2210.C1). Purchasing functions represent the greatest exposure to loss of the items listed and are therefore most likely to be evaluated. The financial exposure in the purchasing function is ordinarily greater than in, for example, the legal and marketing functions. After a merger, risk is heightened because of the difficulty of combining the disparate systems of the two organizations. Thus, the likelihood of an engagement is increased.
Answer (A) is incorrect because imprest funds are typically immaterial in amount. Answer (C) is incorrect because legal functions do not typically represent a risk of loss as great as the purchasing functions. Answer (D) is incorrect because marketing functions do not typically represent a risk of loss as great as the purchasing functions.

13. Writing an engagement work program occurs at which stage of the engagement?

   A. During the planning stage.

   B. Subsequent to evaluating risk management and control systems.

   C. As the engagement is performed.

   D. At the end of each engagement when the standard work program should be revised for the next engagement to ensure coverage of noted problem areas.

Answer (A) is correct. *(CIA, adapted)*
   REQUIRED: The stage of the engagement during which the work program is written.
   DISCUSSION: Standard 2200 states, "Internal auditors should develop and record a plan for each engagement." Thus, Standard 2240 states, "Internal auditors should develop work programs that achieve the engagement objectives. These work programs should be recorded." Furthermore, work programs should be prepared prior to the commencement of engagement work and modified, as appropriate, during the course of the engagement (PA 2200-1). Accordingly, work programs are prepared during the planning stage.
   Answer (B) is incorrect because the work program states the scope, degree, nature, and extent of testing. Hence, it must be written in the planning stage. Answer (C) is incorrect because the internal auditor should write the work program during the planning stage, not as the engagement is performed. However, the work program may be modified during the engagement. Answer (D) is incorrect because, although revising the work program at the end of one engagement for the next engagement is allowed, it should still be written during the planning phase.

14. In the preparation of an engagement work program, which of the following items is not essential?

   A. The performance of a preliminary survey.

   B. A review of material from prior engagement communications.

   C. The preparation of a budget identifying the costs of resources needed.

   D. A review of criteria established by management to determine whether operating goals and objectives have been accomplished.

Answer (C) is correct. *(CIA, adapted)*
   REQUIRED: The item not essential to preparing the work program.
   DISCUSSION: Standard 2230 states, "Internal auditors should determine appropriate resources to achieve engagement objectives. Staffing should be based on an evaluation of the nature and complexity of each engagement, time constraints, and available resources." Hence, it is implicit that the work program should state the resources necessary to carry out the detailed tasks specified. However, quantification of costs is not essential to writing the work program.
   Answer (A) is incorrect because the preliminary survey provides necessary background information about activities, risks, and controls. Answer (B) is incorrect because engagement communications contain, among other things, information about observations from prior engagements and corrective actions taken. Answer (D) is incorrect because internal auditors should ascertain the extent to which management has established adequate criteria to determine whether objectives and goals have been accomplished (Standard 2120.A4).

15. A work program for a comprehensive assurance engagement to evaluate a purchasing function should include

   A. Procedures arranged by relative priority based upon perceived risk.

   B. A statement of the engagement objectives for the operation under review with agreement by the engagement client.

   C. Procedures to accomplish engagement objectives.

   D. A focus on risks affecting the financial statements as opposed to controls.

Answer (C) is correct. *(CIA, adapted)*
   REQUIRED: The content of a work program for a comprehensive engagement to evaluate a purchasing function.
   DISCUSSION: Work programs are a necessary part of engagement planning. They establish the procedures for identifying, analyzing, evaluating, and recording information during the engagement. Work programs should be approved prior to the commencement of work, and any adjustments should be approved promptly (Standard 2240.A1).
   Answer (A) is incorrect because engagement procedures should normally be arranged in an order that will most efficiently complete the work program. Answer (B) is incorrect because engagement objectives should be stated, but they do not need to be agreed to by the engagement client. Answer (D) is incorrect because the engagement should not be narrowly focused on the reliability and integrity of financial information.

16. Which of the following is not ordinarily considered an essential criterion for developing engagement work programs?

A. Description of the objectives of the engagement client operation to be evaluated.

B. Specificity as to the controls to be tested.

C. Specificity as to procedures to be followed.

D. Specificity as to the methodology to be used for the engagement procedures.

Answer (D) is correct. *(CIA, adapted)*
   REQUIRED: The criterion not considered essential for developing engagement work programs.
   DISCUSSION: Work programs are a necessary part of engagement planning. They consist of the specific work steps required for the engagement, but they must allow for some latitude for flexibility in carrying out the steps. Thus, they should be expanded or altered if circumstances warrant (PA 2240-1).
   Answer (A) is incorrect because the objectives of the operation to be evaluated set the parameters of the engagement work. Answer (B) is incorrect because the work program should include the scope, degree, nature, and extent of testing required. Answer (C) is incorrect because the work program must include the engagement procedures necessary to achieve engagement objectives.

17. The engagement work program should be approved

A. No later than the conclusion of engagement work.

B. By the engagement client or designee.

C. Orally in some circumstances.

D. In writing by the board.

Answer (C) is correct. *(Publisher)*
   REQUIRED: The true statement about approval of an engagement work program.
   DISCUSSION: An engagement work program should be approved in writing by the CAE or designee prior to the commencement of engagement work. Adjustments should be approved in a timely manner. Initial approval may be obtained orally if circumstances preclude obtaining written approval prior to commencing engagement work (PA 2240.A1-1).

18. Which of the following is a step in an engagement work program?

A. The engagement will commence in 6 weeks and include tests of compliance with laws, regulations, and contracts.

B. A determination is made concerning whether the manufacturing operations are effective and efficient.

C. Internal auditors may not reveal engagement observations to non-supervisory, operational personnel during the course of this engagement.

D. The methods used to identify defective units produced are observed.

Answer (D) is correct. *(CIA, adapted)*
   REQUIRED: The step in an engagement work program.
   DISCUSSION: An engagement work program is a document that lists the procedures to be followed during an engagement. These procedures are designed to achieve the engagement objectives. Thus, observing the engagement client's execution of methods for identifying defects is an action performed to achieve the engagement objectives and should be included in the work program.
   Answer (A) is incorrect because a partial statement of the scope and the proposed starting time are not engagement procedures. Answer (B) is incorrect because determination of whether operations are effective and efficient is an engagement objective. Answer (C) is incorrect because a prohibition on revealing observations is a rule for the conduct of the internal auditors.

19. One of the primary roles of an engagement work program is to

A. Serve as a tool for planning and conducting engagement work.

B. Document an internal auditor's evaluations of controls.

C. Provide for a standardized approach to the engagement.

D. Assess the risks associated with the activity under review.

Answer (A) is correct. *(CIA, adapted)*
   REQUIRED: The item that states one of the primary roles of an engagement work program.
   DISCUSSION: Work programs document procedures for collecting, analyzing, interpreting, and documenting information; state engagement objectives; set forth the scope and degree of testing needed to achieve objectives in each phase of the engagement; identify technical aspects, risks, processes, and transactions to be examined; state the nature and extent of testing required, and are prepared before work begins, with appropriate modification during the engagement (PA 2200-1).
   Answer (B) is incorrect because engagement working papers include results of control evaluations. Answer (C) is incorrect because the work program should be logical, but it may not be consistent from year to year given the changing conditions to which the engagement client must adapt. The work program should be tailored to the current year's situation; thus, standardization may not be appropriate. Answer (D) is incorrect because the risk assessment in the planning phase helps to identify objectives, a step that must be taken before the work program can be developed.

20. Which of the following statements is an engagement objective?

    A. Observe the deposit of the day's cash receipts.

    B. Analyze the pattern of any cash shortages.

    C. Evaluate whether cash receipts are adequately safeguarded.

    D. Recompute each month's bank reconciliation.

Answer (C) is correct. *(CIA, adapted)*
    REQUIRED: The engagement objective.
    DISCUSSION: Engagement objectives are broad statements developed by internal auditors and define what the engagement is intended to accomplish (PA 2210-1). They should address the risks, controls, and governance processes associated with the activities under review (Standard 2210). Procedures are the means of achieving the objectives. Evaluating whether cash receipts are adequately safeguarded is an objective because it states what the engagement is to accomplish.
    Answer (A) is incorrect because observation is a procedure.
Answer (B) is incorrect because analysis is a procedure.
Answer (D) is incorrect because recomputation is a procedure.

21. The internal audit activity is planning a 3-year effort to perform engagements at all branches of a large international car rental agency. Management is especially concerned with standardized operation of the accounting, car rental, and inventory functions. What type of work program is most appropriate for this project?

    A. A pro forma program developed and tested by the internal audit activity.

    B. Individual programs developed by the internal auditor-in-charge after a preliminary survey of each branch.

    C. A checklist of branch standard operating procedures.

    D. An industry-developed engagement guide.

Answer (A) is correct. *(CIA, adapted)*
    REQUIRED: The type of work program most appropriate for standardized operations at many locations.
    DISCUSSION: A pro forma work program is designed to be used for repeated engagements related to similar operations. It is ordinarily modified over a period of years in response to problems encountered in the field. The "canned" program assures at least minimum coverage, provides comparability, and saves resources when operations at different locations have similar activities, risks, and controls.
    Answer (B) is incorrect because use of tailored work programs would conflict with management's desire for standardization. Answer (C) is incorrect because a checklist of branch standard operating procedures is only one input into the development of a work program. Answer (D) is incorrect because an industry guide might not be tailored to the specific needs of the organization.

22. A standard engagement work program is not appropriate for which situation?

    A. A stable operating environment undergoing only minimal changes.

    B. A complex or changing operating environment.

    C. Multiple locations with similar operations.

    D. Subsequent engagements to provide assurance about inventory performed at same location.

Answer (B) is correct. *(CIA, adapted)*
    REQUIRED: The situation in which a standard work program is not appropriate.
    DISCUSSION: A standard work program is not appropriate for a complex or changing operating environment. The engagement objectives and related procedures may no longer be relevant.
    Answer (A) is incorrect because a standard work program is appropriate for use in a minimally changing operating environment. It may save effort and provide continuity.
Answer (C) is incorrect because a standard work program can be used for engagements at multiple locations with similar operations if the same activities, risks, and controls are present.
Answer (D) is incorrect because a standard work program is acceptable for conducting subsequent inventory engagements at the same location if the inventory functions performed have not varied substantially.

23. Engagement work programs testing controls should

A. Be tailored for each operation evaluated.

B. Be generalized to fit all situations without regard to departmental lines.

C. Be generalized so as to be usable at all locations of a particular department.

D. Reduce costly duplication of effort by ensuring that every aspect of an operation is examined.

Answer (A) is correct. *(CIA, adapted)*
REQUIRED: The true statement about work programs.
DISCUSSION: Work programs document procedures for collecting, analyzing, interpreting, and documenting information; state engagement objectives; set forth the scope and degree of testing needed to achieve objectives in each phase of the engagement; identify technical aspects, risks, processes, and transactions to be examined; state the nature and extent of testing required, and are prepared before work begins, with appropriate modification during the engagement (PA 2200-1). However, a work program must be adapted to the specific needs of the engagement after the internal auditor establishes the engagement objectives and scope and determines the resources required.
Answer (B) is incorrect because a generalized program allows for variations resulting from changing circumstances and varied conditions. Answer (C) is incorrect because a generalized program cannot consider variations in circumstances and conditions. Answer (D) is incorrect because every aspect of an operation need not be examined, only those aspects likely to conceal problems and difficulties.

24. What action should an internal auditor take upon discovering that an area was omitted from the engagement work program?

A. Document the problem in the engagement working papers and take no further action until instructed to do so.

B. Perform the additional work needed without regard to the added time required to complete the engagement.

C. Continue the engagement as planned and include the unforeseen problem in a subsequent engagement.

D. Evaluate whether completion of the engagement as planned will be adequate.

Answer (D) is correct. *(CIA, adapted)*
REQUIRED: The action to take upon discovering that an area was omitted from the engagement work program.
DISCUSSION: Work programs are necessarily tentative because the internal auditors are likely to encounter unexpected situations while carrying out the detailed work. If they learn that an area is not covered, they must determine whether they can achieve the engagement objectives and satisfy their professional responsibilities without modification of the work program. Modification will necessitate consultation with supervisors to obtain authorization to adjust time and financial budgets.
Answer (A) is incorrect because the internal auditor must determine whether changes in the work program are needed. Answer (B) is incorrect because changes in the engagement budgets should be authorized by appropriate persons. Answer (C) is incorrect because an engagement in the unforeseen area may be necessary to achieve current engagement objectives.

7.2 The Preliminary Survey

25. In planning an assurance engagement, a survey could assist with all of the following, except

A. Obtaining engagement client comments and suggestions on control problems.

B. Obtaining preliminary information on controls.

C. Identifying areas for engagement emphasis.

D. Evaluating the adequacy and effectiveness of controls.

Answer (D) is correct. *(CIA, adapted)*
REQUIRED: The planning item with which a survey would not assist.
DISCUSSION: A survey is a process for gathering information, without detailed verification, on the activity being examined. A survey may involve discussions with the client, documenting key control activities, and identifying significant engagement issues (PA 2210.A1-1). A survey does not help in evaluating the adequacy and effectiveness of controls except to the extent the internal auditor gains familiarity with the controls. Evaluation requires testing.

26. An assurance engagement in the quality control department is being planned. Which of the following is least likely to be used in the preparation of a preliminary survey questionnaire?

A. An analysis of quality control documents.

B. The permanent engagement file.

C. The prior engagement communications.

D. Management's charter for the quality control department.

Answer (A) is correct. *(CIA, adapted)*
REQUIRED: The document least likely to be included in preparing a preliminary survey questionnaire.
DISCUSSION: A survey is a process for gathering information, without detailed verification, on the activity being examined (PA 2210.A1-1). An analysis of quality control documents is a part of field work, which follows the preliminary survey.
Answer (B) is incorrect because the permanent engagement file probably contains information, such as problems detected in prior years that will help in the development of appropriate questions to ask this year. Answer (C) is incorrect because the prior engagement communications will likely assist in developing the current year's questionnaire. Answer (D) is incorrect because knowing what the department is supposed to do will help the internal auditor develop knowledgeable questions.

27. The internal-auditor-in-charge has just been informed of the next engagement and the assigned engagement team. What is the appropriate phase for finalizing the time budget?

A. During formulation of the internal audit activity's engagement work schedule.

B. After the preliminary survey.

C. During the initial planning meeting.

D. After the completion of all field work.

Answer (B) is correct. *(CIA, adapted)*
REQUIRED: The appropriate phase for finalizing the engagement time budget.
DISCUSSION: A survey is a process for gathering information, without detailed verification, on the activity being examined. Among other things, the summary of results prepared at the end of the survey identifies preliminary estimates of time and resource requirements and revised dates for reporting phases and completing the engagement (PA 2210.A1-1). Thus, if the survey discloses significant differences from the project that was placed in the long-range plan, budget adjustments should be requested and authorized.
Answer (A) is incorrect because an initial budget is determined during formulation of the engagement work schedule (the long-range plan of the IAA), but revisions based on the survey may be required. Answer (C) is incorrect because the project is not sufficiently well defined during the initial planning meeting to complete the time budget. Answer (D) is incorrect because, after the completion of all field work, the bulk of staff hours have been expended, and the usefulness of the time budget as a control and evaluation tool would be negated.

28. An internal auditor has just completed a survey to become familiar with the organization's payroll operations. Which of the following should be performed next?

A. Assign internal audit personnel.

B. Establish initial engagement objectives.

C. Write the engagement work program.

D. Conduct field work.

Answer (C) is correct. *(CIA, adapted)*
REQUIRED: The step following the survey.
DISCUSSION: The work program is normally prepared after the survey. The survey allows the internal auditor to become familiar with the engagement client and therefore provides input to the work program.
Answer (A) is incorrect because internal audit personnel are usually assigned before the survey. Answer (B) is incorrect because initial engagement objectives are established at the beginning of the planning process. They should be specified before the survey. Answer (D) is incorrect because field work can be performed only after the work program has been written. Thus, field work cannot immediately follow the survey.

29. During which phase of the engagement does the internal auditor identify the objectives and related controls of the activity being examined?

A. Preliminary survey.

B. Staff selection.

C. Work program preparation.

D. Final communication of results.

Answer (A) is correct. *(CIA, adapted)*
REQUIRED: The stage of the engagement in which the internal auditor identifies objectives and related controls.
DISCUSSION: Planning should include performing, as appropriate, a survey to become familiar with activities, risks, and controls; to identify areas for engagement emphasis; and to invite client comments and suggestions (PA 2210.A1-1).
Answer (B) is incorrect because staff selection is the process of deciding which internal auditors will work on the engagement. Answer (C) is incorrect because the work program is prepared after the preliminary survey. Answer (D) is incorrect because final communication of results occurs after the completion of the engagement.

30. The preliminary survey indicates that severe staff reductions at the engagement location have resulted in extensive amounts of overtime among accounting staff. Department members are visibly stressed and very vocal about the effects of the cutbacks. Accounting payrolls are nearly equal to prior years, and many key controls, such as segregation of duties, are no longer in place. The accounting supervisor now performs all operations within the cash receipts and posting process and has no time to review and approve transactions generated by the remaining members of the department. Journal entries for the last 6 months since the staff reductions show increasing numbers of prior-month adjustments and corrections, including revenues, cost of sales, and accruals that had been misstated or forgotten during month-end closing activity. The internal auditor should

A. Discuss these observations with management of the internal audit activity to determine whether further work would be an efficient use of internal auditing resources at this time.

B. Proceed with the scheduled engagement but add personnel based on the expected number of observations and anticipated lack of assistance from local accounting management.

C. Research temporary help agencies and evaluate the cost and benefit of outsourcing needed services.

D. Suspend further engagement work because the observations are obvious and make the final communication of results.

Answer (A) is correct. *(CIA, adapted)*
REQUIRED: The internal auditor action given the absence of many key controls.
DISCUSSION: A preliminary survey allows the internal auditor to become familiar with activities, risks, and controls; to identify areas for engagement emphasis; and to invite engagement client comments and suggestions. Among many other matters, the summary of results prepared at the conclusion of the survey should identify, when applicable, reasons for not continuing the engagement (PA 2210.A1-1). In this case, additional planning is necessary to modify the engagement for the difficult circumstances discovered during the preliminary survey and to address the responsibilities of the IAA.

Answer (B) is incorrect because what additional work will be necessary is not clear in these circumstances. Answer (C) is incorrect because management has not accepted this plan of action. Answer (D) is incorrect because a final communication of results would violate the Standards, including those relating to objectivity, due professional care, and performance of the engagement.

31. Which of the following best describes a preliminary survey?

A. A standardized questionnaire used to obtain an understanding of management objectives.

B. A statistical sample of key employee attitudes, skills, and knowledge.

C. A "walk-through" of the financial control system to identify risks and the controls that can address those risks.

D. A process used to become familiar with activities and risks in order to identify areas for engagement emphasis.

Answer (D) is correct. *(CIA, adapted)*
REQUIRED: The best description of a preliminary survey.
DISCUSSION: Planning includes performing, as appropriate, a survey to become familiar with the activities, risks, and controls; to identify areas for engagement emphasis; and to invite engagement client comments and suggestions (PA 2210.A1-1). Detailed procedures performed during a preliminary survey include use of standard questionnaires, statistical sampling, and a walk-through.

32. The internal auditors of a financial institution are performing an engagement to evaluate the institution's investing and lending activities. During the last year, the institution has adopted new policies and procedures for monitoring investments and the loan portfolio. The internal auditors know that the organization has invested in new types of financial instruments during the year and is heavily involved in the use of financial derivatives to appropriately hedge risks. If the internal auditors were to conduct a preliminary review, which of the following procedures should be performed?

A. Review reports of engagements performed by regulatory and external auditors since the last internal auditing engagement.

B. Interview management to identify changes made in policies regarding investments or loans.

C. Review minutes of board meetings to identify changes in policies affecting investments and loans.

D. All of the answers are correct.

Answer (D) is correct. *(CIA, adapted)*
REQUIRED: The procedure performed in a preliminary review of investing and lending activities.
DISCUSSION: Engagement planning should be documented and should include, among other things, obtaining background information, for example, from prior working papers, results of other engagements, budgetary data, financial statements, organizational information (major system changes, etc.), correspondence, and technical literature. Planning also includes performing, as appropriate, a survey to become familiar with the activities, risks, and controls; to identify areas for engagement emphasis; and to invite engagement client comments and suggestions. A survey involves discussions with the client; interviews with individuals affected by the activity, e.g., users of the activity's output; on-site observations; review of management reports and studies; analytical auditing procedures; flowcharting; functional "walk-through" (tests of specific work activities from beginning to end); and documenting key control activities (PA 2210.A1-1).

33. An internal auditor conducts a preliminary survey and identifies a number of significant engagement issues and reasons for pursuing them in more depth. The engagement client informally communicates concurrence with the preliminary survey results and asks that the internal auditor not report on the areas of significant concern until she has an opportunity to respond to the problem areas. Which of the following engagement responses is not appropriate?

A. Keep the engagement on schedule and discuss with management the need for completing the engagement on a timely basis.

B. Consider the risk involved in the areas involved, and, if the risk is high, proceed with the engagement.

C. Consider the engagement to be terminated with no communication of results needed because the engagement client has already agreed to take constructive action.

D. Work with the engagement client to keep the engagement on schedule and address the significant issues in more depth, as well as the client's responses, during the course of the engagement.

Answer (C) is correct. *(CIA, adapted)*
REQUIRED: The inappropriate response to an engagement client's request not to communicate results.
DISCUSSION: The internal auditor has completed only a preliminary survey. The constructive action by the engagement client may be a delaying device to conceal more serious problems. The internal auditor has identified significant engagement issues. No basis is given for not pursuing the engagement. The internal auditor should always consider the risk associated with the potential observations as a basis for determining the need for more immediate attention.

7.3 Engagement Supervision

34. The purpose of including a time budget in an engagement work program is to

A. Provide an objective means of evaluating the internal auditor's competence.

B. Assure timely completion of the engagement.

C. Provide a means of controlling and evaluating the progress of the engagement.

D. Restrict the scope of the engagement.

Answer (C) is correct. *(CIA, adapted)*
REQUIRED: The purpose of a time budget in an engagement work program.
DISCUSSION: Internal auditors should develop and record work programs to achieve the engagement objectives (Standard 2240). The work program lists the procedures to be followed during the engagement. Accordingly, a work program is a useful tool for scheduling and controlling (supervising) the engagement. Supervision includes, among other things, determining that the approved work program is carried out unless changes are justified and authorized. Moreover, supervision extends to time and expense control (PA 2340-1). For this purpose, a time budget is necessary to evaluate and control the progress of the engagement. It permits comparison of the actual time spent on a procedure with its allotted time.
Answer (A) is incorrect because whether an internal auditor remains within the time budget is affected by many factors other than professional competence. Answer (B) is incorrect because the establishment of a budget cannot assure that work will be completed on a timely basis. Answer (D) is incorrect because a time budget is not intended to limit the scope of the engagement.

35. Which of the following statements is true with respect to a time budget for an internal audit engagement?

A. Requests for time budget adjustments should be approved by the audit committee.

B. Time budgets should be strictly adhered to, regardless of circumstances.

C. Time budgets should be used for financial audits, but not for operational audits.

D. Time budgets should normally be prepared in terms of hours or days.

Answer (D) is correct. *(CIA, adapted)*
REQUIRED: The true statement about a time budget for an internal audit engagement.
DISCUSSION: Supervision extends to time and expense control (PA 2340-1). A budget is a plan that contains a quantitative statement of expected results. It may be defined as a "quantified program." All engagement projects and other assignments should be kept under budgetary control. Time budgets for engagement projects are usually prepared in employee-hours or employee-days.
Answer (A) is incorrect because requests for time budget adjustments should be approved by the CAE, not the audit committee. Answer (B) is incorrect because budgets should be subject to adjustment for unexpected conditions. Answer (C) is incorrect because time budgets are equally applicable to all types of engagements.

36. The best control over the work on which internal auditors' opinions are based is

A. Supervisory review of all engagement work.

B. Preparation of time budgets for internal auditing activities.

C. Preparation of engagement working papers.

D. Staffing of internal audit activities.

Answer (A) is correct. *(CIA, adapted)*
REQUIRED: The best control over the work on which internal auditors' opinions are based.
DISCUSSION: The engagement should be properly supervised to ensure objectives are achieved, quality is assured, and staff is developed (Standard 2340). Supervision includes ensuring that the auditors assigned possess the requisite knowledge, skills, and other competencies to perform the engagement; providing appropriate instructions during the planning of the engagement and approving the engagement work program; seeing that the approved engagement work program is carried out unless changes are both justified and authorized; determining that engagement working papers adequately support the engagement observations, conclusions, and recommendations; ensuring that engagement communications are accurate, objective, clear, concise, constructive, and timely; ensuring that engagement objectives are met; and providing opportunities for developing internal auditors' knowledge, skills, and other competencies. Hence, supervision is a control that encompasses all aspects of engagements (PA 2340-1).
Answer (B) is incorrect because, although useful, time budgets do not assure the adequacy of work supporting opinions. Answer (C) is incorrect because engagement working papers support the conclusions and engagement results, but supervision is necessary to ensure the adequacy of work. Answer (D) is incorrect because proper staffing is required, but supervision is essential to ensure an adequate basis for opinions.

37. Which of the following activities does not constitute engagement supervision?

A. Preparing a preliminary engagement work program.

B. Providing appropriate instructions to the internal auditors.

C. Reviewing engagement working papers.

D. Ensuring that engagement communications meet appropriate criteria.

Answer (A) is correct. *(CIA, adapted)*
REQUIRED: The activity not constituting supervision.
DISCUSSION: The engagement should be properly supervised to ensure objectives are achieved, quality is assured, and staff is developed (Standard 2340). Supervision includes, among other things, providing appropriate instructions during the planning of the engagement and approving the engagement work program; determining that engagement working papers adequately support the engagement observations, conclusions, and recommendations; and ensuring that engagement communications are accurate, objective, clear, concise, constructive, and timely (PA 2340-1). Preparing a preliminary engagement work program is part of engagement planning but not an aspect of engagement supervision.

38. Which of the following best describes what should determine the extent of supervision required for a particular internal auditing engagement?

A. Whether the engagement involves possible fraud on the part of management.

B. Whether the engagement involves possible violations of laws or governmental regulations.

C. The proficiency of the internal auditors and the complexity of the engagement.

D. The internal audit activity's prior experience in dealing with the particular engagement client.

Answer (C) is correct. *(CIA, adapted)*
REQUIRED: The best description of what should determine the extent of supervision of an engagement.
DISCUSSION: The CAE is responsible for providing appropriate engagement supervision. The extent of supervision required will depend on the proficiency and experience of the internal auditors and the complexity of the engagement (PA 2340-1). The engagement's involvement in possible management fraud or possible violations of laws or governmental regulations and the IAA's prior experience with the engagement client are not the primary determinants of the extent of supervision required.

39. Which of the following best describes engagement supervision?

A. The manager of each engagement has the ultimate responsibility for supervision.

B. Supervision is primarily exercised at the final review stage of an engagement to ensure the accuracy of the engagement communications.

C. Supervision is most important in the planning phase of the engagement to ensure appropriate coverage.

D. Supervision is a continuing process beginning with planning and ending with the conclusion of the engagement.

Answer (D) is correct. *(CIA, adapted)*
REQUIRED: The best description of engagement supervision.
DISCUSSION: The CAE is responsible for ensuring that appropriate engagement supervision is provided. Supervision is a process that begins with planning and continues through the examination, evaluation, communication, and follow-up phases of the engagement (PA 2340-1).
Answer (A) is incorrect because the CAE has the ultimate responsibility for supervision. Answer (B) is incorrect because supervision should begin at the planning phase and continue throughout the engagement. Answer (C) is incorrect because supervision is equally important in all phases of the engagement.

40. When engagements are performed for the internal audit activity by nonstaff members, the chief audit executive is responsible for

A. Ensuring that the engagement communications are accurate, objective, clear, concise, constructive, and timely.

B. Reviewing the engagement work programs for approval.

C. Providing appropriate supervision from the beginning to the conclusion of the engagement.

D. None of the work performed by those outside the internal audit activity.

Answer (C) is correct. *(CIA, adapted)*
REQUIRED: The CAE's responsibility for work performed by nonstaff members.
DISCUSSION: All internal auditing engagements, whether performed by or for the IAA, remain the responsibility of the CAE. The CAE is responsible for all significant professional judgments made in the planning, examination, evaluation, communication, and follow-up phases of the engagement (PA 2340-1).
Answer (A) is incorrect because ensuring that the engagement communications are accurate, objective, clear, concise, constructive, and timely is only one of the responsibilities of supervision. Answer (B) is incorrect because supervision is a continuing process beginning with planning and ending with the follow-up phase of the engagement. Answer (D) is incorrect because the CAE is responsible for all work performed by and for the IAA.

41. Supervision of an internal audit engagement should include

   A. Determining that engagement working papers adequately support the engagement observations.

   B. Assigning staff members to the particular engagement.

   C. Determining the scope of the engagement.

   D. Appraising each internal auditor's performance on at least an annual basis.

Answer (A) is correct. *(CIA, adapted)*
REQUIRED: The extent of supervision of an engagement.
DISCUSSION: Supervision includes ensuring that the auditors assigned possess the requisite knowledge, skills, and other competencies to perform the engagement; providing appropriate instructions during the planning of the engagement and approving the engagement work program; seeing that the approved engagement work program is carried out unless changes are both justified and authorized; determining that engagement working papers adequately support the engagement observations, conclusions, and recommendations; ensuring that engagement communications are accurate, objective, clear, concise, constructive, and timely; ensuring that engagement objectives are met; and providing opportunities for developing internal auditors' knowledge, skills, and other competencies (PA 2340-1).
Answer (B) is incorrect because engagement resource allocation is a planning function, not a supervisory function (PA 2230-1). Answer (C) is incorrect because determining the engagement scope is a planning function, not a supervisory function. Answer (D) is incorrect because appraising performance on an annual basis is not a supervisory function of a specific engagement but is part of the management of the human resources of the internal audit activity (PA 2030-1).

42. The chief audit executive is responsible for engagement supervision. The most important form of supervision during the field work phase of engagements involves

   A. Seeing that the approved engagement work program is carried out unless changes are both justified and authorized.

   B. Providing suitable instructions to subordinates at the outset of the engagement and approving the engagement work program.

   C. Appraising each internal auditor's performance at least annually.

   D. Making sure that communications are accurate, objective, clear, concise, constructive, and timely.

Answer (A) is correct. *(CIA, adapted)*
REQUIRED: The most important form of supervision during the field work phase.
DISCUSSION: Supervision includes ensuring that the auditors assigned possess the requisite knowledge, skills, and other competencies to perform the engagement; providing appropriate instructions during the planning of the engagement and approving the engagement work program; seeing that the approved engagement work program is carried out unless changes are both justified and authorized; determining that engagement working papers adequately support the engagement observations, conclusions, and recommendations; ensuring that engagement communications are accurate, objective, clear, concise, constructive, and timely; ensuring that engagement objectives are met; and providing opportunities for developing internal auditors' knowledge, skills, and other competencies (PA 2340-1). Execution of the engagement work program requires supervision during field work. The other supervisory tasks are carried out before or after field work.
Answer (B) is incorrect because "at the outset of the engagement" is not during field work. Answer (C) is incorrect because annual performance appraisal is not specific to a particular engagement. Answer (D) is incorrect because engagement communications are prepared at the conclusion of field work.

43. Determining that engagement objectives have been met is part of the overall supervision of an engagement and is the ultimate responsibility of the

   A. Staff internal auditor.

   B. Audit committee.

   C. Engagement supervisor.

   D. Chief audit executive.

Answer (D) is correct. *(CIA, adapted)*
REQUIRED: The person(s) with ultimate responsibility for determining that engagement objectives have been met.
DISCUSSION: The chief audit executive is responsible for assuring that appropriate engagement supervision is provided. Supervision is a process that begins with planning and continues through the examination, evaluation, communication, and follow-up phases of the engagement (PA 2340-1).

Use Gleim's *CIA Test Prep* for interactive testing with over 2,000 additional multiple-choice questions!

STUDY UNIT EIGHT
MANAGING THE INTERNAL AUDIT ACTIVITY I

(20 pages of outline)

This is the first study unit concerning management of the internal audit activity. According to **General Performance Standard 2000 – Managing the Internal Audit Activity**,

> *The chief audit executive should effectively manage the internal audit activity to ensure it adds value to the organization.*

Practice Advisory 2000-1: Managing the Internal Audit Activity elaborates on this responsibility as follows:

1. *The chief audit executive is responsible for properly managing the internal audit activity so that:*

   - *Engagement work fulfills the general purposes and responsibilities described in the charter, approved by senior management, and accepted by the board.*
   - *Resources of the internal audit activity are efficiently and effectively employed.*
   - *Engagement work conforms to the Standards for the Professional Practice of Internal Auditing.*

The chief audit executive should establish risk-based plans, communicate plans and resource needs to senior management and the board for their approval, develop polices and procedures, coordinate efforts with other service providers, and report periodically to senior management and the board. The CAE must also develop a quality assurance and improvement program for the IAA.

8.1 PLANNING, RISK, AND COMMUNICATIONS

1. This subunit concerns the need for risk-based planning for the IAA, communicating those plans to senior management and the board, and reporting periodically relative to the accomplishment of those plans. These concerns are addressed in three Specific Performance Standards, one Assurance Implementation Standard, one Consulting Implementation Standard, and five Practice Advisories.

   2010   ***Planning*** – *The chief audit executive should establish risk-based plans to determine the priorities of the internal audit activity, consistent with the organization's goals.*

   ### *Practice Advisory 2010-1: Planning*

   1. *Planning for the internal audit activity should be consistent with its charter and with the goals of the organization. The planning process involves establishing:*

      - *Goals.*
      - *Engagement work schedules.*
      - *Staffing plans and financial budgets.*
      - *Activity reports.*

2. The goals of the internal audit activity should be capable of being accomplished within specified operating plans and budgets and, to the extent possible, should be measurable. They should be accompanied by measurement criteria and targeted dates of accomplishment.

3. Engagement work schedules should include the following:

    - What activities are to be performed;
    - When they will be performed; and
    - The estimated time required, taking into account the scope of the engagement work planned and the nature and extent of related work performed by others.

4. Matters to be considered in establishing engagement work schedule priorities should include:

    - The dates and results of the last engagement;
    - Updated assessments of risks and effectiveness of risk management and control processes;
    - Requests by senior management, the audit committee, and the governing body;

    NOTE: Governmental regulatory requirements (for example, an audit of the use of financial assistance provided from public funds) may also be a source of engagements.

    - Current issues relating to organizational governance;
    - Major changes in the enterprise's business, operations, programs, systems, and controls;
    - Opportunities to achieve operating benefits; and
    - Changes to and capabilities of the audit staff. The work schedules should be sufficiently flexible to cover unanticipated demands on the internal audit activity.

Practice Advisory 2010-2: Linking the Audit Plan to Risk and Exposures

1. The internal audit activity's plan should be designed based on an assessment of risk and exposures that may affect the organization. Ultimately, the objective is to provide management with information to mitigate the negative consequences associated with accomplishing the organization's objectives. The degree or materiality of exposure can be viewed as risk mitigated by establishing control activities.

2. The audit universe can include components from the organization's strategic plan. By incorporating components of the organization's strategic plan, the audit universe will consider and reflect the overall business plan objectives. Strategic plans are also likely to reflect the organization's attitude toward risk and the degree of difficulty in achieving planned objectives. It is advisable to assess the audit universe on at least an annual basis to reflect the most current strategies and direction of the organization. The audit universe can be influenced by the results of the risk management process. When developing plans, the outcomes of the risk management process should be considered.

3. Work schedules should be based on, among other factors, an assessment of risk priority and exposure. Prioritizing is needed to make decisions for applying relative resources based on the significance of risk and exposure. A variety of risk models exist to assist the chief audit executive in prioritizing potential engagement subject areas. Most risk models use risk factors to establish the priority of engagements, such as dollar materiality, asset liquidity, management competence, quality of internal controls, degree of change or stability, time of last engagement, complexity, and employee and government relations.

4. Changes in management direction, objectives, emphasis, and focus should be reflected in updates to the audit universe and related plan.

5.   In conducting engagements, methods and techniques for testing and validating exposures should be reflective of the risk materiality and likelihood of occurrence.

6.   Management reporting and communication should convey risk management conclusions and recommendations to reduce exposures. For management to fully understand the degree of exposure, it is critical that reporting identify the criticality and consequence of the risk activity to achieving objectives.

7.   The chief audit executive should, at least annually, prepare a statement of the adequacy of internal controls to mitigate risks. This statement should also comment on the significance of unmitigated risk and management's acceptance of such risk.

2010.A1 – The internal audit activity's plan of engagements should be based on a risk assessment, undertaken at least annually. The input of senior management and the board should be considered in this process.

2010.C1 – The chief audit executive should consider accepting proposed consulting engagements based on the engagement's potential to improve management of risks, add value, and improve the organization's operations. Those engagements that have been accepted should be included in the plan.

2020   **Communication and Approval** – The chief audit executive should communicate the internal audit activity's plans and resource requirements, including significant interim changes, to senior management and to the board for review and approval. The chief audit executive should also communicate the impact of resource limitations.

Practice Advisory 2020-1: Communication and Approval

1.   The chief audit executive should submit annually to senior management for approval, and to the board for its information, a summary of the internal audit activity's work schedule, staffing plan, and financial budget. The chief audit executive should also submit all significant interim changes for approval and information. Engagement work schedules, staffing plans, and financial budgets should inform senior management and the board of the scope of internal auditing work and of any limitations placed on that scope.

2.   The approved engagement work schedule, staffing plan, and financial budget, along with all significant interim changes, should contain sufficient information to enable the board to ascertain whether the internal audit activity's objectives and plans support those of the organization and the board.

2060   **Reporting to the Board and Senior Management** – The chief audit executive should report periodically to the board and senior management on the internal audit activity's purpose, authority, responsibility, and performance relative to its plan. Reporting should also include significant risk exposures and control issues, corporate governance issues, and other matters needed or requested by the board and senior management.

Practice Advisory 2060-1: Reporting to the Board and Senior Management

1.   The chief audit executive should submit activity reports to senior management and to the board at least annually. Activity reports should highlight significant engagement observations and recommendations and should inform senior management and the board of any significant deviations from approved engagement work schedules, staffing plans, and financial budgets, and the reasons for them.

2.   Significant engagement observations are those conditions that, in the judgment of the chief audit executive, could adversely affect the organization. Significant engagement observations may include conditions dealing with irregularities, illegal acts, errors, inefficiency, waste, ineffectiveness, conflicts of interest, and control weaknesses. After reviewing such conditions with senior management, the chief audit executive should communicate significant engagement observations and recommendations to the board, whether or not they have been satisfactorily resolved.

3.   Management's responsibility is to make decisions on the appropriate action to be taken regarding significant engagement observations and recommendations. Senior management may decide to assume the risk of not correcting the reported condition because of cost or other considerations. The board should be informed of senior management's decisions on all significant observations and recommendations.

4.   The chief audit executive should consider whether it is appropriate to inform the board regarding previously reported, significant observations and recommendations in those instances when senior management and the board assumed the risk of not correcting the reported condition. This may be particularly necessary when there have been organization, board, senior management, or other changes.

5.   In addition to subjects covered above, activity reports should also compare (a) actual performance with the internal audit activity's goals and engagement work schedules, and (b) expenditures with financial budgets. Reports should explain the reason for major variances and indicate any action taken or needed.

Practice Advisory 2060-2: Relationship with the Audit Committee

1.   The term "audit committee," as used in this document, refers to the governance body that is charged with oversight of the organization's audit and control functions. Although these fiduciary duties are often delegated to an audit committee of the board of directors, the information in this Practice Advisory is also intended to apply to other oversight groups with equivalent authority and responsibility, such as trustees, legislative bodies, owners of an owner-managed entity, internal control committees, or full boards of directors.

2.   The Institute of Internal Auditors recognizes that audit committees and internal auditors have interlocking goals. A strong working relationship with the audit committee is essential for each to fulfill its responsibilities to senior management, board of directors, shareholders, and other outside parties. This Practice Advisory summarizes The Institute's views concerning the aspects and attributes of an appropriate relationship between an audit committee and the internal audit function. The Institute acknowledges that audit committee responsibilities encompass activities that are beyond the scope of this advisory and in no way intends it to be a comprehensive description of audit committee responsibilities.

3.   There are three areas of activities that are key to an effective relationship between the audit committee and the internal audit function, chiefly through the Chief Audit Executive (CAE):

    - Assisting the audit committee to ensure that its charter, activities, and processes are appropriate to fulfill its responsibilities.

    - Ensuring that the charter, role, and activities of internal audit are clearly understood and responsive to the needs of the audit committee and the board.

    - Maintaining open and effective communications with the audit committee and the chairperson.

Audit Committee Responsibilities

4.   The CAE should assist the committee in ensuring that the charter, role and activities of the committee are appropriate for it to achieve its responsibilities. The CAE can play an important role by assisting the committee to periodically review its activities and suggesting enhancements. In this way, the CAE serves as a valued advisor to the committee on audit committee and regulatory practices. Examples of activities that the CAE can undertake are:

    - Review the charter for the audit committee at least annually and advise the committee whether the charter addresses all responsibilities directed to the committee in any terms of reference or mandates from the board of directors.

- *Review or maintain a planning agenda for the audit committee's meeting that details all required activities to ascertain whether they are completed and that assists the committee in reporting to the board annually that it has completed all assigned duties.*

- *Draft the audit committee's meeting agenda for the chairman's review and facilitate the distribution of the material to the audit committee members and write up the minutes of the audit committee meetings.*

- *Encourage the audit committee to conduct periodic reviews of its activities and practices compared with current best practices to ensure that its activities are consistent with leading practices.*

- *Meet periodically with the chairperson to discuss whether the materials and information being furnished to the committee are meeting their needs.*

- *Inquire from the audit committee if any educational or informational sessions or presentations would be helpful, such as training new committee members on risk and controls.*

- *Inquire from the committee whether the frequency and time allotted to the committee are sufficient.*

Internal Audit Activity's Role

5. *The CAE's relationship to the audit committee should revolve around a core role of the CAE ensuring that the audit committee understands, supports, and receives all assistance needed from the internal audit function. The IIA supports the concept that sound governance is dependent on the synergy generated among the four principal components of effective corporate governance systems: boards of directors, management, internal auditors, and external auditors. In that structure, internal auditors and audit committees are mutually supportive. Consideration of the work of internal auditors is essential for the audit committee to gain a complete understanding of an organization's operations. A primary component of the CAE's role with the committee is to ensure this objective is accomplished and the committee views the CAE as their trusted advisor. The chief audit executive can perform a number of activities to accomplish this role:*

   - *Request that the committee review and approve the internal audit charter on an annual basis.*

   - *Review with the audit committee the functional and administrative reporting lines of internal audit to ensure that the organizational structure in place allows adequate independence for internal auditors (Practice Advisory 1110-2: Chief Audit Executive (CAE) Reporting Lines).*

   - *Incorporate in the charter for the audit committee the review of hiring decisions, including appointment, compensation, evaluation, retention, and dismissal of the CAE.*

   - *Incorporate in the charter for the audit committee to review and approve proposals to outsource any internal audit activities.*

   - *Assist the audit committee in evaluating the adequacy of the personnel and budget, and the scope and results of the internal audit activities, to ensure that there are no budgetary or scope limitations that impede the ability of the internal audit function to execute its responsibilities.*

   - *Provide information on the coordination with and oversight of other control and monitoring functions (e.g., risk management, compliance, security, business continuity, legal, ethics, environmental, external audit).*

   - *Report significant issues related to the processes for controlling the activities of the organization and its affiliates, including potential improvements to those processes, and provide information concerning such issues through resolution.*

- *Provide information on the status and results of the annual audit plan and the sufficiency of department resources to senior management and the audit committee.*

- *Develop a flexible annual audit plan using an appropriate risk-based methodology, including any risks or control concerns identified by management, and submit that plan to the audit committee for review and approval as well as periodic updates.*

- *Report on the implementation of the annual audit plan, as approved, including as appropriate any special tasks or projects requested by management and the audit committee.*

- *Incorporate into the internal audit charter the responsibility for the internal audit department to report to the audit committee on a timely basis any suspected fraud involving management or employees who are significantly involved in the internal controls of the company. Assist in the investigation of significant suspected fraudulent activities within the organization and notify management and the audit committee of the results.*

- *Audit committees should be made aware that quality assessment reviews of the internal audit activity be done every five years in order for the audit activity to declare that it meets The IIA's **Standards for the Professional Practice of Internal Auditing (Standards)**. Regular quality assessment reviews will provide assurance to the audit committee and to management that internal auditing activities conform to **Standards**.*

Communications with the Audit Committee

6. *While not to diminish any of the activities noted above, in a large part the overall effectiveness of the CAE and audit committee relationship will revolve around the communications between the parties. Today's audit committees expect a high level of open and candid communications. If the CAE is to be viewed as a trusted advisor by the committee, communications is the key element. Internal auditing, by definition, can help the audit committee accomplish its objectives by bringing a systematic, disciplined approach to its activities, but unless there is appropriate communications, it is not possible for the committee to determine this. The chief audit executive should consider providing communications to the audit committee in the following areas.*

    - *Audit committees should meet privately with the CAE on a regular basis to discuss sensitive issues.*

    - *Provide an annual summary report or assessment on the results of the audit activities relating to the defined mission and scope of audit work.*

    - *Issue periodic reports to the audit committee and management summarizing results of audit activities.*

    - *Keep the audit committee informed of emerging trends and successful practices in internal auditing.*

    - *Together with external auditors, discuss fulfillment of committee information needs.*

    - *Review information submitted to the audit committee for completeness and accuracy.*

    - *Confirm there is effective and efficient work coordination of activities between internal and external auditors. Determine if there is any duplication between the work of the internal and external auditors and give the reasons for such duplication.*

2. **Audit Committees**. The audit committee is a subcommittee made up of **outside directors** who are independent of management. Its purpose is to help keep external and internal auditors independent of management and to assure that the directors are exercising due care.

   a. The role of an audit committee or an equivalent body in strengthening the position of both internal and external auditing is now widely recognized. The following are some of its **characteristics and responsibilities**:

      1) The appropriate governing authority should develop and approve a **written charter** describing the audit committee's duties and responsibilities.

      2) The audit committee should review the **independence** of the external auditor.

      3) Reports to shareholders or other stakeholders should include a letter from the chair of the audit committee describing its responsibilities and activities.

      4) The audit committee should monitor compliance with codes of conduct and legal and regulatory standards.

      5) The audit committee should have necessary resources available.

      6) The audit committee should oversee the **regulatory reporting process**.

      7) The audit committee should monitor instances in which management seeks second opinions on significant accounting issues.

   b. Many **stock exchanges** require a listed organization to have an audit committee.

   c. An audit committee composed of nonmanagement directors promotes the **independence** of internal as well as external auditors, especially when it selects the external audit firm and the chief audit executive. Thus, a strong audit committee insulates the auditors from influences that may compromise their independence and objectivity.

      1) An audit committee may also serve as a mediator of disputes between the auditors and management.

   d. **Audit Committee Functions**

      1) Select an external auditor and review the audit fee and the engagement letter

      2) Review the external auditor's overall audit plan

      3) Review preliminary annual and interim financial statements

      4) Review results of engagements performed by external auditors, including the management letter (advice and observation not required to be communicated by auditing standards)

      5) Approve the charter of the internal audit activity (Standard 1000)

      6) Review and approve the internal audit activity's plans and resource requirements and receive a summary of the IAA's work schedule, staffing plan, and financial budget (Standard 2020 and PA 2020-1)

      7) Directly communicate with the chief audit executive who regularly attends and participates in meetings (PA 1110-1)

      8) Review evaluations of risk management, control, and governance processes reported by the internal auditors

      9) As an entity able to ensure that engagement results are given due consideration, receive distributions of final engagement communications by the internal auditors (PA 2440-1)

      10) Review policies on unethical and illegal procedures

      11) Review financial statements to be transmitted to regulatory agencies

      12) Participate in the selection of accounting policies

      13) Review the impact of new or proposed legislation or governmental regulations

14) Review the organization's insurance program
15) Consider the effectiveness and efficiency of the organization's information systems
16) Evaluate executive performance and compensation

e. **External auditors** have recognized the importance of **reporting to audit committees**. Among the matters that may be communicated are internal-control-related matters, significant accounting policies, management judgments and accounting estimates, significant audit adjustments, disagreements with management, and difficulties encountered during the audit.

1) One of the factors encompassed by the **control environment** component of internal control is participation by the board, audit committee, or other governing authority. The control consciousness of the entity is improved if the audit committee is independent, composed of experienced and respected people, extensively involved in scrutinizing entity activities, willing to raise and pursue difficult questions with management, and in close communication with the internal and external auditors.

2) **Fraud** involving senior management or fraud that materially misstates the financial statements should be reported directly to the audit committee.

   a) The auditors also should be assured that the audit committee is adequately informed about other **illegal acts** coming to their attention.

f. The following is The IIA's sample charter for the audit committee (Sawyer's Internal Auditing, 5th ed., pages 1328-1332):

Audit Committee Charter

PURPOSE

To assist the board of directors in fulfilling its oversight responsibilities for the financial reporting process, the system of internal control, the audit process, and the company's process for monitoring compliance with laws and regulations and the code of conduct.

AUTHORITY

The audit committee has authority to conduct or authorize investigations into any matters within its scope of responsibility. It is empowered to:

Appoint, compensate, and oversee the work of any registered public accounting firm employed by the organization.

Resolve any disagreements between management and the auditor regarding financial reporting.

Pre-approve all auditing and non-audit services.

Retain independent counsel, accountants, or others to advise the committee or assist in the conduct of an investigation.

Seek any information it requires from employees – all of whom are directed to cooperate with the committee's requests – or external parties.

Meet with company officers, external auditors, or outside counsel, as necessary.

COMPOSITION

The audit committee will consist of at least three and no more than six members of the board of directors. The board or its nominating committee will appoint committee members and the committee chair.

Each committee member will be both independent and financially literate. At least one member shall be designated as the "financial expert," as defined by applicable legislation and regulation.

MEETINGS

The committee will meet at least four times a year, with authority to convene additional meetings, as circumstances require. All committee members are expected to attend each meeting, in person or via tele- or video-conference. The committee will invite members of management, auditors, or others to attend meetings and provide pertinent information, as necessary. It will hold private meetings with auditors (see below) and executive sessions. Meeting agendas will be prepared and provided in advance to members, along with appropriate briefing materials. Minutes will be prepared.

RESPONSIBILITIES

The committee will carry out the following responsibilities:

Financial Statements

- *Review significant accounting and reporting issues, including complex or unusual transactions and highly judgmental areas, and recent professional and regulatory pronouncements, and understand their impact on the financial statements.*
- *Review with management and the external auditors the results of the audit, including any difficulties encountered.*
- *Review the annual financial statements, and consider whether they are complete, consistent with information known to committee members, and reflect appropriate accounting principles.*
- *Review other sections of the annual report and related regulatory filings before release and consider the accuracy and completeness of the information.*
- *Review with management and the external auditors all matters required to be communicated to the committee under generally accepted auditing standards.*
- *Understand how management develops interim financial information, and the nature and extent of internal and external auditor involvement.*
- *Review interim financial reports with management and the external auditors before filing with regulators, and consider whether they are complete and consistent with the information known to committee members.*

Internal Control

- *Consider the effectiveness of the company's internal control system, including information technology security and control.*
- *Understand the scope of internal and external auditors' review of internal control over financial reporting, and obtain reports on significant findings and recommendations, together with management's responses.*

Internal Audit

- *Review with management and the chief audit executive the charter, plans, activities, staffing, and organizational structure of the internal audit function.*
- *Ensure there are no unjustified restrictions or limitations, and review and concur in the appointment, replacement, or dismissal of the chief audit executive.*
- *Review the effectiveness of the internal audit function, including compliance with The Institute of Internal Auditors' Standards.*
- *On a regular basis, meet separately with the chief audit executive to discuss any matters that the committee or internal audit believes should be discussed privately.*

External Audit

- *Review the external auditors' proposed audit scope and approach, including coordination of audit effort with internal audit.*
- *Review the performance of the external auditors, and exercise final approval on the appointment or discharge of the auditors.*
- *Review and confirm the independence of the external auditors by obtaining statements from the auditors on relationships between the auditors and the company, including non-audit services, and discussing the relationships with the auditors.*
- *On a regular basis, meet separately with the external auditors to discuss any matters that the committee or auditors believe should be discussed privately.*

Compliance

- *Review the effectiveness of the system for monitoring compliance with laws and regulations and the results of management's investigation and follow-up (including disciplinary action) of any instances of noncompliance.*
- *Review the findings of any examinations by regulatory agencies, and any auditor observations.*
- *Review the process for communicating the code of conduct to company personnel, and for monitoring compliance therewith.*
- *Obtain regular updates from management and company legal counsel regarding compliance matters.*

Reporting Responsibilities

- *Regularly report to the board of directors about committee activities, issues, and related recommendations.*
- *Provide an open avenue of communication between internal audit, the external auditors, and the board of directors.*
- *Report annually to the shareholders, describing the committee's composition, responsibilities and how they were discharged, and any other information required by rule, including approval of non-audit services.*
- *Review any other reports the company issues that relate to committee responsibilities.*

Other Responsibilities

- *Perform other activities related to this charter as requested by the board of directors.*
- *Institute and oversee special investigations as needed.*
- *Review and assess the adequacy of the committee charter annually, requesting board approval for proposed changes and ensure appropriate disclosure as may be required by law or regulation.*
- *Confirm annually that all responsibilities outlines in this chapter have been carried out.*
- *Evaluate the committee's and individual members' performance on a regular basis.*

g. The **Sarbanes-Oxley Act**, enacted by the U.S. Congress in 2002 as a response to numerous financial reporting scandals involving large public companies, contains provisions relating to corporate governance. The act applies to issuers of publicly traded securities subject to federal securities laws, including foreign companies.

1) It requires that each member of the **audit committee**, including at least one who is a **financial expert**, be an **independent** member of the issuer's **board of directors**.

   a) An independent director is not affiliated with the issuer, and receives no compensation other than for service on the board.

2) The audit committee must be directly responsible for **appointing, compensating, and overseeing** the work of the public accounting firm employed by the issuer.

   a) In addition, this audit firm must **report directly** to the audit committee, not to management.

3) Another function of the audit committee is to implement procedures for the receipt, retention, and treatment of **complaints about accounting and auditing matters**.

4) The audit committee also must be appropriately funded by the issuer and may hire independent counsel or other advisors.

3. Stop and review! You have completed the outline for this subunit. Study multiple-choice questions 1 through 19 beginning on page 263.

8.2 RESOURCE MANAGEMENT

1. This subunit addresses management of human resources of the internal audit activity. It includes one Specific Performance Standard and two Practice Advisories.

2030   *Resource Management* – *The chief audit executive should ensure that internal audit resources are appropriate, sufficient, and effectively deployed to achieve the approved plan.*

Practice Advisory 2030-1: Resource Management

1. *Staffing plans and financial budgets, including the number of auditors and the knowledge, skills, and other competencies required to perform their work, should be determined from engagement work schedules, administrative activities, education and training requirements, and audit research and development efforts.*

2. *The chief audit executive should establish a program for selecting and developing the human resources of the internal audit activity. The program should provide for:*
   - *Developing written job descriptions for each level of the audit staff.*
   - *Selecting qualified and competent individuals.*
   - *Training and providing continuing educational opportunities for each internal auditor.*
   - *Appraising each internal auditor's performance at least annually.*
   - *Providing counsel to internal auditors on their performance and professional development.*

Practice Advisory 2030-2: SEC External Auditor Independence Requirements for Providing Internal Audit Services

NOTE: The following should be considered by organizations subject to U.S. Securities and Exchange Commission (SEC) requirements when evaluating the external auditor's independence if the external auditor both provides internal audit services and audits the organization's financial statements. The SEC auditor independence requirements are summarized for information purposes, but the focus is on the provisions concerning internal audit services. For legal, accounting, or regulatory interpretations of the SEC's requirements, readers should seek appropriate counsel and advice from authoritative sources.

Author's Note: SEC regulations issued under the Sarbanes-Oxley Act of 2002 made changes in the auditor independence requirements. The IIA is therefore reconsidering the guidance in this Practice Advisory. For the new rules, see www.sec.gov.

1. *Effective February 5, 2001, the SEC adopted rule amendments regarding external auditor independence for determining whether an auditor is independent in light of:*
   - *Investments by auditors or their family members in audit clients,*
   - *Employment relationships between auditors or their family members and audit clients*
   - *The scope of services provided by audit firms to their audit clients. The scope of services provisions do not extend to services provided to non-audit clients.*

2. *The rule amendments:*
   - *Significantly reduce the number of audit firm employees and their family members whose investments in audit clients are attributed to the auditor for purposes of determining the external auditor's independence.*
   - *Shrink the circle of family and former firm personnel whose employment impairs an external auditor's independence,*

- *Identify certain non-audit services that, if provided by an external auditor to public company audit clients, impair the auditor's independence.*
- *Require most public companies to disclose in their annual proxy statements certain information related to, among other things, the non-audit services provided by their external auditor during the most recent fiscal year.*
- *Provide accounting firms with a limited exception from being deemed not independent for certain inadvertent independence impairments if they have quality controls and satisfy other conditions.*

3.   *Transition dates for implementing the new rules are:*

- *Until August 5, 2002 – rules relating to providing non-audit services for appraisals, valuations, fairness opinions, and internal audit services will not impair an accountant's independence with respect to the audit client if performing those services did not impair the external auditor's independence under pre-existing requirements of the SEC, the Independence Standards Board, or the accounting profession in the United States.*
- *Until December 31, 2002 – an accounting firm that annually provides audit, review, or attest services to more than 500 companies with a class of securities registered with the SEC under Section 12 of the Securities Exchange Act of 1934 (15 U.S.C. 78L) will not be deemed to lack independence for failing to set up a quality control system with the characteristics identified in the new rules.*

4.   *The SEC rules indicate that an external auditor is not independent if, at any point during the audit and professional engagement period, the accountant provides, subject to certain exemptions and limitations explained in the rules, the following non-audit services to an audit client:*

- *Bookkeeping or other services related to the audit client's accounting records or financial statements.*
- *Financial information systems design and implementation.*
- *Appraisal or valuation services or fairness opinions.*
- *Actuarial services.*
- *Internal audit services.*
- *Management functions.*
- *Human resources.*
- *Broker-dealer services.*
- *Legal services.*

The subjects identified above are discussed in more detail in the SEC rules. The following sections of this Practice Advisory will focus on the rules related to internal audit services.

5.   *Specifically, an external auditor's independence is impaired if:*

- *The external auditor provides internal audit services in an amount greater than 40% of the total hours expended on the audit client's internal audit activities in any one fiscal year, unless the audit client has less than $200 million in total assets. (For purposes of this paragraph, the term internal audit services does not include operational internal audit services unrelated to the internal accounting controls, financial systems, or financial statements.); or*

- *The external auditor provides any internal audit services, or any operational audit services unrelated to the internal accounting controls, financial systems, or financial statements for an audit client, unless:*

  - *The audit client's management has acknowledged in writing to the accounting firm and the audit client's audit committee, or, if there is no such committee, then to the board of directors, the audit client's responsibility to establish and maintain a system of internal accounting controls in compliance with Section 13(b)(2) of the Securities Exchange Act of 1934 (a5 U.S.C. 78m(b)(2));*

  - *The audit client's management designates a competent employee or employees, preferably within senior management, to be responsible for the internal audit function;*

  - *The audit client's management determines the scope, risk, and frequency of internal audit activities, including those to be performed by the accountant;*

  - *The audit client's management evaluates the findings and results arising from the internal audit activities, including those performed by the accountant;*

  - *The audit client's management evaluates the adequacy of the audit procedures performed and the findings resulting from the performance of those procedures by, among other things, obtaining reports from the accountant; and*

  - *The audit client's management does not rely on the accountant's work as the primary basis for determining the adequacy of its internal controls.*

6. *The CAE should facilitate communications among the internal audit activity, management, audit committee, and external auditors concerning the SEC rules regarding external auditor independence requirements. It is critical for all parties involved to understand and reach agreement concerning application of the SEC rules.*

7. *The CAE should confirm that the six criteria contained in the second bullet of paragraph five above and on the previous page are completed and should assist in their completion if necessary. Although the frequency with which these criteria should be communicated or confirmed is not specified, annual assertions are recommended.*

8. *The CAE should determine that appropriate agreement with all relevant parties is achieved concerning definitions and application of the requirements contained in the SEC rules. Appropriate records should be maintained by the organization that document how terms will be defined and how the rule requirements will be applied. It may be deemed advisable to adopt a policy that contains the organization's interpretations and methodology for complying with the SEC rules.*

9. *The following examples are representative, but not all-inclusive, of the types of considerations that should be evaluated and agreed upon:*

  - *How to define "internal audit activities." For example, does this include everything that reports to the CAE? Does it include everything that reports to the audit committee, such as an independent risk management function, compliance function, security function, or ethics officer? It may be necessary to review the organizational charts and charters of the internal audit activity and audit committee.*

  - *In the case of organizations with multiple or decentralized internal audit units, the SEC rules should be applied to the aggregated services of these units. Be aware that the SEC rules will apply to all "registrants," so if an organization has multiple registrants, the requirements will also apply independently at each registrant level.*

- *Organizations should reach agreement on how to define internal accounting controls, financial systems, financial statements, and operational internal audit services. Additionally, organizations should determine those internal audit services that are unrelated to internal accounting controls, financial systems, or financial statements. Note that the rules do not exclude <u>all</u> operational audits, only those that are unrelated to the internal accounting controls, financial systems, or financial statements.*
- *How to calculate the 40% limitation for internal audit services that can be provided by the external auditor. All hours allocated to internal audit services based on a "full-time-equivalent" (FTE) calculation should be included. Note that this rule is effective as of August 5, 2002, and will only include a partial year's hours for the initial implementation period.*
- *The 40% limitation calculation should be performed at the beginning of the audit period based on the planned internal audit activities for the year. The SEC rules will apply to the <u>actual</u> hours and activities performed during the year. The CAE should establish an appropriate monitoring system to periodically evaluate compliance with the 40% limitation and make appropriate adjustments to the internal audit activities to achieve compliance with SEC rules.*

2. **Job descriptions**

   a. Facilitate recruiting by stating explicit job requirements
   b. Provide objective promotion criteria
   c. Are used to justify adequate salaries
   d. Express organizational expectations of employees
   e. Compel the internal audit activity to engage in personnel planning
   f. May be prepared for the chief audit executive and other administrators

   1) The internal audit activity's charter is effectively a job description for the CAE.

   NOTE: The descriptions for the positions of manager, supervisor, and senior are presented beginning below (adapted from Sawyer, Dittenhofer, and Scheiner, *Sawyer's Internal Auditing*, pages 846, 847, and 848, respectively).

   MANAGER

   <u>Purpose</u>
   - *To administer the internal audit activity of an assigned location or operation.*
   - *To develop a comprehensive, practical program of engagement coverage for the assigned location or operation.*
   - *To obtain accomplishment of the program in accordance with acceptable engagement standards and stipulated schedules.*
   - *To maintain effective working relations with executive and operating management.*

   <u>Authority and Responsibility</u>
   Within the general guidelines provided by the chief audit executive:
   - *Prepares a comprehensive, long-range program of engagement coverage for the location to which assigned.*
   - *Identifies those activities subject to engagement coverage, evaluates their significance, and assesses the degree of risk inherent in the activity in terms of cost, schedule, and quality.*
   - *Establishes the related departmental structure.*
   - *Obtains and maintains an audit staff capable of accomplishing the internal audit function.*
   - *Assigns engagement areas, staff, and budget to supervisors.*
   - *Develops a system of cost and schedule control over engagement projects.*
   - *Establishes standards of performance and, by review, determines that performance meets the standards.*

- *Provides executive management within the assigned location with reports on engagement coverage and engagement results, and interprets those results so as to improve the engagement program and the engagement coverage.*
- *Establishes and monitors accomplishment of objectives directed toward increasing the internal audit activity's ability to serve management.*

SUPERVISOR

Purpose

- *To develop a comprehensive, practical program of engagement coverage for assigned areas.*
- *To supervise the activities of staff assigned to the review of various organizational and functional activities.*
- *To ensure conformance with acceptable standards, plans, budgets, and schedules.*
- *To maintain effective working relations with operating management.*
- *To provide for and conduct research and develop manuals and training guides.*

Authority and Responsibility

Under the general guidance of a manager:

- *Supervises the work of staff engaged in the reviews of organizational and functional activities.*
- *Provides a comprehensive, practical schedule of annual engagement coverage within general areas assigned by the manager.*
- *Determines areas of risk and appraises their significance in relation to operational factors of cost, schedule, and quality. Classifies engagement projects as to degree of risk and significance and as to frequency of coverage.*
- *Provides for flexibility in engagement schedules so as to be responsive to management's special needs.*
- *Schedules projects and staff assignments so as to comply with management's needs, within the scope of the internal audit activity's overall schedule.*
- *Coordinates the program with the organization's public accountant.*
- *Reviews and approves the purpose, scope, and approach of each engagement project for assigned areas.*
- *Directs engagement projects to see that professional standards are maintained in the planning and execution and in the accumulation of information.*
- *Counsels and guides staff to see that the approved engagement objectives are met and that adequate, practical coverage is achieved.*
- *Reviews and edits engagement communications and, in organizations with the auditor-in-charge for the assigned project, discusses the communications with appropriate management.*
- *Presents oral briefing to branch-level management.*
- *Provides for and performs research on engagement techniques.*
- *Provides formal plans for the recruiting, selecting, training, evaluating, and supervising of staff personnel. Develops manuals and other training aids.*
- *Accumulates data, maintains records, and prepares reports on the administration of engagement projects and other assigned activities.*
- *Identifies factors causing deficient conditions and recommends courses of action to improve the conditions, including special surveys and audits.*
- *Provides for a flow of communication from operating management to the manager and to the chief audit executive. Assists in evaluating overall results of the engagements.*

SENIOR

Purpose

- *To conduct reviews of assigned organizational and functional activities.*
- *To evaluate the adequacy and effectiveness of the management controls over those activities.*
- *To determine whether organizational units are performing their planning, accounting, custodial, risk management, or control activities in compliance with management instructions, applicable statements of policy and procedures, and in a manner consistent with both organizational objectives and high standards of administrative practice.*
- *To plan and execute engagements in accordance with accepted standards.*
- *To report engagement observations and to make recommendations for correcting unsatisfactory conditions, improving operations, and reducing cost.*
- *To perform special reviews at the request of management.*
- *To direct the activities of assistants.*

Authority and Responsibility

Under the general guidance of a supervisor:

- *Surveys functions and activities in assigned areas to determine the nature of operations and the adequacy of the system of control to achieve established objectives.*
- *Determines the direction and thrust of the proposed engagement effort.*
- *Plans the theory and scope of the engagement, and prepares an engagement work program.*
- *Determines the engagement procedures to be used, including statistical sampling and the use of information technology.*
- *Identifies the key control points of the system.*
- *Evaluates a system's effectiveness through the application of a knowledge of business systems, including financial, manufacturing, engineering, procurement, and other operations, and an understanding of engagement techniques.*
- *Recommends necessary staff required to complete the engagement.*
- *Performs the engagement in a professional manner and in accordance with the approved engagement work program.*
- *Obtains, analyzes, and appraises information as a basis for an informed, objective conclusion (opinion) on the adequacy and effectiveness of the system and the efficiency of performance of the activities being reviewed.*
- *Directs, counsels, and instructs staff assistants assigned to the engagement, and reviews their work for sufficiency of scope and for accuracy.*
- *Makes oral or written presentations to management during and at the conclusion of the engagement, discussing observations and recommending corrective action to improve operations and reduce cost.*
- *Prepares formal written communications, expressing opinions on the adequacy and effectiveness of the system and the efficiency with which activities are carried out.*
- *Appraises the adequacy of the corrective action taken to improve deficient conditions.*

3. **Selection of Staff**

   a. Modern internal auditing demands a superior staff.

      1) Staffing provides the personnel necessary to carry on the work of the internal audit activity.

      2) Mediocre personnel are incapable of carrying out progressive programs.

      3) Each internal auditor must have the capacity to expand his/her abilities as management makes increasing demands for modern services.

   b. The CAE should set high standards for the staff.

   c. Professional education and ability, as well as certain personality characteristics, are essential.

   d. Source of staff

      1) Generating recruits internally has many advantages:

         a) The character, personality, work attitudes, and other personal qualifications of staff members are known.

         b) Internal recruits are familiar with organizational policies and practices.

         c) Internal recruits will have a broader perspective of total organizational operations.

         d) Experience and work qualifications can be closely evaluated.

         e) Internal recruiting can promote good staff morale.

      2) Recruiting experienced personnel externally also has advantages:

         a) The organization can attract specific skills needed.
         b) The range of possible services is broadened.
         c) New ideas are brought to the organization.

3) Recruiting of university graduates is another possibility.

    a) The organization must be able to train and develop personnel.
    b) Benefits include updating accounting and auditing skills.

e. Interviewing and testing techniques

1) The selection of a superior staff is dependent on the ability to evaluate applicants.
2) The interviews should be carefully planned and structured.
3) Competent interviewers should be assigned to the task.
4) Supervisors who will be responsible for the work of the new staff should be present at the interviews.
5) Appropriate questions and forms should be prepared in advance to evaluate

    a) Technical qualifications and educational background
    b) Personal appearance
    c) Ability to communicate
    d) Maturity
    e) Persuasiveness
    f) Self-confidence
    g) Intelligence
    h) Motivation
    i) Potential to contribute to the organization

6) Applicants who have earned the CIA designation have already demonstrated qualifications in internal auditing. Other qualities can be examined by a variety of tests developed by the organization to provide additional insights into abilities of applicants. These tests will vary with the job to be filled.

    a) Test of writing ability. Sawyer, Dittenhofer, and Scheiner suggest requiring a written engagement communication from the applicant based on a prescribed format and a hypothetical situation.
    b) Grading criteria for evaluation of writing ability include clarity, coherence, structure, and vocabulary.
    c) Test of ability to organize thoughts

      i) Sawyer, Dittenhofer, and Scheiner suggest the applicant arrange a series of 25 statements to describe an engagement observation.
      ii) The statements are mixed and given identifying numbers. The applicant is asked to arrange them in proper sequence.

    d) Test of ability to distinguish between fact and conjecture

      i) Applicant must identify the statements of undeniable fact and of mere conjecture in a brief paragraph.

4. Training of Staff

a. Staff orientation

1) An adequate orientation program provides reasonable assurance that the new employee will become productive promptly.

    a) Promotes good employee morale
    b) Deters good employees from leaving

2) The orientation program should be well designed and controlled.
3) Appropriate materials should be devised.

4)   Employees should be familiarized with organizational policies.

5)   Internal auditing familiarization may include

   a)   Introductions to staff personnel and other employees

   b)   Discussion of engagement objectives

   c)   Copies of internal auditing manuals

   d)   Discussion of duties and responsibilities

   e)   Control of work

   f)   General information on the structure of the organization

   g)   Literature on modern internal auditing

   h)   Working paper techniques

   i)   Development of engagement observations

   j)   Communicating

   k)   Instructor's follow-up and feedback after new staff member has performed actual field work

b.   Objectives of staff training are to

1)   Assist internal auditing to do a better job

2)   Add versatility to the internal audit activity

3)   Help develop supervisory skill

4)   Prepare the staff member for promotion

5)   Improve the staff member's job satisfaction, resulting in organizational loyalty and increased productivity

c.   Possible training formats include

1)   Formal classroom training
2)   Self-study
3)   Attendance at IIA and other formal meetings
4)   Industry conferences
5)   University courses
6)   On-the-job training
7)   Research projects

d.   Required components of a successful training program

1)   The trainee's commitment and interest
2)   Sufficient time and resources to permit training objectives to be met
3)   High-quality training materials
4)   Trainee participation
5)   Reinforcement

e.   One aspect of a successful, ongoing training program is the convening of regular staff meetings to explain new techniques, to discuss new administrative policies, and to receive suggestions from staff members.

5.   **Evaluation of Staff**

a.   Appraisal of each internal auditor's performance is required at least annually.

b.   The evaluation provides a basis for counseling subordinates on their strong and weak attributes, opportunities for advancement, and programs for self-improvement.

c.   The evaluation is a basis for promotions, transfers, and compensation adjustments.

d.   The evaluation is done by the person with responsibility for the particular employee.

   e.   Criteria for evaluation are weighted and applied to performance on specific projects. The criteria include type of skill required, extent of responsibility, scope of effort, and nature of working conditions.

   f.   A full explanation of the appraisal process and results should be given to each internal auditor.

6.   Stop and review! You have completed the outline for this subunit. Study multiple-choice questions 20 through 38 beginning on page 270.

8.3 POLICIES AND PROCEDURES

1.   This subunit concerns the formal guidance to be provided by the chief audit executive. This guidance is discussed in one Specific Performance Standard and in one Practice Advisory.

2040   *Policies and Procedures* – *The chief audit executive should establish policies and procedures to guide the internal audit activity.*

Practice Advisory 2040-1: Policies and Procedures

1.   *The form and content of written policies and procedures should be appropriate to the size and structure of the internal audit activity and the complexity of its work. Formal administrative and technical audit manuals may not be needed by all internal auditing entities. A small internal audit activity may be managed informally. Its audit staff may be directed and controlled through daily, close supervision and written memoranda. In a large internal audit activity, more formal and comprehensive policies and procedures are essential to guide the audit staff in the consistent compliance with the internal audit activity's standards of performance.*

2.   **Personnel manuals** describe the overall organization and its relationship to employees, including

   a.   Objectives and goals (also of divisions, subsidiaries, etc.)
   b.   History
   c.   Fringe benefits (medical, pension, life insurance, etc.)
   d.   Vacation and sick-pay policies
   e.   Promotion policies
   f.   Development and training programs

3.   **Audit (technical) manuals** provide guidance on completing specific engagements in compliance with the technical standards and policies of the internal audit activity. Thus, they include

   a.   General and specific guidelines on

      1)   Engagement objectives (may classify types of engagements)
      2)   Theory and purpose of internal auditing
      3)   Scope of engagement, engagement work programs, and time budgets
      4)   Working papers
      5)   Engagement communications
      6)   Internal controls
      7)   Internal administration
      8)   Performance standards

      b.   Special technical topics, such as

          1)   Information technology auditing
          2)   Statistical sampling
          3)   Procedures for suspected fraud
          4)   Fraud investigations

      c.   Matters related to administration of an individual engagement, such as

          1)   Notification of client about a pending engagement
          2)   Preliminary survey and engagement work program
          3)   Engagement time budget and changes therein
          4)   Application of engagement procedures
          5)   Changes in engagement work programs
          6)   Working paper preparation, review, and control
          7)   Communication draft review with clients
          8)   Communication format
          9)   Communication review
          10) Client replies to engagement communication
          11) Follow-up on observations and recommendations

4.   **Administrative policy and procedure manuals** provide guidelines and standards for the operation of the internal audit activity.

      a.   The administrative policy and procedure manual may include

          1)   The internal audit activity charter
          2)   A policy statement setting forth the relationship of the internal audit activity with other organizational units
          3)   The definition of responsibilities of personnel
          4)   An internal audit activity organizational chart
          5)   A delegation guide of approvals required for actions
          6)   Personnel policies unique to the internal audit activity
          7)   Personnel records
          8)   Travel instructions
          9)   Expense reports
          10) Time reports
          11) Staff evaluations
          12) Filing system descriptions for permanent files, temporary files, and working paper retention
          13) Communication preparation and review procedures
          14) Engagement research responsibilities
          15) Training and education programs

      b.   The administrative policy manual should also contain the history of the internal audit activity, including the relationship with management and the board, to provide staff auditors with the activity's philosophy and approach to internal auditing.

5.   Stop and review! You have completed the outline for this subunit. Study multiple-choice questions 39 through 53 beginning on page 276.

QUESTIONS

8.1 Planning, Risk, and Communications

1. The chief audit executive should establish goals as part of the planning process for the internal audit activity. What are the traits of internal auditing goals?

A. Measurable and attainable.

B. Budgeted and approved.

C. Planned and attainable.

D. Requested and approved.

Answer (A) is correct. *(CIA, adapted)*
REQUIRED: The traits of internal auditing goals.
DISCUSSION: Goals should be capable of accomplishment within given operating plans and budgets and should be measurable to the extent possible. They should be accompanied by measurement criteria and targeted dates of accomplishment (PA 2010-1).
Answer (B) is incorrect because goals should be attainable within budget constraints. However, approval is not a trait of goals themselves. Answer (C) is incorrect because goals should be measurable. Answer (D) is incorrect because goals are not usually requested. Instead, they are established by the CAE.

2. At a meeting with engagement managers, the chief audit executive is allocating the engagement work schedule for next year's plan. Which of the following methods will ensure that each manager receives an appropriate share of both the work schedule and internal audit activity resources?

A. Work is assigned to each manager based on risk and skill analysis.

B. Each of the managers selects the individual assignments desired, based on preferences for the area and the management personnel involved.

C. Each manager chooses assignment preferences based on the total staff hours that are currently available to each manager.

D. The full list of scheduled engagements is published for the staff, and work assignments are made based on career interests and travel requirements.

Answer (A) is correct. *(CIA, adapted)*
REQUIRED: The method that ensures proper sharing of engagement work and resources.
DISCUSSION: Engagements should be performed with proficiency and due professional care (Standard 1200). Thus, professional care should be commensurate with the complexities of the engagement, and the IAA should assure that the technical proficiency and educational background of the personnel assigned are appropriate. A skill analysis of tasks to be performed is therefore necessary. Furthermore, matters to be considered in establishing engagement work schedule priorities include (1) updated assessments of risks and effectiveness of risk management and control processes and (2) changes to and capabilities of the staff (PA 2010-1).
Answer (B) is incorrect because choice based on personal preference does not ensure the exercise of due professional care. Answer (C) is incorrect because available staff hours do not correlate with risk or the composite skills necessary for individual assignments. Answer (D) is incorrect because although career interests and travel requirements are considerations for staffing engagements, these factors do not constitute an objective basis for making assignments.

3. The chief audit executive is preparing the engagement work schedule for the next budget year and has limited resources. In deciding whether to schedule the purchasing or the personnel department for an engagement, which of the following is the least important factor?

A. Major changes in operations have occurred in one of the departments.

B. The internal audit staff has recently added an individual with expertise in one of the areas.

C. More opportunities to achieve operating benefits are available in one of the departments than in the other.

D. Updated assessed risk is significantly greater in one department than the other.

Answer (B) is correct. *(CIA, adapted)*
REQUIRED: The least important factor in deciding whether to schedule the purchasing or the personnel department for an engagement.
DISCUSSION: Matters to be considered in establishing engagement work schedule priorities should include (a) the dates and results of the last engagement; (b) updated assessments of risks and effectiveness of risk management and control processes; (c) requests by senior management, audit committee, and governing body; (d) current issues relating to organizational governance; (e) major changes in the enterprise's business, operations, programs, systems, and controls; (f) opportunities to achieve operating benefits; and (g) changes in and capabilities of the staff. The work schedules should be sufficiently flexible to cover unanticipated demands on the IAA (PA 2010-1). The addition of a new staff member is probably less important than the other factors cited.
Answer (A) is incorrect because a major change in operations is a reason for an engagement. Answer (C) is incorrect because potential operating benefits are a reason for an engagement. Answer (D) is incorrect because updated assessed risk is a reason for an engagement.

4. Which of the following factors is not included in determining the engagement work schedule?

    A. Engagement work programs.

    B. The effectiveness of risk management and control processes.

    C. Workload requirements.

    D. Issues relating to organizational governance.

Answer (A) is correct. *(CIA, adapted)*
    REQUIRED: The activity not included in developing the engagement work schedule.
    DISCUSSION: Engagement work schedules should include (a) what activities are to be performed; (b) when they will be performed; and (c) the estimated time required, taking into account the scope of the engagement work planned and the nature and extent of related work performed by others. Matters to be considered in establishing engagement work schedule priorities should include (a) the dates and results of the last engagement; (b) updated assessments of risks and effectiveness of risk management and control processes; (c) requests by senior management, the audit committee, and the governing body; (d) current issues relating to organizational governance; (e) major changes in the enterprise's business, operations, programs, systems, and controls; (f) opportunities to achieve operating benefits; and (g) changes in and capabilities of the staff. The work schedules should be sufficiently flexible to cover unanticipated demands on the IAA (PA 2010-1). Development of work programs occurs during the planning phase of an individual engagement.

5. The chief audit executive routinely presents an activity report to the board as part of the board meeting agenda each quarter. Senior management has asked to review this presentation before each board meeting so that any issues or questions can be discussed beforehand. The CAE should

    A. Provide the activity report to senior management as requested and discuss any issues that may require action to be taken.

    B. Withhold disclosure of the activity report to senior management because such matters are the sole province of the board.

    C. Disclose to the board only those matters in the activity report that pertain to expenditures and financial budgets of the internal audit activity.

    D. Provide information to senior management that pertains only to completed engagements and observations available in published engagement communications.

Answer (A) is correct. *(CIA, adapted)*
    REQUIRED: The action that should be taken regarding the review of internal auditing reports by senior management.
    DISCUSSION: The CAE should submit activity reports to senior management and to the board annually or more frequently as necessary. Activity reports should highlight significant engagement observations and recommendations and should inform senior management and the board of any significant deviations from approved engagement work schedules, staffing plans, and financial budgets, and the reasons for them (PA 2060-1).
    Answer (B) is incorrect because activity reports should be presented to senior management. Answer (C) is incorrect because the report should not be restricted to expenditures and financial budgets. Information about significant deviations from engagement work schedules and staffing plans should be included. Answer (D) is incorrect because the information need not be limited to completed engagements and observations available in published engagement communications.

6. A chief audit executive's activity report should

    A. List the material engagement observations of major engagements.

    B. List uncorrected reported conditions.

    C. Report the weekly activities of the individual internal auditors.

    D. Compare engagements completed with engagements planned.

Answer (D) is correct. *(CIA, adapted)*
    REQUIRED: The true statement about a CAE's activity report.
    DISCUSSION: Activity reports should be submitted periodically to senior management and the board. These reports should compare (a) actual performance with the IAA's goals and engagement work schedules and (b) expenditures with financial budgets. They should explain the reasons for major variances and indicate any action taken or needed (PA 2060-1).
    Answer (A) is incorrect because a list of material engagement observations is not an activity report. Answer (B) is incorrect because a list of uncorrected reported conditions is not an activity report. Answer (C) is incorrect because a report of weekly activities is not an activity report.

7. Recent criticism of an internal audit activity suggested that engagement coverage was not providing adequate feedback to senior management on the processes used in the organization's key lines of business. The problem was further defined as lack of feedback on the recent implementation of automated support systems. Which two functions does the chief audit executive need to improve?

A. Staffing and communicating.

B. Staffing and decision making.

C. Planning and organizing.

D. Planning and communicating.

Answer (D) is correct. *(CIA, adapted)*
    REQUIRED: The functions to be improved.
    DISCUSSION: The lack of feedback indicates the CAE has problems in planning and allocating internal audit resources to communicate necessary information to management. The CAE should establish risk-based plans to determine the priorities of the IAA, consistent with the organization's goals (Standard 2010). Internal auditors should also communicate engagement results promptly (Standard 2400). Moreover, the engagements described are within the scope of the IAA. "Internal auditors should review operations and programs to ascertain the extent to which results are consistent with established goals and objectives to determine whether operations and programs are being implemented or performed as intended" (Standard 2120.A3).
    Answer (A) is incorrect because the facts do not indicate the existence of staffing problems. Answer (B) is incorrect because decision making and staffing are not problems. Answer (C) is incorrect because nothing indicates that the structure of the entity is a problem.

8. During discussions with senior management, the chief audit executive identified several strategic business issues to consider in preparing the annual engagement work schedule. Which of the following does not represent a strategic issue for this purpose?

A. A monthly budgeting process will be implemented.

B. An international marketing campaign will be started to develop product recognition and also to leverage the new organization-based advertising department.

C. Joint venture candidates will be sought to provide manufacturing and sourcing capabilities in European and Asian markets.

D. A human resources database will be established to ensure consistent administration of policies and to improve data retention.

Answer (A) is correct. *(CIA, adapted)*
    REQUIRED: The item not a strategic issue to consider in preparing the annual engagement work schedule.
    DISCUSSION: The audit universe may include components from the organization's strategic plan. By including components of this plan, the audit universe will consider and reflect the overall business plan objectives (PA 2010-2). However, implementing a monthly budgeting process is an operating decision to facilitate the budgeting process and improve information. It does not constitute a strategic issue, but it does entail a major change in operations, etc.
    Answer (B) is incorrect because the CAE will need to ensure that the new marketing process and the centralized advertising department are recognized and monitored in risk assessment and planning activities. Answer (C) is incorrect because the addition of joint-venture partners will add new or additional concerns for risk assessment and planning in the IAA. Answer (D) is incorrect because both the assumptions and ongoing activities related to a human resources database will require consideration in the planning of the IAA.

9. Which of the following factors serves as a direct input to the internal audit activity's financial budget?

A. Engagement work schedules.

B. Activity reports.

C. Past effectiveness of the internal audit activity in identifying cost savings.

D. Internal audit activity's charter.

Answer (A) is correct. *(CIA, adapted)*
    REQUIRED: The direct input to the IAA's financial budget.
    DISCUSSION: The IAA's planning process involves establishing goals, engagement work schedules, staffing plans and financial budgets, and activity reports. The plans and budgets, including the number of internal auditors and the knowledge, skills, and other competencies required to perform their work, should be determined from engagement work schedules, administrative activities, education and training requirements, and research and development efforts (PA 2030-1).
    Answer (B) is incorrect because activity reports compare actual performance with goals and schedules and actual expenditures with financial budgets. Answer (C) is incorrect because past performance is an indicator of the value of internal auditing, but it will not affect the funds committed to current operations. Answer (D) is incorrect because the charter defines the purpose, authority, and responsibility of the IAA.

10. Which of the following is the best source of a chief audit executive's information for planning staffing requirements?

    A. Discussions of internal audit needs with senior management and the board.

    B. Review of internal audit staff education and training records.

    C. Review internal audit staff size and composition of similarly sized organizations in the same industry.

    D. Interviews with existing internal audit staff.

Answer (A) is correct. *(CIA, adapted)*
    REQUIRED: The best source of a CAE's information for planning staffing requirements.
    DISCUSSION: The CAE should establish risk-based plans to determine the priorities of the IAA. These plans should be consistent with the goals of the organization (Standard 2010). The planning process involves establishing goals, engagement work schedules, staffing plans and financial budgets, and activity reports (PA 2010-1). Input from senior management and the board is obviously necessary for determining the resource needs of the IAA.
    Answer (B) is incorrect because the scheduled work is the first consideration in determining the number and qualifications of the staff required. Review of staff education and training records is a subsequent step. Answer (C) is incorrect because the staffing plan must consider the unique needs of a particular organization. The review of staff size and composition of similarly sized organizations in the same industry may not satisfy the engagement objectives for a particular organization. Answer (D) is incorrect because the scheduled work is the first consideration in determining the number and qualifications of the staff required. Interviews with existing staff occur later.

11. Which internal audit planning tool is general in nature and is used to ensure adequate engagement coverage over time?

    A. The long-range plan.

    B. The engagement work program.

    C. The internal audit activity's budget.

    D. The internal audit activity's charter.

Answer (A) is correct. *(CIA, adapted)*
    REQUIRED: The internal audit planning tool used to ensure adequate engagement coverage over time.
    DISCUSSION: The CAE should establish risk-based plans to determine the priorities of the IAA. These plans should be consistent with the goals of the organization (Standard 2010). The planning process involves establishing goals, engagement work schedules, staffing plans and financial budgets, and activity reports (PA 2010-1). The CAE submits annually to senior management for approval, and to the board for its information, summaries of work schedules, staffing plans, and financial budgets (PA 2020-1). Thus, the long-range planning process involves establishing engagement work schedules. These should include (a) what activities are to be performed; (b) when they will be performed; and (c) the estimated time required, taking into account the scope of the work planned and the nature and extent of related work performed by others (PA 2010-1).
    Answer (B) is incorrect because the engagement work program is limited in scope to a particular project. Answer (C) is incorrect because the IAA's budget may be used to justify a head count, but it is not used to ensure adequate engagement coverage over time. Answer (D) is incorrect because the charter is not an engagement planning tool.

12. A chief audit executive may use risk analysis in preparing work schedules. Which of the following is not considered in performing a risk analysis?

    A. Issues relating to organizational governance.

    B. Skills available on the internal audit staff.

    C. Results of prior engagements.

    D. Major operating changes.

Answer (B) is correct. *(CIA, adapted)*
    REQUIRED: The item not considered in performing a risk analysis.
    DISCUSSION: Matters to be considered in establishing engagement work schedule priorities should include (a) the dates and results of the last engagement; (b) updated assessments of risks and effectiveness of risk management and control processes; (c) requests by senior management, audit committee, and governing body; (d) current issues relating to organizational governance; (e) major changes in the enterprise's business, operations, programs, systems, and controls; (f) opportunities to achieve operating benefits; and (g) changes in and capabilities of the staff. The work schedules should be sufficiently flexible to cover unanticipated demands on the IAA (PA 2010-1). The skills of the staff do not affect the risk associated with potential engagement clients.
    Answer (A) is incorrect because issues relating to organizational governance are factors that should be considered. Answer (C) is incorrect because results of prior engagements should be considered. Answer (D) is incorrect because major operating changes should be considered.

13. A manager responsible for the supervision and review of other internal auditors needs the necessary skills, knowledge, and other competencies. Which of the following does not describe a skill, knowledge, or other competency necessary to supervise a particular engagement?

A. The ability to review and analyze an engagement work program to determine whether the proposed engagement procedures will result in information relevant to the engagement's objectives.

B. Assuring that an engagement communication is supported and accurate relative to the information documented in the engagement working papers.

C. Use risk assessment and other judgmental processes to develop an engagement work schedule for the internal audit activity and present the schedule to the board.

D. Determine that staff auditors have completed the engagement procedures and that engagement objectives have been met.

Answer (C) is correct. *(CIA, adapted)*
REQUIRED: The skill, knowledge, or other competency not necessary to supervise a particular engagement.
DISCUSSION: The CAE, not a manager, should establish risk-based plans to determine the priorities of the IAA, consistent with the organization's goals (Standard 2010). The planning process involves establishing goals, engagement work schedules, staffing plans and financial budgets, and activity reports (PA 2010-1). The CAE should communicate the IAA's plans and resource requirements, including significant interim changes, to senior management and the board for review and approval (PA 2020-1). Supervision includes approving the engagement work program; determining that the engagement working papers support observations, conclusions, and recommendations; and making certain that engagement objectives have been met (PA 2340-1).

14. The chief audit executive for an organization has just completed a risk assessment process, identified the areas with the highest risks, and assigned an engagement priority to each. Which of the following conclusions most logically follow(s) from such a risk assessment?

I. Items should be quantified as to risk in the rank order of quantifiable monetary exposure to the organization.

II. The risk priorities should be in order of major control deficiencies.

III. The risk assessment process, though quantified, is the result of professional judgments about both exposures and probability of occurrences.

A. I only.

B. III only.

C. II and III only.

D. I, II, and III.

Answer (B) is correct. *(CIA, adapted)*
REQUIRED: The conclusion(s) logically following from a risk assessment process.
DISCUSSION: Risk is the uncertainty of an event's occurrence that could have an impact on the achievement of objectives. Risk is measured in terms of consequences (exposures) and likelihood (probability)(Glossary appended to the Standards). Engagement work schedules should be based on, among other things, an assessment of risk priority and exposure. Prioritizing is needed to make decisions for applying relative resources based on the significance of risk and exposure. A variety of risk models may assist the CAE in prioritizing potential engagement subject areas. Most of these models use risk factors to establish the priority of engagements, for example, monetary materiality, asset liquidity, management competence, quality of internal controls, degree of change or stability, time of last engagement, complexity, or employee and governmental relations (PA 2010-2). Higher priorities are usually assigned to activities with higher risks. However, this process necessarily involves the exercise of professional judgment. Thus, although risk factors may be weighted to determine their relative significance, a ranking based solely on such specific criteria as monetary exposure or control deficiencies is not always indicated.

15. Which of the following comments is (are) true regarding the assessment of risk associated with two projects that are competing for limited internal audit resources?

I.   Activities that are requested by the board should always be considered higher risk than those requested by management.

II. Activities with higher financial budgets should always be considered higher risk than those with lower financial budgets.

III. Risk should always be measured by the potential monetary or other adverse exposure to the organization.

    A. I only.

    B. II only.

    C. III only.

    D. I and III.

Answer (C) is correct. *(CIA, adapted)*
    REQUIRED: The true statement(s) about risk assessment.
    DISCUSSION: Risk is the uncertainty of an event's occurrence that could have an impact on the achievement of objectives. Risk is measured in terms of consequences (exposures) and likelihood (probability)(Glossary appended to the Standards). Engagement work schedules should be based on, among other things, an assessment of risk priority and exposure. Prioritizing is needed to make decisions for applying relative resources based on the significance of risk and exposure. A variety of risk models may assist the CAE in prioritizing potential engagement subject areas. Most of these models use risk factors to establish the priority of engagements, for example, monetary materiality, asset liquidity, management competence, quality of internal controls, degree of change or stability, time of last engagement, complexity, or employee and governmental relations (PA 2010-2). However, a rigid procedure for conducting the risk assessment, including the assignment of engagement priorities, should not be followed. Thus, a ranking based on the source of a request for performance of an engagement or the financial budget of an engagement client is unlikely to reflect a comprehensive assessment based on a sufficient number of risk factors. A criterion based on the degree of adverse exposure to the organization is preferable.

16. Which of the following factors is considered the least important in deciding whether existing internal audit resources should be moved from an ongoing compliance engagement to a divisional-level engagement requested by management?

    A. A financial audit of the division performed by the external auditor a year ago.

    B. The potential for fraud associated with the ongoing engagement.

    C. An increase in the level of expenditures experienced by the division for the past year.

    D. The potential for significant regulatory fines associated with the ongoing engagement.

Answer (A) is correct. *(CIA, adapted)*
    REQUIRED: The least important factor affecting an allocation of internal audit resources.
    DISCUSSION: Prioritizing is needed to make decisions about applying relative resources based on the significance of risk and exposure. Most risk models use risk factors to establish engagement priorities (PA 2010-2). One such factor is the potential for fraud. Internal auditors traditionally regard fraud as significant even if the immediate exposure is not significant. Increased expenditures also constitute a significant risk factor because they represent an increase in potential loss. For the same reason, potential regulatory fines may also create an exposure sufficiently great to affect the determination of priorities. Thus, the result of an external financial audit performed a year ago is the least likely to affect the current allocation of internal audit resources. Any adverse engagement observations most probably have been acted upon, and, in any case, may not be germane to the ongoing compliance engagement or the proposed divisional-level engagement.

17. Which of the following represent(s) appropriate internal audit action in response to the risk assessment process?

I. The low-risk areas may be delegated to the external auditor, but the high-risk areas should be performed by the internal audit activity.

II. The high-risk areas should be integrated into an engagement work schedule along with the high-priority requests of senior management and the audit committee.

III. The risk analysis should be used in determining an annual engagement work schedule; therefore, the risk analysis should be performed only on an annual basis.

    A. I only.

    B. II only.

    C. III only.

    D. I and III only.

Answer (B) is correct. *(CIA, adapted)*
    REQUIRED: The appropriate internal audit action in response to a risk assessment.
    DISCUSSION: The risk assessment is preliminary to the development of the engagement work schedule. Higher priorities are usually assigned to engagement subject areas with higher risks. Thus, updated assessments of risks and effectiveness of risk management and control processes are considered in establishing engagement work schedule priorities. Other matters to be considered in establishing the engagement work schedule are the dates and results of the last engagement; requests by senior management, the audit committee, and the governing body; current issues relating to organizational governance; major changes; opportunities to achieve operating benefits; and changes in and capabilities of the internal auditor staff (PA 2010-1). Work should be coordinated with the external auditor to avoid duplication of effort and to ensure adequate coverage, but allocation of tasks to the external auditor and the IAA is not necessarily risk based. Moreover, changing conditions may require updating the risk assessment during the year.

18. The internal auditor is considering making a risk analysis as a basis for determining the areas of the organization where engagements should be performed. Which one of the following statements is true regarding risk analysis?

    A. The extent to which management judgments are required in an area could serve as a risk factor in assisting the internal auditor in making a comparative risk analysis.

    B. The highest risk assessment should always be assigned to the area with the largest potential loss.

    C. The highest risk assessment should always be assigned to the area with highest probability of occurrence.

    D. Risk analysis must be reduced to quantitative terms in order to provide meaningful comparisons across an organization.

Answer (A) is correct. *(CIA, adapted)*
    REQUIRED: The true statement about risk analysis.
    DISCUSSION: Most risk models use risk factors to establish the priority of engagements, for example, monetary materiality, asset liquidity, management competence, quality of internal controls, degree of change or stability, time of last engagement, complexity, or employee or governmental relations (PA 2010-2). Hence, the internal auditor could appropriately consider the extent of management competence, including judgment, as a risk factor.
    Answer (B) is incorrect because risk analysis should consider both the potential loss (or damages) and the probability of occurrence. An area with the largest potential loss may have a very low expected loss. Answer (C) is incorrect because a high probability of occurrence may be associated with a small potential loss. Answer (D) is incorrect because the concept of risk analysis is not limited to quantitative measures.

19. The chief audit executive set up a computerized spreadsheet to facilitate the risk assessment process involving a number of different divisions in the organization. The spreadsheet included the following factors:

- Pressure on divisional management to meet profit goals
- Complexity of operations
- Competence of divisional personnel
- The monetary amount of subjectively influenced accounts in the division, such as accounts in which management's judgment can affect the expense, e.g., postretirement benefits.

The CAE used a group meeting of internal audit managers to reach a consensus on the competence of divisional personnel. Other factors were assessed as high, medium, or low by either the CAE or an internal audit manager who had performed an engagement at the division. The CAE assigned a weight ranging from 0.5 to 1.0 to each factor, and then computed a composite risk score. Which of the following statements is correct regarding the risk assessment process?

A. The risk analysis is not appropriate because it mixes both quantitative and qualitative factors, thereby making expected values calculation impossible.

B. Assessing factors at discrete levels such as high, medium, and low is inappropriate for the risk assessment process because the ratings are not quantifiable.

C. The weighting is subjective and should have been determined through a process such as multiple-regression analysis.

D. Using a subjective group consensus to assess personnel competence is appropriate.

Answer (D) is correct.   *(CIA, adapted)*
REQUIRED: The true statement about the risk assessment.
DISCUSSION: The risk assessment should incorporate information from a variety of sources such as discussions with the board and management and with internal audit management and staff. Thus, seeking the consensus of experienced internal audit managers regarding personnel matters is appropriate. This method tends to eliminate the extreme judgments that might be made by a single evaluator.

Answer (A) is incorrect because risk analysis should consider all appropriate factors. It need not be limited to quantitative or expected value calculations. Answer (B) is incorrect because high, medium, and low may be the most precise measures available. Answer (C) is incorrect because subjective analysis is acceptable. Use of multiple-regression analysis to determine a weighted average for the risk-weighting model is not feasible because no criteria exist to determine the weightings.

8.2 Resource Management

20. Audit committees have been identified as a major factor in promoting the independence of both internal and external auditors. Which of the following is the most important limitation on the effectiveness of audit committees?

A. Audit committees may be composed of independent directors. However, those directors may have close personal and professional friendships with management.

B. Audit committee members are compensated by the organization and thus favor an owner's view.

C. Audit committees devote most of their efforts to external audit concerns and do not pay much attention to the internal audit activity and the overall control environment.

D. Audit committee members do not normally have degrees in the accounting or auditing fields.

Answer (A) is correct.   *(CIA, adapted)*
REQUIRED: The most important limitation on the effectiveness of audit committees.
DISCUSSION: The audit committee is a subcommittee made up of outside directors who are independent of management. Its purpose is to help keep external and internal auditors independent of management and to assure that the directors are exercising due care. However, if independence is impaired by personal and professional friendships, the effectiveness of the audit committee may be limited.

Answer (B) is incorrect because the compensation audit committee members receive is usually minimal. They should be independent and therefore not limited to an owner's perspective. Answer (C) is incorrect because although audit committees are concerned with external audits, they also devote attention to the internal audit activity. Answer (D) is incorrect because audit committee members do not need degrees in accounting or auditing to understand engagement communications.

21. The internal audit activity customarily has a dual relationship with management and the audit committee. This means that

A. Management should help the internal audit activity by revising and forwarding engagement communications to the audit committee.

B. The internal audit activity should report directly to the audit committee, without corroborating engagement communications with management.

C. The accuracy of engagement communications should be verified with management, and the internal audit activity should then report to management and the audit committee.

D. Ideally, the internal audit activity works under the audit committee but reports to the chief operating officer on all engagements relating to operations.

Answer (C) is correct. *(CIA, adapted)*
REQUIRED: The meaning of the IAA's dual relationship with management and the audit committee.
DISCUSSION: When communicating engagement results, internal auditors should discuss conclusions and recommendations at appropriate levels of management, a step that permits verifying the accuracy of engagement communications. Final engagement communications should be distributed to members of the organization who are able to ensure that engagement results are given due consideration, such as the audit committee (PA 2440-1).
Answer (A) is incorrect because the IAA should revise and forward engagement communications to the audit committee. Answer (B) is incorrect because engagement communications should be discussed with the client management. Answer (D) is incorrect because the ideal arrangement is to send all engagement communications to the audit committee.

22. The audit committee may serve several important purposes, some of which directly benefit the internal audit activity. The most significant benefit provided by the audit committee to the internal audit activity is

A. Protecting the independence of the internal audit activity from undue management influence.

B. Reviewing annual engagement work schedules and monitoring engagement results.

C. Approving engagement work schedules, scheduling, staffing, and meeting with the internal auditors as needed.

D. Reviewing copies of the procedures manuals for selected organizational operations and meeting with organizational officials to discuss them.

Answer (A) is correct. *(CIA, adapted)*
REQUIRED: The most significant benefit provided by the audit committee to the internal auditor.
DISCUSSION: The audit committee is a subcommittee of outside directors who are independent of corporate management. Its purpose is to help keep external and internal auditors independent of management and to assure that the directors are exercising due care. This committee often selects the external auditors, reviews their overall audit plan, and examines the results of external and internal audits.

23. Which of the following is an appropriate responsibility of an audit committee?

A. Performing a review of the procurement function of the organization.

B. Reviewing the internal audit activity's engagement work schedule submitted by the chief audit executive.

C. Reviewing the engagement records of the public accounting firm to determine the firm's competence.

D. Recommending the assignment of specific internal auditing staff members for specific engagements.

Answer (B) is correct. *(CIA, adapted)*
REQUIRED: The appropriate responsibility for an audit committee.
DISCUSSION: The audit committee consists of outside members of the board of directors (who should be independent of management). Regular communication with this committee helps assure independence and provides a means for the directors and the IAA to keep each other informed. According to Standard 2020 (see Study Unit 7), the CAE should communicate the IAA's plans and resource requirements to senior management and the board for review and approval. Moreover, PA 2020-1 (see Study Unit 7) states that the CAE should submit to senior management for approval, and to the board for its information, a summary of the IAA's work schedule, staffing plan, and financial budget.
Answer (A) is incorrect because reviewing the procurement function of the organization requires detailed technical ability. Answer (C) is incorrect because reviewing the IAA's engagement work schedule requires detailed technical ability. Answer (D) is incorrect because specific assignments should be made by IAA management.

24. To avoid creating conflict between the chief executive officer (CEO) and the audit committee, the chief audit executive should

    A. Submit copies of all engagement communications to the CEO and audit committee.

    B. Strengthen independence through organizational status.

    C. Discuss all pending engagement communications to the CEO with the audit committee.

    D. Request board establishment of policies covering the internal audit activity's relationships with the audit committee.

Answer (D) is correct. *(CIA, adapted)*
    REQUIRED: The measure that avoids conflict between the CEO and the audit committee.
    DISCUSSION: To avoid conflict between the CEO and the audit committee, the CAE should request that the board establish policies covering the IAA's relationships with the audit committee. The CAE should have regular communication with the board, audit committee, or other appropriate governing authority (PA 1110-1). Furthermore, the board should approve a charter that defines the purpose, authority, and responsibility of the IAA (Standard 1000). The CEO and audit committee most likely should receive summary reports. Senior management and the board ordinarily are not involved in the details of internal audit work. Independence is not sufficient to avert conflict unless reporting relationships are well defined.

25. Which of the following actions is an appropriate response by organizations wishing to improve the public's perception of their financial reporting?

    A. Increased adoption of audit committees composed of outside directors.

    B. Viewing internal auditing as a transient profession -- a stepping stone to managerial positions.

    C. Requiring internal auditors to report all significant observations of illegal activity to the chief executive officer.

    D. Keeping external and internal auditing work separated to maintain independence.

Answer (A) is correct. *(CIA, adapted)*
    REQUIRED: The appropriate means of improving the public's perception of financial reporting.
    DISCUSSION: The audit committee consists of outside directors who are independent of management. Its purpose is to help keep external and internal auditors independent of management and to assure that the directors are exercising due care. This committee selects the external auditors, reviews their overall audit plan, examines the results of external and internal auditing engagements, meets regularly with the CAE, and reviews the IAA's engagement work schedule, staffing plan, and financial budget. These functions should increase public confidence that financial statements are fairly presented.
    Answer (B) is incorrect because transience of internal auditors impairs the proficiency of the IAA. Answer (C) is incorrect because if illegal activities involve senior management, distribution of engagement communications should be to the audit committee, not the CEO. Answer (D) is incorrect because the work of the internal and external auditors should be coordinated to minimize duplicate efforts. Coordination does not impair independence or reduce public confidence.

26. Which of the following is not an appropriate member of an audit committee?

    A. The vice president of the local bank used by the organization.

    B. An academic specializing in business administration.

    C. A retired executive of a firm that had been associated with the organization.

    D. The organization's vice president of operations.

Answer (D) is correct. *(CIA, adapted)*
    REQUIRED: The person not an appropriate member of an audit committee.
    DISCUSSION: The audit committee consists of outside directors who are independent of management. Its purpose is to help keep external and internal auditors independent of management and to assure that the directors are exercising due care. This committee selects the external auditors, reviews their overall audit plan, examines the results of external and internal auditing engagements, meets regularly with the CAE, and reviews the IAA's engagement work schedule, staffing plan, and financial budget. Engagements may be performed in the vice president's area of responsibility. Thus, (s)he is not independent of the IAA. The vice president is also not an outside director. The vice president of the local bank used by the organization, an academic specializing in business administration, and a retired executive of a firm that had been associated with the organization are all external parties who are usually independent of the organization's internal operations.

27. Which of the following audit committee activities is of the greatest benefit to the internal audit activity?

A. Review and approval of engagement work programs.

B. Assurance that the external auditor will rely on the work of the internal audit activity whenever possible.

C. Review and endorsement of all internal auditing engagement communications prior to their release.

D. Support for appropriate monitoring of the disposition of recommendations made by the internal audit activity.

Answer (D) is correct. *(CIA, adapted)*
REQUIRED: The audit committee activity of the greatest benefit to the IAA.
DISCUSSION: The organizational status of the IAA is enhanced when it has the support of management and of the board. Internal auditors can thereby gain the cooperation of engagement clients and perform their work free from interference (PA 1110-1).
Answer (A) is incorrect because review and approval of engagement work programs is the responsibility of internal auditing supervisors. Answer (B) is incorrect because whether the external auditor will make use of the work of internal auditing is not for the audit committee to decide. Answer (C) is incorrect because review and approval of internal auditing engagement communications is the responsibility of the chief audit executive or his/her designee.

28. Which of the following features of a large manufacturer's organizational structure is a control weakness?

A. The information systems department is headed by a vice president who reports directly to the president.

B. The chief financial officer is a vice president who reports to the chief executive officer.

C. The audit committee of the board consists of the chief executive officer, the chief financial officer, and a major shareholder.

D. The controller and treasurer report to the chief financial officer.

Answer (C) is correct. *(CIA, adapted)*
REQUIRED: The control weakness in a large manufacturer's organizational structure.
DISCUSSION: The audit committee has a control function because of its oversight of internal as well as external auditing. It should be made up of directors who are independent of management. The authority and independence of the audit committee strengthen the position of the internal audit activity. The board should concur in the appointment or removal of the chief audit executive, who should have direct, regular communication with the board (PA 1110-1).
Answer (A) is incorrect because this reporting relationship is a strength. It prevents the information systems operation from being dominated by a user. Answer (B) is incorrect because it is a normal and appropriate reporting relationship. Answer (D) is incorrect because it is a normal and appropriate reporting relationship.

29. The audit committee strengthens the control processes of an organization by

A. Assigning the internal audit activity responsibility for interaction with governmental agencies.

B. Using the chief audit executive as a major resource in selecting the external auditors.

C. Following up on recommendations made by the chief audit executive.

D. Approving internal audit activity policies.

Answer (C) is correct. *(CIA, adapted)*
REQUIRED: The way in which the audit committee strengthens control processes.
DISCUSSION: Internal auditors should have the support of senior management and the board (board of directors, audit committee, board of trustees of a nonprofit organization, etc.) to gain the cooperation of engagement clients and perform their work free from interference. Such support promotes independence and ensures broad engagement coverage, adequate consideration of engagement reports, and appropriate action on engagement recommendations (PA 1110-1). This enhancement of the position of internal auditing in turn strengthens control processes.

30. An audit committee of the board of directors of an organization is being established. Which of the following is normally a responsibility of the committee with regard to the internal audit activity?

A. Approval of the selection and dismissal of the chief audit executive.

B. Development of the annual engagement work schedule.

C. Approval of engagement work programs.

D. Determination of engagement observations appropriate for specific engagement communications.

Answer (A) is correct. *(CIA, adapted)*
REQUIRED: The responsibility of an audit committee.
DISCUSSION: Independence is enhanced when the board concurs in the appointment or removal of the CAE (PA 1110-1). The audit committee is a subcommittee of outside directors who are independent of management. The term "board" includes the audit committee.
Answer (B) is incorrect because development of the annual engagement work schedule is an operational function of the CAE and the IAA staff. The annual engagement work schedule, staffing plan, and financial budget are submitted to senior management and the board (PA 2020-1). Answer (C) is incorrect because approval of engagement work programs is a technical responsibility of the IAA staff. Answer (D) is incorrect because the determination of engagement observations appropriate for specific engagement communications is a field operation of the IAA staff.

31. According to the Sarbanes-Oxley Act, who is responsible for appointing, compensating, and overseeing the work of the public accounting firm employed by the issuer of the financial statements?

    A. The audit committee.

    B. Management.

    C. The board of directors.

    D. The issuer's shareholders.

Answer (A) is correct. *(Publisher)*
REQUIRED: The responsibility of the audit committee according to the Sarbanes-Oxley Act.
DISCUSSION: The Sarbnes-Oxley Act puts more responsibility in the hands of the audit committee. The audit committee is responsible for appointing, compensating, and overseeing the work of the public accounting firm employed by the issuer. Furthermore, the audit committee is responsible for implementing procedures for the receipt, retention, and treatment of complaints about accounting and auditing matters. The audit committee must also be appropriately funded by the issuer and must be able to hire independent counsel or other advisors.
Answer (B) is incorrect because the audit committee, not management, is responsible for the responsibilities stated. Answer (C) is incorrect because the audit committee, not the board of directors, is responsible for the responsibilities stated. Answer (D) is incorrect because the audit committee, not shareholders, is responsible for the responsibilities stated.

32. The review of findings of regulatory agencies is consistent with which audit committee responsibility?

    A. Reporting responsibilities.

    B. Compliance.

    C. Internal audit.

    D. External audit.

Answer (B) is correct. *(Publisher)*
REQUIRED: the audit committee responsibility related to the findings of regulatory agencies or the external auditor.
DISCUSSION: The audit committee's responsibility with regard to compliance involves reviewing the findings of any examinations by regulatory agencies and any auditor observations. Compliance relates to activities that must be addressed by laws and regulations.
Answer (A) is incorrect because reporting responsibilities involve reporting to parties such as the board of directors, management, and the external auditor. Answer (C) is incorrect because the internal audit involves the structure of the organization and the audit committee itself. Answer (D) is incorrect because the external audit function is concerned with the retention of the external auditor and communication with the external auditor.

33. What part of an audit committee charter states that the audit committee is required to assist the board of directors in fulfilling its oversight responsibilities?

    A. The audit committee's purpose.

    B. The audit committee's authority.

    C. The audit committee's composition.

    D. The audit committee's responsibilities.

Answer (A) is correct. *(Publisher)*
REQUIRED: The components of the audit committee charter.
DISCUSSION: the purpose of the audit committee charter is for the audit committee to assist the board of directors in fulfilling its oversight responsibilities for the financial reporting process, the system of internal control, the audit process, and the company's process for monitoring compliance with laws and regulations and the code of conduct. The statement of purpose is typically the first paragraph of the audit committee charter because it outlines the audit committee's intended function.
Answer (B) is incorrect because the audit committee's authority involves the scope of the audit committee's power to oversee the external audit function, seek information from the issuing firm, and conduct investigations. Answer (C) is incorrect because the audit committee's composition details how many members the audit committee contains and who will be appointed to the audit committee. Answer (D) is incorrect because the audit committee responsibilities involve functions related to the financial statements and internal control.

34. Which of the following communication activities should the chief audit executive provide to the audit committee?

I. Keep the audit committee informed of emerging trends and successful practices in internal auditing.

II. Issue periodic reports to the audit committee and management summarizing results of audit activities.

III. Confirm there is effective and efficient work coordination of activities between internal and external auditors.

    A. I only.

    B. I and II only.

    C. II and III only.

    D. I, II, and III.

Answer (D) is correct. *(Publisher)*
    REQUIRED: The communication to the audit committee recommended for the Chief Audit Executive.
    DISCUSSION: A large part of the effectiveness of the chief audit executive involves communication between the internal audit activity and the audit committee. Therefore, the chief audit executive should keep the audit committee informed of emerging trends and successful practices in internal auditing, issue periodic reports to the audit committee and management summarizing results of audit activities, and confirm there is effective and efficient work coordination of activities between internal and external auditors (PA 2060).

35. Who is responsible for assisting the audit committee so that the charter, role, and activities of the committee are appropriate for it to achieve its responsibilities?

    A. Management.

    B. The board of directors.

    C. The chief audit executive.

    D. The external auditor.

Answer (C) is correct. *(Publisher)*
    REQUIRED: The responsibilities of the chief audit executive.
    DISCUSSION: The chief audit executive should assist the audit committee because the two parties have interlocking goals. Through helping the audit committee, the chief audit executive reviews the audit committee's activities and makes suggestions for improvements. This creates an environment whereby the chief audit executive is considered an advisor to the audit committee (PA 2060).
    Answer (A) is incorrect because management should not be involved in determining the audit committee's charter, role, and activities. Answer (B) is incorrect because the board of directors may not have the technical knowledge to ensure the activities of the audit committee are appropriate to achieve its responsibilities. Answer (D) is incorrect because the external auditor is not responsible for the audit committee's charter, role, and activities.

36. How often does the IIA's Standards require audit committees to undergo quality assessment reviews of the internal audit activity?

    A. Every year.

    B. Every 3 years.

    C. Every 5 years.

    D. Every 10 years.

Answer (C) is correct. *(Publisher)*
    REQUIRED: The frequency of quality assessment reviews of the internal audit to meet the IIA Standards.
    DISCUSSION: The IIA's Standards for the Professional Practice of Internal Auditing requires that quality assessment reviews of the internal audit activity be done every five years.
    Answer (A) is incorrect because the quality assessment reviews are supposed to be done every five years. Answer (B) is incorrect because the quality assessment reviews are supposed to be done every five years. Answer (D) is incorrect because the quality assessment reviews are supposed to be done every five years.

37. Which of the following is the primary purpose of the work of the internal auditors with respect to the audit committee?

- A. To review information submitted to the audit committee for completeness and accuracy.
- B. To gain a complete understanding of the organization's operations.
- C. To provide a summary report of the results or assessments on the results of the audit activities relating to the defined mission and scope of audit work.
- D. To keep the audit committee informed of emerging trends and successful practices in internal auditing.

Answer (B) is correct. *(Publisher)*
REQUIRED: The relationship between the internal auditors and the audit committee.
DISCUSSION: The IIA states that synergy among the board of directors, management, internal auditors, and external auditors is supportive of sound governance, such that the roles of internal auditors and the audit committee are mutually supportive. The work of the internal auditors is essential for the audit committee to gain a complete understanding of an organization's operations.
Answer (A) is incorrect because the review of information is a communications function of the chief audit executive and the audit committee and not the primary purpose of the internal auditor's work. Answer (C) is incorrect because summary reports involve communications between the chief audit executive and the audit committee. Answer (D) is incorrect because the chief audit executive is responsible for keeping the audit committee informed of emerging trends and successful practices in internal auditing.

38. The Sarbanes-Oxley Act applies to all of the following except

- A. A domestic corporation with widely held stock that is traded on a major stock exchange.
- B. A foreign corporation with widely held stock in the United States that is traded on a major stock exchange.
- C. A publicly traded partnership.
- D. A general partnership that practices in more than one state.

Answer (D) is correct. *(Publisher)*
REQUIRED: The entity to which the Sarbanes-Oxley Act does not apply.
DISCUSSION: The Sarbanes-Oxley Act applies to issuers of publicly traded securities subject to federal securities laws, including foreign companies. A general partnership does not issue stock, and therefore, federal securities laws do not apply.
Answer (A) is incorrect because a domestic corporation with widely held stock is required to follow federal securities laws. Answer (B) is incorrect because the stock of the foreign company is traded on a major stock exchange, and therefore required to follow federal securities laws. Answer (C) is incorrect because a publicly traded partnership is similar to a corporation because it often issues shares of stock and is traded on a major stock exchange. Therefore, a publicly traded partnership is required to follow federal securities laws.

8.3 Policies and Procedures

39. In most cases, an internal audit activity should document policies and procedures to ensure the consistency and quality of its work. The exception to this principle is directly related to

- A. Departmentation.
- B. Division of labor.
- C. Size of the internal audit activity.
- D. Authority.

Answer (C) is correct. *(CIA, adapted)*
REQUIRED: The exception to documentation of policies and procedures.
DISCUSSION: Formal administrative and technical manuals may not be needed by all internal audit entities. A small IAA may be managed informally. Its staff may be directed and controlled through daily, close supervision and written memoranda. In a large IAA, more formal and comprehensive policies and procedures are essential to guide the staff in the consistent compliance with the IAA's standards of performance (PA 2040-1).
Answer (A) is incorrect because departmentation can improve communications among team members, but sufficient direct supervision may be lacking if spans of control are large. Answer (B) is incorrect because division of labor produces highly specialized individuals, but formalized guidance is necessary for newer employees if the IAA is large. Answer (D) is incorrect because regardless of the degree of authority wielded by the chief audit executive, formal policies are needed in a large IAA.

40. Which of the following is most essential for guiding the internal audit staff in maintaining daily compliance with the internal audit activity's standards of performance?

    A. Quality program assessments.

    B. Position descriptions.

    C. Performance appraisals.

    D. Policies and procedures.

Answer (D) is correct. *(CIA, adapted)*
    REQUIRED: The item most essential for guiding the internal audit staff in maintaining daily compliance with the IAA's standards.
    DISCUSSION: The chief audit executive should establish policies and procedures to guide the IAA (Standard 2040). The form and content of written policies and procedures should be appropriate to the size and structure of the IAA and the complexity of its work. Formal administrative and technical manuals may not be needed by all IAAs. A small IAA may be managed informally. Its staff may be directed and controlled through daily, close supervision and written memoranda. In a large IAA, more formal and comprehensive policies and procedures are essential to guide the staff in the consistent compliance with the IAA's standards of performance (PA 2040-1) Quality program assessments, position descriptions, and performance appraisals do not provide specific daily guidance to the staff with respect to performance standards.

41. Policies and procedures should be established to guide the internal audit activity. Which of the following statements is false with respect to this requirement?

    A. The form and content of written policies and procedures should be appropriate to the size of the internal audit activity.

    B. All internal audit activities should have a detailed policies and procedures manual.

    C. Formal administrative and technical manuals may not be needed by all internal auditing activities.

    D. A small internal audit activity may be managed informally through close supervision and written memos.

Answer (B) is correct. *(CIA, adapted)*
    REQUIRED: The false statement about written policies and procedures to guide the IAA.
    DISCUSSION: The form and content of written policies and procedures should be appropriate to the size and structure of the IAA and the complexity of its work. A small IAA may be managed informally (PA 2040-1).
    Answer (A) is incorrect because the form and content of written policies and procedures should be appropriate to the size of the IAA. Answer (C) is incorrect because formal administrative and technical manuals may not be needed by all IAAs. Answer (D) is incorrect because a small IAA may be managed informally through close supervision and written memos.

42. Which of the items below most likely reflects differences between the policies of a relatively large and a relatively small internal audit activity? The policies for the large activity should

    A. Define the scope and status of internal auditing.

    B. Contain the authority to carry out engagements.

    C. Be specific as to activities to be carried out.

    D. Be in considerable detail.

Answer (D) is correct. *(CIA, adapted)*
    REQUIRED: The item that most likely reflects differences between the policies of relatively large and small IAAs.
    DISCUSSION: The chief audit executive should establish policies and procedures to guide the IAA (Standard 2040). The form and content of written policies and procedures should be appropriate to the size and structure of the IAA and the complexity of its work. Formal administrative and technical manuals may not be needed by all IAAs. A small IAA may be managed informally. Its staff may be directed and controlled through daily, close supervision and written memoranda. In a large IAA, more formal and comprehensive policies and procedures are essential to guide the staff in the consistent compliance with the IAA's standards of performance (PA 2040-1).
    Answer (A) is incorrect because the scope and status of internal auditing are covered in the charter. Answer (B) is incorrect because the authority to carry out engagements is covered in the charter. Answer (C) is incorrect because whether the IAA is large or small, it must have policies that specifically state its functions.

43. Policies and procedures relative to managing the internal audit activity should

    A. Ensure compliance with its performance standards.

    B. Give consideration to its structure and the complexity of the work performed.

    C. Result in consistent job performance.

    D. Prescribe the format and distribution of engagement communications and the classification of engagement observations.

Answer (B) is correct.   *(CIA, adapted)*
REQUIRED: The true statement about policies and procedures for managing the IAA.
DISCUSSION: The CAE should establish policies and procedures to guide the IAA (Standard 2040). The form and content of written policies and procedures should be appropriate to the size and structure of the IAA and the complexity of its work (PA 2040-1).
Answer (A) is incorrect because engagements should be properly supervised to ensure objectives are achieved, quality is assured, and staff is developed (Standard 2340). Compliance with performance standards is a quality issue, and ensuring quality requires more than establishing policies and procedures. Answer (C) is incorrect because whether policies and procedures are required depends on the size and structure of the IAA. Moreover, these measures alone do not ensure consistent performance. Answer (D) is incorrect because prescribing the format and distribution of engagement communications and the classification of engagement observations is a discretionary measure that depends on the size and structure of the IAA and the complexity of work performed.

44. The chief audit executive is responsible for establishing a program to develop the human resources of the internal audit activity. This program should include

    A. Continuing educational opportunities and performance appraisals.

    B. Counseling and an established career path.

    C. An established training plan and a charter.

    D. Job descriptions and competitive salary increases.

Answer (A) is correct.   *(CIA, adapted)*
REQUIRED: The CAE's responsibilities for the IAA's human resource development program.
DISCUSSION: The CAE should establish a program for selecting and developing the human resources of the IAA. The program should provide for developing written job descriptions for each level of the staff, selecting qualified and competent individuals, training and providing continuing educational opportunities for each internal auditor, appraising each internal auditor's performance at least annually, and providing counsel to internal auditors on their performance and professional development (PA 2030-1).
Answer (B) is incorrect because counseling is an attribute of the program, but an established career path is not. Answer (C) is incorrect because training is part of the development program, but a charter is not specified. Answer (D) is incorrect because written job descriptions are necessary, but salary increases are not.

45. The capabilities of individual staff members are key features in the effectiveness of an internal audit activity. What is the primary consideration used when staffing an internal audit activity?

    A. Background checks.

    B. Job descriptions.

    C. Continuing education.

    D. Organizational orientation.

Answer (B) is correct.   *(CIA, adapted)*
REQUIRED: The primary consideration used when staffing an IAA.
DISCUSSION: The program for selecting and developing the human resources of the IAA should provide for developing written job descriptions for each level of the staff, selecting qualified and competent individuals, training and providing continuing educational opportunities for each internal auditor, appraising each internal auditor's performance at least annually, and providing counsel to internal auditors on their performance and professional development (PA 2030-1). Properly formulated job descriptions provide a basis for identifying job qualifications (including training and experience).
Answer (A) is incorrect because background checks help assure that statements made by prospective employees are accurate. However, they are not the primary requisite. Answer (C) is incorrect because continuing education occurs after the proper people are hired. Answer (D) is incorrect because a thorough orientation helps the new employee become productive more rapidly. However, it will not compensate for hiring the wrong person.

46. Having been given the task of developing a performance appraisal system for evaluating the performance of a large internal auditing staff, you should

- A. Provide for an explanation of the appraisal criteria and methods at the time the appraisal results are discussed with the internal auditor.
- B. Provide general information concerning the frequency of evaluations and the way evaluations will be performed without specifying their timing and uses.
- C. Provide primarily for the evaluation of criteria such as diligence, initiative, and tact.
- D. Provide primarily for the evaluation of specific accomplishments directly related to the performance of the engagement work program.

Answer (D) is correct. *(CIA, adapted)*
 REQUIRED: The characteristic of a performance appraisal system.
 DISCUSSION: A human resources selection and development program should be established that provides for appraising each internal auditor's performance at least annually (PA 2030-1). An effective evaluation system should be based on relevant, reliable, and objective measures closely related to actual job performance (e.g., execution of the engagement work program).
 Answer (A) is incorrect because the personnel whose performance is being appraised should be notified of the criteria and methods at the time they begin employment. Answer (B) is incorrect because the timing and uses of evaluations are important matters that should be clearly communicated. Answer (C) is incorrect because the criteria listed are traits, not accomplishments. Although traits are important, an evaluation system for internal audit performance should primarily focus on specific accomplishments.

47. Which of the following aspects of evaluating the performance of staff members is considered to be a violation of good human resources management techniques?

- A. The evaluator should justify very high and very low evaluations because of their impact on the employee.
- B. Evaluations should be made annually or more frequently to provide the employee feedback about competence.
- C. The first evaluation should be made shortly after commencing work to serve as an early guide to the new employee.
- D. Because there are so many employees whose performance is completely satisfactory, it is preferable to use standard evaluation comments.

Answer (D) is correct. *(CIA, adapted)*
 REQUIRED: The aspect of evaluating the performance of staff members considered a violation of good management techniques.
 DISCUSSION: The CAE should establish a program for selecting and developing the human resources of the IAA. The program should provide for developing written job descriptions for each level of the staff, selecting qualified and competent individuals, training and providing continuing educational opportunities for each internal auditor, appraising each internal auditor's performance at least annually, and providing counsel to internal auditors on their performance and professional development (PA 2030-1). Thus, individualized attention is clearly desirable.
 Answer (A) is incorrect because a very high or very low evaluation has behavioral and other implications that require special consideration. Answer (B) is incorrect because evaluations should be made at least annually. Answer (C) is incorrect because prompt feedback serves to provide the employee with early advice as to the acceptability of performed work.

48. In most organizations, the rapidly expanding scope of internal auditing responsibilities requires continual training. What is the main purpose of such a training program?

- A. To comply with continuing education requirements of professional organizations.
- B. To use slack periods in engagement scheduling.
- C. To help individuals to achieve personal career goals.
- D. To achieve both individual and organizational goals.

Answer (D) is correct. *(CIA, adapted)*
 REQUIRED: The main purpose of a training program.
 DISCUSSION: By being informed and up-to-date, internal auditors are better prepared to reach their personal goals. In addition, IAA responsibilities are more readily discharged by auditors having the required knowledge, skills, and other competencies.
 Answer (A) is incorrect because the CAE should establish a program for selecting and developing human resources, but compliance with continuing education requirements of professional organizations is not the primary purpose. Answer (B) is incorrect because training can be conducted during slack periods, but this is not the primary objective. Answer (C) is incorrect because both personal and IAA goals should be achieved.

49. The key factor in the success of an internal audit activity's human resources program is

    A. An informal program for developing and counseling staff.

    B. A compensation plan based on years of experience.

    C. A well-developed set of selection criteria.

    D. A program for recognizing the special interests of individual staff members.

Answer (C) is correct. *(CIA, adapted)*
    REQUIRED: The key factor in the success of an IAA's human resources program.
    DISCUSSION: Internal auditors should be qualified and competent. Because the selection of a superior staff is dependent on the ability to evaluate applicants, selection criteria must be well-developed. Appropriate questions and forms should be prepared in advance to evaluate, among other things, the applicant's technical qualifications, educational background, personal appearance, ability to communicate, maturity, persuasiveness, self-confidence, intelligence, motivation, and potential to contribute to the organization.
    Answer (A) is incorrect because the human resources program should be formal. Answer (B) is incorrect because the quality of the human resources is more significant than compensation. Answer (D) is incorrect because the quality of the human resources is more significant than special interests of the staff.

50. Which of the following statements most accurately reflects the chief audit executive's responsibilities for human resources management and development?

    A. The CAE is responsible for selecting qualified individuals but has no explicit responsibility for providing ongoing educational opportunities for the internal auditor.

    B. The CAE is responsible for performing an annual review of each internal auditor's performance but has no explicit responsibility for counseling internal auditors on their performance and professional development.

    C. The CAE is responsible for selecting qualified individuals but has no explicit responsibility for the preparation of job descriptions.

    D. The CAE is responsible for developing formal job descriptions for the staff but has no explicit responsibility for administering the organization's compensation program.

Answer (D) is correct. *(CIA, adapted)*
    REQUIRED: The CAE's responsibilities for human resources management and development.
    DISCUSSION: The CAE should establish a program for selecting and developing the human resources of the IAA. The program should provide for developing written job descriptions for each level of the staff, selecting qualified and competent individuals, training and providing continuing educational opportunities for each internal auditor, appraising each internal auditor's performance at least annually, and providing counsel to internal auditors on their performance and professional development (PA 2030-1). Responsibility for administering the organization's compensation program normally resides in the human resources (personnel) area.
    Answer (A) is incorrect because the CAE has responsibility for providing ongoing educational opportunities for the internal auditor. Answer (B) is incorrect because the CAE has responsibility for counseling internal auditors on their performance and professional development. Answer (C) is incorrect because the CAE has responsibility for the preparation of job descriptions.

51. An external auditor of a large organization subject to U.S. Securities and Exchange Commission (SEC) requirements also provides the client with internal audit services. Under rule amendments adopted in 2001 (and without regard to transitional provisions), the external auditor's independence is impaired with respect to the audit client by providing internal audit services if

A. Management of the audit client determines the scope of internal audit activities to be performed by the accountant.

B. The amount of internal audit services exceeds 40% of the total hours expended by the client on such activities in a fiscal year.

C. Management of the audit client does not rely on the external auditor's work to determine the adequacy of its controls.

D. The client has less than $200 million in total assets.

Answer (B) is correct. *(Publisher)*
REQUIRED: The circumstance in which an external auditor's provision of internal services impairs independence with respect to an audit client.
DISCUSSION: Under SEC rules adopted in 2001, an external auditor's independence is impaired by providing internal audit services to an audit client if the external auditor provides internal audit services in an amount greater than 40% of the total hours expended on the audit client's internal audit activities in any one fiscal year, unless the audit client has less than $200 million in total assets. (For purposes of this paragraph, the term internal audit services does not include operational internal audit services unrelated to the internal accounting controls, financial systems, or financial statements.) To determine the 40% limitation, all hours allocated to internal audit services based on a full-time-equivalent calculation should be included. This calculation should be made at the beginning of the audit period based on planned internal audit activities, but the SEC rules apply to actual hours and activities performed (PA 2030-2).
Answer (A) is incorrect because the provision of any internal audit services impairs independence unless the audit client's management determines the scope, risk, and frequency of internal audit activities, including those to be performed by the accountant. Answer (C) is incorrect because the provision of any internal audit services impairs independence unless the audit client's management does not rely on the accountant's work as the primary basis for determining the adequacy of its internal controls. Answer (D) is incorrect because an exemption is allowed if the client has less than $200 million in total assets.

52. According to Specific Attribute Standard 1340, disclosure should be made to senior management and the board whenever

A. The internal audit activity does not comply with the Standards.

B. The internal auditors do not comply with the Code of Ethics.

C. The internal audit activity does not comply with the Standards, or the internal auditors do not comply with the Code of Ethics.

D. Noncompliance with the Standards or the Code of Ethics affects the overall operation of the internal audit activity.

Answer (D) is correct. *(Publisher)*
REQUIRED: The circumstance in which disclosure should be made to senior management and the board.
DISCUSSION: Although the internal audit activity should achieve full compliance with the Standards and internal auditors with the Code of Ethics, there may be instances in which full compliance is not achieved. When noncompliance affects the overall scope or operation of the internal audit activity, disclosure should be made to senior management and the board (Standard 1340).

53. Internal auditors may report that their activities are conducted in accordance with the Standards. They may use this statement only if

A. They demonstrate compliance with the Standards.

B. An independent external assessment of the internal audit activity is conducted annually.

C. Senior management or the board is accountable for implementing a quality program.

D. External assessments of the internal audit activity are made by the external auditors.

Answer (A) is correct. *(Publisher)*
REQUIRED: The condition permitting internal auditors to report that their activities are in accordance with the Standards.
DISCUSSION: Standard 1330 states internal auditors are encouraged to report that their activities are "conducted in accordance with the Standards for the Professional Practice of Internal Auditing." However, internal auditors may use the statement only if assessments of the quality improvement program demonstrate that the internal audit activity is in compliance with the Standards (Standard 1330-1). Internal auditors are encouraged to use the compliance phrase in formal communications with stakeholder groups to demonstrate commitment to quality and to provide assurance to those who rely on the results of such communications (PA 1330-1).
Answer (B) is incorrect because an independent external assessment of the IAA should be conducted at least once every 5 years (Standard 1330-1). Answer (C) is incorrect because the CAE is accountable for implementing a quality program, which should include supervision, periodic internal assessment and ongoing monitoring, and periodic external assessment (PA 1310-1). Answer (D) is incorrect because quality assurance reviews ordinarily should not be performed by the organization's external audit firm, except when such reviews are made under a legislative mandate (PA 1312-1).

STUDY UNIT NINE
MANAGING THE INTERNAL AUDITING ACTIVITY II

(13 pages of outline)

This is the second study unit covering management of the internal audit activity. The first subunit concerns the relationship of the IAA with external providers of assurance and consulting services, including regulators. The second subunit concerns the IAA's quality assurance and improvement program. It addresses internal and external assessments, including benchmarking.

9.1 COORDINATION

1.   Coordination issues include avoiding duplication of effort, work done for external providers and assessment of their performance, and other matters relevant to coordination of efforts. These issues are addressed in one Specific Performance Standard and in two Practice Advisories.

2050   **Coordination** — *The chief audit executive should share information and coordinate activities with other internal and external providers of relevant assurance and consulting services to ensure proper coverage and minimize duplication of efforts.*

NOTE: This Standard applies not only to external auditors but also to other "providers" such as regulatory bodies (e.g., governmental auditors) and certain of the organization's other subunits (e.g., a health and safety department).

Practice Advisory 2050-1: Coordination

1.   *Internal and external auditing work should be coordinated to ensure adequate audit coverage and to minimize duplicate efforts. The scope of internal auditing work encompasses a systematic, disciplined approach to evaluate and improve the effectiveness of risk management, control, and governance processes. The scope of internal auditing work is described within Section 2100 of the Standards. On the other hand, the external auditors' ordinary examination is designed to obtain sufficient evidential matter to support an opinion on the overall fairness of the annual financial statements. The scope of the work of external auditors is determined by their professional standards, and they are responsible for judging the adequacy of procedures performed and evidence obtained for purposes of expressing their opinion on the annual financial statements.*

2.   *Oversight of the work of external auditors, including coordination with the internal audit activity, is generally the responsibility of the board. Actual coordination should be the responsibility of the chief audit executive. The chief audit executive will require the support of the board to achieve effective coordination of audit work.*

3.   *In coordinating the work of internal auditors with the work of external auditors, the chief audit executive should ensure that work to be performed by internal auditors in fulfillment of Section 2100 of the Standards does not duplicate the work of external auditors that can be relied on for purposes of internal auditing coverage. To the extent that professional and organizational reporting responsibilities allow, internal auditors should conduct engagements in a manner that allows for maximum audit coordination and efficiency.*

4.   *The chief audit executive may agree to perform work for external auditors in connection with their annual audit of the financial statements. Work performed by internal auditors to assist external auditors in fulfilling their responsibility is subject to all relevant provisions of the Standards for the Professional Practice of Internal Auditing.*

5. The chief audit executive should make regular evaluations of the coordination between internal and external auditors. Such evaluations may also include assessments of the overall efficiency and effectiveness of internal and external auditing functions, including aggregate audit cost.

6. In exercising its oversight role, the board may request the chief audit executive to assess the performance of external auditors. Such assessments should ordinarily be made in the context of the chief audit executive's role of coordinating internal and external auditing activities, and should extend to other performance matters only at the specific request of senior management or the board. Assessments of the performance of external auditors should be based on sufficient information to support the conclusions reached. Assessments of the external auditors' performance with respect to the coordination of internal and external auditing activities should reflect the criteria described in this Practice Advisory.

7. Assessments of the performance of external auditors extending to matters beyond coordination with the internal auditors may address additional factors, such as:

    - Professional knowledge and experience.
    - Knowledge of the organization's industry.
    - Independence.
    - Availability of specialized services.
    - Anticipation of and responsiveness to the needs of the organization.
    - Reasonable continuity of key engagement personnel.
    - Maintenance of appropriate working relationships.
    - Achievement of contract commitments.
    - Delivery of overall value to the organization.

8. The chief audit executive should communicate the results of evaluations of coordination between internal and external auditors to senior management and the board along with, as appropriate, any relevant comments about the performance of external auditors.

9. External auditors may be required by their professional standards to ensure that certain matters are communicated to the board. The chief audit executive should communicate with external auditors regarding these matters so as to have an understanding of the issues. These matters may include:

    - Issues that may affect the independence of the external auditors.
    - Significant control weaknesses.
    - Errors and irregularities.
    - Illegal acts.
    - Management judgments and accounting estimates.
    - Significant audit adjustments.
    - Disagreements with management.
    - Difficulties encountered in performing the audit.

10. Coordination of audit efforts involves periodic meetings to discuss matters of mutual interest.

    - **Audit Coverage**. Planned audit activities of internal and external auditors should be discussed to assure that audit coverage is coordinated and duplicate efforts are minimized. Sufficient meetings should be scheduled during the audit process to assure coordination of audit work and efficient and timely completion of audit activities, and to determine whether observations and recommendations from work performed to date require that the scope of planned work be adjusted.

- ● **Access to each other's audit programs and working papers**. Access to the external auditors' programs and working papers may be important in order for internal auditors to be satisfied as to the propriety for internal audit purposes of relying on the external auditors' work. Such access carries with it the responsibility for internal auditors to respect the confidentiality of those programs and working papers. Similarly, access to the internal auditors' programs and working papers should be given to external auditors in order for external auditors to be satisfied as to the propriety, for external audit purposes, of relying on the internal auditors' work.

- ● **Exchange of audit reports and management letters**. Internal audit final communications, management's responses to those communications, and subsequent internal audit activity follow-up reviews should be made available to external auditors. These communications assist external auditors in determining and adjusting the scope of work. In addition, the internal auditors need access to the external auditors' management letters. Matters discussed in management letters assist internal auditors in planning the areas to emphasize in future internal audit work. After review of management letters and initiation of any needed corrective action by appropriate members of management and the board, the chief audit executive should ensure that appropriate follow-up and corrective action have been taken.

- ● **Common understanding of audit techniques, methods, and terminology**. First, the chief audit executive should understand the scope of work planned by external auditors and should be satisfied that the external auditors' planned work, in conjunction with the internal auditors' planned work, satisfies the requirements of Section 2100 of the Standards. Such satisfaction requires an understanding of the level of materiality used by external auditors for planning and the nature and extent of the external auditors' planned procedures.

  Second, the chief audit executive should ensure that the external auditors' techniques, methods, and terminology are sufficiently understood by internal auditors to enable the chief audit executive to (1) coordinate internal and external auditing work; (2) evaluate, for purposes of reliance, the external auditors' work; and (3) ensure that internal auditors who are to perform work to fulfill the external auditors' objectives can communicate effectively with external auditors.

  Finally, the chief audit executive should provide sufficient information to enable external auditors to understand the internal auditors' techniques, methods, and terminology to facilitate reliance by external auditors on work performed using such techniques, methods, and terminology. It may be more efficient for internal and external auditors to use similar techniques, methods, and terminology to effectively coordinate their work and to rely on the work of one another.

Practice Advisory 2050-2: Acquisition of External Audit Services

1. The internal auditor's participation in the selection, evaluation, or retention of the organization's external auditors may vary from no role in the process, to advising management or the audit committee, assistance or participation in the process, management of the process, or auditing the process. Since IIA Standards require internal auditors to "share information and coordinate activities with other internal and external providers of relevant assurance and consulting services," it is advisable for internal auditors to have some role or involvement in the selection or retention of the external auditors and in the definition of scope of work.

2.   A board or audit committee approved policy can facilitate the periodic request for external audit services and position such exercises as normal business activities so that the present service providers do not view a decision to request proposals as a signal that the organization is dissatisfied with present services. If a specific policy does not exist, the internal auditor should determine if such services are subject to any other existing procurement policies of the organization. In the absence of appropriate policies, the internal auditor should consider facilitating development of appropriate policies.

3.   Appropriate policies for selection or retention of external audit services should consider addressing the following attributes:

- Board or audit committee approval of the policy
- Nature and type of services covered by the policy
- Duration of contract, frequency of the formal request for services and/or determination to retain the existing service providers
- Participants or members of the selection and evaluation team
- Any critical or primary criteria that should be considered in the evaluation
- Limitations on service fees and procedures for approving exceptions to the policy
- Regulatory or other governing requirements unique to specific industries or countries

4.   A board policy may also address the acquisition of services other than just financial statement audits that may be offered by external audit firms. Those may include:

- Tax services
- Consulting and other non-audit services
- Internal audit outsourcing and/or co-sourcing services (see Practice Advisory 2030-2 SEC External Auditor Independence Requirements for Providing Internal Audit Services for more specific guidance)
- Other outsourced or co-sourced services
- Special services, such as agreed-upon service engagements
- Valuation, appraisal, and actuarial services
- Temporary services such as recruiting, bookkeeping, technology services
- Legal services provided by external audit firms

5.   Appropriate documentation should be retained concerning a periodic, formal decision to retain the existing service providers and forego or delay requests to other potential service providers.

6.   A plan should be developed for the selection process that identifies the selection committee participants, key deliverables and target dates for each phase of the process, candidates from whom to request proposals, nature and extent of services to be requested, and how information will be communicated to potential candidates. Often, at the start of the selection process, an organization may conduct a comprehensive meeting with all potential candidates in which management makes a formal presentation to cover pertinent information for the service request and supplies the candidates with a formal information package or report describing the services being requested. This general meeting can be followed with individual, onsite meetings for each candidate and include appropriate management representatives. Other combinations of meetings and information packages are also practical or appropriate for special situations.

7. *A two-phased request may be necessary to facilitate a screening process to narrow or reduce the field of potential service providers to a reasonable number of final candidates. Initial information requests should be focused on obtaining appropriate statements of qualifications, including background and other general information about the potential candidates. Information should be obtained, such as history of the firm, size of the firm, resources available, firm philosophy and audit approach, special expertise, local or servicing office that would handle the engagement, related industry experience, and biographies of key team members that would be assigned to the engagement.*

8. *After the initial screening process, those candidates selected to advance to the next phase should be sent a second request for information that provides more specifics about the services requested. A detailed service request that itemizes deliverables expected and key target dates should be developed. Candidates should be requested to provide specific details, including pricing for the services. A timetable for the remainder of the process can be supplied that schedules dates for delivery of the additional information requested, meetings for presentations by the candidates to the selection committee, and a date for the final selection. The detailed service request should be specific for each of the services requested and should indicate whether the services may be awarded as one package or split between multiple candidates.*

9. *It may be appropriate to compare and summarize the attributes of the candidates by key criteria and provide it in a format that facilitates consistent evaluation of all the service providers. Questions may be supplied that stimulate thought processes and focus the evaluation on key criteria. An evaluation form can facilitate collection of each participant's analysis and conclusions about each of the candidates. Background information, such as, the organization's past history with the various candidates, type of services previously provided, and fee history, can provide the selection team with an appropriate perspective to begin the evaluation.*

10. *Service arrangements for external audit engagements should be documented in a written agreement and signed by both the service provider and the engagement client.*

11. *If the selection process results in a change in the service providers, appropriate transition plans should be developed to facilitate a smooth and orderly change. Notifications to appropriate parties, including regulatory bodies, if required, should be communicated in a timely manner.*

12. *Internal auditors should determine how the organization monitors ongoing service activities from external auditors. Compliance with the terms of service contracts and other agreements should be assessed on a periodic basis. Assessment of the independence of the external auditors should include internal audit participation, be performed at least annually, and be communicated to the audit committee. Organizations subject to SEC reporting requirements should see Practice Advisory 2030-2 SEC External Auditor Independence Requirements for Providing Internal Audit Services for related guidance.*

2. Stop and review! You have completed the outline for this subunit. Study multiple-choice questions 1 through 9 beginning on page 295.

9.2 QUALITY ASSURANCE

1. This program should provide reasonable assurance that the IAA's work conforms with applicable standards. The relevant pronouncements include one General Attribute Standard, six Specific Attribute Standards, and five Practice Advisories.

1300   ***Quality Assurance and Improvement Programs*** *— The chief audit executive should develop and maintain a quality assurance and improvement program that covers all aspects of the internal audit activity and continuously monitors its effectiveness. The program should be designed to help the internal auditing activity add value and improve the organization's operations and to provide assurance that the internal audit activity is in conformity with the Standards and the Code of Ethics.*

1310   ***Quality Program Assessments*** *— The internal audit activity should adopt a process to monitor and assess the overall effectiveness of the quality program. The process should include both internal and external assessments.*

Practice Advisory 1310-1: Quality Program Assessments

1. ***Implementing Quality Programs*** *— The chief audit executive (CAE) should be accountable for implementing processes that are designed to provide reasonable assurance to the various stakeholders of the internal audit activity that it:*

    - *Performs in accordance with its charter, which should be consistent with the Standards for the Professional Practice of Internal Auditing and Code of Ethics,*
    - *Operates in an effective and efficient manner, and*
    - *Is perceived by those stakeholders as adding value and improving the organization's operations.*

    These processes should include appropriate supervision, periodic internal assessment and ongoing monitoring of quality assurance, and periodic external assessments.

2. ***Monitoring Quality Programs*** *— Monitoring should include ongoing measurements and analyses of performance metrics, e.g., cycle time and recommendations accepted.*

3. ***Assessing Quality Programs*** *— Assessments should evaluate and conclude on the quality of the internal audit activity and lead to recommendations for appropriate improvements. Assessments of quality programs should include evaluation of:*

    - *Compliance with the Standards and Code of Ethics,*
    - *Adequacy of the internal audit activity's charter, goals, objectives, policies, and procedures,*
    - *Contribution to the organization's risk management, governance, and control processes,*
    - *Contribution to the organization's risk management, governance, and control processes,*
    - *Compliance with applicable laws, regulations, and government or industry standards,*
    - *Effectiveness of continuous improvement activities and adoption of best practices, and*
    - *Whether the auditing activity adds value and improves the organization's operations.*

4. ***Continuous Improvement*** — All quality improvement efforts should include a communication process designed to facilitate appropriate modification of resources, technology, processes, and procedures as indicated by monitoring and assessment activities.

5. ***Communicating Results*** — To provide accountability, the CAE should share the results of external, and, as appropriate, internal quality program assessments with the various stakeholders of the activity, such as senior management, the board, and external auditors.

1311   ***Internal Assessments*** — Internal assessments should include:

- Ongoing reviews of the performance of the internal audit activity; and
- Periodic reviews performed through self-assessment or by other persons within the organization, with knowledge of internal auditing practices and the Standards.

Practice Advisory 1311-1: Internal Assessments

1. ***Ongoing Reviews*** — Ongoing assessments may be conducted through

- Engagement supervision as described in Practice Advisory 2340-1 Engagement Supervision,
- Checklists and other means to provide assurance that processes adopted by the audit activity (e.g., in an audit and procedures manual) are being followed,
- Feedback from audit customers and other stakeholders,
- Analyses of performance metrics (e.g., cycle time and recommendations accepted), and
- Project budgets, timekeeping systems, audit plan completion, cost recoveries, and so forth.

2. Conclusions should be developed as to the quality of ongoing performance, and follow-up action should be taken to assure appropriate improvements are implemented.

3. ***Periodic Reviews*** — Periodic assessments should be designed to assess compliance with the activity's charter, the Standards for the Professional Practice of Internal Auditing, the Code of Ethics, and the efficiency and effectiveness of the activity in meeting the needs of its various stakeholders. The IIA's Quality Assessment Manual includes guidance and tools for internal reviews.

4. Periodic assessments may:

- Include more in-depth interviews and surveys of stakeholder groups,
- Be performed by members of the internal audit activity (self-assessment),
- Be performed by CIAs, or other competent audit professionals, currently assigned elsewhere in the organization,
- Encompass a combination of self-assessment and preparation of materials subsequently reviewed by CIAs, or other competent audit professionals, from elsewhere in the organization, and
- Include benchmarking of the internal audit activity's practices and performance metrics against relevant best practices of the internal auditing profession.

5. Conclusions should be developed as to the quality of performance and appropriate action initiated to achieve improvements and conformity to the Standards, as necessary.

6.   The chief audit executive (CAE) should establish a structure for reporting results of periodic reviews that maintains appropriate credibility and objectivity. Generally, those assigned responsibility for conducting ongoing and periodic reviews should report to the CAE while performing the reviews and should communicate their results directly to the CAE.

7.   **Communicating Results** — The CAE should share the results of internal assessments and necessary action plans with appropriate persons outside the activity, such as senior management, the board, and external auditors.

1312   **External Assessments** — External assessments, such as quality assurance reviews, should be conducted at least once every five years by a qualified, independent reviewer or review team from outside the organization.

Practice Advisory 1312-1: External Assessments

1.   **General Considerations** — External assessments of an internal audit activity should appraise and express an opinion as to the internal audit activity's compliance with the Standards for the Professional Practice of Internal Auditing and, as appropriate, should include recommendations for improvement. These reviews can have considerable value to the chief audit executive (CAE) and other members of the internal audit activity. Only qualified persons (paragraph 4 below) should perform such reviews.

2.   An external assessment is required within five years of January 1, 2002. Earlier adoption of the new Standard requiring an external review is highly recommended. Organizations that have had external reviews are encouraged to have their next external review within five years of their last review.

3.   On completion of the review, a formal communication should be provided to the board (as defined in the Glossary to the Standards) and to senior management.

4.   **Qualifications for External Reviewers** — External reviewers, including those who validate self-assessments (paragraph 13 below), should be independent of the organization and of the internal audit activity. The review team should consist of individuals who are competent in the professional practice of internal auditing and the external assessment process. To be considered as external assessment candidates, qualified individuals could include IIA quality assurance reviewers, regulatory examiners, consultants, external auditors, other professional service providers, and internal auditors from outside the organization.

5.   **Independence** — The organization that is performing the external assessment, the members of the review team, and any other individuals who participate in the assessment should be free from any obligation to, or interest in, the organization that is the subject of the review or its personnel. Individuals who are in another department of that organization, although organizationally separate from the internal audit activity, are not considered independent for purposes of conducting an external assessment.

6.   Reciprocal peer review arrangements between three or more organizations can be structured in a manner that alleviates independence concerns. Reciprocal peer reviews between two organizations generally should not be performed.

7.   External assessments should be performed by qualified individuals who are independent of the organization and who do not have either a real or apparent conflict of interest. "Independent of the organization" means not a part of, or under the control of, the organization to which the internal auditing activity belongs. In the selection of an external reviewer, consideration should be given to a possible real or apparent conflict of interest that the reviewer may have due to present or past relationships with the organization or its internal auditing activity.

8. **_Integrity and Objectivity_** — *Integrity requires the review team to be honest and candid within the constraints of confidentiality. Service and the public trust should not be subordinated to personal gain and advantage. Objectivity is a state of mind and a quality that lends value to a review team's services. The principle of objectivity imposes the obligation to be impartial, intellectually honest, and free of conflicts of interest.*

9. **_Competence_** — *Performing and communicating the results of an external assessment requires the exercise of professional judgment. Accordingly, an individual serving as a reviewer should:*

   - *Be a competent, certified audit professional, e.g., CIA, CPA, CA, or CISA, who possesses current knowledge of the Standards.*
   - *Be well versed in the best practices of the profession.*
   - *Have at least three years of recent experience in the practice of internal auditing at a management level.*

10. *The review team should include members with information technology expertise and relevant industry experience. Individuals with expertise in other specialized areas may assist the external review team. For example, statistical sampling specialists or experts in control self-assessment may participate in certain segments of the review.*

11. **_Approval by Management and the Board_** — *The CAE should involve senior management and the board in the selection process for an external reviewer and obtain their approval.*

12. **_Scope of External Assessments_** — *The external assessment should consist of a broad scope of coverage that includes the following elements of the internal audit activity:*

   - *Compliance with the Standards, The IIA's Code of Ethics, and the internal audit activity's charter, plans, policies, procedures, practices, and applicable legislative and regulatory requirements.*
   - *The expectations of the internal audit activity expressed by the board, executive management and operational managers.*
   - *The integration of the internal audit activity into the organization's governance process, including the attendant relationships between and among the key groups involved in that process.*
   - *The tools and techniques employed by the internal audit activity.*
   - *The mix of knowledge, experience, and disciplines within the staff, including staff focus on process improvement.*
   - *The determination whether the audit activity adds value and improves the organization's operations.*

13. **_Self-Assessment with Independent Validation_** — *An alternative process is for the CAE to undertake a self-assessment with independent external validation with the following features:*

   - *A comprehensive and fully documented self-assessment process.*
   - *An independent on-site validation by a qualified reviewer (paragraph 4 above).*
   - *Economical time and resource requirements.*

14. *A team under the direction of the CAE should perform the self-assessment process. The IIA's Quality Assessment Manual contains an example of the process, including guidance and tools for the self-assessment. A qualified, independent reviewer should perform limited tests of the self-assessment so as to validate the results and express an opinion about the indicated level of the activity's conformity to the Standards.*

15. *Communicating the results of the self-assessment should follow the process outlined below (paragraph 17).*

16. While a full external review achieves maximum benefit for the activity and should be included in the activity's quality program, the self-assessment with independent validation provides an alternative means of complying with this Standard 1312.

17. **_Communicating Results_** — The preliminary results of the review should be discussed with the CAE during and at the conclusion of the assessment process. Final results should be communicated to the CAE or other official who authorized the review for the organization.

18. The communication should include the following:

- An opinion on the internal audit activity's compliance with the Standards based on a structured rating process. The term "compliance" means that the practices of the internal audit activity, taken as a whole, satisfy the requirements of the Standards. Similarly, "noncompliance" means that the impact and severity of the deficiency in the practices of the internal audit activity are so significant that it impairs the internal audit activity's ability to discharge its responsibilities. The expression of an opinion on the results of the external assessment requires the application of sound business judgment, integrity, and due professional care.
- An assessment and evaluation of the use of best practices, both those observed during the assessment and others potentially applicable to the activity.
- Recommendations for improvement, where appropriate.
- Responses from the CAE that include an action plan and implementation dates.

19. The CAE should communicate the results of the review and necessary action plan to senior management, as appropriate, and to the board.

1320   **_Reporting on the Quality Program_** — The chief audit executive should communicate the results of external assessments to the board.

Practice Advisory 1320-1: Reporting on the Quality Program

1.   Upon completion of an external assessment, the review team should issue a formal report containing an opinion on the internal audit activity's compliance with the Standards. The report should also address compliance with the internal audit activity's charter and other applicable standards and include appropriate recommendations for improvement. The report should be addressed to the person or organization requesting the assessment. The chief audit executive should prepare a written action plan in response to the significant comments and recommendations contained in the report of external assessment. Appropriate follow-up is also the chief audit executive's responsibility.

2.   The evaluation of compliance with the Standards is a critical component of an external assessment. The review team should acknowledge the Standards in order to evaluate and opine on the internal audit activity's compliance. However, as noted in Practice Advisory 1310-1, there are additional criteria that should be considered in evaluating the performance of an internal audit activity.

1330 <u>*Use of "Conducted in Accordance with the Standards"*</u> — *Internal auditors are encouraged to report that their activities are "conducted in accordance with the Standards for the Professional Practice of Internal Auditing." However, internal auditors may use the statement only if assessments of the quality improvement program demonstrate that the internal audit activity is in compliance with the Standards.*

<u>*Practice Advisory 1330-1: Use of "Conducted in Accordance with the Standards"*</u>

1. <u>*General Considerations*</u> — *External and internal assessments of an internal audit activity should be performed to appraise and express an opinion as to the internal audit activity's compliance with the Standards for the Professional Practice of Internal Auditing and, as appropriate, should include recommendations for improvement. These reviews can have considerable value to the organization's governance processes, the chief audit executive (CAE), and other members of the internal audit activity. Only qualified persons should perform these reviews.*

2. *An external assessment is required within five years of January 1, 2002. Earlier adoption of the new Standard requiring an external review is highly recommended. Organizations that have had external reviews are encouraged to have their next external review within five years of their last review.*

3. <u>*Use of Compliance Phrase*</u> — *Use of the compliance phrase requires periodic assessments of the quality improvement program and a conclusion that the internal audit activity is in compliance with the **Standards**. Instances of noncompliance that impact the overall scope or operation of the internal audit activity, including failure to obtain an **external** assessment by January 1, 2007, should be disclosed to senior management and the board.*

4. *Any significant instances of non-compliance should be remedied before the internal audit activity uses the compliance phrase. Noncompliance that has been disclosed by a quality assessment (internal or external) or covered by related recommendations should be adequately remedied and the remedial actions should be reported and documented to the relevant assessor(s), as well as to senior management and the board, prior to the internal audit activity's use of the compliance phrase.*

1340 <u>*Disclosure of Noncompliance*</u> — *Although the internal audit activity should achieve full compliance with the Standards and internal auditors with the Code of Ethics, there may be instances in which full compliance is not achieved. When noncompliance impacts the overall scope or operation of the internal audit activity, disclosure should be made to senior management and the board.*

2. **Benchmarking** is a tool used in the implementation of a **total quality management approach**. This approach is applicable not only to the business or operating processes of an organization, but also to other activities such as internal or external assessments of the internal audit activity. The following outline describes techniques for improving the effectiveness of benchmarking, which is a means of helping organizations with productivity management and business process reengineering.

   a. **Best practices**. Benchmarking is a continuous evaluation of the practices of the best organizations in their class, and the adaptation of processes to reflect the best of these practices. It entails analysis and measurement of key outputs against those of the best organizations. This procedure also involves identifying the underlying key actions and causes that contribute to the performance difference.

      1) Benchmarking is an ongoing process that entails **quantitative and qualitative measurement** of the difference between the performance of an activity and the performance by the best in the world. The benchmark organization need not be a competitor. It may even be another activity in the same organization.

b.   The first phase in the benchmarking process is to **select and prioritize benchmarking projects**.

   1)   An organization must understand its **critical success factors** and **business environment** to identify key business processes and drivers and to develop parameters defining what processes to benchmark.

      a)   The criteria for selecting what to benchmark arise from the reasons for a process and its importance to the entity's mission, values, and strategy. These reasons relate in large part to satisfaction of end users or customer needs.

c.   The next phase is to organize **benchmarking teams**. A team organization is appropriate because it permits an equitable division of labor, participation by those responsible for implementing changes, and inclusion of a variety of functional expertise and work experience.

   1)   Team members should have knowledge of the function to be benchmarked, respected positions in the organization, good communication skills, teaming skills, motivation to innovate and to support cross-functional problem solving, and project management skills.

d.   The benchmarking team must thoroughly investigate and document the organization's **internal processes**. The organization should be seen as a series of processes, not as a fixed structure.

   1)   A process is a network of related and independent activities joined by their outputs. One way to determine the primary characteristics of a process is to trace the path a request for a product or service takes through the organization.

   2)   The benchmarking team must also develop a **family of measures** that are true indicators of process performance and a process taxonomy. The latter is a set of process elements, measures, and phrases that describes the process to be benchmarked.

e.   **Researching and identifying** best-in-class performance is often the most difficult phase. The critical steps are setting up databases, choosing information-gathering methods (internal sources, external public domain sources, and original research are the possible approaches), formatting questionnaires (lists of questions prepared in advance), and selecting benchmarking partners.

f.   The **data analysis** phase entails identifying performance gaps, understanding the reasons they exist, and prioritizing the key activities that will facilitate the behavioral and process changes needed to implement the benchmarking study's recommendations.

   1)   Sophisticated statistical and other methods may be needed when the study involves many variables, testing of assumptions, or presentation of quantified results.

g.   Leadership is most important in the **implementation** phase of the benchmarking process because the team must be able to justify its recommendations. Moreover, the process improvement teams must manage the implementation of approved changes.

3. A study cited in *Sawyer's Internal Auditing* (5th ed.), page 278, describes **best practices for an internal auditing activity**:

    a. Obtaining an understanding of customers (auditees) so as to satisfy their needs
    b. Treating the IAA as if it were on a service line of a for-profit entity
    c. Applying quality principles and developing performance measures
    d. Auditing operations as well as controls to improve entity performance
    e. Serving as an agent for change in the organization
    f. Communicating regularly within the IAA and with customers (auditees) and shareholders
    g. Integrating information technology and auditing
    h. Emphasizing the professional satisfaction of the internal auditors

4. Stop and review! You have completed the outline for this subunit. Study multiple-choice questions 10 through 16 beginning on page 298.

QUESTIONS

9.1 Coordination

1. Which of the following is a false statement about the relationship between internal auditors and external auditors?

A. Oversight of the work of external auditors is the responsibility of the chief audit executive.

B. Sufficient meetings should be scheduled between internal and external auditors to assure timely and efficient completion of the work.

C. Internal and external auditors may exchange engagement communications and management letters.

D. Internal auditors may provide engagement work programs and working papers to external auditors.

Answer (A) is correct. *(CIA, adapted)*
REQUIRED: The false statement about the relationship between internal and external auditors.
DISCUSSION: Oversight of the work of the independent outside auditor, including coordination with the IAA, is generally the responsibility of the board. Actual coordination should be the responsibility of the CAE. However, the board in the exercise of its oversight role may request that the CAE assess the performance of the external auditors. Ordinarily, this assessment is made in the context of the CAE's function of coordinating internal and external auditing activities (PA 2050-1).
Answer (B) is incorrect because coordination between internal and external auditors involves, among other things, sufficient meetings to assure coordination of engagement work and efficient and timely completion of engagement activities, and to determine whether observations and recommendations from work performed to date require that the scope of planned work be adjusted. Answer (C) is incorrect because coordination between internal and external auditors involves, among other things, exchange of internal audit communications and external auditors' management letters. Answer (D) is incorrect because coordination between internal and external auditors involves, among other things, access to each other's work programs and working papers.

2. In recent years, which two factors have changed the relationship between internal auditors and external auditors so that internal auditors are partners rather than subordinates?

A. The increasing liability of external auditors and the increasing professionalism of internal auditors.

B. The increasing professionalism of internal auditors and the evolving economics of external auditing.

C. The use of computerized accounting systems and the evolving economics of external auditing.

D. The globalization of audit entities and the increased reliance on computerized accounting systems.

Answer (B) is correct. *(CIA, adapted)*
REQUIRED: The two factors that have changed the relationship between internal and external auditors.
DISCUSSION: An external auditor may decide that the internal auditors' work will have an effect on audit procedures if (1) that work is relevant, (2) it is efficient to consider how the work may affect the audit, and (3) the external auditor determines that the internal auditors are sufficiently competent and objective. Hence, internal auditors may be viewed as partners in the audit because of their increasing professionalism. Moreover, the evolving economics of external auditing creates an imperative to control audit fees by eliminating duplication of effort and monitoring more closely the hours worked by external auditors.
Answer (A) is incorrect because increasing liability makes external auditors less likely to determine that the work of the internal auditors has an effect on the external audit procedures. Answer (C) is incorrect because the use of computerized accounting systems would have no significant effect on the relative roles of external and internal auditors. Answer (D) is incorrect because the globalization of audit entities would have no significant effect on the relative roles of external and internal auditors.

3. The foreign subsidiary's auditors would like to rely on some of the work performed by the parent organization's audit firm, but they need to review the working papers first. They have asked you for copies of the working papers of the parent organization's audit firm. What is the most appropriate response to the foreign subsidiary's auditors?

A. Provide copies of the working papers without notifying the parent's audit firm.

B. Notify the parent's auditors of the situation and request that they either provide the working papers or authorize you to do so.

C. Provide copies of the working papers and notify the parent's audit firm that you have done so.

D. Refuse to provide the working papers under any circumstances.

4. The foreign subsidiary's external audit firm wants to rely on an audit of a function at the parent organization. The audit was conducted by the internal audit activity. To place reliance on the work performed, the foreign subsidiary's auditors have requested copies of the working papers. What is the most appropriate response to the foreign subsidiary's auditors?

A. Provide copies of the working papers.

B. Ask the parent's audit firm if it is appropriate to release the working papers.

C. Ask the board for permission to release the working papers.

D. Refuse to provide the working papers under any circumstances.

Answer (B) is correct. *(CIA, adapted)*
REQUIRED: The proper response to a request by one external audit firm for another external audit firm's working papers held by the internal auditors.
DISCUSSION: Coordination of internal and external auditing efforts involves access to each other's work programs and working papers. However, such access carries with it the responsibility to respect the confidentiality of those programs and working papers (PA 2050-1). Hence, the internal auditors should seek the approval of the parent's external auditors before granting access to their working papers to the external auditors of the subsidiaries.
Answer (A) is incorrect because the working papers are the property of the parent's external auditors, and their confidentiality should be respected. Answer (C) is incorrect because the external auditors should give prior authorization for the release of their working papers. Answer (D) is incorrect because the CAE has the responsibility to ensure proper coordination with external auditors.

Answer (A) is correct. *(CIA, adapted)*
REQUIRED: The proper response to a request by external auditors for the internal auditors' working papers.
DISCUSSION: Internal and external auditing efforts should be coordinated to ensure adequate coverage and to minimize duplication of effort. Coordination involves access to each other's work programs and working papers. Access to the internal auditors' work programs and working papers should be given to the external auditors in order for them to be satisfied as to the propriety, for external audit purposes, of relying on the internal auditors' work (PA 2050-1).
Answer (B) is incorrect because the working papers are the property of the organization. The responsibility of the CAE is to maintain the security of the working papers and to coordinate efforts with the external auditors. Thus, the decision belongs not to the parent's external auditors but to the CAE. Answer (C) is incorrect because access to working papers by external auditors should be subject to the approval of the CAE (PA 2330.A1-1). Answer (D) is incorrect because the CAE should ensure proper coordination with external auditors by, among other things, granting the external auditors access to the internal auditors' working papers.

5. To improve their efficiency, internal auditors may rely upon the work of external auditors if it is

- A. Performed after the internal auditing work.
- B. Primarily concerned with operational objectives and activities.
- C. Coordinated with internal auditing work.
- D. Conducted in accordance with the Code of Ethics.

Answer (C) is correct. *(CIA, adapted)*
REQUIRED: The circumstances in which internal auditors may rely upon the work of external auditors.
DISCUSSION: In coordinating the work of internal auditors with the work of external auditors, the CAE should ensure that work to be performed by internal auditors does not duplicate the work of the external auditors that can be relied upon for purposes of internal auditing coverage. To the extent that professional and organizational reporting responsibilities allow, internal auditors should perform services in a manner that allows for maximum coordination and efficiency (PA 2050-1).
Answer (A) is incorrect because duplication of effort may result if the external audit is performed after the internal auditing engagement. Answer (B) is incorrect because internal auditing encompasses both financial and operational objectives and activities. Thus, internal auditing coverage could also be provided by external audit work that included primarily financial objectives and activities. Answer (D) is incorrect because external auditing work is conducted in accordance with auditing standards generally accepted in the host country.

6. Appropriate policies for selection or retention of non-external audit services from independent auditors should consider addressing the following attributes except

- A. Nature and type of services covered by the policy.
- B. The need to limit negotiations to the current external auditor.
- C. Regulatory or other governing requirements unique to specific industries or countries.
- D. Participants or members of the selection and evaluation team.

Answer (B) is correct. *(Publisher)*
REQUIRED: The necessary policies to address for the selection or retention of non-external audit services.
DISCUSSION: Policies for selection or retention of external audits should include all of the issues to be addressed so that procurement results in an economical and efficient outcome for the organization. Also, such listings and services should provide a systematic and complete procurement checklist in addition to the answers listed, except limiting such procurement to the current external auditor. All external auditors that the organization feels may be able to provide good service at a reasonable fee should be considered. In addition to the other answers listed, the procurement policy should address whether Board and/or Auditor Committee approval is required, duration of the contract, frequency of request for services to retain existing service providers, critical or primary criteria that should be considered, limitation on service fees and procedures.
Answer (A) is incorrect because the nature and type of services covered should be addressed by policy statement. Answer (C) is incorrect because regulatory or other governing requirements unique to specific industries or countries should be addressed by policy statement. Answer (D) is incorrect because participants or members of the selection and evaluation team should be addressed by policy statement.

7. Why should internal auditors help develop policies for the selection, evaluation, or retention of external auditor services other than for an external audit?

- A. So that the present external audit service providers do not view a decision to request proposals as a signal that the organization is dissatisfied with present services.
- B. Such services cannot be subject to any other existing procurement policies of the organization.
- C. To facilitate the acquisition of those services economically and effectively.
- D. It is required in the charter of the internal audit function.

Answer (C) is correct. *(Publisher)*
REQUIRED: The reason policies are developed to facilitate external auditor services.
DISCUSSION: PA 2050-2 covers Acquisition of External Audit Services. Non-external audit services consist of tax services, consulting and other non-audit services, internal audit outsourcing and/or co-sourcing services, valuation, appraisal, and actuarial services, temporary services such as recruiting, bookkeeping, technology services, legal services provided by external audit firms. If these services are obtained routinely or non-routinely, their acquisition should be according to a well-conceived set of policies. Most, if not all, of these services can be provided by external auditors other than the present external auditor.
Answer (A) is incorrect because the organization can contract with any independent auditing firm without apologizing to the independent auditor providing independent audit service. Answer (B) is incorrect because presumably, there are procurement policies which affect all procurement and, if need be, additional policies that are prudent for contracting for non-external audit services from independent auditing firms. Answer (D) is incorrect because the internal audit charter usually does not specify detail policies.

8. A quality assurance and improvement program of an internal audit activity provides reasonable assurance that internal auditing work is performed in accordance with its charter. Which of the following are designed to provide feedback on the effectiveness of an internal audit activity?

I. Proper supervision
II. Proper training
III. Internal reviews
IV. External reviews

    A. I, II, and III only.

    B. II, III, and IV only.

    C. I, III, and IV only.

    D. I, II, III, and IV.

Answer (C) is correct. *(CIA, adapted)*
    REQUIRED: The elements designed to provide feedback on the effectiveness of an IAA.
    DISCUSSION: A quality assurance and improvement program should be designed to provide reasonable assurance to the various stakeholders of the IAA that it (1) performs in accordance with its charter, which should be consistent with the Standards and the Code of Ethics; (2) operates effectively and efficiently; and (3) is perceived by the stakeholders as adding value and improving operations. The program should include appropriate supervision, periodic internal assessment and ongoing monitoring of quality assurance and periodic external assessments (PA 1310-1).

9. Quality program assessments may be performed internally or externally. A distinguishing feature of an external assessment is its objective to

    A. Identify tasks that can be performed better.

    B. Determine whether internal auditing services meet professional standards.

    C. Set forth the recommendations for improvement.

    D. Provide independent assurance.

Answer (D) is correct. *(CIA, adapted)*
    REQUIRED: The distinguishing feature of an external assessment.
    DISCUSSION: External assessments should be conducted at least once every 5 years by a qualified, independent reviewer or review team from outside the organization (Standard 1312). Independence means impartiality and fairness not only to the IAA but also to those who may be provided with the results of the review. Assessments by individuals in another department of the organization are not independent. Moreover, reciprocal peer reviews between two organizations, by the external auditor, or by a firm to which internal auditing services have been outsourced ordinarily should not be performed (PA 1312-1).
    Answer (A) is incorrect because an internal assessment will identify tasks that can be performed better. Answer (B) is incorrect because an internal assessment will determine whether internal auditing services meet professional standards. Answer (C) is incorrect because an internal assessment will set forth recommendations for improvement.

9.2 Quality Assurance

10. External assessment of an internal audit activity is not likely to evaluate

    A. Adherence to the internal audit activity's charter.

    B. Compliance with the Standards for the Professional Practice of Internal Auditing.

    C. Detailed cost-benefit analysis of the internal audit activity.

    D. The tools and techniques employed by the internal audit activity.

Answer (C) is correct. *(CIA, adapted)*
    REQUIRED: The purpose not served by external assessment of an IAA.
    DISCUSSION: The external assessment has a broad scope of coverage that includes (1) compliance with the Standards, the Code of Ethics, and the IAA's Charter, plans, policies, procedures, practices, and applicable legislative and regulatory requirements; (2) the expectations of the IAA expressed by the board, senior management, and operational managers; (3) the integration of the IAA into the governance process; (4) the tools and techniques employed by the IAA; (5) the mix of knowledge, experience, and disciplines within the staff, including staff focus on process improvement; and (6) the determination whether the audit activity adds value and improves operations (PA 1312-1). However, the costs and benefits of internal auditing are neither easily quantifiable nor the subject of an external assessment.
    Answer (A) is incorrect because adherence to the IAA's charter is within the broad scope of coverage of the external assessment. Answer (B) is incorrect because compliance with the Standards is within the broad scope of coverage of the external assessment. Answer (D) is incorrect because the tools and techniques of the IAA are within the broad scope of coverage of the external assessment.

11. Ordinarily, those conducting internal quality program assessments should report to

    A. The board.

    B. The chief audit executive.

    C. Senior management.

    D. The internal auditing staff.

Answer (B) is correct. *(CIA, adapted)*
    REQUIRED: The person(s) to whom those conducting internal quality program assessments should report.
    DISCUSSION: An IAA capable of formally conducting internal assessments of its quality program should establish a reporting structure conducive to maintaining appropriate credibility and objectivity. Ordinarily, those assigned responsibility for conducting ongoing and periodic reviews should report to the CAE while performing the assessments and should communicate their results directly to the CAE (PA 1311-1).
    Answer (A) is incorrect because the CAE should periodically share the results of internal assessments with appropriate persons outside the IAA, such as the board. Answer (C) is incorrect because the CAE should periodically share the results of internal assessments with appropriate persons outside the IAA, such as senior management. Answer (D) is incorrect because the CAE should periodically share the results of internal assessments with appropriate persons outside the IAA, such as the external auditors.

12. The chief audit executive (CAE) should communicate the final results of an external assessment review of an internal audit activity (IAA) to senior management, as appropriate, and the board. This communication should include

    A. The reviewer's statement of an action plan in response to the recommendations.

    B. An opinion on whether the practices of the IAA as a whole comply with the Standards.

    C. An opinion on the IAA's compliance with its charter.

    D. The reviewer's assessment of the use of best practices, other recommendations, and statement of implementation dates for responses to the review.

Answer (B) is correct. *(Publisher)*
    REQUIRED: The content of a communication of the final results of an external assessment.
    DISCUSSION: The communication should include an opinion on the IAA's compliance with the Standards based on a structured rating process. Compliance means that the practices of the IAA, taken as a whole, satisfy the requirements of the Standards (PA 1312-1).
    Answer (A) is incorrect because the communication should include responses from the CAE that include an action plan. Answer (C) is incorrect because an opinion on compliance with the Standards should be expressed. Answer (D) is incorrect because the communication should include recommendations and implementation dates.

13. Internal auditors may report that their activities are conducted in accordance with the Standards. They may use this statement only if

    A. They demonstrate compliance with the Standards.

    B. An independent external assessment of the internal audit activity is conducted annually.

    C. Senior management or the board is accountable for implementing a quality program.

    D. External assessments of the internal audit activity are made by the external auditors.

Answer (A) is correct. *(Publisher)*
    REQUIRED: The condition permitting internal auditors to report that their activities are in accordance with the Standards.
    DISCUSSION: Internal auditors are encouraged to report that their activities are "conducted in accordance with the *Standards for the Professional Practice of Internal Auditing.*" However, internal auditors may use the statement only if assessments of the quality improvement program demonstrate that the internal audit activity is in compliance with the Standards (Standard 1330).
    Answer (B) is incorrect because an independent external assessment of the IAA should be conducted at least once every 5 years (Standard 1312). Answer (C) is incorrect because the CAE is accountable for implementing a quality program which should include supervision, periodic internal assessment and ongoing monitoring, and periodic external assessment (PA 1310-1). Answer (D) is incorrect because quality assurance reviews ordinarily should not be performed by the organization's external audit firm, except when such reviews are made under a legislative mandate (PA 1312-1).

14. According to Specific Attribute Standard 1340, disclosure should be made to senior management and the board whenever

   A. The internal audit activity does not comply with the Standards.

   B. The internal auditors do not comply with the Code of Ethics.

   C. The internal audit activity does not comply with the Standards, or the internal auditors do not comply with the Code of Ethics.

   D. Noncompliance with the Standards or the Code of Ethics affects the overall operation of the internal audit activity.

Answer (D) is correct. *(Publisher)*
   REQUIRED: The circumstance in which disclosure should be made to senior management and the board.
   DISCUSSION: Although the internal audit activity should achieve full compliance with the Standards and internal auditors with the Code of Ethics, there may be instances in which full compliance is not achieved. When noncompliance affects the overall scope or operation of the internal audit activity, disclosure should be made to senior management and the board (Standard 1340).

15. Which of the following statements regarding benchmarking is false?

   A. Benchmarking involves continuously evaluating the practices of best-in-class organizations and adapting company processes to incorporate the best of these practices.

   B. Benchmarking, in practice, usually involves a company's formation of benchmarking teams.

   C. Benchmarking is an ongoing process that entails quantitative and qualitative measurement of the difference between the company's performance of an activity and the performance by the best in the world or the best in the industry.

   D. The benchmarking organization against which a firm is comparing itself must be a direct competitor.

Answer (D) is correct. *(Publisher)*
   REQUIRED: The false statement about benchmarking.
   DISCUSSION: Benchmarking is an ongoing process that entails quantitative and qualitative measurement of the difference between the company's performance of an activity and the performance by a best-in-class organization. The benchmarking organization against which a firm is comparing itself need not be a direct competitor. The important consideration is that the benchmarking organization be an outstanding performer in its industry.

16. An example of an internal nonfinancial benchmark is

   A. The labor rate of comparably skilled employees at a major competitor's plant.

   B. The average actual cost per pound of a specific product at the company's most efficient plant.

   C. A $50,000 limit on the cost of employee training programs at each of the company's plants.

   D. The percentage of customer orders delivered on time at the company's most efficient plant.

Answer (D) is correct. *(CIA, adapted)*
   REQUIRED: The internal nonfinancial benchmark.
   DISCUSSION: Benchmarking is a continuous evaluation of the practices of the best organizations in their class and the adaptation of processes to reflect the best of these practices. It entails analysis and measurement of key outputs against those of the best organizations. This procedure also involves identifying the underlying key actions and causes that contribute to the performance difference. The percentage of orders delivered on time at the company's most efficient plant is an example of an internal nonfinancial benchmark.
   Answer (A) is incorrect because the labor rate of a competitor is a financial benchmark. Answer (B) is incorrect because the cost per pound at the company's most efficient plant is a financial benchmark. Answer (C) is incorrect because the cost of a training program is a financial benchmark.

Use Gleim's ***CIA Test Prep*** for interactive testing with over 2,000 additional multiple-choice questions!

STUDY UNIT TEN
ENGAGEMENT PROCEDURES

(7 pages of outline)

10.1 AUDIT PROCEDURES

Internal auditors apply engagement (audit) procedures to obtain sufficient, competent, relevant, and useful information (evidence) to achieve the internal audit engagement's objectives. For example, internal auditors may perform assurance engagements in which they must evaluate the reliability of the output of an accounting information system. Such an engagement involves substantive testing of the balances and transactions. It also involves tests of the adequacy and effectiveness of controls regarding the effectiveness of accounting and control systems/procedures. Consulting engagements require the gathering, analysis, synthesis, and evaluation of information relevant to the engagement objectives.

The CIA exam contains questions that ask for the best, most effective, least appropriate, etc., audit procedures to achieve engagement objectives. The purpose of this study unit is to train you to determine the most (or least) effective procedure under given circumstances. If the question asks for the best, the most effective, etc., there will be one good answer and three incorrect or weak answers. Conversely, if the question asks for the least effective procedure, there will be three "good" procedures and one inappropriate procedure.

Before turning the page, think about and answer the following **questions**:

1.   What are audit or engagement procedures?

2.   How do audit or engagement procedures relate to the information to be gathered?

3.   How is the underlying activity relevant to the audit procedure(s)?

4.   How is the organization's system/processes/procedures related to the audit procedures?

5.   What is risk? What is engagement risk?

6.   Why is the acronym "COVES" useful for financial audits?

7.   Do the audit procedures satisfy the standards imposed by the Professional Standards Framework, legal and regulatory requirements, and/or contractual provisions?

8.   What do you need to do to become more proficient in evaluating audit (engagement) procedures?

Recall that Gleim study materials motivate candidates to become proficient in analysis, synthesis, and evaluation. These are higher levels of knowledge beyond rote memorization, concept learning, and problem solving.

1.   **Analysis** results in an understanding of a situation, set of circumstances, or process. This understanding should apply both to the elements AND to the relationship of the elements of a situation, set of circumstances, or process. Thus, analysis is a means of understanding a "whole" by studying its "parts." Moreover, analysis requires deductive reasoning.

    EXAMPLE: In an engagement to evaluate the effectiveness and efficiency of the organization's use of production capacity, the internal auditor must determine whether customer orders should be accepted at a lower-than-usual price. Variables to consider include contribution margin generated, available production capacity, and psychological and economic effects on other customers.

2.   **Synthesis** involves developing standards and generalizations for a situation, set of circumstances, or a process. It is based on the understanding of individual components, to produce the desired results. Synthesis requires inductive reasoning.

     EXAMPLE: The development of an engagement work program is the documentation of the procedures for collecting, analyzing, interpreting, and documenting information. For this purpose, the internal auditors must synthesize many factors, including the engagement objectives, prior results, organizational changes, legal and regulatory issues, identified risks, technical aspects of the engagement, information obtained during the preliminary survey, budgetary and other resource limits, and many other matters.

3.   **Evaluation** is relating a situation, set of circumstances, or process to predetermined or synthesized standards. Evaluation usually includes both analysis and synthesis.

     EXAMPLE: Internal auditors rely on their training, experience, understanding, and seasoned judgment (if not intuition) to assess the quality of a situation, set of circumstances, or process (or its elements).

     EXAMPLE: Multiple-choice questions consist of a series of either true or false statements with one exception (the correct answer). If the question is evaluative, all of the answer choices will be true or false, but one answer will be better than the others. "The most important nonfinancial issue that a company should consider is . . ." requires evaluation of qualitative variables.

DISCUSSION OF QUESTIONS ON THE PREVIOUS PAGE

Please think about (i.e., visualize) how each of the questions and answers will help you evaluate engagement procedures.

1.   Engagement procedures are designed to gather information that corroborates and documents evidence that specified risk management, control, and governance processes are effective.

2.   Engagement procedures produce information (evidence) about the underlying activity. Both the procedures and the resulting evidence should be documented in the internal auditor's working papers.

3.   To account for or audit any activity (or to account for inactivity), the internal auditor must obtain an understanding of the activity by asking questions about what, why, when, how, and by whom.

4.   Engagement procedures may be applied to an accounting or information system, its processes, and its procedures to develop audit evidence regarding the correctness and reliability of the information.

5.   Risk is the probability of an unfavorable event. Examples are asset loss, incurring a liability, financial statement misstatement, or incorrect analysis/synthesis/evaluation of a situation/set of circumstances/process. Engagement risk is the risk that the information gathered (or its evaluation) may not reflect the true status of the subject of the engagement.

6.   In financial audits, the primary concern is with the assertions explicitly or implicitly made by the information or its presentation, e.g., amounts of revenue or expense and the balances of assets and liabilities. Thus, internal auditors must develop and use engagement procedures to test the assertions. The following assertions model (the acronym is COVES), developed by Dr. Bill Hillison at Florida State University, is from a pronouncement of the American Institute of Certified Public Accountants:

     a.   **C**ompleteness -- whether all transactions and accounts that should be presented in the financial statements or other reports are included.

b. Rights and **O**bligations -- whether, at a given date, all assets are the rights of the entity and all liabilities are the obligations of the entity.

c. **V**aluation or Allocation -- whether the assets, liabilities, revenues, and expenses of an entity have been included in the financial statements at the appropriate amounts in conformity with applicable authoritative accounting principles.

d. **E**xistence or Occurrence -- whether assets/liabilities exist at a given date and whether recorded transactions have occurred during a given period.

e. **S**tatement Presentation and Disclosure -- whether financial statement components have been properly classified, described, and disclosed.

7. The IIA's Professional Standards Framework is covered throughout Parts I, II, and III of the CIA exam and the Gleim CIA books, software, and audios. Your thorough understanding of the standards will make a more effective internal auditor and prepare you for success on the CIA exam.

8. To improve your performance answering "audit procedure" questions, analyze/synthesize/evaluate how you respond to practice questions which are provided here and on your CIA Review CD. It is imperative to answer practice questions and learn from your experience.

ENGAGEMENT PROCEDURES

Sawyer (*Sawyer's Internal Auditing*, 5th ed., The IIA, pp. 282-295) describes six categories of procedures. These procedures are used by internal auditors in their field work to examine (measure and evaluate) selected "documents, transactions, conditions, and processes." The first five categories relate to measurement and the sixth to evaluation.

1. **Observing** is a purposeful visual examination involving a mental comparison with standards and an evaluation of what is seen.

   a. Observations should be documented.

   b. The quality of observations is dependent upon the experience and training of the internal auditor. The greater the experience and the better the training, the more likely that variances from the desirable conditions will be observed.

   c. Observation is usually preliminary to confirmation by other procedures, i.e., analysis and investigation. Confirmation by other procedures prevents observations from being successfully challenged.

   d. Observation occurs during the preliminary survey of the physical plant and work flows. It may also occur when questioning.

   e. Observation may detect risk exposures such as ineffective controls, idle resources, security breaches, or environmental and safety hazards.

2. **Questioning** may be done orally or in writing. It is the most pervasive procedure in reviews of operations.

   a. Oral questioning is the most common form of this procedure. It is also the most difficult. It requires skill in human relations and in phrasing questions so as to elicit the most useful information.

   b. An internal auditor must be able to avoid needlessly antagonizing or intimidating the people interviewed. However, (s)he must not waver from the objective of finding the truth.

   c. Oral information should be confirmed by asking at least one other person.

   d. Quality of service is normally best determined by inquiring of people who use the service, especially when it involves technical matters that only user-technicians understand.

e. A **standard operating procedure questionnaire** helps not only the internal auditor but also clients. Clients may find it more comprehensible than a procedures manual. They also may find it to be an educational device. Thus, a crucial internal audit function is to appraise written operating procedures to determine whether they are current, valid, relevant, and in use.

f. Questionnaires should be limited to material concerns, updated, and cleared with client management. Moreover, an issue may arise as to whether certain sensitive matters should be addressed in questionnaires.

3. **Analysis** means understanding a whole by studying its parts. Analytical procedures are performed to discover "qualities, causes, effects, motives, and possibilities" as a basis for judgment or further examination.

   a. Analytical procedures are valuable whether the subject is an account balance, an operating function, or a process. They are also useful for understanding policy statements, contracts, statutes, the work of committees related to a multifaceted program, and anything else capable of being examined in terms of its significant elements.

   b. Analysis involves making comparisons, noting trends, and identifying variances from expectations. Accordingly, internal auditors must establish standards or benchmarks as a basis for comparisons, investigate variances, and perform any necessary additional tests.

4. **Verifying** is a process of corroboration and comparison, for example, of

   a. One document or oral statement with another;

   b. A general ledger balance with the detail in the subsidiary ledger;

   c. A manager's approval with an authorizing directive issued by a higher level of management; or

   d. A purchase with a purchase requisition, an allowed amount (such as a bill of materials), production schedule, or receiving report.

5. **Investigating** is a systematic search for hidden facts when wrongdoing or otherwise suspect conditions exist.

   a. Investigating should be distinguished from analyzing and verifying, methods that are applied to information that is not (or not yet) suspect.

   b. A **probe** is a type of investigation specifically related to wrongdoing. An example is a fraud investigation. Internal auditors must be cautious in such matters. An improperly conducted probe may have unfortunate legal and criminal ramifications, including injury to the organization because of violations of employees' rights.

6. **Evaluating** is appraisal or estimation of work, i.e., the making of a judgment. This conclusion is a determination of the adequacy, efficiency, and effectiveness of the subject matter.

   a. Evaluating is based on professional judgment, which affects all aspects of the engagement. Typical evaluations include

      1) The risks of not reviewing an activity versus the costs of performing procedures,

      2) Whether detailed procedures are necessary or a simple work-through will suffice, or

      3) Whether sample results are sufficient for the internal auditor's purposes given the risk assessments of the activity being reviewed.

   b. Evaluating determines the significance of results and possibly indicates the corrective action to be taken.

    c.   Evaluating is a step beyond analyzing and verifying (the conclusion of the measurement or fact-finding process). It is the culmination of the internal auditor's consulting responsibility because it gives meaning to the facts found in light of engagement objectives and standards.

    d.   Even an experienced internal auditor should adopt a structured approach to the **evaluation of findings**. For example, Sawyer suggests that the following should be considered when an internal auditor evaluates deviations from standards:

        1)   The significance of the deviations
        2)   Who or what has been damaged
        3)   The degree of damage or possible damage
        4)   Whether the deviations prevented the organization from reaching its objectives
        5)   Whether the deviations are likely to recur in the absence of corrective action
        6)   Why and how the deviations occurred
        7)   What caused the deviations
        8)   Whether the cause has been precisely described and explains all aspects of the deviations

    e.   Internal auditors have a duty to recommend **corrective action**. Recommendations should be based on, among other things, the following considerations:

        1)   The most economical methods of solving the problem
        2)   The objectives of the recommendations
        3)   What management should be trying to achieve
        4)   The choices available and how they match the objectives
        5)   The tentative choice selected and its possible negative effects
        6)   The best choice with the least negative effects
        7)   Methods of control over the corrective action, e.g., to ensure that it is actually and fully implemented and that future deviations will be reported

AUDIT EVIDENCE

1.   **Audit Evidence in Financial Audits**.

    a.   Evidence supporting the financial statements (F/S) consists of underlying accounting data and all corroborating information available to the auditor. **Underlying accounting data** consist of the books of original entry (e.g., journals and registers), the general and subsidiary ledgers, related accounting manuals, and records such as work sheets and spreadsheets supporting cost allocations, computations, and reconciliations, often in electronic form.

        1)   Accounting data alone cannot be considered sufficient support for financial statements.

        2)   The auditor tests underlying accounting data by

            a)   Analysis and review
            b)   Retracing the procedural steps followed in the accounting process and in developing the work sheets and allocations involved
            c)   Recalculation
            d)   Reconciling related types and applications of the same information

b. **Corroborating evidential matter** includes both written and electronic information (e.g., checks, invoices, EFTs, contracts, and minutes of meetings); confirmations and other written representations by knowledgeable people; information obtained by the auditor from inquiry, observation, inspection, and physical examination; and other information developed by, or available to, the auditor that permits conclusions through valid reasoning.

c. Accounting data and corroborating evidence may be available only in electronic form (e.g., EDI systems or image processing systems) and may exist only at a certain moment in time. When choosing engagement procedures, the auditor should consider that evidence may not be retrievable after a specified period of time.

d. The diagram below illustrates the relationship of data in the accounting process on the left and the related direction of the completeness and existence tests on the right.

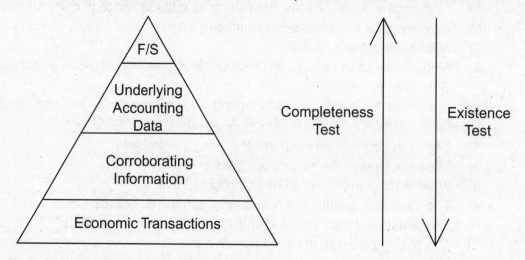

2. **Competence of Evidential Matter**. Competent evidence, regardless of its form, must be both valid (objective and reliable) and relevant (i.e., timely and related to the issue). Its validity is dependent on the circumstances under which it is obtained. Subject to exceptions, the following presumptions can be made about the validity of evidence:

a. Evidence obtained from independent sources outside an entity provides greater assurance of reliability for the purposes of an independent audit than evidence secured solely within the entity.

b. The more effective the internal control, the more assurance it provides about the reliability of the accounting data and financial statements.

c. The independent auditor's direct personal knowledge, obtained through physical examination, observation, computation, and inspection, is more persuasive than information obtained indirectly.

3. **Sufficiency of Evidential Matter**

a. The amounts and kinds of evidence needed are matters to be determined in the exercise of the professional judgment of the auditor.

b. The auditor typically has to rely on persuasive, rather than convincing, evidence.

c. The auditor must decide whether the evidence available within time and cost limits is sufficient to justify the opinion.

d. A rational relationship should exist between the cost of obtaining evidence and the usefulness of the information obtained. However, the difficulty and the expense involved in testing a particular item are not in themselves a valid basis for omitting the test.

4. **Evaluation of Evidential Matter**. Through this evaluation, the auditor considers whether the specific audit objectives have been achieved.

   a. The independent auditor should be thorough in the search for evidence and unbiased in its evaluation.

   b. The auditor should recognize the possibility that the financial statements may not be in conformity with applicable authoritative accounting principles when designing engagement procedures.

   c. In developing an opinion, the auditor should consider relevant evidence regardless of whether it appears to corroborate or contradict the financial statement assertions.

   d. If the auditor has substantial doubt about any assertion of material significance, (s)he must refrain from forming an opinion until (s)he has obtained sufficient competent evidence to remove the doubt, express a qualified opinion, or disclaim an opinion.

5. Stop and review! You have completed the outline for this subunit. Study multiple-choice questions 1 though 19 beginning below.

QUESTIONS

10.1 Audit Procedures

1. Internal auditors must use both inductive and deductive reasoning when gathering information and reaching conclusions. They must also understand the differences between the two types of reasoning in order to assess the strengths and weaknesses of each. Which of the following procedures uses deductive reasoning?

A. The internal auditor uses generalized audit software to select a sample of items for confirmation. Based on the confirmation responses, the auditor concludes that accounts receivable as recorded exist.

B. The internal auditor performs analytical procedures to estimate the accuracy of the sales account balance. No material differences are noted. Based on this, the internal auditor assumes that the underlying record-keeping must be correct.

C. The internal auditor observes the client's physical inventory process and records test counts of inventory. Those test counts are traced to the year-end inventory compilation and no exceptions are noted. The internal auditor concludes that the compiled inventory exists.

D. The internal auditor examines sales transactions recorded during January 2002 and finds that none of those sales represent 2001 sales. The internal auditor concludes that 2001 sales are recorded properly.

Answer (B) is correct. *(CIA, adapted)*

REQUIRED: The audit procedure using deductive reasoning.

DISCUSSION: Deductive reasoning is the inference of a conclusion about particulars from general or universal premises. In contrast, inductive reasoning is the inference of a generalized conclusion from particular instances. Analytical procedures are based on the general premise that plausible relationships among the data may reasonably be expected to continue in the absence of known conditions to the contrary. For example, absent unusual circumstances, the sales balance is relatively predictable given its known relationship to other factors, such as cost of sales. Thus, the process is one of deductive reasoning because a general premise (the known relationship of sales to other data) is applied to draw a conclusion about a particular instance (the sales balance).

Answer (A) is incorrect because sampling receivables is an example of an inductive process. It entails gathering empirical data about particular items and then determining the general principle that the evidence supports. Answer (C) is incorrect because test counting inventory is an example of an inductive process. It entails gathering empirical data about particular items and then determining the general principle that the evidence supports. Answer (D) is incorrect because examining sales recorded after the balance sheet date is an example of an inductive process. It entails gathering empirical data about particular items and then determining the general principle that the evidence supports.

2. The internal auditor is concerned about whether all the debits to the computer security expense account are appropriate expenditures. The most appropriate engagement procedure is to

A. Take an attribute sample of computing invoices and determine whether all invoices are properly classified.

B. Perform an analytical review comparing the amount of expenditures incurred this year with the amounts incurred on a trend line for the past 5 years.

C. Take an attribute sample of employee wage expenses incurred by the outsourcing organization and trace to the proper account classification.

D. Take a sample of all debits to the account and investigate by examining source documents to determine the nature and authority of the expenditure.

Answer (D) is correct. *(CIA, adapted)*
REQUIRED: The most appropriate audit procedure to determine the validity of computer security expenses.
DISCUSSION: The sample should be taken from the population of interest, that is, debits to the expense account. The proper engagement procedure is to vouch the accounting records to the source documents.
Answer (A) is incorrect because the sample would be too broad to be efficient. The auditor is specifically interested in the debits to the account. Answer (B) is incorrect because analytical procedures provide information as to whether the total expense is reasonable. They do not determine whether specific debits are correct. Answer (C) is incorrect because this procedure furnishes some information about the wage component of costs, but it is not relevant to other computer security costs.

3. A production manager for a moderate-sized manufacturer began ordering excessive raw materials and had them delivered to a wholesaler he runs as a side business. He falsified receiving documents and approved the invoices for payment. Which of the following engagement procedures most likely will detect this fraud?

A. Take a sample of cash disbursements; compare purchase orders, receiving reports, invoices, and check copies.

B. Take a sample and confirm the amount purchased, purchase price, and date of shipment with the vendors.

C. Observe the receiving dock and count materials received; compare your counts to receiving reports completed by receiving personnel.

D. Prepare analytical tests comparing production, materials purchased, and raw materials inventory levels and investigate differences.

Answer (D) is correct. *(CIA, adapted)*
REQUIRED: The audit procedure most likely to detect the fraud.
DISCUSSION: Because the materials are shipped to and used in another business, the analytic comparisons (variance analysis) will show an unexplained increase in materials used.
Answer (A) is incorrect because documents have been falsified, and all supporting documents should match for each cash disbursement. Answer (B) is incorrect because all transactions will appear to be valid from the perspective of vendors. Answer (C) is incorrect because fraudulent orders are shipped to another location. Thus, the receiving dock activities will appear to be satisfactory.

Question 4 is based on the following information. The internal audit activity has been assigned to perform an engagement involving a division. Based on background review, the internal auditor knows the following about management policies:

- Organizational policy is to rapidly promote divisional managers who show significant success. Thus, successful managers rarely stay at a division for more than 3 years.
- A significant portion of division management's compensation comes in the form of bonuses based on the division's profitability.

The division was identified by senior management as a turnaround opportunity. The division is growing, but is not scheduled for a full audit by the external auditors this year. The division has been growing about 7% per year for the past 3 years and uses a standard cost system.

During the preliminary review, the internal auditor notes the following changes in financial data compared with the prior year:

- Sales have increased by 10%.
- Cost of goods sold has increased by 2%.
- Inventory has increased by 15%.
- Divisional net profit has increased by 8%.

4. It is November and the internal auditing manager is finalizing plans for a year-end engagement at the division. Based on the data, the engagement procedure with highest priority is to

A. Select sales transactions and trace shipping documents to entries into cost of goods sold to determine whether all shipments were recorded.

B. Schedule a complete count of inventory at year-end and have the internal auditor observe and test the year-end inventory.

C. Schedule a complete investigation of the standard cost system by preparing cost buildups of a sample of products.

D. Schedule a year-end sales cutoff test.

Answer (B) is correct. *(CIA, adapted)*
REQUIRED: The audit procedure with the highest priority.
DISCUSSION: Given that sales increased by 10% and inventory by 15% while cost of goods sold increased by only 2%, the data indicate that inventory is overstated and cost of goods sold is understated. Inventory might be overstated because of either quantity or cost differences. Because year-end is near, the most appropriate procedure is to begin a physical observation of inventory and extend the engagement to price tests after establishing the existence of inventory.
Answer (A) is incorrect because testing sales is appropriate, but the major problem appears to be the existence of inventory, and the internal auditor should start there. Answer (C) is incorrect because investigating the standard cost system is appropriate, but the major problem appears to be the existence of inventory, and the internal auditor should start there. Answer (D) is incorrect because the problem is occurring during normal operations. Because of the red flags, the internal auditor should schedule a cutoff test, but the existing red flags point primarily to a problem with inventory overstatement.

5. Assume the internal auditor becomes concerned that significant fraud may be taking place by dentists who are billing the health care processor for services that were not provided. For example, employees may have their teeth cleaned, but the dentist charges the processor for pulling teeth and developing dentures. The most effective procedure to determine whether such a fraud exists is to

A. Develop a schedule of payments made to individual dentists. Verify that payments were made to the dentists by confirming the payments with the health care processor.

B. Take a random sample of payments made to dentists and confirm the amounts paid with the dentists' offices to determine that the amounts agree with the amounts billed by the dentists.

C. Take a random sample of claims submitted by dentists and trace through the system to determine whether the claims were paid at the amounts billed.

D. Take a discovery sample of employee claims that were submitted through dentist offices, and confirm the type of service performed by the dentist through direct correspondence with the employee who had the service performed.

Answer (D) is correct. *(CIA, adapted)*
REQUIRED: The most effective audit procedure to reveal overcharging by districts.
DISCUSSION: A discovery sample is used to identify critical errors or irregularities, that is, when a single deviation is critical. This method cannot be used to evaluate the results statistically if deviations are found. Because dentists are suspected of filing fraudulent claims, the auditor should take a discovery sample of employee claims. The internal auditor should then confirm the work done by the dentist according to the claim with the employee. The employee is the best source of information as to whether the service was provided.
Answer (A) is incorrect because developing a schedule of payments and verifying that the payments were made does not reveal whether the claims were proper or fraudulent. Answer (B) is incorrect because verifying that dentists were paid the amounts that they billed does not reveal whether the claims were proper or fraudulent. Answer (C) is incorrect because verifying that claims were paid at the amounts billed does not reveal whether the claims were proper or fraudulent.

6. The internal auditor found that the purchasing department has a policy of setting all purchasing lead times to the highest number of days experienced within each product subassembly, even though some subassemblies required 3 or more months to complete. To address the objective of reducing inventory holding costs related to this policy, the internal auditor should focus on

A. Reviewing production requirements for a sample of products to determine at which point in the production process materials and subassemblies are needed.

B. Evaluating whether product-line assignments were rotated among the members of the purchasing department.

C. Identifying signature approval authority among members of the purchasing department in relation to any computer system controls.

D. Testing those products having the highest sales to determine the average number of days that the completed products were held in inventory.

Answer (A) is correct. *(CIA, adapted)*
REQUIRED: The audit procedure to address the objective of reducing inventory holding costs given that purchasing uses a uniform lead time.
DISCUSSION: The effect of this policy is to increase inventory holding costs. Using the longest lead time avoids stockout costs but ensures that many items will be delivered long before they are needed.
Answer (B) is incorrect because rotating assignments would not directly affect holding costs. Answer (C) is incorrect because approval requirements would not increase holding costs. Answer (D) is incorrect because this would address holding costs for finished goods, but not for raw materials and subassemblies.

7. Which of the following is a false statement about the relationship between internal auditors and external auditors?

A. External auditors must assess the competence and objectivity of internal auditors.

B. There may be periodic meetings between internal and external auditors to discuss matters of mutual interest.

C. There may be an exchange of engagement communications and management letters.

D. Internal auditors may provide engagement work programs and working papers to external auditors.

Answer (A) is correct. *(CIA, adapted)*
REQUIRED: The false statement regarding the relationship between internal and external auditors.
DISCUSSION: The external auditor assesses the objectivity and competence of the internal auditors if their activities are relevant to the external audit and it is efficient to consider how that work may affect the nature, timing, and extent of external audit procedures. If the internal auditors are found to be sufficiently competent and objective, the external auditor then considers how their work will affect the external audit. Thus, external auditors are not required to assess the competence and objectivity of internal auditors.
Answer (B) is incorrect because the relationship should involve a sufficient number of meetings (PA 2050-1). Answer (C) is incorrect because the relationship should involve reasonable mutual access to engagement communications and management letters (PA 2050-1). Answer (D) is incorrect because the relationship should involve reasonable mutual access to engagement work programs and working papers (PA 2050-1).

8. To determine whether credit controls are inconsistently applied, preventing valid sales to creditworthy customers, the internal auditor should

A. Confirm current accounts receivable.

B. Trace postings on the accounts receivable ledger.

C. Analyze collection rates and credit histories.

D. Compare credit histories for those receiving credit and for those denied credit.

Answer (D) is correct. *(CIA, adapted)*
REQUIRED: The audit procedure to determine if credit controls are inconsistently applied.
DISCUSSION: Credit policy should maximize profits by balancing bad debt losses and the increase in sales derived from granting credit. One concern in an engagement involving credit management is whether credit policies and procedures are fairly administered.
Answer (A) is incorrect because, if credit is not granted, there would be no balance to confirm. Answer (B) is incorrect because, if credit is not granted, there would be no posting to trace. Answer (C) is incorrect because, if credit is not granted, there would be no receivable to collect.

9. A large manufacturer has a transportation division that supplies gasoline for the organization's vehicles. Gasoline is dispensed by an attendant who records the amount issued on a serially prenumbered gasoline disbursement form, which is then given to the accounting department for proper recording. When the quantity of gasoline falls to a certain level, the service station attendant prepares a purchase requisition and sends it to the purchasing department where a purchase order is prepared and recorded in a gasoline purchases journal. Which of the following engagement procedures will best determine whether gasoline disbursements are fully and completely recorded?

A. Compare the gasoline purchase requisitions with the gasoline disbursement records.

B. Select a number of gasoline purchases from the gasoline purchases journal and compare them with their corresponding purchase orders and ascertain that they are serially prenumbered, are matched with purchase requisitions, and are authorized by someone independent of employees of the service station.

C. Perform analytical procedures comparing this period's gasoline consumption with prior periods.

D. Match the quantity of gasoline disbursed according to disbursement forms with an independent reading of quantity disbursed at the pump.

Answer (D) is correct. *(CIA, adapted)*
REQUIRED: The best audit procedure to determine whether gasoline disbursements are fully and completely recorded.
DISCUSSION: Physical information is best obtained through direct observation or inspection by the internal auditor. Because the gasoline disbursement forms are prenumbered, the internal auditor is able to match them with the independent reading of quantity disbursed at the pump to test the completeness of disbursement records.
Answer (A) is incorrect because matching the gasoline purchase requisitions with the gasoline disbursement records is not a meaningful procedure. Temperature-related expansion and contraction can cause significant differences between purchases and disbursements. Answer (B) is incorrect because matching entries from the gasoline purchases journal with the corresponding purchase orders ascertains that purchases are supported by proper source documents but does not assure the completeness of the disbursement records. Answer (C) is incorrect because performing analytical procedures does not provide any information regarding proper controls over gasoline purchases.

10. Which of the following engagement techniques would be most persuasive in determining that significant inventory values on the books of an acquiree are accurately stated?

A. Obtain a management representation letter stating that inventory values are correctly stated.

B. Flowchart the inventory and warehousing cycle and form an opinion based on the quality of internal controls.

C. Conduct a physical inventory and bring in an independent expert if necessary to value inventory items.

D. Interview purchasing and materials control personnel to ascertain the quality of internal controls over inventory.

Answer (C) is correct. *(CIA, adapted)*
REQUIRED: The audit procedure providing the most persuasive evidence that inventory is accurately stated.
DISCUSSION: A physical inventory should almost certainly be requested for an acquisition involving significant inventory values. The internal auditor's direct observation of inventory provides the most reliable information. Appraisal by an outside service provider may be necessary if the internal audit activity lacks the necessary expertise.
Answer (A) is incorrect because management certification as a means of attesting inventory values does not provide sufficient, reliable, relevant, and useful information. Answer (B) is incorrect because flowcharting the internal controls is not an accurate test of inventory value. Answer (D) is incorrect because testimonial information is not sufficient to determine the correctness of inventory values.

11. One of the engagement objectives of a financial audit of the organization's accounts receivable function is to determine whether prescribed standard procedures are followed when credit is granted. Which of the following engagement procedures will produce the most reliable information?

A. Ask management of the credit department if specific policies and procedures are followed when granting credit.

B. Select a statistical sample of credit applications and test them for conformance with prescribed procedures.

C. Analytically review the relationships between trends in credit sales and bad debts.

D. Review procedures for periodically aging accounts receivable.

Answer (B) is correct. *(CIA, adapted)*
REQUIRED: The audit procedure resulting in the most competent evidence regarding the accounts receivable function.
DISCUSSION: To determine whether the accounts receivable function is following prescribed standards for the granting of credit, the internal auditor should select a statistical sample of credit applications and test them for conformance with prescribed procedures. Detailed testing of actual credit applications produces direct information about the application (or the lack of application) of specific procedures, for example, authorization of credit by an appropriate individual.
Answer (A) is incorrect because interviews with credit department management produce testimonial information that is more useful in gaining an understanding of operations or providing insight into the reasons for exceptions. Answer (C) is incorrect because analytical procedures can be used to isolate unusual or unexplained fluctuations but do not locate the cause. Answer (D) is incorrect because an aged accounts receivable schedule provides information about whether a particular account might be collected, not the application of credit procedures.

12. Cash receipts should be deposited on the day of receipt or the following business day. Select the most appropriate engagement procedure to determine that cash is promptly deposited.

A. Review cash register tapes prepared for each sale.

B. Review the functions of cash handling and maintaining accounting records for proper separation of duties.

C. Compare the daily cash receipts totals with the bank deposits.

D. Review the functions of cash receiving and disbursing for proper separation of duties.

Answer (C) is correct. *(CIA, adapted)*
REQUIRED: The most appropriate audit procedure to determine that cash is promptly deposited.
DISCUSSION: A standard control over the cash receipts function is to require that daily cash receipts be deposited promptly and intact. Hence, the total of cash receipts for a day should equal the bank deposit because no cash disbursements are made from the daily receipts. To determine whether cash receipts are promptly deposited, the internal auditor should compare the daily cash receipts totals with bank deposits.
Answer (A) is incorrect because cash register tapes will not ensure that cash is deposited. Answer (B) is incorrect because separating functions will not ensure that cash is deposited. Answer (D) is incorrect because separate receiving and disbursing functions will not ensure that cash is promptly deposited.

13. In a review of the accounting department's bank reconciliation unit, which of the following is an appropriate engagement procedure to test canceled checks for authorized signatures?

A. Compare the check date with the first cancelation date.

B. Determine that all checks are signed by individuals authorized by the board.

C. Examine a representative sample of signed checks and determine that the signatures are authorized in the organization's signature book.

D. Complete the tests of controls over check signatures in 4 hours.

Answer (C) is correct. *(CIA, adapted)*
REQUIRED: The audit procedure step for the review of canceled checks for authorization.
DISCUSSION: Cash disbursements must be properly authorized. The issuance of checks is performed by the treasury function after review of supporting documents, including a payment voucher prepared by the accounts payable department. Proper control procedures require that check-signing responsibility be limited to a few persons whose signatures are kept on file at the financial institutions where the organization has accounts.
Answer (A) is incorrect because comparing the check date with the first cancelation date has no bearing on a review for authorized signatures. Answer (B) is incorrect because a statement of an engagement objective is not an engagement procedure. Answer (D) is incorrect because a time budget goal is not an engagement procedure.

Question 14 is based on the following information. During an engagement to review the December 31, 2003, accounts payable balance of a division, the internal auditor has received from the division controller's office a schedule listing the creditors and the amount owed to each at December 31, 2003.

14. Which of the following engagement procedures best determines that no individual account payable has been omitted from the schedule?

A. Send confirmation requests to a randomly selected sample of creditors listed on the schedule.

B. Send confirmation requests to creditors listed on the schedule that were not listed on the corresponding December 31, 2002, schedule.

C. Examine support for selected January 2004 payments to creditors, ascertaining that those relating to 2004 are not on the schedule.

D. Examine support for selected January 2004 payments to creditors, ascertaining that those relating to 2003 are on the schedule.

Answer (D) is correct. *(CIA, adapted)*
REQUIRED: The best audit procedure to detect unrecorded payables.
DISCUSSION: The greatest danger in an engagement involving accounts payable is that unrecorded liabilities exist. Omission of an entry to record a payable is an irregularity more difficult to detect than an inaccurate or false entry. The search for unrecorded payables should include examining cash disbursements made after the balance sheet date for expenditures for goods and services received prior to year-end and comparing them with the accounts payable trial balance, sending confirmations to vendors with zero balances, and reconciling payable balances with vendors' documentation.
Answer (A) is incorrect because confirmation is unlikely to detect unrecorded amounts owed to creditors not listed on the schedule. Answer (B) is incorrect because confirmation of zero balances might be more useful to detect unrecorded amounts than confirming amounts owed currently. Answer (C) is incorrect because this procedure is intended to detect overstatement, not understatement, of 2003 payables.

15. Which is the best engagement procedure to obtain information to support the legal ownership of real property?

A. Examination of board resolutions with regard to approvals to acquire real property.

B. Examination of closing documents, deeds, and ownership documents registered and on file in local government records.

C. Discussion with the organization's legal counsel concerning the acquisition of a specific piece of property.

D. Confirmation with the title company that handled the escrow account and disbursement of proceeds on the closing of the property.

Answer (B) is correct. *(CIA, adapted)*
REQUIRED: The best audit procedure for obtaining evidence to support the legal ownership of real property.
DISCUSSION: Examination of title documents, the deed, and any other supporting documents, such as closing documents, will be helpful in verifying ownership. But these records are not conclusive. An inspection of public records will determine whether any interests in the property (e.g., mortgages, judgment liens, or claims to the title) exist that do not appear in the engagement client's records.
Answer (A) is incorrect because an examination of board resolutions will not provide information about actual ownership, only approval to acquire the property. Answer (C) is incorrect because the testimony of legal counsel provides only corroborating information. Answer (D) is incorrect because confirmation with an escrow agent provides information only about the closing. It does not provide information regarding subsequent transactions, such as a mortgage liability not recorded in the accounting records.

16. To ascertain that all credit sales are recorded in accounts receivable, an internal auditor should

A. Confirm selected accounts receivable balances by direct correspondence with customers.

B. Vouch a sample of subsidiary ledger entries to related sales invoices and to related shipping documents.

C. Compare a sample of customer purchase orders with related shipping documents.

D. Trace a sample of shipping documents to related sales invoices and the subsidiary ledger.

Answer (D) is correct. *(CIA, adapted)*
REQUIRED: The audit procedure to ascertain that all credit sales are recorded in accounts receivable.
DISCUSSION: Customer orders should be approved and sales invoices prepared before shipping documents are created. To determine that all credit sales are recorded, the proper direction of testing is from the shipping records, such as bills of lading, to the sales invoices and the accounts receivable subsidiary ledger.
Answer (A) is incorrect because confirming accounts receivable will not detect an unrecorded and unbilled receivable. Answer (B) is incorrect because vouching entries will not detect an unrecorded and unbilled receivable. Answer (C) is incorrect because comparing customer orders with shipping documents does not determine whether goods shipped were billed.

Question 17 is based on the following information. The internal auditor of a construction enterprise that builds foundations for bridges and large buildings performed a review of the expense accounts for equipment (augers) used to drill holes in rocks to set the foundation for the buildings. During the review, the internal auditor noted that the expenses related to some of the auger accounts had increased dramatically during the year. The internal auditor inquired of the construction manager who offered the explanation that the augers last 2 to 3 years and are expensed when purchased. Thus, the internal auditor should see a decrease in the expense accounts for these augers in the next year but would expect an increase in the expenses of other augers. The internal auditor also found out that the construction manager is responsible for the inventorying and receiving of the augers and is a part owner of a business that supplies augers to the organization. The supplier was approved by the president to improve the quality of equipment.

17. Which of the following procedures would be the least appropriate engagement procedure to address these analytical observations?

A. Note the explanation in the working papers for investigation during the next engagement and perform no further work at this time.

B. Develop a comparative analysis of auger expense over the past few years to determine if the relationship held in previous years.

C. Take a sample of debits to the auger expense account and trace to independent shipping documents and to invoices for the augers.

D. Arrange to take an inventory of augers to determine if the augers purchased this year were on hand and would be available for use in the next 2 years.

Answer (A) is correct. *(CIA, adapted)*
REQUIRED: The least appropriate audit procedure to address the findings.
DISCUSSION: Performing no further work is the least appropriate engagement procedure because it defers the investigation to the following year. The construction manager's conflict of interest provides the motive for fraud, and the ineffective controls allow its commission and concealment.
Answer (B) is incorrect because a comparative analysis is an effective procedure to establish the reasonableness of the manager's explanation. If the relationship is valid, it should also have held in previous years. Answer (C) is incorrect because the internal auditor should obtain independent information as to whether the goods invoiced were received. The internal auditor should search for receiving reports signed by parties other than the construction manager and should verify that those individuals exist. The construction manager is in a position to bill the organization for more augers than are actually received and to conceal the shortage. Answer (D) is incorrect because taking an inventory of the augers enables the internal auditor to verify their existence and condition.

18. The internal auditors are evaluating the adequacy of the new policies and procedures in maintaining an appropriate risk profile. Which of the following engagement procedures is least relevant to the accomplishment of the engagement objective?

A. Meet with operational management to determine its interpretation of those procedures that are not clear.

B. Meet with senior management or a board member, if necessary, to clarify policy issues.

C. Test a sample of investments for compliance with the new procedures.

D. Review recent regulatory pronouncements to determine whether the new procedures are consistent with regulatory requirements.

Answer (C) is correct. *(CIA, adapted)*
REQUIRED: The audit procedure least relevant to the evaluation of new controls over investing and lending activities.
DISCUSSION: Based on the results of the risk assessment, the internal audit activity should evaluate the adequacy and effectiveness of controls (for example, the new policies and procedures for monitoring investments and loans) encompassing the organization's governance, operations, and information systems. This should include, among other things, the reliability and integrity of financial information (Standard 2120.A1). Adequacy of risk management, control, and governance processes is present when management plans and designs them so that they provide reasonable assurance that organizational objectives and goals will be achieved efficiently and economically. Testing for compliance with controls is a procedure to determine their effectiveness, that is, whether management has directed processes so that they provide reasonable assurance that organizational objectives and goals will be achieved (PA 2100-1).
Answer (A) is incorrect because the internal auditors must seek authoritative interpretations of vague operating standards. Answer (B) is incorrect because policy issues that are not clear should be clarified by upper management or the board. Answer (D) is incorrect because the auditors should determine whether the criteria used by the organization comply with laws, regulations, and contracts.

19. The audit committee has expressed concern that the financial institution has been taking on higher-risk loans in pursuit of short-term profit goals. Which of the following engagement procedures provides the least amount of information to address this concern?

A. Perform an analytical review of interest income as a percentage of the investment portfolio in comparison with a group of peer financial institutions.

B. Take a random sample of loans made during the period and compare the riskiness of the loans with that of a random sample of loans made 2 years ago.

C. Perform an analytical review that involves developing a chart to compare interest income plotted over the past 10 years.

D. Develop a multiple-regression time-series analysis of income over the past 5 years including such factors as interest rate in the economy, size of loan portfolio, and dollar amount of new loans each year.

Answer (C) is correct. *(CIA, adapted)*
REQUIRED: The audit procedure least useful in addressing the concern about making riskier loans for short-term purposes.
DISCUSSION: Plotting the changes in interest income over the past 10 years is the least useful procedure. It does not consider other important factors, such as size of the portfolio, changes in interest rates, the development of new financial instruments, the level of inflation, and government regulation.
Answer (A) is incorrect because higher-risk loans should generate higher short-term interest income compared with that earned by comparable institutions. Higher-risk loans have higher yields. Answer (B) is incorrect because a historical comparison of loan risk for the institution addresses the engagement objective. Answer (D) is incorrect because multiple regression explains the change in a dependent variable (interest income) attributable to two or more independent variables. Thus, it allows the internal auditor to estimate how much of the change might be due to a change in the riskiness of the loans.

Use Gleim's *CIA Test Prep* for interactive testing with over 2,000 additional multiple-choice questions!

APPENDIX A
THE IIA CONTENT SPECIFICATION OUTLINES (CSOs)

We have reproduced The IIA's Content Specification Outlines (CSOs) verbatim from their website (www.theiia.org) for your convenience. Please visit The IIA's website for updates and more information about the exam. Rely on the Gleim book and software to pass each part of the exam. We have researched and studied The IIA's CSOs as well as questions from prior exams to provide you with an excellent review program.

PART I – THE INTERNAL AUDIT ACTIVITY'S ROLE IN GOVERNANCE, RISK, AND CONTROL

A. **COMPLY WITH THE IIA'S ATTRIBUTE STANDARDS (15 - 25%)** (proficiency level)

1. Define purpose, authority, and responsibility of the internal audit activity.

   a. Determine if purpose, authority, and responsibility of internal audit activity are clearly documented/approved.
   b. Determine if purpose, authority, and responsibility of internal audit activity are communicated to engagement clients.
   c. Demonstrate an understanding of the purpose, authority, and responsibility of the internal audit activity.

2. Maintain independence and objectivity.

   a. Foster independence.

      1) Understand organizational independence.
      2) Recognize the importance of organizational independence.
      3) Determine if the internal audit activity is properly aligned to achieve organizational independence.

   b. Foster objectivity.

      1) Establish policies to promote objectivity.
      2) Assess individual objectivity.
      3) Maintain individual objectivity.
      4) Recognize and mitigate impairments to independence and objectivity.

3. Determine if the required knowledge, skills, and competencies are available.

   a. Understand the knowledge, skills, and competencies that an internal auditor needs to possess.
   b. Identify the knowledge, skills, and competencies required to fulfill the responsibilities of the internal audit activity.

4. Develop and/or procure necessary knowledge, skills, and competencies collectively required by internal audit activity.

5. Exercise due professional care.

6. Promote continuing professional development.

   a. Develop and implement a plan for continuing professional development for internal audit staff.
   b. Enhance individual competency through continuing professional development.

7. Promote quality assurance and improvement of the internal audit activity.

   a. Establish and maintain a quality assurance and improvement program.
   b. Monitor the effectiveness of the quality assurance and improvement program.
   c. Report the results of the quality assurance and improvement program to the board or other governing body.
   d. Conduct quality assurance procedures and recommend improvements to the performance of the internal audit activity.

8. Abide by and promote compliance with The IIA Code of Ethics.

B.   **ESTABLISH A RISK-BASED PLAN TO DETERMINE THE PRIORITIES OF THE INTERNAL AUDIT ACTIVITY (15 - 25%)** (proficiency level)

   1.   Establish a framework for assessing risk.
   2.   Use the framework to:

      a.   Identify sources of potential engagements (e.g., audit universe, management request, regulatory mandate)
      b.   Assess organization-wide risk
      c.   Solicit potential engagement topics from various sources
      d.   Collect and analyze data on proposed engagements
      e.   Rank and validate risk priorities

   3.   Identify internal audit resource requirements.
   4.   Coordinate the internal audit activity's efforts with:

      a.   External auditor
      b.   Regulatory oversight bodies
      c.   Other internal assurance functions (e.g., health and safety department)

   5.   Select engagements.

      a.   Participate in the engagement selection process.
      b.   Select engagements.
      c.   Communicate and obtain approval of the engagement plan from board.

C.   **UNDERSTAND THE INTERNAL AUDIT ACTIVITY'S ROLE IN ORGANIZATIONAL GOVERNANCE (10 - 20%)** (proficiency level)

   1.   Obtain board's approval of audit charter.
   2.   Communicate plan of engagements.
   3.   Report significant audit issues.
   4.   Communicate key performance indicators to board on a regular basis.
   5.   Discuss areas of significant risk.
   6.   Support board in enterprise-wide risk assessment.
   7.   Review positioning of the internal audit function within the risk management framework within the organization.
   8.   Monitor compliance with the corporate code of conduct/business practices.
   9.   Report on the effectiveness of the control framework.
   10. Assist board in assessing the independence of the external auditor.
   11. Assess ethical climate of the board.
   12. Assess ethical climate of the organization.
   13. Assess compliance with policies in specific areas (e.g., derivatives).
   14. Assess organization's reporting mechanism to the board.
   15. Conduct follow-up and report on management response to regulatory body reviews.
   16. Conduct follow-up and report on management response to external audit.
   17. Assess the adequacy of the performance measurement system, achievement of corporate objective.
   18. Support a culture of fraud awareness and encourage the reporting of improprieties.

D.   **PERFORM OTHER INTERNAL AUDIT ROLES AND RESPONSIBILITIES (0 - 10%)** (proficiency level)

   1.   Ethics/compliance

      a.   Investigate and recommend resolution for ethics/compliance complaints.
      b.   Determine disposition of ethics violations.
      c.   Foster healthy ethical climate.
      d.   Maintain and administer business conduct policy (e.g., conflict of interest).
      e.   Report on compliance.

   2.   Risk management

      a.   Develop and implement an organization-wide risk and control framework.
      b.   Coordinate enterprise-wide risk assessment.
      c.   Report corporate risk assessment to board.
      d.   Review business continuity planning process.

   3.   Privacy

      a.   Determine privacy vulnerabilities.
      b.   Report on compliance.

   4.   Information or physical security

      a.   Determine security vulnerabilities.
      b.   Determine disposition of security violations.
      c.   Report on compliance.

E. **GOVERNANCE, RISK, AND CONTROL KNOWLEDGE ELEMENTS (15 - 25%)**

    1. Corporate governance principles (awareness level)
    2. Alternative control frameworks (awareness level)
    3. Risk vocabulary and concepts (proficiency level)
    4. Risk management techniques (proficiency level)
    5. Risk/control implications of different organizational structures (proficiency level)
    6. Risk/control implications of different leadership styles (awareness level)
    7. Change management (awareness level)
    8. Conflict management (awareness level)
    9. Management control techniques (proficiency level)
    10. Types of control (preventive, detective, input, output) (proficiency level)

F. **PLAN ENGAGEMENTS (15 - 25%)** (proficiency level)

    1. Initiate preliminary communication with engagement client.
    2. Conduct a preliminary survey of the area of engagement.

        a. Obtain input from engagement client.
        b. Perform analytical reviews.
        c. Perform benchmarking.
        d. Conduct interviews.
        e. Review prior audit reports and other relevant documentation.
        f. Map processes.
        g. Develop checklists.

    3. Complete a detailed risk assessment of the area (prioritize or evaluate risk/control factors).
    4. Coordinate audit engagement efforts with

        a. External auditor
        b. Regulatory oversight bodies

    5. Establish/refine engagement objectives and identify/finalize the scope of engagement.
    6. Identify or develop criteria for assurance engagements (criteria against which to audit).
    7. Consider the potential for fraud when planning an engagement.

        a. Be knowledgeable of the risk factors and red flags of fraud.
        b. Identify common types of fraud associated with the engagement area.
        c. Determine if risk of fraud requires special consideration when conducting an engagement.

    8. Determine engagement procedures.
    9. Determine the level of staff and resources needed for the engagement.
    10. Establish adequate planning and supervision of the engagement.
    11. Prepare engagement work program.

FORMAT: 125 Multiple-choice questions

PART II – CONDUCTING THE INTERNAL AUDIT ENGAGEMENT

A. **CONDUCT ENGAGEMENTS (25 - 35%)** (proficiency level)

    1. Research and apply appropriate standards:

        a. IIA Professional Practices Framework (Code of Ethics, Standards, and Practice Advisories)
        b. Other professional, legal, and regulatory standards

    2. Maintain an awareness of potential for fraud when conducting an engagement.

        a. Notice indicators or symptoms of fraud.
        b. Design appropriate engagement steps to address significant risk of fraud.
        c. Employ audit tests to detect fraud.
        d. Determine if any suspected fraud merits investigation.

    3. Collect data.
    4. Evaluate the relevance, sufficiency, and competence of evidence.
    5. Analyze and interpret data.
    6. Develop workpapers.
    7. Review workpapers.
    8. Communicate interim progress.
    9. Draw conclusions.
    10. Develop recommendations when appropriate.

11.   Report engagement results.

    a.   Conduct exit conference.
    b.   Prepare report or other communication.
    c.   Approve engagement report.
    d.   Determine distribution of report.
    e.   Obtain management response to report.

12.   Conduct client satisfaction survey.
13.   Complete performance appraisals of engagement staff.

B.   CONDUCT SPECIFIC ENGAGEMENTS (25 - 35%) (proficiency level)

1.   Conduct assurance engagements.

    a.   Fraud investigation

        1)   Determine appropriate parties to be involved with investigation.
        2)   Establish facts and extent of fraud (e.g., interviews, interrogations, and data analysis).
        3)   Report outcomes to appropriate parties.
        4)   Complete a process review to improve controls to prevent fraud and recommend changes.

    b.   Risk and control self-assessment

        1)   Facilitated approach

            a)   Client-facilitated
            b)   Audit-facilitated

        2)   Questionnaire approach
        3)   Self-certification approach

    c.   Audits of third parties and contract auditing
    d.   Quality audit engagements
    e.   Due diligence audit engagements
    f.   Security audit engagements
    g.   Privacy audit engagements
    h.   Performance (key performance indicators) audit engagements
    i.   Operational (efficiency and effectiveness) audit engagements
    j.   Financial audit engagements
    k.   Information technology (IT) audit engagements

        1)   Operating systems

            a)   Mainframe
            b)   Workstations
            c)   Server

        2)   Application development

            a)   Application authentication
            b)   Systems development methodology
            c)   Change control
            d)   End user computing

        3)   Data and network communications/connections (e.g., LAN, VAN, and WAN)
        4)   Voice communications
        5)   System security (e.g., firewalls, access control)
        6)   Contingency planning
        7)   Databases
        8)   Functional areas of IT operations (e.g., data center operations)
        9)   Web infrastructure
        10)   Software licensing
        11)   Electronic Funds Transfer (EFT)/Electronic Data Interchange (EDI)
        12)   E-Commerce
        13)   Information protection/viruses
        14)   Encryption
        15)   Enterprise-wide resource planning (ERP) software (e.g., SAP R/3)

    l.   Compliance audit engagements

2.   Conduct consulting engagements.

    a.   Internal control training
    b.   Business process review
    c.   Benchmarking
    d.   Information technology (IT) and systems development
    e.   Design of performance measurement systems

C. **MONITOR ENGAGEMENT OUTCOMES (5 - 15%)** (proficiency level)

    1.   Determine appropriate follow-up activity by the internal audit activity
    2.   Identify appropriate method to monitor engagement outcomes
    3.   Conduct follow-up activity
    4.   Communicate monitoring plan and results

D. **FRAUD KNOWLEDGE ELEMENTS (5 - 15%)**

    1.   Discovery sampling (awareness level)
    2.   Interrogation techniques (awareness level)
    3.   Forensic auditing (awareness level)
    4.   Use of computers in analyzing data (awareness level)
    5.   Red flag (proficiency level)
    6.   Types of fraud (proficiency level)

E. **ENGAGEMENT TOOLS (15 - 25%)**

    1.   Sampling (awareness level)

        a.   Nonstatistical (judgmental)
        b.   Statistical

    2.   Statistical analyses (process control techniques) (awareness level)
    3.   Data gathering tools (proficiency level)

        a.   Interviewing
        b.   Questionnaires
        c.   Checklists

    4.   Analytical review techniques (proficiency level)

        a.   Ratio estimation
        b.   Variance analysis (e.g., budget vs. actual)
        c.   Other reasonableness tests

    5.   Observation (proficiency level)
    6.   Problem solving (proficiency level)
    7.   Risk and control self-assessment (CSA) (awareness level)
    8.   Computerized audit tools and techniques (proficiency level)

        a.   Embedded audit modules
        b.   Data extraction techniques
        c.   Generalized audit software (e.g., ACL, IDEA)
        d.   Spreadsheet analysis
        e.   Automated workpapers (e.g., Lotus Notes, Auditor Assistant)

    9.   Process mapping including flowcharting (proficiency level)

    FORMAT: 125 multiple-choice questions

PART III – BUSINESS ANALYSIS AND INFORMATION TECHNOLOGY

A. **BUSINESS PROCESSES (15 - 25%)**

    1.   Quality management (e.g., TQM) (awareness level)
    2.   The International Organization for Standardization (ISO) framework (awareness level)
    3.   Forecasting (awareness level)
    4.   Project management techniques (proficiency level)
    5.   Business process analysis (e.g., workflow analysis and bottleneck management, theory of constraints) (proficiency level)
    6.   Inventory management techniques and concepts (proficiency level)
    7.   Marketing- pricing objectives and policies (awareness level)
    8.   Marketing- supply chain management (awareness level)
    9.   Human Resources (individual performance management and measurement, supervision, environmental factors that affect performance, facilitation techniques, personnel sourcing/staffing, training and development, and safety) (proficiency level)
  10.   Balanced Scorecard (awareness level)

B. **FINANCIAL ACCOUNTING AND FINANCE (15 - 25%)**

    1.   Basic concepts and underlying principles of financial accounting (statements, terminology, relationships) (proficiency level)
    2.   Intermediate concepts of financial accounting (e.g., bonds, leases, pensions, intangible assets, R&D) (awareness level)
    3.   Advanced concepts of financial accounting (e.g., consolidation, partnerships, foreign currency transactions) (awareness level)

4.   Financial statement analysis (proficiency level)
5.   Cost of capital evaluation (awareness level)
6.   Types of debt and equity (awareness level)
7.   Financial instruments (e.g., derivatives) (awareness level)
8.   Cash management (treasury functions) (awareness level)
9.   Valuation models (awareness level)

   a.   Inventory valuation
   b.   Business valuation

10.   Business development life cycles (awareness level)

C.   **MANAGERIAL ACCOUNTING (10 - 20%)**

1.   Cost concepts (e.g., absorption, variable, fixed) (proficiency level)
2.   Capital budgeting (awareness level)
3.   Operating budget (proficiency level)
4.   Transfer pricing (awareness level)
5.   Cost-volume-profit analysis (awareness level)
6.   Relevant cost (awareness level)
7.   Costing systems (e.g., activity-based, standard) (awareness level)
8.   Responsibility accounting (awareness level)

D.   **REGULATORY, LEGAL, AND ECONOMICS (5 - 15%)** (awareness level)

1.   Impact of government legislation and regulation on business
2.   Trade legislation and regulations
3.   Taxation schemes
4.   Contracts
5.   Nature and rules of legal evidence
6.   Key economic indicators

E.   **INFORMATION TECHNOLOGY (IT) (30 - 40%)** (awareness level)

1.   Control frameworks (e.g., SAC, COBIT)
2.   Data and network communications/connections (e.g., LAN, VAN, and WAN)
3.   Electronic funds transfer (EFT)
4.   E-Commerce
5.   Electronic data interchange (EDI)
6.   Functional areas of IT operations (e.g., data center operations)
7.   Encryption
8.   Viruses
9.   Information protection
10.   Evaluate investment in IT (cost of ownership)
11.   Enterprise-wide resource planning (ERP) software (e.g., SAP R/3, Peoplesoft)
12.   Operating systems
13.   Application development
14.   Voice communications
15.   Contingency planning
16.   Systems security (e.g., firewalls, access control)
17.   Databases
18.   Software licensing
19.   Web infrastructure

FORMAT: 125 multiple-choice questions

PART IV – BUSINESS MANAGEMENT SKILLS

A.   **STRATEGIC MANAGEMENT (20 - 30%)** (awareness level)

1.   Global analytical techniques

   a.   Structural analysis of industries
   b.   Competitive strategies (e.g., Porter's model)
   c.   Competitive analysis
   d.   Market signals
   e.   Industry evolution

2.   Industry environments

   a.   Competitive strategies related to:

      1)   Fragmented industries
      2)   Emerging industries
      3)   Declining industries

      b.   Competition in global industries

           1)   Sources/impediments
           2)   Evolution of global markets
           3)   Strategic alternatives
           4)   Trends affecting competition

   3.   Strategic decisions

      a.   Analysis of integration strategies
      b.   Capacity expansion
      c.   Entry into new businesses

   4.   Portfolio techniques of competitive analysis
   5.   Product life cycles

B.   **GLOBAL BUSINESS ENVIRONMENTS (15 - 25%)** (awareness level)

   1.   Cultural/legal/political environments

      a.   Balancing global requirements and local imperatives
      b.   Global mindsets (personal characteristics/competencies)
      c.   Sources and methods for managing complexities and contradictions
      d.   Managing multicultural teams

   2.   Economic/financial environments

      a.   Global, multinational, international, and multilocal compared and contrasted
      b.   Requirements for entering the global market place
      c.   Creating organizational adaptability
      d.   Managing training and development

C.   **ORGANIZATIONAL BAHAVIOR (20 - 30%)** (awareness level)

   1.   Motivation

      a.   Relevance and implication of various theories
      b.   Impact of job design, rewards, work schedules, etc.

   2.   Communication

      a.   The process
      b.   Organizational dynamics
      c.   Impact of computerization

   3.   Performance

      a.   Productivity
      b.   Effectiveness

   4.   Structure

      a.   Centralized/decentralized
      b.   Departmentalization
      c.   New configurations (e.g., hourglass, cluster, network)

D.   **MANAGEMENT SKILLS (20 - 30%)** (awareness level)

   1.   Group dynamics

      a.   Traits (cohesiveness, roles, norms, groupthink, etc.)
      b.   Stages of group development
      c.   Organizational politics
      d.   Criteria and determinants of effectiveness

   2.   Team building

      a.   Methods used in team building
      b.   Assessing team performance

   3.   Leadership skills

      a.   Theories compared/contrasted
      b.   Leadership grid (topology of leadership styles)
      c.   Mentoring

   4.   Personal time management

E.   **NEGOTIATING (5 - 15%)** (awareness level)

1.   Conflict resolution

a.   Competitive/cooperative
b.   Compromise, forcing, smoothing, etc.

2.   Added-value negotiating

a.   Description
b.   Specific steps

FORMAT: 125 multiple-choice questions

APPENDIX B
THE IIA EXAMINATION BIBLIOGRAPHY

The Institute has prepared a listing of references for the CIA exam, reproduced beginning below. These publications have been chosen by the Board of Regents as reasonably representative of the common body of knowledge for internal auditors. However, all of the information in these texts will not be tested. When possible, questions will be written based on the information contained in the suggested reference list. This bibliography is reorganized in an alphabetical listing by part to give you an overview of the scope of each part. The IIA also indicates that the examination scope includes

1. Articles from *Internal Auditor* (The IIA periodical)
2. IIA research reports
3. IIA pronouncements, e.g., The IIA Code of Ethics and SIASs
4. Past published CIA examinations

The IIA bibliography is reproduced for your information only. The texts you will need to acquire (use) to prepare for the CIA exam will depend on many factors, including

1. Innate ability
2. Length of time out of school
3. Thoroughness of your undergraduate education
4. Familiarity with internal auditing due to relevant experience

SUGGESTED REFERENCES FOR THE CIA EXAM

PART I: THE INTERNAL AUDIT ACTIVITY'S ROLE IN GOVERNANCE, RISK, AND CONTROL

Sawyer, et al, *Sawyer's Internal Auditing*, 5th Ed., The Institute of Internal Auditors.

OR Sears, *Internal Auditing Manual*, WG&L Financial Reporting & Management.

The American Institute of Certified Public Accountants, *Internal Control - Integrated Framework*, 1994.

The Institute of Internal Auditors, Inc., *Professional Practices Framework*, 2002.

OR *Other Control and Governance Frameworks*.

Supplemental:

Albrecht, Wernz, and Williams, *Fraud: Bringing Light to the Dark Side of Business*, Irwin Professional Publishing.

Murphy and Parker, *Handbook of IT Auditing*, Warren, Gorham & Lamont.

Reider, *Complete Guide to Operational Auditing*, John Wiley & Sons, Inc.

PART II: CONDUCTING THE INTERNAL AUDIT ENGAGEMENT

Sawyer, et al, *Sawyer's Internal Auditing*, 5th Ed., The Institute of Internal Auditors.

OR Sears, *Internal Auditing Manual*, WG&L Financial Reporting & Management.

The Institute of Internal Auditors, Inc., *Professional Practices Framework*, 2002.

Supplemental:

Kreitner, *Management*, 9th Ed., Houghton Mifflin Co., 2004.

PART III: BUSINESS ANALYSIS AND INFORMATION TECHNOLOGY

Information Systems and Control Foundation, *Cobit: Governance, Control, and Audit for Information and Related Technology*, 3rd Ed., 2000.

International Accounting Standards Committee, *International Accounting Standards*, 2002.

Kieso, Warfield, and Weygandt, *Intermediate Accounting*, 11th Ed., John Wiley & Sons, Inc., 2004.

Kreitner, *Management*, 9th Ed., Houghton Mifflin Co., 2004.

Sawyer, et al, *Sawyer's Internal Auditing*, 5th Ed., the Institute of Internal Auditors.

OR Sears, *Internal Auditing Manual*, WG&L Financial Reporting & Management.

The Institute of Internal Auditors Research Foundation, *Systems Assurance and Control*, 2003.

Weber, *Information Systems Control and Audit*, Prentice Hall, 1998.

PART IV: BUSINESS MANAGEMENT SKILLS

Bruner, Eaker, Freeman, Spelkman, Teisberg, and Venkataraman, *The Portable MBA*, 4th Ed., John Wiley & Sons, 2002.

Fisher, Ury, and Patton, *Getting to Yes, Negotiating Agreement Without Giving In*, Penguin USA.

Hill, *International Business with Global Resource CD, Powerweb and World Map*, 4th Ed., McGraw-Hill/Irwin, 2002.

Kreitner, *Management*, 9th Ed., Houghton Mifflin Co., 2004.

Kotler, *Marketing Management*, 11th Ed., Prentice Hall, 2002.

PUBLICATIONS AVAILABLE FROM THE IIA

The listing on the previous pages presents only some of the current technical literature available. Quantity discounts are provided. Inquiries should be sent to

Customer Service
Institute of Internal Auditors
249 Maitland Avenue
Altamonte Springs, FL 32701-4201

Request a current catalog by mail or call
(407) 830-7600, ext. 1

Book orders can be placed directly by calling (877) 867-4957 (toll-free) or (770) 442-8633, extension 275.

ORDERING TEXTUAL MATERIAL

The IIA does not carry all of the reference books. Write directly to the publisher if you cannot obtain the desired texts from your local bookstore. Begin your study program with *CIA Review*, Parts I through IV, which most candidates find sufficient. If you need additional reference material, borrow books from colleagues, professors, or a library.

Addison-Wesley Publishing
Company
Reading, MA 01867

Basic Books, Inc.
Harper & Row Publishers
10 East 53rd Street
New York, NY 10022

Business Publications, Inc.
1700 Alma, Suite 390
Plano, TX 75075

The Dryden Press
One Salt Creek Lane
Hinsdale, IL 60521-2902

Harcourt Brace Jovanovich
1250 Sixth Avenue
San Diego, CA 92101

Harper & Row
10 East 53rd Street
New York, NY 10022

Holt, Rinehart, Winston
383 Madison Avenue
New York, NY 10017

Houghton Mifflin Company
One Beacon Street
Boston, MA 02108

Richard D. Irwin, Inc.
1818 Ridge Road
Homewood, IL 60430

Kent Publishing Company
20 Park Plaza
Boston, MA 02116

McGraw-Hill Book Company
1221 Avenue of the Americas
New York, NY 10020

Mitchell Publishing, Inc.
915 River Street
Santa Cruz, CA 95060

Prentice-Hall, Inc.
Englewood Cliffs, NJ 07632

Reston Publishing Company
11480 Sunset Hills Road
Reston, VA 22090

South-Western Publishing
Company
5101 Madison Road
Cincinnati, OH 45227

West Publishing Company
P.O. Box 55165
St. Paul, MN 55101

John Wiley & Sons, Inc.
605 Third Avenue
New York, NY 10016

INDEX

COMPLETE GLEIM CPA SYSTEM with REVIEW ONLINE
☐ $924.95 $_____

All 4 parts, including 5 books, 4 audios, CPA Test Prep software, **Review Online**[1], plus bonus book bag.

Also available by exam part — Auditing ☐ $256.95   Business ☐ $256.95

(Does not include book bag.) — Financial ☐ $256.95   Regulation ☐ $256.95 $_____

GLEIM CPA SET
☐ $539.95 $_____

All 4 parts, including 5 books, 4 audios, CPA Test Prep software, plus bonus book bag.

CPA REVIEW

	Online Simulations (included in Review Online)	Book/Software/ Audio Package Save 18%	Book/Software Package Save 16%	Audio Reviews	Software	Books	
Auditing	☐ @$99.95	☐ @$143.95	☐ @$74.95	☐ @$89.95	☐ @$49.95	☐ @$39.95	$____
Business	☐ @$99.95	☐ @$143.95	☐ @$74.95	☐ @$89.95	☐ @$49.95	☐ @$39.95	____
Regulation	☐ @$99.95	☐ @$143.95	☐ @$74.95	☐ @$89.95	☐ @$49.95	☐ @$39.95	____
Financial	☐ @$99.95	☐ @$143.95	☐ @$74.95	☐ @$89.95	☐ @$49.95	☐ @$39.95	____
A System for Success		☐ @$19.95 (FREE with the purchase of any Gleim CPA Review book.)					____

COMPLETE GLEIM CMA/CFM SYSTEM
☐ $566.95 $_____

Includes: 5-part set (book, software, and audio), plus bonus book bag.

GLEIM 4-Part Set

Includes: 4-part set (book, software, and audio), plus bonus book bag.   ☐ CMA@$453.95   ☐ CFM@$453.95 $_____

CMA/CFM REVIEW

	Book/Software/ Audio Package Save 15%	Book/Software Package Save 10%	Audio Reviews	Software	Books	
Part 1 Eco., Fin., & Mgmt.	☐ @$120.95	☐ @$64.95	☐ @$69.95	☐ @$44.95	☐ @$26.95	$____
Part 2CMA Fin. Acc. & Rep.	☐ @$120.95	☐ @$64.95	☐ @$69.95	☐ @$44.95	☐ @$26.95	____
Part 2CFM Corp. Fin. Mgmt.	☐ @$120.95	☐ @$64.95	☐ @$69.95	☐ @$44.95	☐ @$26.95	____
Part 3 Mgmt. Rep./Behav. Iss.	☐ @$120.95	☐ @$64.95	☐ @$69.95	☐ @$44.95	☐ @$26.95	____
Part 4 Dec. Anal. & Info. Sys.	☐ @$120.95	☐ @$64.95	☐ @$69.95	☐ @$44.95	☐ @$26.95	____

CIA REVIEW

	Book/Software Package Save 10%	Software	Books	
All 4 Parts	☐ @$279.80	☐ @$199.80	☐ @$119.80	$____
Part I Internal Audit Role in Governance, Risk, & Control	☐ @$69.95	☐ @$49.95	☐ @$29.95	____
Part II Conducting the Internal Audit Engagement	☐ @$69.95	☐ @$49.95	☐ @$29.95	____
Part III Business Analysis and Information Technology	☐ @$69.95	☐ @$49.95	☐ @$29.95	____
Part IV Business Management Skills	☐ @$69.95	☐ @$49.95	☐ @$29.95	____

EA REVIEW

	Book/Software Package Save 10%	Software	Books	
All 4 Parts	☐ @$279.80	☐ @$199.80	☐ @$119.95	$____
Part 1 Individuals	☐ @$69.95	☐ @$49.95	☐ @$29.95	____
Part 2 Sole Prop. & Partnerships	☐ @$69.95	☐ @$49.95	☐ @$29.95	____
Part 3 Corp./Fid./Est. & Gift Tax	☐ @$69.95	☐ @$49.95	☐ @$29.95	____
Part 4 IRS Adm/Other Topics	☐ @$69.95	☐ @$49.95	☐ @$29.95	____

"THE GLEIM SERIES" EXAM QUESTIONS AND EXPANATIONS BOOKS, SOFTWARE, AND CPE[2]

	Book/Software Package (Save 25%)	Software	Books	Books & CPE	
Auditing & Systems	☐ @$29.95	☐ @$20.00	☐ @$19.95	☐ @200.00	$____
Business Law/Legal Studies	☐ @$29.95	☐ @$20.00	☐ @$19.95		____
Federal Tax	☐ @$29.95	☐ @$20.00	☐ @$19.95	☐ @200.00	____
Financial Accounting	☐ @$29.95	☐ @$20.00	☐ @$19.95	☐ @200.00	____
Cost/Managerial Accounting	☐ @$29.95	☐ @$20.00	☐ @$19.95		____

[1]For more information on our **CPA Review Online**, please visit **www.gleim.com/CPAOL/**

[2]For our online **CPE** courses and course catalog, please visit **www.gleim.com/CPE/**

SUBTOTAL $_____

Complete your order on the next page.

GLEIM Publications, Inc.

P. O. Box 12848   Gainesville, FL 32604

TOLL FREE:	(888) 87-GLEIM	Customer service is available (Eastern Time):
LOCAL:	(352) 375-0772	8:00 a.m. - 7:00 p.m., Mon. - Fri.
FAX:	(888) 375 -6940 (toll free)	9:00 a.m. - 2:00 p.m., Saturday
INTERNET	www.gleim.com	Please have your credit card ready,
E-MAIL:	sales@gleim.com	or save time by ordering online!

For audio purchases, please select: ☐ CD ☐ Cassette

SUBTOTAL (from previous page) $_____

Add applicable sales tax for shipments within Florida. _____

Shipping (nonrefundable): **First Item* = $5; each additional item = $1** _____

*Sets and package deals contain multiple items. Each book, audio, and software counts as 1 item; online courses have no shipping charges.

TOTAL $_____

Fax or write for prices/instructions on shipments outside the 48 contiguous states, or simply order online.

NAME (please print) _____

ADDRESS _____ Apt. _____
(street address required for UPS)

CITY _____ STATE _____ ZIP _____

____ MC/VISA/DISC ____ Check/M.O.   Daytime Telephone (____)_____

Credit Card No. _____ - _____ - _____ - _____

Exp. ____/____ Signature _____
     Month / Year

E-mail address _____

1. We process and ship orders daily, within one business day over 98.8% of the time. Call by noon for same day service.
2. Please PHOTOCOPY this order form for others.
3. No CODs. Orders from individuals must be prepaid. Library and company orders may be purchased on account.
4. Gleim Publications, Inc. guarantees the immediate refund of all resalable texts and unopened software and audios if returned within 30 days. Applies only to items purchased direct from Gleim Publications, Inc. Our shipping charge is nonrefundable.
5. Components of specially priced package deals are nonrefundable.

Printed 11/03. Prices subject to change without notice.

For updates and other important information, visit our website.

GLEIM
KNOWLEDGE
TRANSFER
SYSTEMS®

www.gleim.com

337

The GLEIM CPA System Works!

Just thought I would let you know that I passed all four parts of the CPA Exam during my first attempt! I had only three months to study and a very limited budget. Your program proves that it has the greatest value available anywhere. I had friends who spent over a thousand dollars on other materials and still failed to pass. Thank you for such a great product. I highly recommend it to everyone who is preparing for this challenging experience.

- James G. Vaughn

"I would like to thank you for your CPA Software. It did wonders for me. I passed all 4 parts! In fact, your software was the best of ALL the other companies my friends and I tested. Not just me, but all agreed to that fact. Your CPA products were great. It sure helped me PASS!"

- Faizur Bakshi

I passed the entire CPA exam in November! It was my first attempt and I was really excited about that. I thought the Gleim CPA Review materials worked great. I recommend it to everyone that I know who is studying for the CPA exam. I think it followed the exam format very well and covered all the important material. I liked the multiple-choice questions the most. I just kept going through those questions until I understood the material. As you can see, your software worked for me! I was very pleased with the results. Thanks.

- John J. Hedahl, CPA

I just received notification that I passed all 4 parts of the November 2002 CPA Exam. This was my first time taking the exam. I used Gleim's study materials and I would recommend your product to anyone. There were no surprises on the exam. Gleim Study Materials + Hard Work and Dedication = Passing the CPA Exam on the first try.

- Luis Mendez

I passed the CPA exam with the help of Gleim. Thanks for a great product. I've used other products and even went to a review course, but I think Gleim products assisted me in focusing on the areas where I was weak.

- Kathy Napier

COMPLETE GLEIM CPA SYSTEM with REVIEW ONLINE

☐ $924.95 $_____

All 4 parts, including 5 books, 4 audios, CPA Test Prep software, **Review Online**[1], plus bonus book bag.

Also available by exam part
(Does not include book bag.)

Auditing ☐ $256.95		Business ☐ $256.95	
Financial ☐ $256.95		Regulation ☐ $256.95	$_____

GLEIM CPA SET

All 4 parts, including 5 books, 4 audios, CPA Test Prep software, plus bonus book bag.

☐ $539.95 $_____

CPA REVIEW

	Online Simulations (included in Review Online)	Book/Software/ Audio Package Save 18%	Book/Software Package Save 16%	Audio Reviews	Software	Books	
Auditing	☐ @$99.95	☐ @$143.95	☐ @$74.95	☐ @$89.95	☐ @$49.95	☐ @$39.95	$_____
Business	☐ @$99.95	☐ @$143.95	☐ @$74.95	☐ @$89.95	☐ @$49.95	☐ @$39.95	_____
Regulation	☐ @$99.95	☐ @$143.95	☐ @$74.95	☐ @$89.95	☐ @$49.95	☐ @$39.95	_____
Financial	☐ @$99.95	☐ @$143.95	☐ @$74.95	☐ @$89.95	☐ @$49.95	☐ @$39.95	_____
A System for Success		☐ @$19.95 (FREE with the purchase of any Gleim CPA Review book.)					_____

COMPLETE GLEIM CMA/CFM SYSTEM

Includes: 5-part set (book, software, and audio), plus bonus book bag.

☐ $566.95 $_____

GLEIM 4-Part Set

Includes: 4-part set (book, software, and audio), plus bonus book bag.   ☐ CMA@$453.95   ☐ CFM@$453.95 $_____

CMA/CFM REVIEW

	Book/Software/ Audio Package Save 15%	Book/Software Package Save 10%	Audio Reviews	Software	Books	
Part 1 Eco., Fin., & Mgmt.	☐ @$120.95	☐ @$64.95	☐ @$69.95	☐ @$44.95	☐ @$26.95	$_____
Part 2CMA Fin. Acc. & Rep.	☐ @$120.95	☐ @$64.95	☐ @$69.95	☐ @$44.95	☐ @$26.95	
Part 2CFM Corp. Fin. Mgmt.	☐ @$120.95	☐ @$64.95	☐ @$69.95	☐ @$44.95	☐ @$26.95	
Part 3 Mgmt. Rep./Behav. Iss.	☐ @$120.95	☐ @$64.95	☐ @$69.95	☐ @$44.95	☐ @$26.95	
Part 4 Dec. Anal. & Info. Sys.	☐ @$120.95	☐ @$64.95	☐ @$69.95	☐ @$44.95	☐ @$26.95	

CIA REVIEW

	Book/Software Package Save 10%	Software	Books	
All 4 Parts	☐ @$279.80	☐ @$199.80	☐ @$119.80	$_____
Part I Internal Audit Role in Governance, Risk, & Control	☐ @$69.95	☐ @$49.95	☐ @$29.95	_____
Part II Conducting the Internal Audit Engagement	☐ @$69.95	☐ @$49.95	☐ @$29.95	_____
Part III Business Analysis and Information Technology	☐ @$69.95	☐ @$49.95	☐ @$29.95	_____
Part IV Business Management Skills	☐ @$69.95	☐ @$49.95	☐ @$29.95	_____

EA REVIEW

	Book/Software Package Save 10%	Software	Books	
All 4 Parts	☐ @$279.80	☐ @$199.80	☐ @$119.95	$_____
Part 1 Individuals	☐ @$69.95	☐ @$49.95	☐ @$29.95	_____
Part 2 Sole Prop. & Partnerships	☐ @$69.95	☐ @$49.95	☐ @$29.95	_____
Part 3 Corp./Fid./Est. & Gift Tax	☐ @$69.95	☐ @$49.95	☐ @$29.95	_____
Part 4 IRS Adm/Other Topics	☐ @$69.95	☐ @$49.95	☐ @$29.95	_____

"THE GLEIM SERIES" EXAM QUESTIONS AND EXPANATIONS BOOKS, SOFTWARE, AND CPE[2]

	Book/Software Package (Save 25%)	Software	Books	Books & CPE	
Auditing & Systems	☐ @$29.95	☐ @$20.00	☐ @$19.95	☐ @200.00	$_____
Business Law/Legal Studies	☐ @$29.95	☐ @$20.00	☐ @$19.95		_____
Federal Tax	☐ @$29.95	☐ @$20.00	☐ @$19.95	☐ @200.00	_____
Financial Accounting	☐ @$29.95	☐ @$20.00	☐ @$19.95	☐ @200.00	_____
Cost/Managerial Accounting	☐ @$29.95	☐ @$20.00	☐ @$19.95		_____

[1]For more information on our **CPA Review Online,** please visit **www.gleim.com/CPAOL/**

[2]For our online **CPE** courses and course catalog, please visit **www.gleim.com/CPE/**

SUBTOTAL $_____

Complete your order
on the next page.

GLEIM Publications, Inc.

P. O. Box 12848   Gainesville, FL 32604

TOLL FREE:	(888) 87-GLEIM	Customer service is available (Eastern Time):
LOCAL:	(352) 375-0772	8:00 a.m. - 7:00 p.m., Mon. - Fri.
FAX:	(888) 375 -6940 (toll free)	9:00 a.m. - 2:00 p.m., Saturday
INTERNET	www.gleim.com	Please have your credit card ready,
E-MAIL:	sales@gleim.com	or save time by ordering online!

For audio purchases, please select: ☐ CD ☐ Cassette

SUBTOTAL (from previous page) $_____

Add applicable sales tax for shipments within Florida. _____

Shipping (nonrefundable): **First Item* = $5; each additional item = $1** _____

*Sets and package deals contain multiple items. Each book, audio, and software counts as 1 item; online courses have no shipping charges.

TOTAL $_____

Fax or write for prices/instructions on shipments outside the 48 contiguous states, or simply order online.

NAME (please print) _____

ADDRESS _____ Apt. _____
(street address required for UPS)

CITY _____ STATE _____ ZIP _____

____ MC/VISA/DISC ____ Check/M.O. Daytime Telephone (____) _____

Credit Card No. _____ - _____ - _____ - _____

Exp. ____ / ____ Signature _____
Month / Year

E-mail address _____

1. We process and ship orders daily, within one business day over 98.8% of the time. Call by noon for same day service.
2. Please PHOTOCOPY this order form for others.
3. No CODs. Orders from individuals must be prepaid. Library and company orders may be purchased on account.
4. Gleim Publications, Inc. guarantees the immediate refund of all resalable texts and unopened software and audios if returned within 30 days. Applies only to items purchased direct from Gleim Publications, Inc. Our shipping charge is nonrefundable.
5. Components of specially priced package deals are nonrefundable.

Printed 11/03. Prices subject to change without notice.

For updates and other important information, visit our website.

www.gleim.com

CIA Review: Part I, Eleventh Edition, First Printing -- Please complete and mail to us pages 343 and 344 the week following the CIA exam.

343

Please forward your suggestions, corrections, and comments concerning typographical errors, etc., to **Irvin N. Gleim • c/o Gleim Publications, Inc. • P.O. Box 12848 • University Station • Gainesville, Florida • 32604.** Please include your name and address so we can properly thank you for your interest.

1. _____

2. _____

3. _____

4. _____

5. _____

6. _____

7. _____

8. _____

9. _____

10. _____

11. _____

12. _____

13. _____

14. _____

15. _____

16. _____

17. _____

18. _____

Remember for superior service: Mail, e-mail, or fax questions about our books or software.
Telephone questions about orders, prices, shipments, or payments.

Name: _____

Address: _____

City/State/Zip: _____

Telephone: Home: _____ Work: _____ Fax: _____

E-mail: _____